Essential Texts for Nonprofit and Public Leadership and Management

The Handbook of Nonprofit Governance, by BoardSource

Strategic Planning for Public and Nonprofit Organizations, third edition, by John M. Bryson

The Effective Public Manager, fourth edition, by Steven Cohen et al.

Handbook of Human Resources Management in Government, third edition, by Stephen E. Condrey

The Responsible Administrator, fifth edition, by Terry L. Cooper

Conducting a Successful Capital Campaign, revised and expanded edition, by Kent E. Dove

The Public Relations Handbook for Nonprofits, by Arthur Feinglass

The Jossey-Bass Handbook of Nonprofit Leadership and Management, second edition, by Robert D. Herman

Benchmarking in the Public and Nonprofit Sectors, second edition, by Patricia Keehley et al.

Museum Marketing and Strategy, second edition, by Neil Kotler et al.

The Ethics Challenge in Public Service, second edition, by Carol W. Lewis et al.

Working Across Boundaries, by Russell M. Linden

Designing and Planning Programs for Nonprofit and Government Organizations, by Edward J. Pawlak

Measuring Performance in Public and Nonprofit Organizations, by Theodore H. Poister

Human Resources Management for Public and Nonprofit Organizations: A Strategic Approach, third edition, by Joan E. Pynes

Understanding and Managing Public Organizations, fourth edition, by Hal G. Rainey

Designing and Conducting Survey Research, third edition, by Louis M. Rea et al.

Fundraising Principles and Practice, by Adrian Sargeant et al.

Making Critical Decisions, by Roberta M. Snow et al.

Hank Rosso's Achieving Excellence in Fundraising, second edition, Eugene R. Tempel

Handbook of Practical Program Evaluation, second edition, by Joseph S. Wholey et al.

THE HANDBOOK OF NONPROFIT GOVERNANCE

JOSSEY-BASS
A Wiley Imprint
www.josseybass.com

BOARDSOURCE®
Building Effective Nonprofit Boards

Published by Jossey-Bass
A Wiley Imprint
989 Market Street, San Francisco, CA 94103-1741—www.josseybass.com

Readers should be aware that Internet Web sites offered as citations and/or sources for further
information may have changed or disappeared between the time this was written and when it is read.

Jossey-Bass books and products are available through most bookstores. To contact Jossey-Bass directly
call our Customer Care Department within the U.S. at 800-956-7739, outside the U.S. at 317-572-3986,
or fax 317-572-4002.

Jossey-Bass also publishes its books in a variety of electronic formats. Some content that appears in print
may not be available in electronic books.

Library of Congress Cataloging-in-Publication Data

The handbook of nonprofit governance / Boardsource.
 p.   cm.—(Nonprofit and public leadership and management)
Includes bibliographical references and index.
ISBN 978-0-470-45763-4 (cloth)
  1. Nonprofit organizations—Management.   2. Corporate governance.   3. Boards of
directors.   4. Nonprofit organizations—Management—Case studies.   5. Corporate
governance—Case studies.   6. Boards of directors—Case studies.   7. BoardSource (Organization)
I. BoardSource (Organization)
 HD62.6.H345 2010
 658.4'22—dc22
                                                                                          2010004073
Printed in the United States of America
FIRST EDITION
HB Printing   10 9 8 7 6 5 4 3 2

BOARDSOURCE®
Building Effective Nonprofit Boards

BoardSource is dedicated to advancing the public good by building exceptional nonprofit boards and inspiring board service.

BoardSource was established in 1988 by the Association of Governing Boards of Universities and Colleges (AGB) and Independent Sector (IS). In the early 1980s, the two organizations had conducted a survey and found that although 30 percent of respondents believed they were doing a good job of board education and training, the rest of the respondents reported little, if any, activity in strengthening governance. As a result, AGB and IS proposed the creation of a new organization whose mission would be to increase the effectiveness of nonprofit boards.

With a lead grant from the Kellogg Foundation and funding from five other donors, BoardSource opened its doors in 1988 as the National Center for Nonprofit Boards. It had a staff of three and an operating budget of $385,000. On January 1, 2002, BoardSource took on its new name and identity. These changes were the culmination of an extensive process of understanding how we were perceived, what our audiences wanted, and how we could best meet the needs of nonprofit organizations.

Today BoardSource is the premier voice of nonprofit governance. Its highly acclaimed products, programs, and services mobilize boards so that organizations fulfill their missions, achieve their goals, increase their impact, and extend their influence. BoardSource is a 501(c)(3) organization.

BoardSource provides

- Resources to nonprofit leaders through workshops, training, and an extensive Web site (www.boardsource.org)
- Governance consultants who work directly with nonprofit leaders to design specialized solutions to meet an organization's needs
- The world's largest, most comprehensive selection of material on nonprofit governance, including a large selection of books and CD-ROMs
- An annual conference that brings together approximately nine hundred governance experts, board members, and chief executives and senior staff from around the world

For more information, please visit our Web site at www.boardsource.org, e-mail us at mail@boardsource.org, or call us at 800-883-6262.

Have You Used These BoardSource Resources?

The Governance Series

Ten Basic Responsibilities of Nonprofit Boards, second edition
Financial Responsibilities of Nonprofit Boards, second edition
Structures and Practices of Nonprofit Boards, second edition
Fundraising Responsibilities of Nonprofit Boards, second edition
Legal Responsibilities of Nonprofit Boards, second edition
The Nonprofit Board's Role in Mission, Planning, and Evaluation, second edition

The Committee Series

Transforming Board Structure: Strategies for Committees and Task Forces
Governance Committee
Executive Committee
Financial Committees
Development Committee
Advisory Councils

Other Books

The Board Building Cycle: Nine Steps to Finding, Recruiting, and Engaging Nonprofit Board Members, second edition
The Board Chair Handbook, second edition
The Business Professional's Guide to Nonprofit Board Service
Chief Executive Succession Planning: Essential Guidance for Boards and CEOs, second edition
Chief Executive Transitions: How to Hire and Support a Nonprofit CEO
Culture of Inquiry: Healthy Debate in the Boardroom
Driving Strategic Planning: A Nonprofit Executive's Guide, second edition
Exceptional Board Practices: The Source in Action
Fearless Fundraising for Nonprofit Boards, second edition
Generating Buzz: Strategic Communications for Nonprofit Boards
Getting the Best from Your Board: An Executive's Guide to a Successful Partnership
Governance as Leadership: Reframing the Work of Nonprofit Boards
Managing Conflicts of Interest: A Primer for Nonprofit Boards, second edition
Meeting, and Exceeding Expectations: A Guide to Successful Nonprofit Board Meetings, second edition
Moving Beyond Founder's Syndrome to Nonprofit Success

Navigating the Organizational Lifecycle: A Capacity-Building Guide for Nonprofit Leaders

The Nonprofit Board Answer Book: A Practical Guide for Board Members and Chief Executives, second edition

The Nonprofit Board's Guide to Bylaws: Creating a Framework for Effective Governance

The Nonprofit Chief Executive's Ten Basic Responsibilities

Nonprofit Executive Compensation: Planning, Performance, and Pay, second edition

The Nonprofit Dashboard: A Tool for Tracking Progress

Nonprofit Governance: Steering Your Organization with Authority and Accountability

The Nonprofit Legal Landscape

The Nonprofit Policy Sampler, second edition

The Source: Twelve Principles of Governance That Power Exceptional Boards

Taming the Troublesome Board Member

Trouble at the Top: The Nonprofit Board's Guide to Managing an Imperfect Chief Executive

Understanding Nonprofit Financial Statements, third edition

Who's Minding the Money? An Investment Guide for Nonprofit Board Members, second edition

Online Assessments

Assessment of the Chief Executive

Board Self-Assessment

CONTENTS

ACKNOWLEDGMENTS

BoardSource wishes to acknowledge the authors of the material used in producing this handbook:

Nancy R. Axelrod, *Advisory Councils* (BoardSource Committee Series); *Chief Executive Succession Planning: Essential Guidance for Boards and CEOs* (second edition); *Culture of Inquiry: Healthy Debate in the Boardroom;* "Curious Boards," *Board Member* 15, no. 3 (May/June 2006).

Steven Berger, *Understanding Nonprofit Financial Statements* (third edition).

BoardSource, *The Nonprofit Board Answer Book: A Practical Guide for Board Members and Chief Executives* (second edition).

BoardSource, *The Source: Twelve Principles of Governance That Power Exceptional Boards.*

Marla J. Bobowick, Sandra R. Hughes, and Berit M. Lakey, *Transforming Board Structure: Strategies for Committees and Task Forces* (BoardSource Committee Series).

Janet Boguch, "Enforcing Give, Get, or Get Off," *Board Member* 17, no. 1 (January/February 2008).

Lawrence M. Butler, *The Nonprofit Dashboard: A Tool for Tracking Progress.*

Richard P. Chait, William P. Ryan, and Barbara E. Taylor, *Governance as Leadership: Reframing the Work of Nonprofit Boards.*

Paul M. Connolly, *Navigating the Organizational Lifecycle: A Capacity-Building Guide for Nonprofit Leaders*.

Charles F. Dambach, MBA, Melissa Davis, and Robert L. Gale, *Structures and Practices of Nonprofit Boards* (second edition) (BoardSource Governance Series).

Charles F. Dambach, MBA, Oliver Tessier, and Carol E. Weisman, *The Business Professional's Guide to Nonprofit Board Service*.

M. Christine DeVita, "Constructing a Partnership," *Board Member* 15, no. 5 (September/October 2006).

Outi Flynn, *Meeting, and Exceeding Expectations: A Guide to Successful Nonprofit Board Meetings* (second edition).

Robert P. Fry Jr., *Who's Minding the Money? An Investment Guide for Nonprofit Board Members* (second edition).

Kay Sprinkel Grace, MA, "Fundraising in the 21st Century," *Board Member* 17, no. 3 (May/June 2008).

Kay Sprinkel Grace, MA, Amy McClellan, MNO, and John A. Yankey, PhD, *The Nonprofit Board's Role in Mission, Planning, and Evaluation* (second edition) (BoardSource Governance Series).

James M. Greenfield, *Fundraising Responsibilities of Nonprofit Boards* (second edition), ACFRE, FAHP (BoardSource Governance Series).

Peter Dobkin Hall, "A History of Nonprofit Boards in the United States."

Deborah S. Hechinger and Marla J. Bobowick, "Governance Matters," Board Member 14, no. 3 (June/July 2005).

Bruce R. Hopkins, JD, LLM, *Legal Responsibilities of Nonprofit Boards* (second edition) (BoardSource Governance Series).

Richard T. Ingram, *Ten Basic Responsibilities of Nonprofit Boards* (second edition) (BoardSource Governance Series).

Katha Kissman, *Taming the Troublesome Board Member*.

Katha Kissman, *Trouble at the Top: The Nonprofit Board's Guide to Managing an Imperfect Chief Executive*.

Daniel L. Kurtz and Sarah E. Paul, *Managing Conflicts of Interest: A Primer for Nonprofit Boards* (second edition).

Berit M. Lakey, *The Board-Building Cycle: Nine Steps to Finding, Recruiting, and Engaging Nonprofit Board Members* (second edition); *Nonprofit Governance: Steering Your Organization with Authority and Accountability*.

Berit M. Lakey, Sandra Hughes, and Outi Flynn, *Governance Committee* (BoardSource Committee Series).

Andrew S. Lang, CPA, *Financial Responsibilities of Nonprofit Boards* (second edition) (BoardSource Governance Series).

Barbara Lawrence and Outi Flynn, *The Nonprofit Policy Sampler* (second edition).

Mark Light, *Executive Committee* (BoardSource Committee Series).

Thomas A. McLaughlin, *Financial Committees* (BoardSource Committee Series).

Thomas A. McLaughlin and Addie Nelson Backlund, *Moving Beyond Founder's Syndrome to Nonprofit Success.*

Richard L. Moyers, *The Nonprofit Chief Executive's Ten Basic Responsibilities.*

Ober | Kaler, *The Nonprofit Legal Landscape.*

Sally J. Patterson, *Generating Buzz: Strategic Communications for Nonprofit Boards.*

Maureen K. Robinson, "Declaration of Independence," *Board Member* 16, no. 2 (March/April 2007).

Irene Rozansky, "Communicating in a Crisis," *Board Member* 16, no. 2 (March/April 2007).

Dave Sternberg, *Fearless Fundraising for Nonprofit Boards* (second edition).

Don Tebbe, *Chief Executive Transitions: How to Hire and Support a Nonprofit CEO.*

Eugene R. Tempel, *Development Committee* (BoardSource Committee Series).

D. Benson Tesdahl, Esq., *The Nonprofit Board's Guide to Bylaws: Creating a Framework for Effective Governance.*

Brian H. Vogel and Charles W. Quatt, *Nonprofit Executive Compensation: Planning, Performance, and Pay* (second edition).

Susan A. Waechter, *Driving Strategic Planning: A Nonprofit Executive's Guide* (second edition).

Vernetta Walker, "Beyond Political Correctness: Building a Diverse Board," *Board Member* 18, no. 3 (May/June 2009).

Mindy R. Wertheimer, *The Board Chair Handbook* (second edition).

Sherill K. Williams and Kathleen A. McGinnis, *Getting the Best from Your Board: An Executive's Guide to a Successful Partnership.*

Terry Williams, "Thinking Outside the Boardroom," *Board Member* 15, no. 2 (March/April 2006).

Peter York, "Are We There Yet? The Board's Role in Evaluating Mission Achievement," *Board Member* 14, no. 6 (December 2005).

INTRODUCTION

Service on a nonprofit board was once perceived as an honorary role requiring nothing more than periodic attendance at meetings and generous annual donations. But vibrant growth in the nonprofit sector has helped to change the nature of board service. Board members need to do more than just show up. They must understand and promote the organization's work, define measures of success, and assess how well the organization performs, using both subjective and objective standards. They must generate and allocate resources, hire the chief executive, develop plans, establish policies and programs, and monitor activities—all with a sharp focus on producing meaningful results.

Within these broad roles, board members have many functions. They are guardians of the mission, they ensure compliance with legal and financial requirements, and they enforce ethical guidelines for their organization. They are policymakers, fundraisers, ambassadors, partners with the chief executive, and strategic thinkers. They monitor progress, evaluate the performance of the organization and the chief executive, and demonstrate integrity in everything they do on behalf of the organization. Because of their many roles, board members need more than enthusiasm for a cause, passion for a mission, or just good intentions. They need to understand all of their stewardship responsibilities and perform all of their duties.

Board service entails serious obligations, to be sure, but it can also deliver immense satisfaction. A board that knows what is expected of it and performs at the highest level is a strategic resource for its organization and chief executive. And ultimately, this commitment by dedicated board members translates into mission impact in our communities.

About This Book

The Handbook of Nonprofit Governance is a comprehensive overview of the principles and practices of nonprofit boards. To compile this handbook, BoardSource drew on its extensive selection of books, articles, and topic papers by leading experts on nonprofit governance.

The book is organized in two parts. Part One (Chapters One through Five) addresses basic governance history, roles, and structures. Part Two (Chapters Six through Sixteen) examines nonprofit governance practices, drawing on the experience and wisdom of BoardSource experts to review basic approaches to board responsibilities and board self-management. Consulting the handbook provides answers to the following questions:

What is the nonprofit sector, and how does governance fit in? Chapters One and Two review the history of the nonprofit sector, its function in society, and the basic tenets of nonprofit governance.

What roles do nonprofit boards serve? Chapter Three explains the governance roles of the full board and of individual board members, broadly described as setting organizational direction, ensuring the necessary resources, and providing oversight. It links to other chapters in this handbook that explore elements of these governance roles in greater depth. Chapter Four examines board structure, including board size and the functions of committees, task forces, and other work groups. Chapter Five describes the board–chief executive relationship and offers suggestions to ensure its success.

Part Two examines nonprofit governance practices, drawing on the experience and wisdom of BoardSource experts to review basic approaches to board responsibilities and board self-management:

How does a nonprofit organization build and sustain a strong, active board? Chapter Six reviews the cyclical process of finding the best people, bringing them onto the board, and then creating an environment for board service that invites them to reach their full potential as board members. Building a board involves more than enlisting new members and training them. This chapter describes the full cycle: identifying, cultivating, and recruiting board members; providing orientation; involving all board members in meaningful work; promoting continuing education; evaluating the effectiveness of the full board and of individuals;

refreshing the board through term limits and regular rotation; and celebrating board accomplishments.

What are the legal and ethical responsibilities of the board and its members? Governance is serious business, with a set of duties that are defined by law. Chapter Seven opens with a discussion of fiduciary responsibility—the board's obligations for financial accountability and effective oversight of the organization. Exceptional boards not only follow legal requirements, but also ensure that the organization's work is conducted in an ethical, open, and responsive manner. Legal and ethical compliance, conflict of interest, legal liability, and the concepts of private benefit and private inurement are among the issues covered in this chapter.

How does the board carry out its financial oversight responsibilities? Ultimately, the board is responsible for the financial viability, the program success, and the survival of the organization. Chapter Eight reviews what board members need to know about financial integrity and solvency, safeguards and procedures to protect the organization, and signs of financial trouble. It explains the implications of the Sarbanes-Oxley Act for nonprofits, the importance of an external audit, and the financial systems that organizations need for safe, efficient operations.

What is the board's role in fundraising? Fundraising begins with the board, because board members understand the organization well and are committed to helping it fulfill its mission. Chapter Nine outlines the board's involvement in fundraising, step by step. Joining with staff to generate necessary resources, the board provides strategic guidance and direction, participates as donors and as fundraisers, and is responsible for stewardship and oversight of the funds raised. Beginning with an explanation of board members' personal obligation for giving, the chapter reviews fundraising types, policies, and techniques, with tips for raising board members' comfort level for joining in this important activity.

How does the board engage in strategic thinking and participate in strategic planning? Strategic thinking and planning move an organization toward fulfilling its mission and creating its future. Both processes—as described in Chapter Ten—are potentially enriching and energizing for the board. When strategic thinking becomes a habit, board meetings are dynamic, discussions are challenging and thought pro-voking, and the board identifies crucial issues that lead to more relevant, timely, and constructive decisions. This chapter outlines the rationale for strategic planning, describes basic steps in the process, and emphasizes the need to blend planning and evaluation.

What does the board contribute to communications and outreach? For nonprofit boards, strategic communications involves big-picture thinking, a clear understanding of appropriate roles, and hands-on participation when appropriate. Chapter Eleven reviews how board members can contribute to the staff's work through public speaking, relationship building, and advocacy. It explains lobbying and political activity by nonprofits, and it addresses communications during a crisis or controversy.

How do boards ensure effective chief executive transitions? The board's responsibility for hiring and supporting the chief executive can have an extraordinary impact on organizational effectiveness. Chapter Twelve explains that there's more to this responsibility than executive search. It begins with the proactive step of having a succession plan and compensation policy in place. This chapter describes the steps in a careful, thorough executive search, describes some characteristics to look for, and emphasizes the essential support that new chief executives need from their boards.

Why is evaluation important, and how is the board involved? Evaluation is a learning tool that, when embedded in an organization's culture, promotes the achievement of mission. Chapter Thirteen stresses the board's role in promoting continuing evaluation. Measuring organizational effectiveness, self-assessment for the full board, self-assessment for individual board members, and performance evaluation for the chief executive are all board responsibilities, described in this chapter. The staff is also responsible for evaluating an organization's core programs and practices.

How do bylaws and policies promote sound board decisions? Chapter Fourteen reviews the details of a nonprofit organization's governing documents (bylaws) and operating principles (policies). It explains the context for bylaws and policies and provides an overview of the issues and areas they should address. The chapter includes recommendations and examples to serve as a starting point for the documents that each organization should tailor to its own needs and circumstances.

What are the ingredients of a productive board meeting? At meetings, the board carries out its role as policy maker, sets direction for the organization, defines and follows its own ethical guidelines, oversees operations, and takes care of its own well-being. Chapter Fifteen offers recommendations for planning fast-paced, efficient meetings while maintaining the spirit of teamwork and collegiality among board members. Topics include deciding on frequency of meetings, developing an agenda, facilitating the meeting, preparing minutes, holding executive sessions, and evaluating the meeting.

How do board dynamics influence board effectiveness? The dynamics of working together on behalf of the organization can be complex, but boards need to promote a working environment that encourages collaboration, partnership, engagement, trust, respect, flexibility, and interaction. Chapter Sixteen addresses five key issues in board dynamics: building trust to support collaborative governance, developing a culture of inquiry, recognizing and avoiding micromanagement, ensuring independent-mindedness, and dealing with the problem of troublesome board members.

Reflecting on board dynamics is a fitting way to conclude this handbook. While many principles and practices of nonprofit governance are well established, the essence of board interactions is often more difficult to express. When all is said and done, the board is a group of individuals with a collective commitment. How they engage with one another can make the difference between governance that is simply good and governance that is truly exceptional. The stakes are high, but the dynamic role of nonprofit organizations in our society attests to the fact that the women and men who serve on nonprofit boards fulfill their responsibilities with seriousness of purpose, dedication to service, and passion for their organizations' missions.

PART ONE

GOVERNANCE PRINCIPLES,
ROLES, AND STRUCTURE

CHAPTER ONE

IN THE SPIRIT OF SERVICE: INTRODUCTION TO THE NONPROFIT WORLD

The only ones among you who will be really happy are those who will have sought and found how to serve.

—ALBERT SCHWEITZER

Virtually every society shows its voluntary spirit and philanthropic instinct by creating informal community groups, charitable nongovernmental organizations, or faith-based organizations and places of worship. In countries around the world, nonprofits are a vibrant, essential element of national life. They struggle to reduce poverty and bring an end to homelessness. They strive to build safe places to learn and play, create inspiring art and music, and protect natural resources.

Nonprofit organizations span a wide spectrum of mission areas, resources, values, history, and stakeholders—from small, local homeless shelters to large, international trade associations; from community foundations operating within a geographic region to educational institutions that attract students from around the country. Their funding may come from just a handful of sources or from an array of charitable contributions, membership dues, grants, fees from programs and services, and more. According to the Internal Revenue Service, the United States alone has more than 1.8 million voluntary, nonprofit, and nongovernmental organizations, with more recognized every month by the federal government as tax-exempt entities.

Economic life in the United States and many other countries consists of three sectors:

- *Public-sector organizations* exist to serve the public good. They are part of governmental structures and are financed largely by tax revenues.

- *Private-sector organizations* exist to produce a profit for their owners. To do so they must meet the needs of a constituency who will pay for their goods or services.
- *Nonprofit-sector organizations* exist to serve a social purpose, a constituency, or a cause. To do so successfully, they must earn or raise sufficient funds to cover expenses and safeguard the organization's future. They are not prohibited from creating excess revenue over expenses, but such surplus must be used to support the organization's mission, not to be distributed as private gain. In nonprofit organizations there are no individual owners who can claim organizational assets for their own benefit.

An Overview of the Nonprofit Sector

The nonprofit sector sometimes is called the not-for-profit sector, the third sector, the independent sector, the philanthropic sector, the voluntary sector, or the social sector. Outside the United States, nonprofits are often called nongovernmental organizations (NGOs) or civil society organizations.

These other names emphasize the characteristics that distinguish nonprofits— *voluntary sector* to acknowledge the importance of volunteers and voluntary action, *independent sector* to distinguish nonprofits from business and government, and *social sector* to underscore how the activities of nonprofits enhance the social fabric of our country.

The nonprofit sector in the United States is vast and diverse and touches all our lives. The nonprofit organizations in this country in 2008 employed 10.5 percent of the country's work force—close to ten million paid workers.

Almost all nonprofits are exempt from federal, state, and local income taxes; state and local property taxes; and state and local sales taxes. They are, however, required to pay taxes on income derived from activities that are unrelated to their mission. Nonprofits are not exempt from withholding payroll taxes for employees. Section 501(c) of the Internal Revenue Code, which outlines the types of organizations eligible for tax exemption, lists more than twenty-five classifications of nonprofits, which include the major subcategories described in the following section.

Public Charities

Nonprofits that are exempt under Section 501(c)(3) of the tax code are often called charities, but these organizations do far more than provide free care and services to the needy. Hospitals, museums, orchestras, independent schools, public television and radio stations, and many other organizations are 501(c)(3) nonprofits. Most U.S. nonprofits are classified as public charities, and in 2008 nearly 1.2 million were registered with the Internal Revenue Service.

To be recognized as a public charity, a nonprofit must be organized and operated for purposes that are beneficial to the public interest. These purposes include

- Relief of the poor, distressed, or underprivileged
- Advancement of religion
- Advancement of education and science
- Creation or maintenance of public buildings or monuments
- Lessening of the burden of government
- Elimination of prejudice and discrimination
- Defense of human and civil rights
- Combating of community deterioration and juvenile delinquency

A public charity must be able to show broad public support, rather than funding from an individual source. Upon dissolution, its assets must be distributed to another 501(c)(3) charity. It is not allowed to engage in any partisan political activity. Lobbying is accepted but cannot be a substantial part of its activities. Individuals and corporations that give money to these organizations can deduct the value of gifts from their taxable income, provided they file itemized tax returns.

Foundations

Many individuals, families, businesses, and communities establish foundations as a way to support causes and programs that benefit society. Foundations, which are also 501(c)(3) charitable nonprofits, are one of the most complex components of the nonprofit sector. As a result of federal legislation passed in 1969, private foundations are subject to more stringent regulation and reporting requirements than other types of nonprofits. They are required to make grants equal to at least 5 percent of their net investment assets each year, and they generally pay a 2-percent excise tax on net investment earnings. There are more than seventy thousand foundations in the United States:

- *Private* foundations usually have a single source of funding (an individual, a family, or a business), and use income from investments to make grants to charitable nonprofit organizations. The Ford Foundation, the Carnegie Corporation of New York, and the W. K. Kellogg Foundation are well-known examples.

Corporate foundations are private foundations that receive funding from—and make grants on behalf of—a corporation. The MetLife Foundation and the American Express Foundation are examples. Many corporations have in-house corporate giving programs instead of or in addition to corporate foundations.

- *Operating* foundations are "hybrid" foundations that use the bulk of their resources to carry out their own charitable programs, while also making grants to other charities. The Carnegie Endowment for International Peace and the J. Paul Getty Trust are examples of operating foundations.
- *Community* foundations pool the resources of many donors and focus their grantmaking on a particular city or region. The Cleveland Foundation and the New York Community Trust are examples of community foundations. The IRS classifies community foundations as publicly supported charities, not private foundations. These groups are not subject to excise taxes or distribution requirements like private foundations, and donations made to them by individuals are tax deductible.

Some nonprofits, such as hospitals and public colleges, create related or supporting 501(c)(3) organizations that may be called foundations; these groups are fundraising (rather than grantmaking) organizations, and they typically raise money from a broad range of donors and then distribute the proceeds to the parent organization. In addition, some other charities include the word *foundation* in their names even though they are not considered foundations according to legal definitions.

Social Welfare Organizations

To be tax-exempt as a 501(c)(4) organization, a nonprofit must not be organized for profit and must be operated exclusively for the promotion of social welfare. This means that the organization must operate primarily to further, in some way, the common good and general welfare of the people of the community (such as by bringing about civic betterment and social improvements). Nonprofits such as the NAACP, the National Rifle Association, and the National Organization for Women are examples of social welfare or advocacy organizations. Contributions to 501(c)(4) organizations are not tax deductible, and 501(c)(4) nonprofits have greater latitude to participate in legislative advocacy, lobbying, and political campaign activities.

Professional and Trade Associations

Organizations whose missions focus on the advancement of the conditions of a particular trade or the interests of a community, an industry, or a profession generally qualify for tax exemption under Section 501(c)(6) of the tax code.

Although contributions to these organizations are not tax deductible, membership dues may be deductible as business expenses.

Many people believe that nonprofits receive most of their funds from private contributions. In reality, many nonprofits (hospitals and universities are good examples) generate revenue by charging fees for the services they provide, earning interest on investments, or producing and selling goods. Many organizations also receive funding from government, either in the form of outright subsidies or for providing services on a contract basis.

The idea of the nonprofit sector may be abstract, but the sector's role in our society is tangible and easily recognized. Freed from the profit motive that dominates business and from the constraints of government, the nonprofit sector is a forum for the creation and dissemination of new ideas, an efficient vehicle for delivering social services, and a guardian of our environment, values, and heritage.

Monitoring, Regulating, and Governing Nonprofits

Nonprofits are not immune from damage that can be caused by unscrupulous and fraudulent solicitors, financial improprieties, and executives and board members who care more about their own financial welfare than the mission of the organization. Problems, when they do arise, are particularly disturbing because of the nature of nonprofits themselves—organizations created to provide some public benefit.

Most people are familiar with the mechanisms that safeguard the integrity of government and business. Disenchanted voters can throw politicians out of office, and the branches of government view each other with watchful eyes. Businesses have shareholders or owners and are monitored by government agencies such as the Securities and Exchange Commission and the Occupational Safety and Health Administration. The media monitor both sectors and are quick to point out cases of corruption and poor performance.

Far fewer people understand how nonprofits are monitored and regulated. For much of its history, the nonprofit sector has operated outside the realm of harsh public scrutiny. No government agency exists exclusively to monitor the activities of nonprofits, most nonprofits aren't required to hold public meetings, and few journalists report on nonprofits with the same depth and focus devoted to business and government.

Nevertheless, nonprofits have many lines of defense against fraud and corruption:

- *Boards*. All nonprofits are governed by a board of directors or trustees (there's no real difference)—a group of volunteers that is legally responsible for making sure the organization remains true to its mission, safeguards its assets, and operates in the public interest. The board is the first line of defense against fraud and abuse.

- *Private watchdog groups.* Several private groups (which are themselves nonprofits) monitor the behavior and performance of other nonprofits. Some see their mission as advising donors who want to ensure that their gifts are being used effectively; others are industry or "trade" groups that provide information to the public and encourage compliance with generally accepted standards and practices.

- *State charity regulators.* The attorney general's office or some other part of the state government maintains a list of registered nonprofits and investigates complaints of fraud and abuse. Often the state attorney general serves as the primary investigator in cases of nonprofit fraud or abuse. Almost all states have laws regulating charitable fundraising.

- *Internal Revenue Service.* A small division of the IRS (the exempt organizations division) is charged with ensuring that nonprofits comply with the eligibility requirements for tax-exempt status. IRS auditors investigate the financial affairs of thousands of nonprofits each year. As a result, a handful have their tax-exempt status revoked; others pay fines and taxes. In 1996, legislation authorized the IRS to penalize individuals who abuse positions of influence within public charities and social welfare organizations. Before that change, the only weapon available to the IRS was to revoke tax-exemption, which resulted in the denial of service to the clients and constituents the organization was created to help. Because they fall short of revocation of tax-exempt status, these provisions are called intermediate sanctions.

- *Donors and members.* Some of the most powerful safeguards of nonprofit integrity are individual donors and members. By giving or withholding their financial support, donors and members can cause nonprofits to reappraise their operations.

- *Media.* Most of the major scandals involving nonprofit organizations in recent years have come about as a result of media investigations and resulting news stories. Although many nonprofit leaders feel misunderstood or even maligned by negative media coverage, this media watchdog role has resulted in increased awareness and accountability throughout the sector.

Starting a Nonprofit Organization

Americans are known for their pioneer temperament, community spirit, and help-thy-neighbor attitude. We show social consciousness, concern for the environment, commitment to saving historic sites, responsibility to advocate individual rights, and an urgency to do this all as a personal vocation for a cause. This commitment often leads to a desire to start a nonprofit organization.

Forming a nonprofit requires more than passion or devotion. One needs understanding of financial management, knowledge of legal requirements, managerial skills, community relations, familiarity with issues in the field, friends and supporters, and more than anything, time, energy and endless patience.

Questions to Ask Before Starting a Nonprofit

1. Is somebody already doing what I would like to do?

   There is no sense in duplicating an effort that already exists. Maybe there is a possibility of working with an existing organization as a consultant, fund-raiser, employee, direct-service volunteer, or board member.

2. Is this the right time and place for starting a new organization?

   How will the idea be received by the community? Is there a true need for my services? Have I tested the idea, or am I the only one who thinks it is essential? Who are the constituents?

3. How would I finance my organization?

   Do I have the necessary seed money? If not, where can I get the initial funding? Have I developed relations with the leaders in the community? How much fundraising will I have to do? Do I understand that grant funding is highly competitive and therefore not dependable? Should the services of my organization be free, or is this how I will produce earned income? Should I form a membership organization and charge a fee? Could I associate my group with an already established organization?

4. Do I understand the steps of forming a nonprofit organization?

   There are a multitude of procedures to take care of before a nonprofit organization is ready to function: forming a board, drafting bylaws, developing a strategic plan, incorporating, applying for tax-exempt status, securing funding, setting up an accounting system, locating an office, applying for licenses, recruiting staff, and so on.

5. Are my financial ambitions appropriate for the cause?

   Running a nonprofit or serving as a nonprofit board member is not going to fill my pockets with cash. Staff members can be compensated justly; board members normally serve as volunteers and should not seek any personal benefit from this affiliation. Will I be content to serve and work for my cause, get satisfaction from the results of my labor, and always put my organization first before thinking of my personal gain?

To be effective at fulfilling its purpose, every nonprofit organization must have a carefully developed structure and operating procedures. Good governance starts with helping the organization begin on a sound legal and financial footing in compliance with the numerous federal, state, and local requirements affecting nonprofits.

1. *Determine the purpose of the organization.* Every organization should have a written statement that expresses its reason for being. *Resources:* Board members, potential clients and constituents.

2. *Form a board of directors.* The initial board will help translate the ideas behind the organization into reality through planning and fundraising. As the organization matures, the nature and composition of its board will also change. *Resources:* BoardSource, planning and management consultant.

3. *File articles of incorporation.* Not all nonprofits are incorporated. For those that do wish to incorporate, the requirements for forming and operating a nonprofit corporation are governed by state law. *Resources:* State secretary of state or attorney general's office.

4. *Draft bylaws.* Bylaws—the operating rules for the board—should be drafted and approved by the board early in the organization's development. *Resources:* Attorney experienced in nonprofit law.

5. *Develop a strategic plan.* Strategic planning helps express a vision of the organization's potential. Outline the steps necessary to work toward that potential, and determine the staffing needed to implement the plan. Establish program and operational priorities for at least one year. *Resources:* Board members, planning and management consultant.

6. *Develop a budget and resource development plan.* Financial oversight and resource development (for example, fundraising, earned income, and membership) are critical board responsibilities. The resources needed to carry out the strategic plan must be described in a budget and financial plan. *Resources:* Fundraising consultant.

7. *Establish a recordkeeping system for the organization's official records.* Corporate documents, board meeting minutes, financial reports, and other official records must be preserved for the life of the organization. *Resources:* State secretary of state or attorney general's office.

8. *Establish an accounting system.* Responsible stewardship of the organization's finances requires the establishment of an accounting system that meets both current and anticipated needs. *Resources:* Bookkeeper experienced in nonprofit accounting.

9. *File for an Internal Revenue Service determination of federal tax-exempt status.* Nonprofit corporations with charitable, educational, scientific, religious, or cultural purposes have tax-exempt status under section 501(c)(3)—or sometimes section 501(c)(4)—of the Internal Revenue Code. To apply for recognition of tax-exempt status, obtain form 1023 (application) and publication 557 (detailed instructions) from the local Internal Revenue Service office or from the IRS Web site http://www.irs.gov/charities/index.html. Though it is not essential to consult an attorney when preparing this document, many organizations do seek the assistance of an attorney experienced in nonprofit law. *Resources:* Local IRS office, attorney.

10. *File for state and local tax exemptions.* In accordance with state, county, and municipal law, apply for exemption from income, sales, and property taxes. *Resources:* State, county, or municipal department of revenue.

11. *Meet the requirements of state, county, and municipal charitable solicitation laws.* Many states and local jurisdictions regulate organizations that solicit funds within that state, county, or city. Usually compliance involves obtaining a permit or license and then filing an annual report and financial statement. *Resources:* State attorney general's office, state department of commerce, state or local department of revenue, or county or municipal clerk's office.

12. *Other steps:*
    • Obtain an employer identification number (EIN) from the IRS.
    • Register with the state unemployment insurance bureau.
    • Apply for a nonprofit mailing permit from the U.S. Postal Service.
    • Obtain directors' and officers' liability insurance.

The Board of a Start-up Nonprofit

When setting up a nonprofit, the founder or founders form the first board for an organization. Start with a small but committed group that has the skills and expertise necessary to get started. Here are some suggestions:

• Include people who are familiar with constituents and their needs.
• Include people who have served on a nonprofit board or staff.
• If the organization depends on outside funding, engage someone who can help develop a fundraising plan.
• Find someone who understands the field or mission area.
• Include someone who is comfortable with technology.
• Bring in innovative people who have new ideas.
• Make sure all board members can work as a team.

Incorporation and Tax Exemption

Most nonprofits choose to organize themselves as corporations—a legal form of organization that is available to nonprofits under every state's laws. A corporation offers some desirable advantages, such as limited liability protection for its managers, directors, and officers. And, because of the relatively stable environment in which incorporated nonprofits function, business contractors and funders tend to prefer working with them. State statutes and common law govern the formation, organization, and ongoing operations of corporations.

Incorporation is not the same as applying for tax-exempt status. Through tax exemption, federal, state, and local governments provide an indirect subsidy to nonprofits and receive a direct benefit in return. Tax exemption is an acknowledgment of an organization performing an activity that relieves some burden that would otherwise fall to federal, state, or local government. Churches are automatically provided tax exemption as a safeguard to preserve separation of church and state by preventing governments from using taxation to favor one religion over another. Categories of tax-exempt organizations are described earlier in this chapter.

Articles of Incorporation

A corporation is a legal entity that exists in perpetuity until it is dissolved. It is a "fictitious person," separate from its managers or governors, and it is usually given many of the same rights and obligations as natural persons. A nonprofit corporation is able to conduct charitable, educational, or scientific activities; it can enter into contracts; it can incur debts; it can hire employees who are eligible for fringe benefits; and it is legally liable for its actions.

Nonprofit corporations are "created" by one or more incorporators—usually selected from among the initial board members—who sign and file the corporation's articles of incorporation with the appropriate state agency. The incorporators' role ends at that moment, and the board assumes the responsibility for the organization. Each state's law prescribes the content and form of this binding legal document. Articles of incorporation generally include the following:

- Name of the corporation
- The organization's specific purpose (this should be brief and broad to allow for future evolution, but should clearly indicate its tax-exempt focus)
- Duration of the corporation's existence (often perpetuity)
- Location of the organization's office

- Number, names, and addresses of the initial board of directors
- Whether or not it is a membership organization
- Provisions for distribution of assets when the corporation is dissolved

---

Amending the Articles of Incorporation

Articles of incorporation should remain as general as possible within the framework of state law. The bylaws provide further detail on the governance structure, and additional policies and procedures secure the rest of the necessary guidelines for effective and ethical functioning of the organization. Sometimes major changes in status, activities, or structure of the organization require the articles to be amended. These changes include

- Changing the organization's name or address
- Substantially changing the organization's mission
- Altering the provision for the disposition of assets if the organization is dissolved
- Changing the way board members are elected (formal membership structure or self-perpetuating board)

Special Types of Nonprofit Organizations

Not all nonprofit organizations are structured similarly with independent, self-perpetuating boards. Other types include a federated system with a national office and local chapters or formal membership organizations whose members are the main beneficiaries of the services and in return have a say in the internal affairs of the organization.

Federated Organizations

A federated organization is a national umbrella organization that has smaller chapters or affiliates with a regional or local reach. It typically is a membership organization whose members are the chapters, but it is possible to have individual members as well. Chapters may also be membership organizations with individual members, but they may function as separate and independent public charities.

The national organization typically acts as the spokesperson for the cause and sets the overall strategic vision for the federated structure. It also provides support for the local chapters. The chapters provide mission-related programs or services to a local area. Examples of federated organizations include the American Lung Association, Boy Scouts of America, and Habitat for Humanity.

Formal Membership Organizations

Many nonprofits have members who might also be described as supporters, donors, or friends who believe in the mission of the organization. They receive benefits such as discounts, newsletters, and helpful information. This is a membership structure that has no legal implications, and it does not need to be defined in the organizational documents of the nonprofit. However, if members are granted a say in the structure and priorities of the organization, they are part of a "formal" membership organization, and their categorization and authority levels must be clarified in the articles of incorporation and in the bylaws. Formal members usually elect board members and officers, and they can approve amendments to the bylaws. A trade association usually is structured as a formal membership organization. Other examples of formal membership organizations include the United Way of America and the National Association of Social Workers.

Chapter Exercises

- Describe how nonprofits intersect with your daily life.
- What circumstances might influence the growth or shrinkage of the nonprofit sector?
- Define *public trust*, and discuss why it should be important for a tax-exempt organization.
- Discuss what a productive collaboration between a nonprofit, a for-profit, and the public sector might look like.
- If you wanted to establish a homeless shelter in your community, what are the decisions and choices you would have to make along the way?
- List the different ways nonprofit tax-exempt organizations can or should self-regulate.

CHAPTER TWO

WHAT IS GOVERNANCE?

Whatever its size, scope, or funding, every nonprofit organization has a governing board composed of people who believe in and support the mission. Board members have the pleasure—and the responsibility—of monitoring, overseeing, and providing direction for the organization's pursuit of that mission. Those responsibilities, which have legal ramifications, call on board members to develop or hone understanding in many areas, from financial management to organizational communication, from fundraising to strategic planning. Although it is impossible to calculate the precise number of people who are members of these governing boards at any given moment—nearly all of them without compensation—we do know that millions of women and men accept the fiduciary and other responsibilities of board service.

Governance Defined

Governance is the board's legal authority to exercise power and authority over an organization on behalf of the community it serves. The board is authorized to establish policies and make decisions that will affect the life and work of the organization. The board is where the proverbial "buck" stops; it is also held accountable for the actions that follow those policies and decisions. Governance is group action. Individual board members do not govern the organization. Rather, meeting as a group confers governing status to the board as a whole.

Authority to govern an organization may be granted by a variety of sources, from organizational members and supporters to public officials. When an organization is incorporated, the state in which the incorporation takes place assigns responsibility for the organization's affairs to a governing board. An organization's articles of incorporation or constitution (see Chapter One) and its bylaws (see Chapter Fourteen) will specify how its board is to be constituted and organized.

Sometimes groups other than the board carry the authority to control certain board decisions. For instance, in some membership organizations, a representative house of delegates must approve bylaws changes. In subsidiaries, certain decisions may require the approval of the parent organization board or must conform to a policy framework established by the parent board. Examples of such decisions include election of board members, changes in bylaws, sale or acquisition of property, hiring of the chief executive, or choice of management service provider.

There are some similarities—but many differences—between corporate boards and nonprofit boards. Both for-profit and nonprofit organizations need strong board leadership and must adhere to certain legal principles that are outlined in state corporation laws. But for-profits answer primarily to their shareholders and focus on generating profits for those people. In contrast, nonprofits are accountable to their members, constituents, supporters, donors, and the public; their missions are not to make money but to make a difference in someone's life or the world.

This chapter reviews fundamental responsibilities and principles of governance: the board's fiduciary responsibilities, the difference between collective and individual responsibilities, the critical place of mission at the center of governance, and the guiding principles of effective governance.

Why Nonprofits Need Boards

There are legal, ethical, and practical reasons to build a board when a nonprofit is created. These reasons shape the foundation for good governance.

Legal Reasons

State laws require that nonprofit corporations have a board to assume the fiduciary role for the organization's well-being. These laws assign overall responsibility and liability to that board. In addition to the board's responsibilities as a governing body, individual board members are bound by their legal obligations: the duties of care, loyalty, and obedience (see "Collective and Shared Responsibilities," later in this chapter).

State laws generally stipulate the minimum size for a board—mostly between one and three members—and other requirements that define how boards may function or be structured. Some state laws define the smallest acceptable number of independent board members (that is, members without specific personal benefits or attachment), but usually the laws do not address board composition. The articles of incorporation and bylaws define the internal authority within the nonprofit and clarify the board's role on top of the decision-making hierarchy. (Naturally, in a formal membership organization the members have certain rights to approve major board decisions.)

Federal law is less specific about board structure, but it does expect the board to serve as the gatekeeper for the organization. When applying for recognition of tax-exempt status, board members for a nonprofit must be listed to allow the IRS to determine whether proper oversight has been established. In complying with federal law, one of the board's roles is to ensure that no inappropriate private inurement takes place—a situation when an insider with decision-making power misdirects organizational assets into the hands of individuals who don't provide commensurate products or services in return (see Chapter Seven, Legal and Ethical Responsibilities).

Ethical Reasons

The board functions, in part, to assure the public and all stakeholders that the organization is in good hands. It assumes responsibility for the organization's achievements or lack thereof. It goes beyond the legal requirements to ensure that the organization not only does things right, but does the right thing.

The board acts as the agent for the organization's constituents. When a supporter, client, or customer relies on the organization to use its funds appropriately or provide trustworthy and quality services, the board sees to it that these expectations are met. Board members are not there to benefit personally from their affiliation; during decision making they are expected to place the interests of the organization above any other considerations.

Oversight is a primary duty for all boards. They work closely with management to ensure that goals are met and that ethical principles guide all activities. As overseers, board members also spell out the expectations and evaluate the results. The board is there to go above and beyond the status quo, keeping the organization viable by reacting to and anticipating stakeholders' needs.

Practical Reasons

A board is made up of individuals who, at one time or another, dedicate their efforts to help the organization get its work done. Especially in start-up organizations, boards draft the organizational documents, hunt for supplies and equipment, and procure funding. Before a staff is hired, board members usually manage the daily affairs and run the programs of an all-volunteer organization.

In most nonprofits, as soon as the situation allows, the board hires the first staff member—often a chief executive—and delegates the daily affairs to him or her, with the necessary support and guidance. At this point the board can devote its time to governing, providing direction, and ensuring that the mission of the organization stays on course.

Detached from daily affairs, the board is able to differentiate the trees from the forest—to look at the organization as part of its larger sphere and not just as an office that carries out the strategic plan. The perspectives that board members bring to the boardroom complement those of the chief executive. Together, they should be able to ask the probing questions necessary to avoid stagnation and keep the organization moving forward.

Finally, the board provides continuity. Individuals come and go, but the board as an entity remains. When good practices are institutionalized, the changing of the guard does not adversely affect the good work that has been accomplished.

Board Members as Fiduciaries

Contemporary law regarding the responsibilities of nonprofit board members is grounded in English common-law rules for administrators of charitable trusts. This framework assigned a great deal of responsibility to individual trustees and tended to foster a fairly cautious approach to organizational affairs. A number of court cases have since placed interpretation of nonprofit board accountability within the framework of corporate law. Now, legal responsibility in general rests with the board as a body rather than with individual board members. (For more about the legal responsibilities of nonprofit boards, see Chapter Seven.)

Board members today are fiduciaries of the organization's resources and guardians of its mission. Most state laws, by statute or court opinion, impose on board members the standards of conduct and management that, together, constitute fiduciary responsibility. Thus personal liability can result when a board member, officer, or key employee of a nonprofit organization breaches the standards of fiduciary responsibility.

A chief responsibility of board members is to maintain financial accountability and effective oversight of the organization they serve. As stewards of the organization's resources, board members must exercise due diligence to see that it is well managed and that its financial situation remains sound. (For more about financial oversight, see Chapter Eight.) Fiduciary duty requires board members to be objective, unselfish, responsible, honest, trustworthy, and efficient. They should always act for the good of the organization, rather than for their personal benefit. They need to exercise reasonable care in all decision making, without placing the organization under unnecessary risk.

Collective and Shared Responsibilities

- The distinction of legal liability between the board and an individual board member relates to the responsibility of *the board* for the organization and responsibility of *individual board members* for their actions. The board as a collective entity is responsible and liable for what happens in and to the organization. As the ultimate authority, it must ensure that the organization operates in compliance with the law and its own policies. Boards make decisions in a legally structured meeting.
- All actions taken by a board are held to three legal standards: the duty of care, the duty of loyalty, and the duty of obedience. These collective duties, which apply to the entire board, require the active participation of all individual board members. If the board or individual board members are sued, their actions or inaction are judged against these legal obligations. These three duties set the basic guidelines for the board to act as the fiduciary and the steward of the organization. (See Chapter Seven for an expanded discussion of these standards.)
  - *Duty of care.* A standard of care in decision making that can be expected of all prudent individuals under similar circumstances. Each board member is to act in good faith and actively participate in governance.
  - *Duty of loyalty.* A standard of faithfulness to the organization's priorities. Board members put the interests of the organization ahead of their own professional or personal interests or those of another, and they speak with one voice in their decision-making capacity.
  - *Duty of obedience.* A standard of faithfulness to the organization's mission and purpose, which requires that nonprofit board members comply with applicable federal, state, and local laws; adhere to the organization's bylaws; and remain the guardians of the mission.

Generally, board members who carry out their duties faithfully and in adherence to the duties of care, loyalty, and obedience will not be found personally liable. However, the demarcation between individual and collective responsibility can often be indistinct, and in legal action under certain circumstances, an individual board member may end up paying the penalties or having other sanctions applied.

Mission at the Center

To meet the challenges of the nonprofit environment, boards need members who understand governance as a dynamic activity. They need members who are fully and actively engaged in promoting the organization's achievement of its mission, developing and refining its vision, and upholding its values. The first order of business for board members is to understand and endorse these defining elements of the organization's identity.

Everything begins with the mission. Mission is the foremost organizing tool for a nonprofit, helping to build common understanding and ensuring that programs and activities are aligned toward the same goal. As part of their governance responsibilities, nonprofit board members are the keepers, watchers, challengers, revisers, and champions of the mission.

The center-stage role of mission in the nonprofit sector has a strong conceptual basis. Nonprofit organizations are founded to meet a need, and people invest time and money in these organizations to help them meet that need. People often identify first with the need and the values it represents—for example, equal access to education; intelligent media; or the rights of children, seniors, or people with disabilities. They show interest in the organization's work because of its expressed mission. Trade associations or professional societies have missions related to advancing the needs of their members. Individuals or corporations join membership organizations because these groups represent their interests and provide unique products, services, and information.

Nonprofit organizations are generally described as mission driven, mission focused, and values based. A mission-driven or mission-focused organization is motivated in its programs, activities, and decision making by remembering why it exists: to meet the needs of the community. To be values based means that a set of core values inspires and guides the involvement of board members, other volunteers, staff, and donors. Mission, vision, and values are the givens in establishing the framework for organizational involvement, investment, and advancement:

- *Mission* is the reason an organization exists, the need it is meeting in the community. A mission statement captures the reason and the need and communicates succinctly what inspires the organization to meet those needs.

- *Vision* is what the organization sees in the future for its community if the organization succeeds at its mission.
- *Values* are the deeply held beliefs that guide all aspects of the organization's programs and operations and provide the litmus test for all decisions.

For further discussion of mission, vision, and values in the context of strategic planning, see Chapter Twelve; in the context of evaluation, see Chapter Thirteen.

Characteristics of Exceptional Governance

Good governance is about providing critical capital—intellect, reputation, resources, and access—to strengthen the organization and in turn the community it serves. But a board may meet every legal requirement, adhere to proper procedures, and still be ineffective if it is not engaged in setting strategic direction and supporting the organization. If a board neglects the full range of its responsibilities, it may preclude the organization from reaching its potential. An exceptional board recognizes the impact of its leadership, and board members understand that they must be thoughtful and engaged leaders—not merely competent but passive stewards.

Boards often represent underperforming assets for nonprofit organizations that need every resource they can muster. Drawing on observations, academic knowledge, and proven practices, BoardSource identified the common traits and actions of boards that have made discernible differences to their organizations.

These boards behaved differently from other boards. To highlight these differences, BoardSource distinguishes between *responsible* boards and *exceptional* boards. A responsible board is capable and dutiful in carrying out its responsibilities. This is not always an easy feat, nor should it be taken for granted by board or staff members. A responsible board understands its fiduciary obligations, and it adds value to the organization by approving strategic plans and budgets, regularly reviewing financial statements, evaluating the chief executive annually, and participating in fundraising.

An exceptional board operates on a higher level. Its members give more of their time, talent, and treasure. But they also give differently. Their time may be spent more wisely, their skills and social networks better leveraged, and their treasure more strategically deployed. Exceptional boards measure organizational impact and evaluate their own performance, discuss and debate issues, and open doors and make connections. The difference between responsible and exceptional lies in thoughtfulness and intentionality, action and engagement, knowledge and communication.

Three common denominators enable the board to operate at an exceptional level:

1. *A frank and open relationship.* The chief executive is more than competent and confident. He or she is also open and honest with the board. The board, in turn, is committed to ensuring success, while recognizing that nonprofit organizations are complex and constantly changing. As interlocking pieces in a jigsaw puzzle that together create a complete picture, the chief executive and the board are complements, with mutual trust, respect, and appreciation building the foundation for a leadership team that can handle short- and long-term challenges.

2. *Intentional.* Great governance doesn't just happen by accident. It takes the right people in the right place at the right time. Who serves on a board matters, and board composition is an important indicator of an exceptional board. An exceptional board is also thoughtful, self-aware, and proactive. It balances the need for long-term stability with the need to adapt its own structures and practices as circumstances change and the organization evolves.

3. *Engaged.* Board work requires more than mere attendance at meetings. It requires personal motivation and commitment, as well as intellectual curiosity and an appetite for challenge. Board members must share a passion for the organization's cause. In turn, the chief executive must be ready, willing, and able to engage board members in making sense of situations, in determining what matters, and in solving dilemmas. Neither the board nor the chief executive can simply go through the governance motions and expect great results.

Effective Governance in Action

FRANK AND OPEN

Working together, the board and head of an independent school created a leadership succession plan a few years before the head of the school was to retire. Board and staff members participated in a collaborative, holistic review process that included articulating the institution's values, evaluating the school's other internal infrastructure needs, and assessing the board—all before the executive search officially started.

INTENTIONAL

A university foundation board, after asking how it could add real value to the institution, shifted the foundation's focus from fundraising to commercialization of intellectual property. In turn, the board populated itself with individuals who have significant professional expertise in law, finance, and research and development. Given the foundation's new role, the board also redefined its relationship with the university's administration and governing board, as well as with foundation and fundraising staff.

ENGAGED

A board member led a process that resulted in an emotionally powerful vision statement at an environmental organization. The board and the staff were inspired to reframe strategies, elevate goals, and embark on an ambitious fundraising campaign. The campaign raised significantly more money than expected, fueling even greater conservation success.

Exceptional boards add significant value to their organizations, making a discernible difference in advancing the mission. Good governance requires the board to balance its role as an oversight body with its role as a force supporting the organization.

The following twelve principles offer a description of an empowered board that is a strategic asset to be leveraged. They provide board members with a vision of what is possible and a way to add lasting value to the organization they lead.

1. *Constructive partnership.* Exceptional boards govern in constructive partnership with the chief executive, recognizing that the effectiveness of the board and chief executive are interdependent. They build this partnership through trust, candor, respect, and honest communication.
2. *Mission driven.* Exceptional boards shape and uphold the mission, articulate a compelling vision, and ensure the congruence between decisions and core values. They treat questions of mission, vision, and core values not as exercises to be done once, but as statements of crucial importance to be drilled down and folded into deliberations.
3. *Strategic thinking.* Exceptional boards allocate time to what matters most and continually engage in strategic thinking to hone the organization's direction. They not only align agendas and goals with strategic priorities but also use them for assessing the chief executive, driving meeting agendas, and shaping board recruitment.

4. *Culture of inquiry.* Exceptional boards institutionalize a culture of inquiry, mutual respect, and constructive debate that leads to sound and shared decision making. They seek more information, question assumptions, and challenge conclusions so that they may advocate for solutions based on analysis.

5. *Independent mindedness.* Exceptional boards are independent minded. They apply rigorous conflict-of-interest procedures, and their board members put the interests of the organization above all else when making decisions. They do not allow their votes to be unduly influenced by loyalty to the chief executive or by seniority, position, or reputation of fellow board members, staff, or donors.

6. *Ethos of transparency.* Exceptional boards promote an ethos of transparency by ensuring that donors, stakeholders, and interested members of the public have access to appropriate and accurate information regarding finances, operations, and results. They also extend transparency internally, ensuring that every board member has equal access to relevant materials when making decisions.

7. *Compliance with integrity.* Exceptional boards promote strong ethical values and disciplined compliance by establishing appropriate mechanisms for active oversight. They use these mechanisms, such as independent audits, to ensure accountability and sufficient controls; to deepen their understanding of the organization; and to reduce the risk of waste, fraud, and abuse.

8. *Sustaining resources.* Exceptional boards link bold visions and ambitious plans to financial support, expertise, and networks of influence. Linking budgeting to strategic planning, they approve activities that can be realistically financed with existing or attainable resources, while ensuring that the organization has the infrastructure and internal capacity it needs.

9. *Results oriented.* Exceptional boards are results oriented. They measure the organization's progress toward mission goals and evaluate the performance of major programs and services. They gauge efficiency, effectiveness, and impact while simultaneously assessing the quality of service delivery, integrating benchmarks against peers, and calculating return on investment.

10. *Intentional board practices.* Exceptional boards purposefully structure themselves to fulfill essential governance duties and to support organizational priorities. Making governance intentional, not incidental, exceptional boards invest in structures and practices that can be thoughtfully adapted to changing circumstances.

11. *Continuous learning.* Exceptional boards embrace the qualities of a continuous learning organization, evaluating their own performance and assessing the value they add to the organization. They embed learning opportunities into routine governance work and in activities outside of the boardroom.

TABLE 2.1. RESPONSIBLE BOARDS AND EXCEPTIONAL BOARDS

Responsible Boards . . .	Exceptional Boards . . .
Establish and review strategic plans.	Allocate time at meetings and between meetings to address what matters most and engage in strategic thinking on a regular basis.
Adopt a conflict-of-interest policy.	Adopt a conflict-of-interest policy that includes guidelines for disclosure, review, and recusal; require board members to sign the conflict-of-interest statement annually; and rigorously adhere to the policy.
Monitor financial performance and receive programmatic updates.	Measure overall organizational efficiency, effectiveness, and impact using various tools including dashboards.
Design board meetings to accomplish the work of the board.	Make meetings matter by improving meeting efficiency, using consent agendas and meeting regularly in executive sessions—with and without the chief executive—to allow for confidential discussion.
Orient new board members.	Invest in ongoing board development to deepen the commitment of board members, and have board members reflect on their own performance by conducting regular board self-assessments.

12. *Revitalization.* Exceptional boards energize themselves through planned turnover, thoughtful recruitment, and inclusiveness. They see the correlations among mission, strategy, and board composition, and they understand the importance of fresh perspectives and the risks of closed groups. They revitalize themselves through diversity of experience and through continuous recruitment.

Table 2.1 compares the actions of responsible and exceptional boards. It highlights acceptable and good practices and illustrates how an exceptional board goes beyond the call of duty.

Governance Through the Organizational Life Cycle

Nonprofit organizational development is similar to human development in that each nonprofit passes through stages that have foreseeable features and characteristics. Like life for humans, life for nonprofits is often messy and unpredictable.

The basic life-cycle model encompasses five stages. This model is only a framework that shows the typical nonprofit's journey. All organizations do not go through each stage or even need to, and the rate at which they pass through the stages varies. Organizational development has an organic, nonlinear flow, and an organization can make dramatic leaps—forward or back—at any point in its life cycle. The ability to achieve the mission through delivery of effective programs and services is the main determinant of the life-cycle stage. The level, quality, reach, and impact of programs and services are a better measurement of development stage than age, budget size, or number of staff.

Stage One: Start-up

A nonprofit organization is usually conceived when one or more people see a need, formulate an idea to address it, and decide to form an organization to do the necessary work. The start-up phase generally lasts a few years, and the annual operating budget is small but growing during this period.

The founder or group of founders usually is visionary, has a passionate commitment to the mission, and brings a high level of energy to initiating the first simple programs. If there is a single founder, this person usually acts as staff leader and assembles a small group of enthusiastic volunteers who follow and encourage the founder. If more than one person initiates the organization, they may serve as the core of the board. Most start-ups operate initially as all-volunteer organizations, meaning that there are no paid staff or managers, and the board members manage volunteers, handling all other duties themselves.

Typically, the board of a start-up organization plays a hands-on role in oversight and management. The organization is especially vulnerable during this early period, so the leaders need to be persistent, flexible, and resilient to allow programs to take root and begin to blossom.

Stage Two: Adolescent

Nonprofit adolescence is often accompanied by uncertainty and angst. Although age and size can vary widely, this stage often occurs between the third and sixth year of an organization's existence, as the annual operating budget grows from approximately $250,000 to about one or two million dollars. This phase normally entails expansion of programs, broader outreach, more staff, and larger quarters. Frequently, the adolescent nonprofit experiences instability when it does not adequately anticipate the systems required to support this growth.

During expansion, the chief executive and board focus on meeting early programmatic goals for quantity of clients served and quality of services. They also undertake a formal self-assessment process to be sure all board members are clear about their roles and responsibilities, develop simple systems for gathering and using data about programmatic outcomes, and incorporate all of this valuable information into a strategic planning process. As the staff expands and takes on more responsibility for day-to-day tasks, the board will relinquish its operational role and focus more on advice, oversight, and long-term planning. To adapt and stay relevant, the board and chief executive need to monitor the organization's progress and relate it to developments in the outside world that could influence its effectiveness and viability. By broadening connections with constituents and evaluating programs in simple ways, an organization can keep its pulse on how needs are shifting and whether programs are working or not working.

Stage Three: Mature

Any group that aims to deliver successfully on its mission must attain the mature stage—and sustain itself there. An organization can be said to have entered maturity when its programs are established and well regarded in the marketplace or community, its operations and systems are formalized, and its executive and board leadership are capable of directing a complex organization. Typical nonprofits reach this point some time after five or six years of operations and when the budget exceeds one or two million dollars.

At this stage, the board further reduces its operational role and increases its policy, oversight, and fundraising role. It usually expands, becomes more diverse and more specialized, and formalizes its structure. The mature board continually assesses its own performance and modifies its composition, roles, responsibilities, and structure to stay effective.

Maturity is a mission-driven stage. A fully actualized, mature nonprofit should remain vital and continue to improve the quality of its programs so that it makes significant progress in fulfilling the defined need.

Stage Four: Stagnant

Each year, many nonprofits fall into stagnation. Savvy board members or executives can recognize the signs: funding support diminishes, demand for services wanes, the number of volunteers declines, staff morale suffers, and key leaders and managers leave the organization. A nonprofit may descend rapidly into this crisis, or the decline can take years as the organization begins to wither almost imperceptibly. Stagnation can occur at any stage, from start-up through maturity.

The good news is that even seriously ailing organizations may be able to renew themselves—a difficult, sometimes unpleasant, and usually thankless job to accomplish. The board, with cooperation and support from the chief executive, is usually required to take the first steps to initiate recovery. Because adaptability and leadership are so often at fault, often the process must begin with a board shake-up. Board leaders may want to retire some disengaged veteran board members and add new people who will support the renewal effort. Board development will need to be directed toward bridging skill gaps, removing unproductive members, and creating new structures and processes to improve decision making and performance. The board will need new members who function well in adverse circumstances and who savor a challenge. (See Chapter Six, Building a Board, for principles and strategies that work when renewing the board.)

Stage Five: Defunct

Literally thousands of nonprofits close their doors every year. In a few situations, a group may disband because it has actually fulfilled its mission. In most cases, however, nonprofits dissolve for less positive reasons, such as loss of a compelling mission focus, a chronic inability to operate programs effectively, or a lack of technical expertise in marketing and fundraising.

How do the organizational leaders determine when it is best to disband the organization rather than attempt renewal? The following conditions are important indicators:

- Programs are widely considered to be ineffective, and the client base has declined significantly.
- The board of directors is moribund, taking little interest in the problems of the organization and showing no will or ability to initiate needed change.
- The current chief executive is unable or unwilling to take on the task of renewal, and the board can find no one else to do the job.
- The organization's public reputation is poor and seems beyond resurrection.
- Management systems are not supporting the organization's work.

Although the decline into obsolescence usually occurs over a period of time, sometimes one significant change, internal or external, is all that is needed to send a distressed operation into a swift downward spiral.

The work of improving the performance of a nonprofit organization is difficult and complex—there is no single right way to do it and no predetermined timeframe for completing it. Understanding where an organization falls in its cycle of development and how to build capacity along the way is an effort worth making.

Chapter Exercises

- What might be the differences between a nonprofit's initial board and the board that has been in place for twenty years?
- How would you define the difference between a responsible board and an exceptional board?
- Formulate some hypothetical examples of organizations in each stage of the life cycle.

CHAPTER THREE

GOVERNANCE ROLES

There's no denying that nonprofit organizations in the United States play a vital role in society, from assisting victims of natural disasters to beautifying our neighborhoods, from educating our children to healing the sick. To ensure that their organizations have the resources, leadership, and oversight necessary to carry out these and other vital activities, nonprofit boards must understand and fulfill their governance responsibilities.

This chapter explains the governance roles assumed by the full board and by individual board members. Each section links to other chapters in this handbook that explore elements of these governance roles in greater depth. It is important to remember that because every organization is unique, no one-size-fits-all model of governance applies. There are, however, certain fundamental responsibilities common to nearly all boards. These responsibilities in turn provide a frame of reference for assessing the board's performance periodically. It is equally important to clearly articulate expectations for those who serve on boards and to use those standards to assess individual board member performance.

Board Roles

The board as a whole has three primary roles: setting organizational direction, including ensuring effective planning; ensuring the necessary resources, both financial and human; and providing oversight of the chief executive, assets, and programs and services.

Set Organizational Direction

The demand for organizational effectiveness and efficient use of resources is increasing. The public in general, and funding sources in particular, are challenging nonprofit organizations to prove their worth. It is clearer than ever before that boards must take responsibility for establishing organizational direction so that all efforts are geared toward shared ends.

Some nonprofit organizations appear to work hard but fail to make a great deal of difference. Busy-ness and constant activity can mask a lack of direction. People burn out because they are moving in circles rather than forward toward shared goals. Different people or groups within an organization must operate with common assumptions about what is important and what the organization as a whole needs to accomplish. Resources should be effectively apportioned so that every program or approach builds on the efforts of the others. An organization will rarely make a significant difference unless it pays careful attention to the ends and outcomes of its programs. Instead of thinking only about what to *do*, organizational leaders should also be thinking about what to *achieve*.

Setting direction requires looking beyond the immediate horizon. It means asking questions. *What are the issues the organization must confront in order to serve our mission in the years ahead? Where should it be in five years? What is it committed to achieving?* Setting direction means making a habit of strategic thinking and taking the time to engage in strategic planning to establish a framework for the organization's efforts. Developing a shared vision, articulating guiding values for organizational action, establishing major goals, and outlining strategies for achieving goals are all part of direction setting.

Determine Mission, Vision, and Values

The board is responsible for ensuring that the organization's mission is clearly stated and advanced. A commitment to mission should drive the board's and management's priorities. Organizations need a relatively brief written mission statement (the reason the organization exists and the need it meets), sometimes supplemented with a more detailed statement of vision (what the community's future will look like if the mission is achieved) and values (the organization's deeply held beliefs).

The board and management should review the mission statement periodically to ensure that it is useful, honest, valid, and current. The mission statement should articulate whom the organization serves and explain what makes it distinctive. The board is ultimately responsible for the mission statement. Still, before developing or revising the mission, wise chief executives and boards consult with the organization's stakeholders—for example, its members, volunteers, staff, clients served, or the leaders of any subsidiary enterprises.

Good statements of mission, vision, and values also serve to guide and benchmark such undertakings as organizational planning and assessment, board and staff decisions about programs and services, volunteer initiatives, and priorities among competing demands for scarce resources. The board should periodically assess what the organization does to ensure that it is not drifting away from its intended mission and purposes. The mission, which will vary widely from one organization to the next, also sets the stage for developing fundraising strategies and serves as a benchmark for sustaining the confidence and support of those who support the organization.

For more about mission and the board's role in articulating it, see Chapter Two, What Is Governance? For a discussion of mission and strategic planning, see Chapter Ten, Strategic Thinking and Strategic Planning.

Engage in Strategic Thinking

Effective boards hone the organization's direction by making strategic thinking a part of regular, ongoing board work. With guidance from management, they stay current with internal and external forces that drive change. They look backward and forward to understand what has emerged and imagine what is possible. By engaging in strategic thinking, they are able to explore the frameworks within which the organization operates and ask far-ranging questions that drive deeper, value-enriched decisions.

In collaboration with the chief executive, the board should allocate the lion's share of its time to issues of substantial consequence. Moving away from report-driven formats, agendas carve out time for meaningful discussion that shapes organizational strategy and actions. Meetings are well attended, agendas feature only a few issues, and rich debate ensues. Working with senior staff, board members help clarify thorny problems, offer breakthrough insights on pressing issues, present new ways of framing challenges and opportunities, and actively generate important strategic ideas.

See Chapter Ten, Strategic Thinking and Strategic Planning, for a discussion of the concept of strategic thinking, and Chapter Sixteen, Board Dynamics, for more about incorporating strategic thinking into a culture of inquiry.

Ensure Effective Planning

Strategically focused planning enables the board and staff to translate the mission and purposes into meaningful and manageable goals and objectives, which then focus its resources and energy. Goals, which usually require new resources, also become the benchmarks for assessing the organization's progress over time. Although the chief executive and staff are responsible for designing and conducting a process that provides what is, in effect, a business plan for the organization, the board participates in and approves all decisions that set strategic direction.

Members of governing boards—who are, after all, part-time volunteers—often ask, "Where and how do we participate meaningfully and appropriately in the process?" The short answer is that board members are at their best when they ask good questions and offer ideas of their own about the organization's operating environment. The board's responsibilities are to

- Insist that comprehensive organizational planning occurs
- Participate with staff in the planning process
- Assess the merits of the process and its results
- Approve the agreed-upon outcomes
- Use the goals as a guide for budgeting and other priorities
- Track the plan's implementation and the organization's progress

When board members are involved extensively in planning, they own responsibility for helping to implement appropriate goals and priorities, acquire new resources, and much more. Their participation helps to ensure that the big picture—how the organization fits within its larger community of interest—is considered, along with key competitive and environmental factors. By bringing their experience and professional talents to appropriate parts of the planning process, by asking good questions of other participants, and by diligently demonstrating that the governing board takes planning seriously, board members add a great deal to the process.

There are nearly as many opinions about planning and how it should be done as there are different sizes and shapes and missions of organizations, both for-profit and not-for profit. Each organization should determine its own approach to planning, based on the needs and life cycle of the organization. What is most important is that planning be done and that it be tailored to the organization's culture, the staff's competence, and the experience and wishes of the chief executive, who is mostly responsible for getting the job done.

Chapter Ten explores planning in more detail.

Ensuring the Necessary Resources

Once the board has established a sense of direction, it must make sure that the organization has four principal types of resources for achieving its goals: board members with appropriate competencies, people to do the work, money to pay salaries and other expenses, and credibility with the public on whose support the organization will depend. The organization's size and complexity, structure, culture, and environment will determine how resource development responsibilities are allocated.

Build a Competent Board

A nonprofit board represents talent that the organization can draw on to further its mission. For this reason, board composition is critical to success. Many boards revitalize themselves through term limits and a well-defined process for recruitment that assesses future organizational needs and current board member competencies. They seek diversity in terms of personal and professional backgrounds and experiences, and they welcome differing voices and an array of perspectives. They are acutely aware of the need for members who have knowledge of the nonprofit sector, superior financial acumen, ability to secure funding, and personal characteristics and experiences that positively enrich group interaction. They also use board composition as a strategy to increase understanding of their constituencies and community needs. Board composition matters if others are to see the organization as a responsible and civic-minded enterprise in the service of all people.

Most boards delegate recruitment, orientation, and ongoing education to a committee—usually called the governance committee—whose purview extends beyond nominations to board development. Along with the chief executive, they recruit candidates to strengthen board capacity in terms of expertise and group dynamics. Recruitment is continuous, with individual members sharing responsibility for identifying and cultivating new candidates. They consciously and conscientiously inform candidates and new members of their responsibilities and expectations. It follows that clarifying expectations for individual board members before they are asked to join the board can greatly influence how energetic and effective they are likely to be. Recognizing the importance of board leadership development and succession planning, governance committee members also groom board chairs and officers purposefully through a transparent, participatory process.

Fresh perspectives energize the work of nonprofit boards; in contrast, closed groups within the board risk the opposite effect. Evaluation of individual board members' participation, as well as term limits, are important techniques for keeping board members aware of their responsibilities and rejuvenating the board when necessary. Boards should not hesitate to remove ineffective members to maintain a sense of shared responsibility. They can also find creative alternatives—such as membership in committees, task forces, and advisory councils—for keeping valuable members associated with the organization after their terms expire.

Consult Chapter Four, Governance Structure, for the governance committee's job description. Chapter Six, Building a Board, outlines the cycle of recruitment, orientation, and ongoing education. Board evaluation is reviewed in Chapter Thirteen.

Ten Resolutions That Promote Board Development

1. Remember that mission and stakeholders come first.
2. Ensure the organization's relevance and value to stakeholders and to society as a whole.
3. Openly debate policies, practices, and choices that further our mission.
4. Plan for a marathon, not a sprint.
5. When new members join the board, pass the baton to them, using their unique strengths to advance the mission.
6. Apply each team member's assets to fit organizational needs.
7. Contribute time and money for the organization's good works.
8. Plan for the continuing contribution of those rotating off the board who still wish to be involved with the social and philanthropic goals of the organization.
9. Focus on the organization's future. Don't just fall in love with its past.
10. Exhibit courage, flexibility, and willingness to change as challenges and opportunities emerge.

Select the Chief Executive

After determining the organization's mission and purposes, selecting the chief executive has the next greatest impact on the success of the organization. With the right person in the position, the organization will be better equipped to succeed. Choosing the wrong person will have long-lasting adverse consequences. The board must choose carefully and wisely.

The process of choosing a new chief executive begins well before the search itself. It is essential to start from a clear consensus on the organization's nature and current circumstances, its strategic and most pressing priorities and goals that are expected to be addressed—that is, what does the board expect a new chief executive to achieve? It is easy to fall back on job announcement clichés—"We seek an effective communicator" or "The outstanding candidate will be an effective speaker" or "We seek an experienced and proven fundraiser"—when true leadership is actually more than the sum of a simple list of skill sets.

Addressing the kinds of issues and needs that will constitute the challenge for the new leader—and seeking the mix of experience and personal style that fits the organization's mission and culture—is more likely to produce outstanding candidates. There is no single prescription that works for all organizations; the simple facts are (1) it is very difficult to define leadership, and yet we know it when we see or have it, and (2) we often don't know how effective our new leader is until he or she has been in the job for many months.

Especially in large and complex organizations, board leaders should remain open to the idea of identifying, developing, and promoting promising talent from within—and even encourage it, to provide a wider pool of candidates. On the other hand, the board should not conclude too quickly that internal promotion is the only possible course of action. Succession planning is part of the board's responsibility to ensure that the organization is prepared for the future. When done properly—with the full commitment and assistance of the current chief executive—the odds of making a smooth transition to new leadership increase dramatically. (For more about succession planning, see Chapter Twelve, Succession Planning and Chief Executive Transition.)

When a vacancy occurs in the chief executive position, the board appoints a search committee, which may decide to hire an executive search firm or to conduct the search on its own. Although the committee takes the lead, the full board should be kept well informed as the search proceeds. Of course, the full board makes the final decision, based on the committee's recommendation. (For discussion of the chief executive search and transition, see Chapter Twelve.)

Ensure Adequate Financial Resources

Although much can and should be expected of the chief executive and management on this score, the board works closely with the chief executive to diversify and maximize sustainable revenue sources so that the organization can achieve its goals. It is up to the board to engage with management to develop and monitor a portfolio of income streams, which may range from fundraising and sponsorship, to earned income and for-profit subsidiaries, to program-related and market investments.

Relying on just one or two of these areas to generate the majority of the organization's income can be risky: what would happen, for instance, if the number of dues-paying members dropped precipitously? The board should be willing to advocate or approve creation of appropriate new products, services, or activities that not only have the potential for net income growth but also are consistent with the organization's purposes.

The board also establishes clear expectations for member participation in development activities and individual giving. Members not only make personally meaningful annual contributions but also stretch further for special campaigns. They extend the reach of the organization by actively using their own reputations and networks to secure funds, expertise, and access.

In raising private support, the board works in partnership with the chief executive and the director of development (if the organization has one). Specifically, the board should assess its own involvement in meeting fundraising targets and goals and should have clear obligations regarding personal philanthropy. In addition to being able to report 100-percent board participation to potential and current supporters, board members are better fundraisers when they set their own good example. After all, if board members don't substantially support their own organization, why should anyone else?

The board should also be ready to help open doors, when they can, to secure resources. They can assist staff by identifying potential donors, helping to solicit support, and thanking donors and maintaining cordial relationships with them.

Resource development is a function of the full board, not just its development committee. The committee is simply the board's agent to help oversee the work of all board members, the chief executive, and the development staff.

Chapter Nine addresses the board's role in the critical area of fundraising.

Enhance the Organization's Public Standing

Board members serve as a link between the organization and its members, stakeholders, constituents, or clients. They should think of themselves as the organization's ambassadors and advocates—ideally, even after they leave the board. The challenge for the board, together with management, is how to communicate the organization's story strategically and contribute to a healthy and accurate public image for the organization.

Constituents, members, and clients are invaluable resources that help to bring useful information back to the organization. Serving as an ambassador works both ways: board members are also representatives of those they presume to serve through the organization's mission and activities. The executive staff and board leaders should welcome feedback, suggestions for improving what board members do, ideas for doing some things better, even complaints or concerns. A healthy organization is always in touch, and board members are the vital link.

Elements of a comprehensive public awareness process include:

- Clearly articulated achievements, described using a variety of electronic and print media
- Contributions to the public good, communicated to community and government leaders
- Explanations of how gifts and grants and other revenue sources are accounted for and allocated
- Speeches by board members to civic and community groups

Communication plans are an important part of organizational planning and strategic thinking. When asked what the organization is and does, all board members should have an elevator speech—an interesting and compelling explanation, deliverable in less than a minute, of the organization's mission and purpose. There is no substitute for enthusiastic, even passionate board members who always manage to insert something wonderful about the organization into conversations with friends and colleagues.

Board members should also remember that whatever they say about the organization carries great weight, whether intended or not. Thus confidential information must be protected as confidential, even from close friends and relatives.

For more about the board's role in communications and outreach, see Chapter Eleven.

Provide Oversight

All of a board's work involves both authority and accountability. However, in its oversight role, the emphasis is on accountability. As far as much of the public is concerned, a board's most important role is to provide oversight, not only of finances and programs, but also of an organization's legal and moral conduct and its overall effectiveness. People want to know that somebody is checking to be sure that the organization is making a difference and that resources are being used wisely. A board must take its oversight role seriously, and the organization's constituencies must be made aware that the board is doing so. The organization's Web site is the ideal way to provide information about the board and its work, as is an annual report.

Support and Evaluate the Chief Executive

Selecting the chief executive is only the beginning of what everyone hopes will be a long and productive relationship with the governing board that will bring real achievement and long service to the organization. Providing personal and organizational support for executive leadership, periodically assessing the chief executive's performance, and acknowledging superb service through appropriate compensation are key board responsibilities. A high-performing board gives ongoing attention to these matters.

The chief executive's success is linked to the board's determination to do its part to sustain an effective relationship—one marked by mutual respect on both sides and an understanding of the distinction between board and executive responsibilities—a distinction determined, first and foremost, by open communication. The board chair has an especially important responsibility, as does the chief executive, to provide the board with the bad news as well as the good. Their respect for one another's different but complementary responsibilities affects how well the board itself functions. Again, there can only be one chief executive and one chair of the board; their respective responsibilities should not be confused. (For more about the relationship between the chief executive and the board, see Chapter Five.)

Specifically, the board ensures that the chief executive

- Receives frequent, substantive, and constructive feedback (not just at the time of the annual performance review)
- Has confidence that the board chair will intervene with any board members who may misunderstand or abuse their positions
- Feels that on-the-job performance is being assessed fairly and appropriately, without resorting to oversimplified checklists, rating scales, or invitations for constituents or staff to offer critiques
- Is introduced by board members to key community leaders who can assist and support the organization
- Receives invitations to important social events, opening opportunities for the chief executive to speak at significant or high-profile community functions
- Receives compliments for exceptional initiatives (every chief executive appreciates the occasional "pat on the back" from board members, especially the board's leaders)
- Is encouraged to use professional and personal leave time for renewal
- Feels that, at the least, the board chair is aware of and sensitive to any personal situations or needs and respects the confidentiality of their private conversations

For more about the board's role in supporting and evaluating the chief executive, see Chapters Twelve and Thirteen.

Protect Assets and Provide Financial Oversight

Safeguarding organizational assets, or holding them "in trust" on behalf of others, is one of the most important board functions. The board ensures that the organization has a clear financial plan that is aligned with strategic, operating, and development or philanthropic grantmaking plans. Linking budgeting to strategic planning, it approves activities that can be realistically financed with existing or attainable resources.

Financial oversight includes a constellation of concepts. The board, often working in concert with the chief executive,

- Reviews and approves how the organization budgets, spends, and makes money
- Establishes and follows monetary policies that balance short- and long-term needs
- Verifies that the organization's financial systems and practices meet accepted standards
- Ensures that the organization has adequate operational reserves for rainy days and to take advantage of unexpected opportunities
- Safeguards the organization's reputation by making sure it operates in a transparent, accountable manner, including conducting an annual independent audit
- Ensures that the organization is not subjected to unnecessary risk

The board can delegate some details to a finance committee and some to an audit committee, but the full board always retains the final responsibility. For more about the finance and audit committees, see Chapter Four, Governance Structure, and Chapter Eight, Financial Oversight.

Board members must understand the issues important to financial integrity and solvency, safeguards and procedures to protect the organization, and signs of financial trouble. That means knowing how to read and understand the financial information—such as distinguishing the important numbers and relationships—and, most important, making decisions based on the information. Developing this knowledge enables board members to recognize impending problems and tell the difference between minor ripples and major crises.

Of course, a board shouldn't expect every one of its members to become a financial expert. Board members inevitably will have differing levels of expertise. But, at a minimum, it is a good idea to ask an expert to provide training so every member can attain at least a basic understanding of nonprofit accounting and the organization's financial side. In addition, all board members need to feel comfortable asking questions when they don't understand something and need to be able to make sense of the answers (and realize when the answer doesn't make sense). Simply put, there are no dumb questions.

Financial information is not the only type of information used in decision making. But it plays an essential part in all important decisions, even those that may, at first glance, appear nonfinancial in nature (for example, should the organization keep its clinic open an extra hour in the evening so people can get there after work?). Armed with this knowledge, decision makers can better protect and enhance the organization's capacity to serve the community.

In 2002, after several high-profile instances of corporate financial mismanagement, the U.S. Congress passed the Sarbanes-Oxley Act. For the most part, this law does not impose legal requirements on nonprofits (though two parts of it do; see Chapter Eight for more information). But its passage profoundly influenced debate and discussion about the practice of nonprofit governance. Several states have proposed or passed regulations that extend some provisions of the Sarbanes-Oxley Act to nonprofit organizations. For instance, the California Nonprofit Integrity Act of 2004 requires charities with gross revenues of $2 million or more to have an audit committee. Many of the provisions of the federal Sarbanes-Oxley Act—especially those related to internal controls—are generally good practices for nonprofits to adopt, because doing so enhances financial reporting and accountability to stakeholders.

Monitor and Strengthen Programs and Services

This board responsibility begins with ensuring that current and proposed programs and services align with the organization's stated mission and purposes. Given limited dollars and unlimited demands on them, the board ultimately decides among competing priorities.

What the organization actually does, and how well it does it, should be at the heart of board curiosity. Board work focuses primarily on the organization's impact, as determined by indicators expressed in the strategic plan. These indicators include the number of clients served, number of attendees at particular events, the extent to which program participants achieved the desired results, revenues and expenditures for individual services, and changes in behaviors or conditions over the long term. Board members should always ask these questions:

- What data and information will help us assess our operational effectiveness, financial condition, and programmatic activity?
- What difference are we trying to make?

- How do we know whether we are making a difference or succeeding at our mission?

Because most volunteer, nonprofit, and tax-exempt organizations do not have board members who are program experts, professional service providers, or practitioners, they usually hire qualified staff to execute programs and gather such data. They aim for a balance between the board's responsibility to ensure quality, cost-effective programs and services and the staff's responsibility to creatively initiate, conduct, and evaluate them.

At times, these different roles of board and staff can become confused—particularly when board members of small organizations must, of necessity, volunteer extensively to conduct and manage programs. In particular, membership-based professional societies and trade associations often struggle with where to draw the line between staff and board functions because their board members are usually practitioners in the field the organization serves. When board members' knowledge and work experience relate directly to what the organization does, ambiguity, confusion, and tension may arise unless the board remains focused on its responsibility to align the organization's programs with its mission and purposes.

How does a board monitor and otherwise contribute to strengthening the organization's endeavors, especially when a well-qualified staff is in place? For most boards, fulfilling this responsibility is always a work in progress. It includes

- Periodically assessing the efficacy of program and service offerings (some boards establish a committee to evaluate programs and services)
- Asking good questions about proposed programs and services, especially as they relate to the organization's unique mission and purposes
- Studying cost-benefit ratios and outcome-based measurement data to facilitate an exchange of information and learning
- Occasionally recommending or authorizing management to invite qualified third-party consultants to study programs or services that may be causing concern

Effective chief executives work with their boards to explore ideas, generate questions for meeting agendas, and identify the benchmark data that will show at a glance how the organization is doing. For more about the board's role in evaluation, see Chapter Thirteen.

Ensure Legal and Ethical Integrity

Because the board is ultimately responsible for ensuring adherence to legal standards and ethical norms, its members must collectively exhibit diligence, commitment, and vigilance to keep their house in order. This board responsibility, like several others, begins with hiring and retaining a chief executive whose moral compass and integrity are above reproach. The organization's reputation and public standing require everyone to take three watchwords seriously: compliance, transparency, and accountability.

The term *compliance* is shorthand for the local, state, and federal regulatory and legal requirements that are considered part of a board's fiduciary responsibility. As a result of the Sarbanes-Oxley Act (mentioned earlier), boards are taking care to

- Ensure that the organization adheres to local, state, and federal laws and regulations that apply to nonprofit organizations
- Ensure that the organization registers with appropriate state agencies as required before beginning organized fundraising campaigns
- Act in accordance with the provisions of the organization's bylaws and articles of incorporation, amending them when necessary

Transparency refers to the need to provide accurate information about an organization's revenue, how it is expended, and its due diligence. Organizations should document how executive compensation is linked to performance, and they should keep records about what other peer and other similar-sized organizations pay their top staff officers. Clear policies and procedures should be in place for destruction of documents, gifts from vendors and suppliers, and competitive bids for products and services. The organization should publish annual reports, and it should respond willingly to requests for information from individuals and organizations, including the media. Board members should also familiarize themselves with the wide range of questions asked on Internal Revenue Service Form 990, which is a public document and available to any citizen who requests it (for information about Form 990, see Chapter Seven, Legal and Ethical Responsibilities).

Although the board sets and periodically assesses the adequacy of major organizational policy, *accountability* measures will ordinarily and appropriately fall to management. But the board needs to ensure that the organization

- Adopts a code of conduct or ethical standards for board members and officers
- Defines what constitutes possible conflicts of interest, establishes procedures to deal with real or possible conflicts, and annually discloses any such possible conflicts for board members and officers
- Implements the organization's whistle-blower policy, which should include procedures for how and to whom to report allegations of wrongdoing

- Looks at annual board member and officer disclosure statements and acts on them through an appropriate board committee, as required by established policy
- Keeps detailed records of any lobbying expenditures and activities
- Maintains official records for the time periods required
- Develops and maintains up-to-date personnel policies and procedures (including staff grievance protocols)
- Conducts annual audits of all revenues, assets, expenditures, and liabilities
- Publishes and widely distributes annual reports that detail the organization's mission, programs, achievements, board members, and finances

Chapter Seven explores the board's role in ensuring integrity in the legal and ethical realms.

Individual Roles

While the board as a whole has certain roles and responsibilities, the board is, after all, composed of individuals. These individuals (board member, board chair, chief executive, other board officers, and former board members) each play a part in ensuring that the board functions effectively; their roles are explored in the following sections.

The Board Member's Role

Although governing boards have the legal authority to exercise their responsibilities as their organization's fiduciaries, individual board members do not. Indeed, while individual board members have considerably different yet complementary responsibilities to those held by the board, they do not have the board's legal authority (except when the board votes to give its officers or other members certain and limited authority to act on its behalf).

Clearly articulating the board's corporate responsibilities and authority (preferably in the bylaws) and the responsibilities and expectations of board members (preferably codified as a separate policy statement) is a best practice. It can be helpful to ask leading peer organizations with similar missions for copies of what they have developed. As an alternative, the list of responsibilities in this chapter (see sidebar on next page) can serve as a framework.

A clear statement of individual board member responsibilities adapted to the organization's mission and needs serves at least two purposes. First, when recruiting new board members, it helps to clarify what the organization expects before candidates accept the invitation to be nominated. Second, it can provide criteria for identifying and recruiting prospective nominees and reviewing the performance of current board members who are eligible for reelection or reappointment.

Individual Board Member Responsibilities

GENERAL EXPECTATIONS

- Know the organization's mission, purpose, goals, policies, programs, services, strengths, and needs.
- Serve in leadership positions and undertake special assignments willingly and enthusiastically.
- Avoid prejudiced judgments on the basis of information received from individuals; urge staff members with grievances to follow established policies and procedures through their supervisors. All significant matters coming to you should be called to the attention of the chief executive and/or the board's elected leader as appropriate.
- Follow trends in the organization's field of interest and keep informed.
- Bring goodwill and a sense of humor to the board's deliberations.
- Suggest to the appropriate committee possible nominees for board membership who are women and men of achievement and distinction and who would make significant contributions to the board and organization.

MEETINGS

- Prepare for and conscientiously participate in board and committee meetings, including appropriate organizational activities when possible.
- Ask timely and substantive questions at board and committee meetings, consistent with your conscience and convictions.
- Maintain confidentiality of the board's executive sessions and any confidential information given to you. Never speak for the board or organization unless authorized to do so, but also remember that all utterances from board members carry great weight with those within and outside of the organization. Private opinion on any matter is often construed by others as the board's official posture whether it really is or isn't.
- Occasionally suggest board and committee meeting agenda items to board leaders and the chief executive to ensure that significant policy-related and strategic matters are discussed.
- Follow and support the decisions of the board. Do not undermine those decisions if you disagree.

RELATIONSHIP WITH STAFF

- Counsel the chief executive as appropriate, providing support through difficult relationships with groups or individuals.

- Avoid asking the staff for favors, including special requests for extensive information that may take extraordinary time to gather and is not part of ongoing board or committee work—unless you have consulted with the chief executive, board chair, or appropriate committee chair.
- Remember that the chief executive—not board members or the board—is responsible for assessing staff performance.

AVOIDING CONFLICTS

- Serve the organization as a whole rather than any special interest group or constituency. Even if you were invited to serve by virtue of your relationship with a certain constituency or organization, your first obligation is to avoid any preconception that you "represent" anything other than the overall organization's best interests.
- Avoid even the appearance of a conflict of interest that might embarrass the board or the organization; disclose any possible conflicts to the board in a timely fashion.
- Maintain independence and objectivity and do what a sense of fairness, ethics, and personal integrity dictate.
- Never accept (or offer) favors or gifts from (or to) anyone who does business with the organization.

FIDUCIARY RESPONSIBILITIES

- At all times, exercise prudence with the board in the control and transfer of funds.
- Faithfully read and understand the organization's financial statements and otherwise help the board fulfill its fiduciary responsibility.

FUNDRAISING

- Give an unrestricted annual gift and restricted program or project support in line with your particular interests and personal means. Always do your best to set an example for other board members.
- Assist the development committee and staff by helping to identify potential givers and implement fundraising strategies through personal influence where you have it (corporations, individuals, and foundations).

AMBASSADORIAL SERVICE

- Represent your organization responsibly and diligently in the community it serves by telling the organization's story and presenting its accomplishments as well as its needs and current challenges.
- Represent your community to your organization. Bring back concerns, ideas, suggestions, and compliments when you believe they have merit or possibility.

The Board Chair's Role

The board chair is responsible for leading the board in the oversight and support responsibilities that are critical to good governance. Serving the organization's interests and needs is the foundation from which a board chair operates. A visionary board chair understands this practice and puts it into action. He or she is a generative and strategic thinker who is vigilant about asking questions and seeking knowledge to understand the opportunities, challenges, and threats that affect the organization's big picture.

Visionary leaders attract followers and motivate people, focus on the big issues, make effectiveness a top objective, have the capability to set direction, and are willing to take calculated risks. A visionary leader empowers the board to move forward and to build organizational capacity. He or she understands that the board chair role is not about serving personal ego and preference. It is about serving the organization.

The board chair must be knowledgeable about the organization—its mission, vision, values, programs, services, constituents, and resources—and understand its place in the larger framework of the community and the still-larger sphere of local and national peer organizations. With a respect for and understanding of the organization, the context for the board chair role emerges. The role incorporates exhibiting leadership skills (how the chair carries out the duties) and adhering to strong governance practices (what duties are expected). The following list works as a board chair job description incorporating this dual focus.

Responsibilities of the Board Chair

LEADERSHIP SKILLS

Personal Qualities

- Be approachable and available.
- Be a good listener and communicator.
- Show integrity, respect, and humility.
- Be a strategist and a visionary and generative thinker.
- Develop group facilitation skills.
- Encourage open communication and constructive debate.

Commitment to the Board

- Engage board members to take ownership for the work of the board.

- Celebrate the hard work and achievements of individual board members and the collective board.
- Promote outstanding board development and governance practices.

Commitment to the Organization

- Show an understanding of and passion for the mission, values, and work of the organization.
- Engage board members to show the same commitment.
- Uphold legal and ethical standards of conduct.

DUTIES

Chief Executive

- Cultivate a working partnership with the chief executive (see Chapter Five).
- Oversee the hiring, monitoring, and evaluation of the chief executive.

Board Members

- Ensure that every board member carries out the roles and responsibilities of board service.
- Be the contact for board members on board issues.
- Oversee a board assessment process.

Meetings

- Preside at all meetings of the board and executive committee and at other meetings or events as necessary.
- Promote meaningful dialogue at board meetings, and give every board member an opportunity to contribute.

Board Committees

- Appoint board committee and task force chairs.
- Ensure ongoing communication with the board.
- Serve as ex officio member of all committees except the governance committee.

Community

- Cultivate relationships with individual donors, funders, and other community stakeholders.
- Serve as a community ambassador and advocate for the organization.
- Speak at the annual meeting, organizational programs, and community events, and contribute to the organization's Web site, newsletter, and other communications pieces.

(Continued)

> *Partnership with the Chief Executive and Board Members*
>
> • Oversee fiscal affairs and organizational assets.
> • Participate in strategic planning and program evaluation.
> • Ensure legal and ethical compliance of all board work.
> • Practice fiscal and programmatic transparency.
> • Install and maintain risk management safeguards.

The board chair's role is framed by the accepted legal and ethical standards of conduct for nonprofit boards. The chair needs to stay well informed about any legal changes that will affect the functioning of the nonprofit and communicate in a clear and timely way with board members about how the changes will affect them. As the board's leader, the chair must set the example in adhering to legal and ethical standards of conduct. Ensuring compliance with these standards requires the chair to

• Apply effective communication and facilitation skills in all board discussions and deliberations
• Operate according to what's best for the organization
• Show transparency with full personal/professional disclosure
• Ensure that board members have all the necessary facts and figures (pro and con) when making decisions

The Chief Executive's Role

The relationship with the board is paramount in the life of every nonprofit chief executive. In high-performing organizations, the interdependent team of board chair and chief executive develops a close working partnership. This partnership—which is critical to effective governance—is addressed in depth in Chapter Five. The chief executive's management responsibilities, which are not linked directly to the partnership with the board, form a large and important part of the chief executive's job.

Chief executives have many responsibilities that are distinct from those of the board, and also manage many other important partnerships—with staff, donors, public officials, and leaders of other nonprofits. Chapter Five elaborates on the following essential responsibilities of the nonprofit chief executive:

• Commit to the mission.
• Lead the staff and manage the organization.

- Exercise responsible financial stewardship.
- Lead and manage fundraising.
- Follow the highest ethical standards, ensure accountability, and comply with the law.
- Engage the board in planning and lead the implementation.
- Develop future leadership.
- Build external relationships and serve as an advocate.
- Ensure the quality and effectiveness of programs.
- Support the board.

Other Board Officers' Roles

Besides the chair, the most typical board officers are vice chair, secretary, and treasurer. State laws frequently define these positions. The law may also indicate whether one individual can hold more than one officer position. In addition, some organizations have a chair-elect, which is one way to secure future leadership.

Specific officer duties vary from board to board and are generally defined in the organization's bylaws. Responsibilities may also be outlined in separate job descriptions. Particularly as the organization hires new and different staff, it is important to review and update officer job descriptions to reflect any changes in their focus.

Vice chair. The office of vice chair gives the board additional and substitute leadership. The vice chair generally fills in when the chair is absent and/or must leave the position permanently and without warning. The vice chair often takes on special projects, and some boards may divide various duties among two or more vice chairs. On some boards, the vice chair may naturally assume the role of chair.

Chair-elect. In some cases, a board may determine a candidate to succeed the board chair before the chair's term in office has concluded. The chair-elect may be given specific tasks, such as heading up the strategic planning task force. This position may provide a useful leadership development training ground and help to ensure a smoother transition to the role of board chair. In many professional associations, the chair-elect may be elected or appointed by the membership at large.

Treasurer. The treasurer is responsible for overseeing financial operations to make certain that things are done in an appropriate fashion. In staffed organizations, the chief financial officer, controller, or accountant keeps the financial records. In smaller organizations with few staff, the treasurer may have hands-on responsibilities. For more on the treasurer's role, see Chapter Eight, Financial Oversight.

Secretary. Depending on the organization's size and staff, the actual task of recording minutes can belong to either a board member or a staff member. In the event that a staff member fills the position, the board's official secretary should review the minutes before distributing them to the rest of the board. In addition, traditionally the board secretary acts as the custodian of the board's records, although in most circumstances the board's important documents are kept in the organization's offices. In many organizations, the board combines the positions of secretary and treasurer.

Former Board Members' Roles

Many organizations try to keep valued board members involved when their terms expire by inviting them to continue their commitment in a different capacity. Involving them after they leave the board shows appreciation for their service and lets them know that the organization continues to need and value their wisdom, insights, and knowledge.

Boards use four typical options for continuing involvement. A *board member emeritus* or *honorary board member* is usually a former member of the board who deserves to be recognized publicly because of his or her active participation, financial contribution, or strong interest in the organization. An honorary board member may also be a distinguished outsider who has an affinity for the organization and whose affiliation would be beneficial to the organization. An *advisory council* is another way to keep former board members engaged in the organization. Groups that focus on fundraising, outreach, or public relations are excellent opportunities for dynamic retired board members to participate. (See Chapter Four, Governance Structure, for a discussion of advisory councils.)

Inviting a departing board member to serve on a *board committee* is a practical way to extend affiliation past the official term limit. This gives the board member a chance to focus on a specific interest without the other obligations that come with full board membership. The committee also benefits by maximizing the use of a board member's particular skill or ability. (For more about committees, see Chapter Four.)

Through *informal involvement*, all former board members can remain advocates and goodwill ambassadors for the organization if the organization cultivates their willingness. The staff should keep retired members informed through special mailings and invitations to events. For many former board members, keeping social contacts active is enough of an incentive to maintain firm ties with the organization.

Staying Involved:
Clarifying Former Board Members' Roles

To avoid misunderstandings, the board needs to make sure that the new role of former board members is understood:

- Determine tenure. Advisory councils may set terms and renew them periodically. Emeritus positions may be for life.
- Articulate attendance requirements. Committee members are expected to attend meetings regularly.
- Clarify the fundraising relationship. As friends of the organization, honorary board members may be solicited for gifts and/or asked to solicit gifts.

Unless specifically provided in the bylaws, honorary board members and outside committee members do not have voting rights. Although this changes their role in decision making, it does not preclude their participation in discussions. Remember, only voting members' presence counts toward a quorum. Nonvoting members do not have the same liabilities as voting members. When discussing confidential matters or in executive sessions, it may be necessary to exclude nonvoting members.

Chapter Exercises

- Define the differences between the respective authorities, responsibilities, and liabilities of an individual board member and those of the full board.
- What are some ideal ways for the board and staff to communicate with each other?
- What is meant by "board-driven" and "CEO-driven" organizations? What might be the distinctive characteristics of each?
- What might cause board members to micromanage?
- When a board member leaves the board, when is it desirable or wise to keep this person involved with the organization? How could this be accomplished?

CHAPTER FOUR

GOVERNANCE STRUCTURE

Every board has a fundamental responsibility for self-management: for creating a structure, policies, and procedures that support good governance. The term *board structure* encompasses a variety of matters, from routine activities, such as preparing a schedule of board meetings, to actions with broader consequences, such as developing a policy about terms of service.

When aligned with the strategic priorities of the organization, an efficient structure allows board and staff to apply their skills in concert to fulfill the mission. This formula is neither complex nor profound, but few organizations apply it consistently or thoroughly. Those that do find that while effective governance takes time, flexibility, intention, and attention, it makes all the difference in the world to the nonprofit organization and to the community it serves.

Board Size

According to BoardSource's *Nonprofit Governance Index 2007*, the average board has sixteen members. By no means does this number represent the optimal size for every board. Each organization needs to look at its mission and the initiatives that it will carry out in pursuit of that mission, then determine how large a board it needs to operate effectively. That is, the board needs to be purposefully constructed; it must strike a balance in which each member feels valued and appreciated, no member feels overburdened, and all board functions can be fully carried out. If the board decides to adjust the size, it must amend the bylaws to reflect the change.

Not every board has the opportunity to determine its own size. In many formal membership organizations, external factors influence the board's size. For example, special mandates may require that a certain number of board seats be reserved for various constituencies or geographic regions. Or outside authorities may have the opportunity to nominate board members to represent their specific interests. Some of these boards may be large and may need to figure out their own solutions to deal with accompanying challenges.

Large Boards: Pros and Cons

One rationale for larger boards is rooted in the notion that more is better. A larger board can provide both broader representation of the organization's constituency and a larger base of donors and fundraisers. The more people there are to share the workload, the less burnout and stress individual board members experience. Furthermore, with a larger board, more people who want to serve have the opportunity—even if willingness to join the board does not necessarily bring with it the needed expertise and perspectives that the board seeks.

Larger boards, however, are not necessarily more effective or productive. The more members who are available to contribute ideas and opinions, the longer it tends to take to build consensus—and the more slowly the board may move from discussion to action. In addition, large boards tend to leave many members feeling underutilized and unappreciated. On large boards, members may have few opportunities to speak at meetings; because their votes are diluted by so many other votes, they may feel their participation doesn't matter or their time has not been valued. The chair has the responsibility to determine when the issue has been handled thoroughly, with all the sides having been presented fairly.

Small Boards: Pros and Cons

Smaller groups tend to expedite communication. The smaller the board, the more important each individual member is to the organization, and the more is expected of each member—and the more each can contribute to boardroom discussions. With smaller boards, members can communicate more personally and achieve consensus more easily, facilitating the move from discussion to action.

If the board is too small, however, it may lack the people needed to carry out all board tasks effectively. The board's outreach capability—so essential for building community relations, raising funds, and recruiting new board members—will diminish as the number of active board members decreases. Furthermore, the lower the number of active board members, the greater the risk of board member burnout.

Committees and Task Forces

To manage their work, most boards create work groups to accomplish tasks that need to be done outside board meetings. These work groups—committees and task forces—may be charged with developing proposals for board action or with acting on behalf of the board. In many organizations, they do most of the board's work and allow the board to keep its attention on the big picture and on decision making.

Committees and task forces foster board-staff interaction and cooperation and deepen the board's understanding of the issues that have an impact on the organization's life. They can be as beneficial to board members as they are to the organization as a whole. They enable board members to contribute in ways they can't often do in regular board meetings, to use their expertise to benefit the organization, and to learn from each other and get to know each other better.

As helpful as committees can be, they can also be a hindrance to the board if they are not set up or used appropriately. Frequently reevaluating a board's committee structure and keeping it flexible will allow the board to address structural problems as they occur or even before they start.

Committee Structure

The structure a board chooses depends on its individual needs, its strategic plan, and the board's and the organization's stage of development. A start-up board may have a lot of committees because the organization most likely has no staff. A small or active board may not need committees at all. When establishing its committee structure, the board determines not only the number of work groups it needs and their functions, but also the life span of each group. Not every board work group is permanent; in fact, most are not.

Each work group needs a job description, or charter, that explains its role, what it is responsible for achieving, and to whom it is accountable. This description—agreed upon by the full board—reflects an organization's vision and mission. In the case of a task force, the charter should include any deadlines and the time frame to complete the work. In addition, each work group needs an annual work plan, a timeline, and, in some cases, a staff member assigned to it.

Standing committees deal with ongoing issues, such as financial oversight or investments. Committee members rotate on and off, but the committees themselves last indefinitely because there is a continuous flow of work for them to accomplish. It is beneficial for most boards to have a few standing committees because they ensure consistency in certain board practices and can serve as organizational memory. The most common standing committees are the executive, governance, and finance committees. Their functions are described in greater detail later in this chapter.

Task forces are established to accomplish a specific objective—such as reviewing bylaws or planning retreats—within a specific time frame. When the work is done, the group disbands. Using task forces allows boards and board members greater flexibility. Boards can tackle immediate issues more quickly without rethinking the whole committee structure or assignments. Board members can contribute their expertise and interest in more specialized areas or more concentrated time than they may have been able to by serving on a standing committee. Traditionally these temporary work groups have been called *ad hoc committees*, but using the term *task force* can help make it clear to board members that this assignment is temporary.

Zero-Based Committee Structure

A zero-based committee structure prevents committee structures from becoming cumbersome and forces boards to constantly reevaluate their work groups. Here's how it works:

1. The board starts each year (or every two years, depending on the needs of the board) with a clean slate of no committees.
2. At the beginning of the year, the board determines its organizational strategy and priorities. Then the board establishes committees and task forces based on its current needs. These groups are formed with the understanding that the group will disband once the objective is met or when the board decides they should at the next annual review of committees.

A zero-based committee structure may seem extreme, but it helps prevent a board from getting trapped in an outdated system. Many boards are more comfortable maintaining a limited number of standing committees while using the zero-based approach for all other committees.

Board Committees Versus Organizational Committees

Committees can be defined by whether they are *board committees*, which report to the board, or *organizational committees*, which work with and sometimes report to the staff. Board committees take on policy and strategic work. Organizational committees work on issues that usually are part of the staff's responsibility. They advise the staff, or they can help in program implementation. Marketing and public relations committees are two examples. In organizations with few or no staff, these committees often do most of the program work. Members of organizational committees can include board and nonboard members. They typically involve people from the community with special interests or expertise.

How to Keep Committee Structure Simple

- Limit the number of standing committees to the bare minimum, and supplement them with a few less permanent work groups.
- Make sure each committee has a significant amount of ongoing and important work to do. Disband them when they do not.
- For flexibility and efficiency, rely on task forces for short-term or special projects.
- Keep the committee structure, except for the description of the executive committee, out of the bylaws to ensure that committee powers are limited. Consider including a phrase in the bylaws that says the board may establish and disband committees as needed to support its work.

Creating New Committees and Task Forces

Before creating a new task force or committee, boards will want to consider the following questions:

- How does this work group relate to the organization's mission and to the organization's current strategy and priorities?
- How will it benefit the board and the organization?
- Will it provide information that will help the board in decision making?
- Who will it report to: board, staff, or both?
- Who will implement its decisions?
- What risks will this task force or committee face? What liability issues are likely to come up?
- Could the work be done just as easily by one board member working with the staff?
- Is the group's purpose an ongoing concern? If not, when will the work group be dissolved?

Sample Committee Structures

The following samples are not necessarily typical, in that they don't include separate audit/finance or governance committees. In some nonprofits, the entire board may handle these functions.

A Jewish Voice for Peace (Berkeley, California) is a young, incorporated organization that works for peace in the Middle East and has no paid staff. It does all its work informally through work groups, which have between four and twelve members each. None are standing committees; all are task forces lasting various lengths of time and meeting as often as needed. These groups are as follows:

- Education committee
- Committee to prepare for upcoming events
- Committee to consider what kinds of direct actions to have during the Days of Awe (High Holy Days)
- Direct action committee
- Jewish Voice for Peace strengthening committee (focuses on how to support people in leadership positions within the group)
- Incorporation committee

Women's Health Rights Coalition (Oakland, California) offers information, referrals, and support for women seeking reproductive health care information in northern and central California. It has three staff members, six board members, and no committees. Individual board members have specific assignments, taking charge of issues that committees often handle in larger organizations, such as the following:

- Board development (recruiting and training potential board members)
- Financial issues
- Fundraising
- Human resources (creating a job description for the executive director and leading the executive director's evaluation)

Reports to the board have been informal, but now the board often receives packets with written reports before the board meetings.

Crow River Habitat for Humanity (Hutchinson, Minnesota) builds affordable houses for people in need. The one paid staff member, the executive director, works part time. Not all committee members—or even committee chairs—are board members. The executive committee meets on an as-needed basis. The board has the following standing committees that do much of the hands-on program work:

- Family selection (social workers and bankers who publicize the search for potential homeowners and screen applicants)
- Family support (assigns mentors and provides support for the homeowners)

- Site selection committee
- Building committee (plans and implements the building of the house)
- Development committee
- Golf outing task force (organizes a fundraiser)
- Executive committee
- Appreciation/barbecue task force (organizes a thank-you event after a project is done)

Committee Chairs and Members

Bylaws usually define how committee chairs are appointed—for standing committees, generally by the board chair, and for organizational committees, by the chief executive in consultation with relevant staff member. Authority for making committee assignments is also spelled out in the bylaws or in other board policies. Usually, the board chair, in consultation with the committee chair and chief executive, makes committee member assignments, though sometimes chairs appoint their own members.

Committee appointments usually are a mutual decision. Some committee members will be chosen for their expertise in the committee's function, whereas others will bring a different perspective or fresh eye to the issue. For example, it is important for the finance committee to have some members with financial expertise, but new board members with little financial know-how could also learn a lot about the organization's finances and the board's fiduciary responsibility by serving on the finance committee.

Every board member should have an opportunity to serve on a committee or task force at least once during a term. Because committee meetings are usually less formal than meetings of the full board, they often allow a higher level of personal engagement and therefore can be more rewarding. Incoming board members who join committees must understand that their contributions to committees are just as important as their work with the full board. They should also understand that committee work, because it may be research or action oriented, may take extra time, even beyond attending meetings.

Non–Board Members on Committees

By involving some committee members from outside the board, the organization can realize the following benefits:

- Bringing in new expertise and diversity and expanding the number of people involved in the organization without increasing the board to an unwieldy size

- Serving as a good testing and training ground for potential board members
- Giving more people a chance to get to know the organization, and adding legitimacy in the community to the nonprofit's work
- Providing a chance for people to be involved who don't have the time to commit to board service, who cannot afford to give financially at the level required by some organizations, or who do not want the liability of a full-fledged board member

Committees and Staff

Board committees often—but not always—have a staff member assigned to them to provide context, explain standards in the field, or help with background information. The staff member, who may be someone other than the chief executive, may also serve as secretary to the committee to take notes, follow up on administrative tasks, and coordinate logistics. However, because committee meetings can take staff time away from their focus on mission-related programs, the trend is toward fewer meetings with less extensive staff support.

The relationship between committee members and staff on an organizational committee is notably different. In an organizational committee, staff provide the leadership, and the members assist in the implementation. Although this arrangement is often perceived as a partnership, staff are ultimately accountable (to the chief executive) for the work of an organizational committee.

Committee Size and Term Limits

The size of any work group is related to the issue or task at hand, within reason. Large groups are usually cumbersome and may suffer from a lack of member involvement. Small groups often have an easier time making decisions; on the other hand, if a committee is too small, the board may risk overlooking significant questions or the perception that considerable power is resting in the hands of too few. A committee should be large enough to provide the required skills, knowledge, and perspectives, but small enough so that all members can be involved.

Boards usually limit service on standing committees—often to two-year terms—to allow people to serve on different committees, thereby broadening board members' understanding of the whole organization. When board members are appointed to committees, they should be aware of the term limits. However, in committees that deal with complicated issues that require greater expertise, it can be helpful to retain committee members for more than one term to give them time to acquire and use specialized knowledge.

Essential Standing Committees

Many boards regard several standing committees as essential, in particular those focusing on the board's own development and the organization's financial and ethical integrity. According to BoardSource's *Nonprofit Governance Index 2007*, the most common are governance, finance, and executive.

Governance Committee

The governance committee is the board's mechanism for looking after itself. This committee is more active and dynamic than its traditional precursor, the nominating committee. Rather than focusing on nominations for annual elections, the governance committee works year-round to guarantee that the board takes responsibility for its own development, learning, and behavior; sets and enforces its own expectations; and allots time, attention, and resources to understanding its stewardship role. The governance committee does not run the board, but it makes it possible for the board to be run well.

The governance committee's charge is to find accomplished, enthusiastic people with the assets the board needs; teach these high performers what it means to be on the board and continually engage them in its work; evaluate the work of the board and each member's contribution, watching for leadership potential; and make sure that the board is living up to its potential.

Governance committee membership. Because the governance committee will, to an extent, perpetuate the board, its members should be both visionary and strategic as well as a microcosm of the board. The governance committee should include people who

- Have a broad range of backgrounds
- Are active in the community and in various circles
- Can provide wide contacts in the community
- Hold a variety of experiences
- Understand human dynamics and relationship building
- Have experience with organizational development
- Are not afraid to speak up
- Are respected by the board
- Have good judgment and insight to leave a legacy to the board
- Know the organization well and understand the needs of the board
- Have integrity
- Can leave personal agendas behind
- Are willing to bring in new thoughts and perspectives—even to question present practices

The governance committee can especially benefit by drawing on people with particular areas of expertise, including management consultants and organizational development experts, human resource professionals, nonprofit executives, and community activists. Individuals with this type of experience may fall more easily into the softer side of group dynamics, organizational management, and community outreach that is necessary for the committee's work.

The governance committee chair needs to have experience with the board and the organization but not necessarily be a veteran. He or she should have plenty of energy, enthusiasm, and openness to new ideas, while maintaining an understanding of good governance practices. The committee chair works closely with the board chair.

Exhibit 4.1 presents an example of a job description for a governance committee.

EXHIBIT 4.1. SAMPLE GOVERNANCE COMMITTEE JOB DESCRIPTION

The governance committee is responsible for ongoing review and recommendations to enhance the quality of the board of directors. The work of the committee revolves around five major areas:

1. Help create board roles and responsibilities.
   - Lead the board in regularly reviewing and updating the board's description of its roles and areas of responsibility and what is expected of individual board members.
   - Assist the board in periodically updating and clarifying the primary areas of focus for the board, and help shape the board's agenda for the coming year or two, based on the strategic plan.
   - Establish and monitor policies for board performance, such as confidentiality, participation in fundraising, and conflict of interest.
2. Pay attention to board composition.
   - Recruit new members who will be able to help achieve the organization's strategic and annual goals. To know what types of skills to look for in potential board members, first analyze the skills current board members have, and then recruit to fill the gaps.
   - Develop a profile of the board as it should evolve.
   - Identify potential board member candidates, and explore their interest and availability for board service.
   - Nominate individuals to be elected as members of the board.
   - In cooperation with the board chair, contact each board member eligible for reelection to assess his or her interest in continuing board membership, and work with each board member to identify what he or she might be able to contribute to the organization.

3. Encourage board development.
   - Provide candidates with information needed prior to election to the board.
   - Design and oversee a process of board orientation, sharing information needed during the early stages of board service.
   - Design and implement an ongoing program of board information, education, and team building.
4. Assess board effectiveness.
   - Initiate an assessment of the board's performance approximately every two years, and propose, as appropriate, changes in board structure and operations.
   - Provide ongoing counsel to the board chair and other board leaders on steps they might take to enhance board effectiveness.
   - Regularly review the board's practices regarding member participation, conflict of interest, confidentiality, and so on, and suggest needed improvements.
   - Periodically review and update the board policy and practices.
5. Prepare board leadership.
   - Take the lead in succession planning, taking steps to recruit and prepare for future board leadership.
   - Nominate board members for election as board officers.

Finance Committee

The finance committee is responsible for making certain that the organization is in good fiscal health. This committee oversees expenditures and provides information and recommendations related to the annual budget and its implementation, as well as projections for the future. It recommends policies to the full board to safeguard the organization's assets, ensures the completeness and accuracy of its financial records, and oversees proper use of resources. It also sees to it that the organization has appropriate internal controls, conducts proper financial analysis, and reports any concerns to the full board.

Financial oversight is different from budgeting, and sometimes the finance committee gets too involved in budget preparation, which in all but the smallest organizations is the job of the staff. The finance committee's job is to see that the board's policies and strategic priorities are reflected in the budget. When reviewing financial reports, the finance committee asks the questions, "Are we on track? If not, why not?"

The finance committee sometimes works with the independent auditor, who is hired by the board to examine the organization's books. As a form of internal control, more boards are separating the audit from general financial oversight and using another work group to oversee the audit.

The finance committee may provide oversight relating to investments, or a separate investment committee may be created for this purpose. Foundations and organizations with large portfolios might find it especially useful to separate the two committees.

Beginning with the orientation of new members, the finance committee facilitates the board's understanding of the budget and fiscal issues. The committee also makes sure that all board members get the financial statements in a timely manner and that board members know how to examine and understand the reports. All board members should have a term on the finance committee to learn about their financial responsibilities.

Finance committee members may include the following:

- The board treasurer, usually as the chair or as an active member
- Members of the development committee, if there is one
- Members with expertise in accounting, banking, or business
- Members who are familiar with programs

If the organization has a chief financial officer, he or she works closely with the finance committee by answering questions and preparing reports for committee review. However, because staff and the committee work so closely together, committee members need to distinguish their roles from the staff's to avoid micromanaging. In general, staff monitor income and expenditures on a daily basis and prepare the budget. The finance committee provides oversight by reviewing financial statements and the budget.

Exhibit 4.2 presents an example of a job description for a finance committee.

Executive Committee

The executive committee is a small group, commonly with authority to act on behalf of the full board between meetings or in an urgent situation. Usually the executive committee includes the board chair and other officers. Committee chairs may also sit on the executive committee, and the chief executive serves as an ex officio member. If the executive committee is allowed to act on behalf of the board, its membership, functions, and authority level must be specifically stated in the organization's bylaws.

Not all nonprofit organizations need an executive committee. Small boards and the boards of start-up organizations, for instance, rarely do, because all board members can be convened relatively easily and need to be involved in decision making. For large and/or geographically dispersed boards, the existence of an executive committee whose membership can be convened quickly and make decisions efficiently may prove critical in emergency situations. However, the full

EXHIBIT 4.2. SAMPLE FINANCE COMMITTEE JOB DESCRIPTION

The finance committee helps the board ensure that the organization is in good fiscal health. The committee's work revolves around six areas:

1. Ensure that accurate and complete financial records are maintained.
   - Monitor income and expenditures against projections.
   - Review and recommend financial policies to the board, including ensuring adequate internal controls and maintaining financial records in accordance with standard accounting practices.
2. Ensure that accurate, timely, and meaningful financial statements are prepared and presented to the board, quarterly or monthly.
3. Oversee budget preparation and financial planning.
   - Propose for board approval a budget that reflects the organization's goals and board policies.
   - Ensure that the budget accurately reflects the needs, expenses, and revenue of the organization.
4. Safeguard the organization's assets.
   - Review proposed new funding for ongoing financial implications, recommending approval or disapproval to the board.
   - Ensure that the organization has the proper risk-management provisions in place.
5. Help the full board understand the organization's financial affairs.
   - Ensure that the board as a whole is well informed about the organization's finances.
   - Educate the board about financial matters.
6. Ensure compliance with federal, state, and other requirements related to the organization's finances.
   - Ensure that the organization maintains adequate insurance coverage.
   - Ensure that the IRS Form 990, other forms, and employment and other taxes required by government entities are filed completely, correctly, and on time.

board—not the executive committee alone—always makes significant decisions such as amending the bylaws, electing or removing board members, hiring or firing the chief executive, and approving the budget.

An executive committee has two inherent dangers:

- Because a smaller group is more efficient, the board may be inclined to delegate responsibilities to the executive committee that are properly handled by the full board.

- When a select group handles many of the major deliberations and decisions, other board members may begin to feel underutilized, unwanted, or disenfranchised.

Recognizing these dangers, some nonprofit organizations have amended their bylaws to eliminate the executive committee as a standing committee of the board. Others have refined the executive committee's role so that it carries out specific functions, such as the performance review of the chief executive, that are best handled by a small, knowledgeable group that can act efficiently and maintain confidentiality. Still others have redefined the executive committee's role significantly. One board, for example, recast its executive committee as a strategic think tank for the board itself, not to make decisions in the board's place. Composed of committee vice-chairs, this redefined executive committee models a think tank practice for all other committees to emulate.

The reasons why some boards choose to have an executive committee include the following:

- If the board is large, a smaller group authorized to act on its behalf in certain circumstances can speed up decision making.
- If board members are scattered all over the country or the world, it is easier for a core group to get together to make quick decisions during an emergency, although this problem can sometimes be solved by using e-mail or teleconferencing involving the whole board.
- The executive committee can approve an action after issues raised by the board have been resolved.
- The executive committee can be involved in approving grant requests.
- When the board needs a place to test controversial ideas, an executive committee can study important issues and present the findings to the full board. A task force could also accomplish this purpose.
- If the board needs to make frequent decisions, an executive committee that can meet more often may help. Certain financial and legal matters may not require full board meetings and can easily be attended to by an executive committee.

Often the role of the executive committee is defined by what it *cannot* do. To avoid delegating essential powers away from the full board, the executive committee should not

- Amend bylaws
- Determine its role in the organization

- Elect or remove board members
- Hire or fire the chief executive
- Approve or change the budget
- Make major structural decisions (add or eliminate programs, approve mergers, or dissolve the corporation)

The bylaws determine who is on the executive committee. Often it is the board chair, other officers, and sometimes committee chairs. The board chair usually chairs the executive committee, and the chief executive usually serves as an ex officio member. Whether or not the chief executive has a vote on the committee is up to each board. Some organizations choose to elect other representatives to ensure diversity in decision making and to avoid concentrating too much power in the hands of too few board members.

When there is no executive committee. Every board does not need an executive committee. In fact, every board should fully justify its identified need to form one. If the board is small enough, the work can be done by a committee of the whole. Board officers, or any board member with a special acumen, can act as advisors for the chief executive or the board as an entity. If there is a formal standing committee structure, the duties can be dispersed to other board committees. Here are some other alternatives:

- An informal group of committee chairs to coordinate committee work and ensure efficiency of structure and activities.
- A board leadership group made up of board officers to provide guidance to the chief executive in between meetings, to focus the attention of the board, and to address their roles in the leadership of the board.
- A task force of board officers and committee chairs who can convene quickly in the case of an emergency. Consider involving some key community members in this task force that can add value to the group.

Exhibit 4.3 presents an example of a job description for an executive committee.

EXHIBIT 4.3. SAMPLE EXECUTIVE COMMITTEE JOB DESCRIPTION

The executive committee is responsible for working in support of, or occasionally in place of, the full board. The work of the committee revolves around three and possibly five major areas.

1. Handle urgent issues, resolving any emergency or organizational crisis (such as a loss of funding or the unexpected loss of the chief executive).

(Continued)

2. Perform policy work, carrying out specific directions of the board, and taking action on policies when they affect the work of the executive committee or when the full board directs the committee to do so.
3. Act as liaison to the chief executive.
   - Nurture the chief executive by providing counsel, feedback, and support when needed.
   - Facilitate annual assessment of the chief executive by the board and report the results of the assessment to the chief executive.
   - Review compensation and benefits for the chief executive.

In some organizations, the executive committee takes the lead in two additional areas:

4. Help develop a strategic plan.
   - Initiate the board's involvement in establishing a strategic framework or direction.
   - In organizations with no staff, lead the board's efforts in developing the strategic plan.
5. Conduct executive searches.
   - Assume the lead in the search for a new chief executive or delegate the responsibility to a task force.
   - Conduct the research necessary to determine an appropriate salary for the chief executive.
   - Seek approval from the full board before hiring a new chief executive.

Best Practices for Executive Committees

A board must find an appropriate balance between the efficiency of the executive committee and the larger value of the full board. Here are some best practices to ensure that the committee adds value without overstepping its bounds.

- *Make board decisions intentional:* The full board determines whether an executive committee is needed and if so, what its role should be.
- *Clarify authority levels:* The full board agrees to the authority given to the committee, and the bylaws clearly state the limitations given to the committee.
- *Understand the special nature of this committee:* Unlike other board committees, the roles and boundaries of the executive committee should be defined in the board's bylaws.
- *Delegate cautiously:* The board should be judicious and specific about the powers that it delegates to the executive committee.
- *Separate the committee from the board:* The board should avoid having committee meetings act as dress rehearsals for full board meetings.
- *Communicate:* The board should establish policies and procedures for communications between the executive committee and the full board.

Other Work Groups

In reviewing the work required to accomplish the organization's strategic goals and prepare for a healthy future, a board may need committees other than its standing committees. Some of the more common additional work groups are described in this section.

Development Committee or Task Force

Development committee members are active in planning for and conducting fundraising. The group works closely with development staff, and the committee chair boosts the participation of the rest of the board. This particular structure for a development committee is still the most common in fundraising nonprofits.

Some boards, however, simply decide to act as a fundraising committee of the whole. The entire board shares the duties and carries the load. Eliminating a separate development committee is sometimes a deliberate effort to stress each board member's duty to participate in fundraising and not simply leave it to development committee members.

An *organizational* development committee works directly with the development staff and may be composed of staff members, community leaders, fundraising specialists, helpful volunteers who want to be involved and who have special skills, and board members who have particular expertise and aptitude in representing the organization to their funders.

Audit Committee or Task Force

This work group arranges to hire an independent auditor and serves as a link between the auditor and the board. It ensures that the auditor has full access to financial and related records, reviews the auditor's report and submits it to the board, and arranges for the full board to meet with the auditor once a year. Once the board has reviewed the audit, the task force is disbanded. An audit task force is usually a small group—typically three to five people—appointed by the board chair with an eye to involving a mix of people with audit task force experience and those who have not served in the recent past.

See the discussion of finance committee responsibilities, earlier in this chapter, for a rationale for separating the audit responsibility from regular financial oversight responsibility.

Investment Committee

The investment committee ensures that the board's investment policies are up-to-date and appropriately implemented. The committee proposes policies, but the board is responsible for adopting them. The investment committee oversees investment performance and recommends changes to the investment approach, as appropriate. It may also be authorized to make decisions within the scope of policies established by the board, such as hiring a professional to manage the organization's investments.

Investment committee members often have related expertise, such as investment managers, bankers, and tax attorneys with knowledge of nonprofit law. Sometimes that expertise can be found among non–board members. Investment committee members should not have a financial interest in the way the organization's funds are invested.

Public Policy or Legislative Committee

An organization involved in public policy matters may decide to have a work group to sort out the issues involved, advise the board on recommended positions, or alert the board or staff to possible effects of impending changes in public policy. If staff are assigned to public policy and/or legislative matters, the committee is defined as an *organizational committee*. If public policy is important to the overall mission but not an integral part of programs and services, this committee might be a board committee assigned the responsibility of tracking and raising public policy issues.

Marketing and public relations committee. This committee develops, oversees, and often implements a plan for reaching the community with the organization's message and involving segments of the public in its work. An important function for committee members is to serve as eyes and ears in the community to help evaluate the organization's image and the effectiveness of its public relations strategy. Because marketing and public relations are staff functions, if a special committee is seen as necessary, it should be an organizational committee reporting to staff, not a board committee. It can serve in an advisory and support capacity to staff or as adjunct volunteer staff.

Other Special Committees

Special committees can meet certain ongoing board needs that do not fit into the scope of other committees. They never should micromanage the related staff functions. Examples include the following:

- A program review task force established in preparation for strategic planning to identify the strengths and weaknesses of current programs and propose changes for the future

- An institutional relations committee that might assist the board of a national federated organization in promoting appropriate communication with the affiliate or different constituent parts
- An accreditation committee established to prepare for and maintain organizational accreditation
- A strategic planning task force charged with preparing for the board's participation in strategic planning and for ensuring the appropriate follow-up

Advisory Councils

Some boards enlarge their organization's reach by creating advisory councils: voluntary collections of individuals typically assembled to supplement the governance activities carried out by governing boards or the management tasks carried out by staff members. Overall, advisory councils provide a specialized expertise that may be missing from the board or staff. Advisory council members can serve as ambassadors for the organization, building bridges into the community and fostering a sense of accountability. They can bring outside support and expertise to an organization and link it to everything from grassroots community concerns to celebrities and potential funders. When well organized and given a clear sense of its goals, a successful advisory council can do much to help an organization fulfill its mission.

It is important to remember that advisory councils are not boards. They are not legal bodies and cannot assume responsibility for the governance of an organization. Advisory council members generally have no legal responsibilities. They have no vested right to serve and no immunity from removal.

Most nonprofits find it helpful to include language pertaining to advisory councils in their bylaws. The language should *not* spell out all of the conditions governing formation of an advisory council—that might paint the board into a corner when an unforeseen incident arises and lead to the laborious task of rewriting the bylaws. It is advisable, however, to give the board the option of creating advisory councils when appropriate.

Advisory councils can perform a variety of jobs, many of which are central to an organization's activities. They can provide technical expertise and survey the need for new programs. They can also review funding applications, make resource allocation recommendations, raise funds themselves, and conduct evaluation and oversight activities. Advisory councils may help organizations maintain accountability or meet the demands of an external constituency. Sometimes they serve more as an honorary than a functional group.

Advisory Council Functions

Advisory councils have been established by educational institutions, museums, performing arts groups, human service and advocacy organizations, health care agencies, and other nonprofits to serve many functions. Here are some examples:

- Provide oversight and accountability for projects, programs, and services funded by government agencies and foundations.
- Raise money for unrestricted use or for a specific program.
- Serve as advocates, facilitate access to policy makers, and help shape public policy that benefits the organization.
- Serve as ambassadors for the organization to the community.
- Provide credibility, especially for start-up organizations.
- Review, monitor, or assess a specific program.
- Evaluate the performance of the organization as a whole.
- Provide a means for involving people who are willing to give critical assistance but have limited time (such as public officials, celebrities, influential business-persons, or individuals with access to potential large donors).
- Enlist help from others without enlarging the governing board.
- Create an oversight mechanism when an organization launches a new venture or converts to national or international scope before the composition of the governing board changes.
- Provide technical expertise.
- Gather input from or serve as a liaison with key constituencies.
- Build a corps of outside, experienced experts whose interest and support are important (including possible future board members or former board members who can continue to make a contribution to the organization).
- Provide an independent, unbiased sounding board for brainstorming, creating new ventures, or identifying institutional strengths and weaknesses as well as external opportunities and threats.
- Review applications for funding.
- Incorporate additional layers of diversity and new perspectives within the organization.

Characteristics of Successful Advisory Councils

An advisory council can be almost any size and perform almost any task. The only generalization that can accurately be tied to thriving advisory councils is that each must meet the expectations of both the nonprofit and the group itself.

High-functioning advisory groups often share the following characteristics:

- A clearly written statement of purpose that explains the goal of the advisory council. It notes the size as well as the membership selection, process, terms of office, and responsibilities.
- A strong and knowledgeable chair who understands the group's purpose, is committed to giving more time than others, and is skilled at conducting meetings.
- Clear and consistent communication between the board and the advisory council. Although the board should not micromanage, it shouldn't ignore the group either. The board should be apprised of developments and should check that the group is not duplicating staff work. Good communication can also help identify group members who might make strong candidates for future board seats. Even after a group disbands, the board should continue to show gratitude for its members' hard work.

Advisory Council Structure and Membership

The exact structure of an advisory council—size, meeting frequency, reporting mechanisms—varies from organization to organization and from advisory council to advisory council. An advisory council's purpose should determine its membership. In general, members are people in the community who can add value to the organization. Advisory council membership can give potential board members an inside look at the organization, which may help them decide whether they want to continue their affiliation and take their commitment deeper into board service. For board members, an advisory council can be a way to identify board prospects. Observing people in the advisory council setting before they are considered for nomination is a good way to get a sense for their energy, enthusiasm, and level of interest.

Staffing an Advisory Council

A crucial ingredient in building a successful advisory council is the involvement of staff. When the professional staff member charged with staffing the advisory council devotes time to orient, educate, motivate, and engage members, these busy advisors will make progress on the group's goals and feel a sense of connection to the organization. Too many nonprofits overlook the staff time and expenses required to inform, educate, and nurture advisory councils. The costs (particularly in staff time) should be projected in advance. Advisory council development should be viewed as an ongoing process that must be established and maintained, rather than a single event that produces transformation.

When Not to Form an Advisory Council

Many advisory councils make substantial contributions, but others never have a meaningful impact. An unsuccessful advisory council may well have been formed for the wrong reason. It might have simply sounded like a good idea. Or it may have provided a useful "parking lot" without a defined constructive purpose for former office holders such as board members who have served their maximum terms. The fervor with which these groups are established can ebb quickly. They suffer from a gap between expectations and performance.

Nonprofits cannot mistakenly believe that an advisory council is the answer to their diversity issues. Forming a diverse advisory council simply to satisfy demands from foundations or communities to enhance diversity efforts does little to promote a truly diverse organization. It leads to a group whose advice is neither sought nor valued. An isolated attempt to diversify an organization is meaningless. True change requires an organization-wide commitment to a shift in culture.

Membership Organization Boards

A formal membership organization (see Chapter One) grants its members specific rights to participate in its internal affairs. (This structure should not be confused with "supporter" memberships, whereby individuals, for a fee, receive special discounts, newsletters, or other benefits.) These rights are established in the articles of incorporation and are defined in more detail in the bylaws. Usually, members elect the board and/or officers, approve changes in the bylaws, and authorize major transactions such as mergers and dissolution of the organization. Members have a strong interest and voice in the future of the organization, not only in the tangible benefits that they may receive as members. For example, trade associations and business leagues are membership organizations in which the members rely on the organization to advocate for better business opportunities for their line of business.

The board is the governing body of a membership organization. Members have significant input in the governance of the organization by electing at least part of the board. But for any board to be effective, it is important to have a cohesive group that works well together. In purely representational boards, to which members elect representatives from their own regions or sectors, consensus building may become tougher. It is important to seek competent candidates and inform members objectively about board member expectations to facilitate the election of qualified board members.

Board members in a membership organization need to see the association as an entity, not as an agent for their particular constituents. Political favors and strict representational quotas may not produce an effective board. Elected board members need to be able to leave their personal and professional agendas behind and make decisions only for what is best for the entire organization.

Members elect the board during annual meetings. Proxy voting is a common practice because it is often impossible to get the entire membership together at the same time. Preparing the slates and administering the meeting is a major task in a membership organization. The costs and time involved can be a demanding feature of this governance structure.

National Boards of Federated Systems

A federated system consists of a national organization and its affiliates or chapters. A board governs the parent organization, and each chapter has its own local board. Working together, the objective for the parent and its affiliates is to accomplish their mandate more efficiently and effectively than would be possible for several independent organizations working alone. Examples of federated organizations include United Way of America, Habitat for Humanity, and Planned Parenthood.

Role of the National Board

As the governing body of the parent organization, the national board

- Defines the mission and mandate for the federated system, which is adopted by the affiliates.
- Clarifies how the parent organization fits into the federated system and how it will carry out its mission.
- Envisions the future of the organization. The board ties the organization to its environment, to society in general, and to the external forces that may have an impact on its future.
- Serves as the primary advocate for the cause. The board pioneers the message and purpose of the organization. Its concern is about the organization's impact using the most effective tools to campaign for its beliefs, principles, and convictions.
- Defines the brand and standards for the organization, communicating them to affiliates and monitoring their implementation.

- Supports the affiliates by providing helpful resources (funds, materials, information, training) that aid the work of the chapters.
- Pays attention to its own development. If it does not care about its own capacity, it will have difficulties in fulfilling the responsibilities just enumerated.

Board Composition

One of the toughest challenges for federated organizations is to find the right balance between the needs of constituents and the development of the governing body. There are numerous approaches, from multilayered governing bodies to affiliate members appointing and electing their own agents to the national board. Here are some examples of how federated organizations link to their chapters:

- Separate representational membership bodies (national council, house of delegates) may have varying powers but work closely with the governing board to incorporate the affiliate view.
- Chapters or regional areas may have board representative quotas. The board may also include at-large members.
- Chapters elect all board members.
- Local or regional advisory councils provide feedback to a self-perpetuating board.

Board Focus

The chapter-elected members of the parent board must differentiate their roots from their present function. They do not serve merely as the advocates for their own causes. Rather, they bring to the table all the ideas, concerns, opinions, and feedback received from the home front, listen openly to similar presentations and views by fellow board members, and, after appropriate deliberation, help to form the direction the full board adopts in its efforts to fairly and wisely serve the entire constituency.

Every chapter-elected member of the board has a duty of loyalty to the parent organization. When he or she accepts the call to board service there is the expectation of a transformation from local advocate to national spokesperson—a focus change from local problems to major strategic issues. If a board member is not able to make this transition because of the incapacity to work with the big picture or difficulty in dealing with any duality of interest, that person may not be the best possible choice for serving the parent organization.

Education

The federated system board's governance committee has a big task. It educates board members on their roles, clarifies the expectations of their service, and provides the necessary tools and training to ensure that the full board is able to fulfill its mandate effectively and without bias. But the education needs to begin with the bodies that nominate board member candidates and determine the slate for election. If the local chapters are not able to envision the demands of serving on the parent organization's board, they are not able to choose the best individual for the job. The governance committee needs to reach out to the field and articulate the ideal characteristics of its board members and educate nominating and electing bodies on the burdens of conflicts of interest or duality of interest.

Chapter Exercises

- How should a board define its optimal size? What issues influence this choice?
- When should a board consider forming a governance, development, audit, membership, and compensation committee? Or should any of these be task forces?
- What might be the challenges of a board member serving on an organizational committee?
- What can happen when an executive committee has too much power and autonomy?
- What are some potential roles for advisory councils? How can organizations use these groups effectively?
- Why would a founder decide to form a membership organization rather than choosing a self-perpetuating board? When might this structure be essential? When might it be an unnecessary challenge?
- Discuss the ways in which a federated system can be formed. What are the key roles of the national board and the chapter boards? How do the national staff and the chapter staff best relate to this structure?

CHAPTER FIVE

THE BOARD–CHIEF EXECUTIVE RELATIONSHIP

Creating a climate of openness, and the transparency that accompanies it, is critical to nonprofit organizational success—especially in an era marked by heightened accountability for performance and, in many cases, increased competition for resources. That climate depends on agreement about the distinctive roles of the board and the chief executive and, by extension, of the staff. When roles are clear, these players can take steps to create the environment for constructive leadership partnerships.

A successful working partnership between the board chair and the chief executive is at the heart of board-staff partnership. In combining resources, any partnership's whole becomes greater than its individual parts. This partnership has the capacity to transform an organization and move it forward. A positive, productive partnership signals direction, purpose, and excitement about the organization's mission, whereas a lackluster or confrontational relationship will have a detrimental effect on the board and on individual members' commitment. While being mindful that the board hires the chief executive, who serves at the pleasure of the board, both the chair and the chief executive need to make their partnership work and use it to the organization's advantage.

The chief executive's relationship with the board as a whole should also be a constructive partnership in which the executive provides essential leadership that engages and involves the board in governance. An effective chief executive is the catalyst whose active participation ignites the partnership and helps board performance move from ordinary to extraordinary. The board can't do its job without information, direction, administrative support, and encouragement from the chief executive. Carefully crafted meeting agendas, committee structures that are aligned with the needs of the organization, and thoughtful and strategic discussions will not spring into existence out of the raw material supplied by the board members, no matter how much energy and goodwill they bring to the table.

The Board Chair and the Chief Executive

The power and potential of the board chair–chief executive team rests with mission. These two leaders are the foremost stewards of the mission. The most successful leadership teams find organizational approaches that continually revisit and reaffirm the mission of the organization. They find ways of inspiring passion for the mission, communicating the organization's core purpose, and measuring performance relative to the mission. In short, they find a way to live the mission and to make it part of the organizational DNA.

Principles and Goals for Success

Like any relationship, the board chair–chief executive partnership requires commitment and effort from both partners. Each should take responsibility for his or her behaviors and actions and be open to constructive feedback not just on the tasks at hand, but on the partnership itself.

Three basic principles are the foundation of a strong partnership: mutual respect, trust, and support for each other and the partnership; reciprocal communications; and shared purpose. With these principles in place, the board chair and chief executive should be equipped to understand one another's perspectives as they build the leadership partnership. Their goals include the following:

- Adapting to differences in personality, temperament, work style, communication style, and time commitment
- Keeping ongoing tasks and responsibilities running smoothly during board leadership transitions
- Setting mutual expectations for the working relationship
- Establishing clear boundaries for roles and responsibilities and understanding where they overlap
- Agreeing on what sound governance practices are and how to apply them
- Developing a shared interpretation of what constitutes the best interests of the organization

The two leaders will not always agree on the issues they face (and that is not necessarily the objective), but each voice should be heard and respected while framed by a shared purpose. The chief executive may already have expectations for how his or her relationship with the board chair operates based on past experience and personal preference. These expectations may be different from the board chair's perception of a working relationship. It is up to the board chair to take the initiative to articulate his or her view of the working relationship and go over the three guiding principles.

Establishing a Foundation

When conditions are right, the relationship between board chair and chief executive begins long before the chair takes the job. In many organizations, committed and capable board members progress to the position of board chair. The board chair should have experience with the organization and a track record of working successfully with the chief executive on a variety of projects and issues. A board chair can increase his or her success by serving as chair-elect for one or more years, preparing for the position, shadowing the current board chair, and being included in strategic discussions that cut across a variety of issues and topics of importance to the organization.

This foundation provides an excellent platform on which to build the leadership partnership. Early on, the two leaders should establish their expectations of each other in areas such as communication style and values, frequency of reporting and meetings, functions in which the board chair is expected to participate, and shared and individual priorities. The chief executive may encourage the new board chair to adopt a platform for his or her term, similar in concept to the platforms adopted by candidates for political office. The platform should reflect the organization's strategic goals and the unique interests and skills that the board chair can offer (for an example, see Exhibit 5.1).

Increased interaction with the incoming chair will also give the chief executive the information and experience needed to create a successful partnership. Often the new chair is a committee chair or a key committee member. The chief executive should make a point of attending meetings in which the chair-elect is involved and observe him or her in action. In this way, the executive can take stock of strengths and weaknesses and provide opportunities to enhance leadership skills. This observation process will also alert the chief executive to skills he or she may need to develop to complement the new chair. Veteran chief executives know that flexibility and adaptability are important attributes in determining the balance of leadership that the organization needs.

EXHIBIT 5.1. SAMPLE BOARD CHAIR PLATFORM

(This example is based on a statement created by a health care advocacy organization.)

- Build greater board engagement.
- Show how board involvement makes a difference to the organization in advocacy, collaboration, and cooperation.
- Build a closer relationship with the national organization.
- Reward accomplishments in diversity.
- Preserve and protect the organization's government granting agency.
- Position the organization as a key player in the public health arena through inter-organizational collaboration and partnerships.
- Focus on partnerships with organizations on aging to build mission and funding relationships.

Before the board chair takes office, a discussion about expectations will help the two leaders review their job descriptions and craft a communications and accountability pact. This agreement can cover issues ranging from honest feedback about the chief executive's performance to a schedule of weekly telephone calls or monthly in-person meetings (see sidebar below).

Communication and Accountability Pact

The chief executive will

- Share both good news and bad news immediately
- Provide time for weekly telephone and monthly in-person updates
- Alert the board chair to any information or issue that has the slightest chance of escalating into a risk for the organization

The board chair will

- Make time to develop the agenda of each board meeting in concert with the chief executive
- Provide honest feedback to the chief executive in regard to the purview of his or her responsibilities and performance
- Develop a platform of issues in concert with the chief executive to be advanced during his or her term
- Be timely and responsive to the requests of the chief executive, recognizing that, at least in some instances, it is not appropriate for the chief executive to determine organizational direction or response without participation of the governing body

---

In a recently formed organization that has not yet established a "career path" for the board chair, the chief executive will help the governance committee select a candidate who has previous experience in nonprofit governance. It is important to take particular care in providing opportunities for the new board chair to interact with board members (to build the team), with colleagues in the field (to build knowledge of the external environment), and with customers that the organization serves (to build the passion).

Defining Separate and Shared Functions

Sometimes tensions between the chair and chief executive stem from confusion over who is responsible for what. Even board members and staff may have trouble distinguishing between the two leaders' responsibilities. Job responsibilities should be clarified from a solid governance perspective, not based on individual preferences.

In general, the board chair's responsibilities divide into two distinct yet inseparable areas: board process and board tasks. Board process applies to building a strong team, and board tasks refer to the board team's plan of work. In close collaboration with the chief executive and the governance committee, the chair fosters team building by continuously educating board members, spotting leadership promise among them, and nurturing that promise by providing leadership opportunities and personal mentoring. The chair ensures that the work of the board is aligned with the strategic plan and addressed appropriately in partnership with the staff.

The chief executive's responsibilities are not so easily categorized, because they are influenced by the changing skills and personalities of the board chair and board members. Whatever the variations, however, the chief executive's core responsibility is to lead the staff and manage the organization, along with

- Monitoring the quality and effectiveness of the organization and individual programs
- Developing future board and staff leadership
- Engaging in financial stewardship of the organization, within parameters established by the board
- Building external relations and advocacy
- Supporting the board

Each board chair–chief executive relationship will produce a unique variation; Table 5.1 summarizes the general responsibilities of the two positions. For each key function, the board chair and the chief executive support one another in maintaining focus on the mission and ensuring that the organization operates in alignment with its values.

TABLE 5.1. SEPARATE AND SHARED RESPONSIBILITIES
OF THE BOARD CHAIR AND CHIEF EXECUTIVE

Function	Board Chair	Chief Executive	Shared
Policy and Planning	Facilitates board's involvement in approving guiding principles, policies, and mission	Carries out mission; implements strategic plan; provides administrative support for board policymaking	Create policies and guidelines; develop mission and vision statements; outline organizational values
Budget and Finances	Guides board in approving and overseeing budget; oversees outside audits; ensures that the board holds ultimate responsibility for integrity of organization's finances	Proposes budget to board; manages programs according to board-adopted financial policies and budget guidelines	N/A
Board Meetings	Leads and facilitates board meetings	Ensures that board members have meeting materials and needed information; attends meetings, except specific executive sessions	Develop meeting agenda
Committee Work	Structures overall committee system; is ex officio member of all committees	Sits in on appropriate committee meetings; ensures that committee members have staff support and needed materials and information	Review committee system and individual committees to ensure alignment with mission and strategic goals
Board Development	Leads development of a strong board; sets goals and expectations for the board; cultivates leadership in individual board members; makes board development a priority	Shares appropriate information to keep board informed and educated	Keep all board members engaged in the work of the organization
Board Recruitment and Orientation	Works with governance committee to identify and recruit new board members	Assists in identifying and cultivating new board members; works with governance committee to structure board orientation	Identify skills, expertise, and attributes needed for the board

TABLE 5.1. (Continued)

Function	Board Chair	Chief Executive	Shared
Board Assessment	Ensures regular opportunities for board self-assessment; oversees comprehensive board assessment every two to three years	Assists in development of board assessment process	Assess results and consider improvements in collaboration with governance committee
Staff Oversight, Compensation, Evaluation	Oversees hiring, compensation, and evaluation of chief executive; ensures chief executive success on plan exists	Oversees and evaluates all staff; sets staff salaries within budget constraints	N/A
Fundraising and Development	Solicits contributions from board members and ensures all board members do their share	Coordinates overall fundraising effort; ensures staff support for fundraising	Solicit contributions from outside donors; set the case for—and the amount of—a capital campaign based on determined strategic objectives
Public Relations and Communications	Promotes the work of the organization and encourages board members to do so; speaks for the board when controversy or crisis arises	Official spokesperson for the organization; coordinates public relations and communications	With board and staff, develop message that conveys the organization's mission effectively and can be used consistently by board and staff

Communication

Supporting the chief executive is one way the board chair can also support the organization. Open communication on a weekly basis is highly important, whether by e-mail, telephone, videoconferencing, in person, or some combination. The two leaders may discuss a specific item or simply check in to see how things are going. In national organizations with the board chair and chief executive living in different places, arranging in-person meetings may be a challenge, so establishing other forms of communication is necessary.

Communication involves keeping the board abreast of problems as they occur, along with trends, opportunities, or general concerns that are worthy of discussion. No board chair likes surprises. Transparency and accountability will flow from ongoing communication. Similarly, the board chair owes it to the chief executive to keep him or her informed of any board concerns about the effective operations of the board and the organization. It is the board's chair's responsibility to ensure that board members who may have direct contact with the chief executive, such as the treasurer or other committee chairs, bring any concerns about their relationships with the executive to the chair instead of voicing them directly. If it seems that the chief executive is under constant bombardment by board members, then it is the chair's responsibility to act as a gatekeeper and determine a more concise flow of information.

If communication difficulties with the chief executive escalate to the point where only the intervention of an objective third party can help, it could be useful to ask a consultant to mediate and help arrive at a solution. If the conflict relates to a governance issue, a board governance consultant may be helpful.

Professional Boundaries

The board chair and chief executive must have a professional relationship with clear boundaries. However, as the partnership develops, they may share personal information as they get to know one another, adding a humanizing element and creating a less perfunctory relationship. They may also gain a larger context of understanding about what each of them brings to their respective roles.

It's important to be aware of how the personal may affect the professional. For example, if either the chief executive or board chair faces an emergency with a family member, how will the other person's responsibilities be handled? How can they help one another, and, if necessary, how can another staff or board member temporarily step up to assist the organization? Avoid allowing the personal relationship to dominate the professional one.

Hierarchy Versus Partnership

It is important to understand when to make joint decisions and when to exert authority. The chief executive works at the pleasure of the board, possibly creating an imbalance in the chair-executive partnership. Tension may be discernible when the executive's contract is up for renewal or when it is time for an annual salary review. The board chair should engage a compensation committee (including counsel) to negotiate the contract and recommend a salary increase based on preset variables stated in the executive's contract, such as the performance evaluation and annual goals. When there is any sense of imbalance in the partnership, it's time to make conscious use of partnership principles.

Partnership Challenges

The manner in which the board chair and chief executive resolve the challenges in their relationship sets the tone for the board chair's term in office and may affect other board and staff relationships. Board chairs and chief executives often have respectful and positive relationships, but when those relationships are negative, there is the potential to create additional tensions, divided loyalties, and unwelcome schisms. If differences are allowed to smolder, unresolved, the work of the board will suffer.

Part of the challenge in forging a partnership is dealing with uncomfortable issues and problems. Often, new board chairs are not quite sure how to use their authority. At times this uncertainty can look like simply accepting and continuing the status quo. For example, one incoming board chair remarked that her chief executive routinely chooses the members of the nominating committee and was a member himself. She was content to follow the current organizational practices and assumed it was acceptable. By simply accepting a "routine" practice without assessing it from the perspective of good governance practices, this board chair let personal issues take precedence over good governance.

Challenging a strong chief executive is not an easy task for a new board chair (or even an existing one), but in the context of good governance and effective leadership, it may indeed be necessary to question old practices. Both individuals bring their personal histories to the partnership, creating interactions different from those of the past. To further complicate the board chair–chief executive partnership, variables such as the following may enter into the equation:

- Gender similarities or differences
- Age similarities or differences
- Ethnic, cultural, or religious similarities or differences
- Tenure of the chief executive (new or veteran)
- Work and volunteer history, occupation of the board chair
- Personality type (quiet or overbearing)
- Range of communication skills
- Assertiveness or lack thereof
- Degree of confidence in oneself and in the other person
- Personal integrity or lack thereof
- Fear of hurting one another's feelings, making waves, opening a Pandora's box, or undermining current practices
- Feeling overwhelmed or being in over one's head
- Feeling uncertain, intimidated, unmotivated, anxious

Consciously or unconsciously, these variables can easily undermine the working relationship and the balance of power between the chair and the chief executive. Building a collaborative relationship requires finding common ground from which to operate while respecting differences. The board chair's and chief executive's attention to the partnership must focus on both the reality and the perception.

The Chief Executive and the Board

In their insightful 1991 book *Executive Leadership in Nonprofit Organizations*, Robert Herman and Richard Heimovics noted that the most effective chief executives have discovered that they can get more done for the organization by embracing their responsibility for helping the board do its job. Herman and Heimovics described these effective executives as "board-centered." Chief executives who embrace their responsibility for supporting the board exhibit the following behaviors (adapted loosely from the work of Herman and Heimovics):

• *Initiate and maintain a structure for board work.* In most organizations, the chief executive (sometimes through other staff, but sometimes directly) sends out meeting notices, coordinates meeting times and locations, orders refreshments, sends out the agenda and other advance materials, and makes sure that accurate minutes are taken and eventually distributed. The chief executive may do the same for some or all board committees. These superficial duties are not worth much further discussion, except to reaffirm that they are almost universally accepted and practiced as executive responsibilities. Performed poorly, they can have a surprisingly large impact on overall board performance.

The board-centered chief executive also works in close partnership with the board chair to plan efficient and productive meetings. This goes beyond simply putting together an agenda; it may include a premeeting session with the chair to discuss goals and desired outcomes for the meeting; creating a timed and annotated agenda to help the board chair run the meeting well; designing, administering, and tabulating results from a meeting evaluation form; and having a post-meeting session to review decisions and next steps. An overcommitted board chair may not have enough time for all these steps, in which case the chief executive needs to find less time-consuming ways to accomplish the same things. Many chief executives also work with the chair to create an annual calendar to guide the board's work.

• *Show consideration and respect toward board members; facilitate interaction in board relationships.* The board-centered chief executive works to ensure that all board members feel equally valued and participate fully in the work of the board. He or she takes the time to understand the positions, concerns, and interests of individual board members, which reduces the likelihood that the chief executive will be surprised or sidelined during board discussions. He or she also seeks to understand what each board member finds rewarding or valuable in serving on the board and then responds to those needs.

• *Provide helpful and useful information to the board.* The chief executive works with the board chair and other officers to make sure that the board receives the right information—and the right quantity of information—at the right time to support its work. While a few executives provide too little information, many others provide too much. Successful chief executives manage to find a balance, which will vary from organization to organization and is also likely to change over time. The chief executive's goal should be to help board members feel smart, not to stupefy them with overwhelming amounts of unedited material. One of the most valuable ways chief executives can spend their time is editing, simplifying, and clarifying information that is given to the board.

• *Promote board accomplishments and productivity.* One of the characteristics of an effective team is a culture of mutual accountability. Although chief executives are not well positioned to point out the shortcomings of the board as a whole or of individual directors, they can do so indirectly by making sure that good performance is recognized and acknowledged. If board members or board committees who do their jobs and produce results receive no more recognition than those who consistently fall short, over time the performance of the entire board is likely to fall to the lowest acceptable level of productivity. Board members are more likely to follow through on their commitments if they consistently see examples of other board members who do so. And the board as a whole is more likely to produce meaningful results if it is reminded of past successes and convinced that its work is vital to the organization.

• *Envision change and innovation with the board.* An effective chief executive keeps the board informed about trends and changes in the external environment and their implications for the organization and the work of the board. In addition to the formal planning process, discussed earlier, the executive should play this role on an ongoing basis. Executives should lay the groundwork for change over time, so that major shifts or decision points don't come as a surprise to the board. This applies to both the work of the organization and that of the board itself. Effective chief executives are not content with business as usual, and they use their position to encourage ongoing adaptation and improvement.

Recommending that the chief executive take responsibility for the success of the board is not equivalent to suggesting that the chief executive manipulate or dominate the board. Executives who do can sometimes be successful over the short term or even for many years, but the opportunity cost is huge. Chief executives who dominate their organizations' boards not only fail to capitalize on a potential asset but also create a climate of reduced accountability and increased risk. As a result, the executive's leadership role is lonelier and more precarious than it needs to be.

Handling the Chief Executive's Annual Assessment

The chief executive's role in supporting the board extends, sometimes awkwardly, to supporting the board in conducting the executive's annual performance assessment and salary review. Thus many chief executives find themselves helping the board identify an assessment tool, gathering comparable salary information, and reminding the board chair that the review needs to take place. Even chief executives who understand their responsibility for the board's success may still feel sheepish reminding the board chair that they haven't had a performance review in two years or suggesting that a long-overdue raise be made retroactive.

Working with the board chair to create an annual work plan for the board and making sure the performance and salary review are part of that plan will drain some of the awkwardness from the interaction.

Chapter Thirteen includes a discussion of assessing the chief executive's performance.

Board Self-Assessment

The chief executive may also need to help the board initiate a periodic assessment of its own effectiveness, as many boards find the idea of self-assessment threatening or off-putting. Chief executives who fully embrace the behaviors described in the earlier list will recognize the importance of board self-assessment as a tool for improving the systems and structures that support board work, increasing board productivity, and stimulating innovation and change. The executive may need to help the board find a consultant or a self-assessment tool, develop a plan for conducting the self-assessment, provide some administrative support, and offer reassurance that the process can be positive and productive.

Chapter Thirteen addresses board self-assessment in more detail.

The Value of Mutual Support

When considering their role in supporting the board, chief executives should review the concept of servant-leadership. If the board and executive focus on their roles in serving and supporting each other, rather than traditional hierarchical ideas about who's in charge, a balanced partnership is more likely to emerge. The chief executive will sometimes lead the board but will often create the space and provide the tools for the board to lead.

Effective executives recognize that their own success—and the organization's—depends on the board's effectiveness. Those who embrace their own responsibility for the board's success, rather than passively complaining about a weak board, are more likely to succeed themselves.

What to Do When the Board and Chief Executive Aren't Working as a Team

When a board and chief executive have a problematic relationship, turning to outside help is often the easiest way to find a path to creating team understanding and effectiveness. An external consultant can

- Provide a structured process for productive discussion and resolution
- Assess strengths and weaknesses
- Provide facilitation skills and help to define preferred outcomes
- Bring objectivity and a fresh perspective
- Provide access to additional business experience and acumen
- Follow up and hold the team accountable
- Evaluate and recommend

Planned strategic thinking discussions, formal team-building experiences, and self- and group assessment are all tools that can be used to increase the effectiveness of the board–chief executive team.

The Chief Executive as Board Member

Most nonprofits have the chief staff executive as an ex officio nonvoting member of the board. A 2007 BoardSource survey reported that just 14 percent of the chief executives among the respondents were voting members of their boards, but the vast majority of chief executives attend and regularly participate in board meetings.

Is the chief executive's impact affected by whether he or she has a vote on the board? Do board members relate to their chief executive differently if he or she has an opportunity to vote on board issues? These are some of the questions that every board should ask while defining the role of the chief executive. First clarifying the role of management and governance within the organization may help the board define its relationship with the chief executive.

Conflicts Created by Voting Rights

Serving on the board while being responsible for the daily management of the organization often places the chief executive in a complicated situation, which may include:

- The introduction of a potential for conflict of interest
- Blurring of the distinction between the board's responsibilities and the chief executive's responsibilities
- Chief executive's for-pay status versus the board's volunteer status
- Board assessment of the chief executive's performance and determination of compensation
- Exclusionary nature of executive sessions—often meeting without staff members
- Propriety of membership in certain committees (audit, personnel)
- Potential for some relationships between the chief executive and certain board members to become strained if the chief executive votes against a particular initiative or idea

Benefits of Voting Rights

Having a vote on the board may create some concrete but mostly symbolic advantages to the chief executive. As a voting member, the chief executive can

- Have a tangible method of voicing an opinion or a concern to the board
- Feel he or she has earned the full trust of the board and can function as a peer, albeit not hierarchically
- Enhance his or her position of authority inside and outside of the organization
- Strengthen the working partnership with the board
- Bring continuity to board service (because board members normally have term limits, staff often stay longer in their positions)

Other Considerations

When determining the chief executive's voting status, ask and answer the following questions:

- Could the chief executive's contribution to the board work more efficiently as an ex officio nonvoting member?

- What are the underlying reasons for why the chief executive wants to become a voting member? Does he or she feel out of the loop or feel that the board is showing a lack of confidence in his or her performance?
- How would granting voting rights affect the relationship between the chief executive and other staff members?
- If the chief executive becomes a voting member, the organization should establish clear policies on the chief executive's participation on issues such as determining executive salary, evaluation procedures, and the like.

Chapter Exercises

- A constructive partnership between the chair and the chief executive is vital to every nonprofit. Why is this true—or does it always matter?
- For the most part, chairs change regularly, but the chief executive stays in place for a longer period of time. How can this situation affect the dynamics of the two positions?
- If the chief executive insists on a vote on the board, what questions should the board ask before making the decision?

PART TWO

GOVERNANCE PRACTICES

CHAPTER SIX

BUILDING A BOARD

The job of building a nonprofit board is more than just filling slots. It is about being strategic in the way a board looks at its composition and its operations. Today, nonprofit organizations are taking a closer look not only at how business is conducted, but at how decisions are made and by whom.

An effective board is not only a legal requirement, but a strategic necessity. The most effective boards—those whose members are deeply committed to the mission, who bring expertise in key areas, and who represent diverse points of view—evolve over time through careful planning. Board building is a cycle, not an annual event.

Organizations with strong, active boards often spend significant time and attention on each part of the board building cycle. Good boards wanting to become great boards continually consider how to strengthen their performance at each step of the cycle. They ensure that every board member is on the same page in terms of responsibilities, both collective and individual. The board-building process has two major purposes: to replenish the board's people power by bringing in new members and to strengthen the board's performance.

The Governance Committee

The role of the governance committee is to find enthusiastic people with the skills the board needs, help teach these people what it means to be on the board, continually engage them, evaluate the board's work, and make sure the board is living up to its potential. The committee may also convey the legal side of board service and the liabilities included in it. Board candidates need to understand the seriousness of their responsibilities. In addition to making a personal commitment of time, they are making both a legal and a financial commitment. It may sound like a lot to do, but forming a great governance committee is essential in laying a solid foundation for a strong and dynamic board. For more about the roles and responsibilities of the governance committee, see Chapter Four, Governance Structure.

Building a board is a continuous process with nine essential steps:

Step 1: Identify the needs of the board: the skills, knowledge, perspectives, and connections needed to achieve goals. What are its current strengths? What necessary characteristics are missing?

Step 2: Cultivate sources of potential board members and identify people with the desired characteristics. Ask current board members, senior staff, and others to suggest potential candidates. Find ways to connect with those candidates, get them interested in the organization, and keep them informed of progress.

Step 3: Recruit prospects. Describe why prospective members are wanted and needed. Explain expectations and responsibilities of board members, and don't minimize the requirements. Invite questions, elicit prospects' interest, and find out whether they are prepared to serve.

Step 4: Orient new board members both to the organization and to the board, explaining the history, programs, pressing issues, finances, facilities, bylaws, and organizational chart. Describe committees, board member responsibilities, and lists of board members and key staff members.

Step 5: Involve all board members. Discover their interests and availability. Involve them in committees or task forces. Assign them a board "buddy." Solicit feedback. Hold everyone accountable. Express appreciation for work well done.

Step 6: Educate the board. Provide information concerning the mission area. Promote exploration of issues facing the organization. Hold retreats and encourage board development activities by sending board members to seminars and workshops. Don't hide difficulties.

Step 7: Evaluate the whole board, as well as individual board members. Examine how the board and chief executive work as a team. Engage the board in assessing its own performance. Identify ways in which to improve. Encourage individual self-assessment.

Step 8: Rotate board members. Establish term limits. Do not automatically reelect for an additional term; consider the board's needs and the board member's performance. Explore advisability of resigning with members who are not active. Develop new leadership.

Step 9: Celebrate victories and progress, no matter how small. Appreciate individual contributions to the board, the organization, and the community. Make room for humor and a good laugh.

Step 1: Identify the Board's Needs

The search for new board members is a strategic activity driven by consideration of what resources the board needs among its members to serve the organization well during the next few years. Cyril O. Houle—the author of a seminal work, *Governing Boards: Their Nurture and Their Nature*— observed that "most of the time . . . the selection of board members should be made by deciding who is 'right' for a particular board, who can strengthen it, and who can give it the distinctive qualities that it needs at the present moment."

Having a strategic plan or annual goals is key to identifying the special skills and resources required on the board. For example, an organization planning to develop more of an online presence or enhance its internal technology capacities may need to recruit board members with a technology background. A symphony orchestra struggling with declining concert attendance may need board members who represent constituencies that are currently missing from the audience and who may understand these constituencies' needs and interests.

A board matrix (see Table 6.1) can help the governance committee identify recruitment needs, which will depend on the organization's mission and its stage of development. For example, the board of an independent school established five years ago has very different requirements than the board of a similar school with a fifty-year track record. The board of the newer school probably will want members who can take on jobs to supplement the work of a small staff, whereas the board of the well-established school may face major responsibilities for fundraising. During the early years, most board members may turn out to be parents, whereas the mature school may realize the importance of expertise and perspectives that must be found in the wider community.

TABLE 6.1. BOARD MATRIX WORKSHEET

	Current Members						Prospective Members					
	1	2	3	4	5	6	A	B	C	D	E	F
Age												
Under 18												
19–34												
35–50												
51–65												
Over 65												
Gender												
Male												
Female												
Race/Ethnicity												
African American/Black												
Asian/Pacific Islander												
Caucasian												
Hispanic/Latino												
Native American/Indian												
Other												
Resources												
Money to give												
Access to money												
Access to other resources (foundations, corporate support)												
Availability for active participation (solicitation visits, grant writing)												
Community Connections												
Religious organizations												
Corporate												
Education												
Media												
Political												
Philanthropy												
Small business												
Social services												
Other												

TABLE 6.1. (Continued)

	Current Members						Prospective Members					
	1	2	3	4	5	6	A	B	C	D	E	F
Qualities												
Leadership skills/Motivator												
Willingness to work/ Availability												
Personal connection with the organization's mission												
Personal Style												
Consensus builder												
Good communicator												
Strategist												
Visionary												
Bridge builder												
Areas of Expertise												
Administration/ Management												
Entrepreneurship												
Financial management												
Accounting												
Investments												
Fundraising												
Government												
Law												
Marketing, public relations												
Human resources												
Strategic planning												
Physical plant (architect, engineer)												
Real estate												
Representative of clients												
Special program focus (such as education, health, public policy, social services)												
Technology												
Other												
Number of years (or terms) on the board												

Identify Necessary Skills

Every board needs people who have leadership skills, work well as part of a team, ask good questions, and follow through on commitments. Community involvement, political connections, and fundraising abilities will be important for most organizations. A commitment to the organization's mission and values is a must. Financial expertise and professional expertise related to the organization's mission are two other valuable qualities. People with an understanding of information technology, entrepreneurial talent, and public relations and marketing skills may also add value. By identifying candidates with proven leadership skills, the board creates a pool of potential future leaders. Someone with organizational leadership experience may have demonstrated skills in managing groups of people, strategic planning, or finances.

Some organizations are required to fill a certain number of board seats with people who reflect the needs of specific geographic locations or other organizations or who are directly affected by the organization's services. Others choose to do so because they recognize the need for the perspectives that come from different experiences and interests. A statewide organization may need board members from different parts of the state. An organization serving people with developmental disabilities may be required to have clients' family members on the board.

Add Value with Diversity

The chief reason for developing a heterogeneous board is to promote exploration of a wider range of ideas and options, to reach forward-looking decisions, and to better represent community needs and interests. Research has shown that systems perform best when internal diversity reflects the diversity of the environment. Boards that include men and women with different skills and professional backgrounds, ages, financial situations, and cultural and ethnic backgrounds may be better positioned to steer the organization through frequently turbulent environments than may boards whose membership is more homogeneous.

For example, more boards are including young people in their ranks because they tend to bring different assumptions to the board table. Their ideas about technology use can be creative and practical. They won't feel constrained by a "we tried this already" mentality, and may, by their questions and comments, help identify "the elephant in the room." A study conducted in 2000 at the University of Wisconsin-Madison found that adults who worked with young people in making decisions about an organization reported a higher level of commitment and energy around the room.

In ethnically and racially diverse communities, it can be crucial that boards diversify their membership to respond effectively to the needs and aspirations of the community. For example, a retirement community struggling with declining enrollment might be disadvantaged by a board that does not incorporate the perspectives of the major population groups in the area. Not only does demographic diversity add depth and nuance to the board's discussions, but it also serves as a symbol of the organization's values. People will consciously or unconsciously draw conclusions about what an organization stands for based on the composition of its board.

Diversity includes, but is not limited to, gender, age, religion, sexual orientation, race or ethnicity, language, socioeconomic status, legal status, disability, geographic base, and political viewpoint.

Avoid Tokenism When Building the Board

Building a diverse board is not about tokenism. No board member wants to fill a quota, and no one is able to represent an entire subsection of the population. Organizations are often more successful integrating new voices when the new group makes up 30 percent of the total—or, at a minimum, three people. This approach helps change the culture, and the new participants will not feel isolated. To better integrate new members, incorporate informal social time and training on diversity and inclusiveness into board meetings. Also consider whether the board and organization would benefit from cultural competency training.

Round Out the Board

Once it is clear what kind of composition the board will need over the next several years, it's time to assess what characteristics and attributes current board members bring to the table. Consider the traditional "Ws" that every board depends on: work, wealth, and wisdom. Every board needs people who are willing to roll up their sleeves to get things done, who have access to financial resources, and who have the wisdom to ask the right questions, provide the needed knowledge, and support healthy discussion. But there are two other Ws essential to an effective board: wit and witness. Humor can make it easier and more enjoyable for the board to work together, and all board members need to be able to give witness to the organization's valuable work, to tell the story so that others will add their support.

Balance Diversity and Size

Gauging the board's ideal size takes careful thought. If it is too large, some members may feel disengaged, and decision making becomes cumbersome. If the board is too small, board members may be overwhelmed and the board will not have sufficient breadth of perspective, expertise, and other resources. To learn more about determining board size, see Chapter Four, Governance Structure.

To maximize the board's effectiveness, all board members should represent more than one skill or attribute. For example, the governance committee of a nursing home board determined that it was going to need members with financial expertise, connections to the local African American community, and understanding of issues facing frail elderly people. As a result, the board identified a promising prospect in an African American man who served as chief financial officer of a major community organization. His father was also a former resident of the nursing home.

Another way to expand the resources available to the board is to use advisory councils: groups of people who agree to make themselves available by providing consultation pro bono. Chapter Four, Governance Structure, addresses the purpose, structure, and functions of advisory groups.

Step 2: Cultivate Relationships

Cultivation has two parts: creating a pool of prospective board members and developing relationships with them that will lead to either board membership or to some other form of supportive interaction. The outcome of the cultivation process should increase the likelihood that someone with the right qualifications will be waiting in the wings when the need arises.

The governance committee manages cultivation, making sure that the entire board is involved and that everyone understands how best to participate. No board member should ask potential candidates whether they want to serve on the board; the governance committee is responsible for delegating that task. On the other hand, board members ought to feel free to share information about the organization's work, invite people to events, and discover their levels of support for the mission. The governance committee should collect information about individuals who might become likely candidates, maintain a prospects file, and take next steps, if appropriate.

Look for Prospects

Every board member, the chief executive, senior staff, and former board members should be engaged in looking for prospects. Others who will be helpful are donors who could think of people who might be interested in board service, professionals in related fields, and colleagues and board members of other nonprofit groups. The chief executive will also have important contacts in the community.

The board needs to look beyond its usual "local" view of board prospects. For instance, a health-related charity might look for leads among medical professionals, social workers, clergy, and family members of people who have benefited from the organization's services. A local Boys and Girls Club board might develop relationships with recent graduates who have exhibited strong leadership abilities.

The following may be good sources of suggestions for prospective board members:

- Colleagues
- Former board members and staff of other nonprofits
- Members of the organization
- Chief executive and other senior staff
- Board members
- Volunteer centers
- Local leadership programs
- Current volunteers
- Current advisory council members or task force members
- Articles and reports in the local media

People with these attributes are likely to be good board candidates:

- Those with a demonstrated affinity with the mission
- Community leaders
- Executives of local or national corporations, including those not at a senior level
- Owners of small businesses
- Individuals in professions related to the organization's mission
- Current and prospective major donors
- People who have benefited from the organization's services, or their relatives
- Current or past volunteers

These are promising places to look for board candidates:

- Religious institutions and congregations
- Major corporations' outreach programs
- Trade, professional, and fraternal associations
- Local businesses

- Organizations representing various racial and ethnic groups
- Local colleges and universities, community colleges
- Electronic databases (www.guidestar.org, www.volunteermatch.org, www.boardnetusa.org)
- Hobby centers, clubs, community centers

As boards consider possible candidates, they may want to look for these personal characteristics that are particularly desirable in a board member:

- Ability to listen, analyze, think clearly and creatively, and work well with individuals and groups
- Commitment to preparing for and participating in board and committee meetings, asking relevant questions, taking responsibility and following through on assignments, contributing personal and financial resources according to circumstances, opening doors in the community, and self-evaluation
- Willingness to develop certain skills, such as cultivating and soliciting funds, cultivating and recruiting board members and other volunteers, reading and understanding financial statements, and learning more about the substantive program areas of the organization
- A character that is honest, sensitive, patient, and tolerant of differing views
- Personal integrity, a sense of values, concern for the organization's development, and a sense of humor

Nurture Relationships

As soon as prospective candidates are identified, it is time to begin bringing them into the fold. They need basic information, including annual reports, brochures, newsletters, and links to media coverage. Many organizations invite prospects to special events and ask whether they would like to observe the organization's programs. Or they can join committees and task forces or participate in other volunteer activities.

Some organizations require that prospective board members serve in some volunteer capacity for as much as a year before they are invited to join. As they become more familiar with the institution and the board, it may become apparent that they have additional skills or interests that could benefit the organization—or it may turn out that they would not be the right people for the board.

People who serve on other boards or whose schedules are busy may not be able to join the board right away. It's important to keep them on the prospect list, stay in touch, and update them on the organization's activities and achievements.

Practice Diplomacy

The governance committee can avoid misunderstandings by being clear with prospects that not everyone who is invited to take an active interest in the organization's work—including the possibility of board service at some point in the future—will end up as a board member. If someone seems to meet some of the criteria listed in the desired profile, it may be wise to say that the governance committee might be interested in talking with them at some point about possible board service and ask whether this would be of interest to them. The committee considers a variety of factors, including getting the right mix of talents, perspectives, and experiences on the board.

Follow Written Procedures

When the board clearly documents its needs, selection criteria, and process for recruiting and nominating new board members, it is in a better position to protect itself from accusations of unfair discrimination. Because board service does not involve an employment contract, there is generally no legal recourse that can be taken. However, an organization may still be open to public criticism if disgruntled constituents sense that the selection process was unfair or unbalanced.

Should Board Members Provide Professional Services?

Should every board recruit an attorney, an accountant, and a financial manager? Should technical specialty be a necessary criterion for board service? It is true that boards often deal with legal, financial, or other specialist issues that require more expertise than a nonspecialized board member may be able to give. In all-volunteer organizations, professional skills are particularly helpful. However, experts and representatives of specific fields can find themselves in a difficult position of trying to define their role as an active and contributing board member while being expected to perform professional services for the organization. In most cases, board members with a technical background benefit the board best as advisors rather than as direct service providers.

Step 3: Recruit Prospective Board Members

Because of the time-consuming nature of board work, it is important to talk to prospective board members about their interest in serving and to listen carefully to their answers. These conversations will provide indications of prospective members' commitment to the important job for which they are being considered.

Eliciting Interest

Some direct questions will help gauge whether a prospect is interested in serving on a board.

- Why are you interested in our organization?
- Why are you interested in serving on a board?
- Do you have any previous board service, leadership, or volunteer experience?
- How will the organization benefit from your participation?
- How do you think we could best take advantage of your expertise?
- What do you expect us to do for you so that your experience is satisfying?
- What kind of time and financial commitment will you be able to make?
- Are you willing to serve on committees and task forces?
- Can we expect you to come to board meetings regularly? Would you be able to make a personal contribution?

The governance committee narrows the list of prospects by reviewing their qualifications against the board matrix and expectations. Confidential research reveals more about their past performance on boards, the extent of their expertise, and their willingness to be a team player. Board members ought to have a clean legal slate as well as a good reputation in the community, the capacity to carry out their duties, and the ability to contribute financial support according to their individual means.

Nominating Candidates

The governance committee identifies viable and interested candidates and presents a slate of nominees to the board, the membership, or the appointing authorities. The chief executive will usually participate in the deliberations and have a voice, but not necessarily a determining voice, in the selection of nominees. Some organizations have more than one candidate for each open position; in others, the board prefers to be presented with just one nominee per position. If the bylaws stipulate one method or the other, the bylaws must be followed.

Reelection to the board should not be automatic. If the board matrix indicates that the board needs someone with very different qualifications, the governance committee might recommend against renominating a current member in favor of bringing in someone with much-needed expertise.

As a final step before formal nomination, it is wise for the board chair, the governance committee chair, and/or the chief executive to talk with the person to review in detail what board membership entails.

Formal Nomination and Election

Although some boards ask the governance committee to present a slate of fully vetted candidates, this practice may suggest that the governance committee, not the full board, controls the election. Other boards may prefer to have more influence over the final slate and ask the governance committee to present more than one candidate per slot. The procedure the board chooses to follow should be clearly outlined in its bylaws or policies.

As soon as the board has elected new members, the board chair contacts them to issue a warm welcome. Although a phone conversation may suffice as preliminary notification, candidates should be informed in writing about their election to the board and asked to indicate their acceptance in writing. Some boards ask board members to sign a formal agreement or statement of understanding that outlines mutual expectations between the board and its members (see Exhibit 6.1 for an example). Some may also hold an official swearing-in ceremony at new members' first board meeting, at which they pledge their service to the organization and its mission and formally acknowledge their responsibilities as board members.

Step 4: Orient New Board Members

Orientation begins when a prospective board member is first approached about the possibility of serving—or, for membership organizations that nominate and elect board members, before potential board members decide to put their names up for election. The formal orientation is a continuation of that process. Ideally, orientation is held before new board members attend their first board meeting and is organized by the governance committee with the chief executive and the board chair.

Unfortunately, board orientation is often a weak area. It is not uncommon for board members to learn what they need to know almost entirely on the job. Establishing a policy that makes participation in board orientation mandatory will go a long way toward strengthening board performance, especially if an effective process supports the policy.

Each new board member should receive a board manual or handbook before the board orientation session. Many organizations store this information online in

EXHIBIT 6.1. SAMPLE BOARD MEMBER AGREEMENT

As a board member of the XYZ, I am fully committed to the mission and have pledged to help carry it out. I understand that my duties and responsibilities include the following:

1. I will be fiscally responsible, with other board members, for this organization. I will know what our budget is and take an active part in reviewing, approving, and monitoring the budget.
2. I know my legal responsibilities for this organization as a member of the board and will take an active part in establishing and overseeing the organization's policies and programs.
3. I will act in accordance with the bylaws and operating principles outlined in the manual and understand that I am morally responsible, as a member of the board, for the health and well-being of this organization.
4. I will give what is for me a substantial annual financial donation.
5. I will actively participate in fundraising in whatever ways are best suited for me and agreed on with those in charge of the organization's fundraising. These may include individual solicitations, undertaking special events, writing mail appeals, and the like. I am making a good faith agreement to do my best and to help raise as much money as I can.
6. I will actively promote XYZ in the community and will encourage and support its staff.
7. I will prepare for and attend board meetings, be available for phone consultation, and serve on at least one committee, as needed.
8. If I am not able to meet my obligations as a board member, I will offer my resignation.
9. In signing this document, I understand that no quotas are being set and that no rigid standards of measurement and achievement are being formed; rather, all board members are trusted to carry out the above agreements to the best of their ability.

Date_____ Signed _____
                                                          Board Member
Date_____ Signed _____
                                                          Board Chair

a password-protected section of the Web site designed just for board members. The handbook contains information pertinent to the board and its members, organized as an easy reference. The contents depend on the board's and the organization's processes and needs; see Exhibit 6.2 for an example of what the handbook could include.

EXHIBIT 6.2. SAMPLE BOARD HANDBOOK CONTENTS

A. The board
- Board member names and contact information
- Board member bios, using standard format (not formal resumes)
- Board member terms
- Statement of board responsibilities
- Board member responsibilities
- Committee descriptions

B. Historical references for the organization
- Brief written history and/or fact sheet
- Articles of incorporation
- IRS determination letter
- Listing of past board members

C. Bylaws

D. Strategic framework
- Mission, vision, and values statements
- Strategic framework or plan
- Current annual operating plan
- Programs list

E. Finance
- Prior year's annual report
- Prior year's audit report
- Chart outlining financial growth (sales, membership, programs, and so on for the past five to ten years)
- Current annual budget
- IRS Form 990
- Banking resolutions
- Policies related to investments, reserves, endowments, and the like
- Risk management policies

F. Policies pertaining to the board
- Policy on potential conflicts of interest
- Insurance coverage
- Legal liability policies
- Travel and meeting expense reimbursements
- Accreditation documents (if applicable)
- Whistle-blower policy
- Others

G. Staff
- The chief executive's job description
- Staff listing (at least senior staff and those with whom the board might interact)
- Organization and team charts

(Continued)

H. Resource development
- Case statement
- Current funder list
- Sample grant proposal
- Sponsorship policy

I. Other Information
- Annual calendar
- Programs list
- List of common acronyms and terms (with explanations)
- Current brochure(s)
- Web site information

J. Procedures to update board handbook

Orientation introduces board members to the work of the organization and the work of the board. Staff members usually lead segments on the organization; the board chair or governance committee members facilitate segments on the board. Some organizations invite current board members to attend all or part of orientation sessions as ongoing board education. Long-time board members may be particularly helpful in sharing stories about the past, and even the most experienced board members may find the sessions helpful for keeping them current on new developments or reminding them of things they may have forgotten.

Subjects to be covered include the roles and responsibilities of board members, the organization's mission and programs, its strategic plan, finances, fundraising initiatives, and the structure of the board and staff. The orientation should touch on financial statements and the most recent audit, explain liability and insurance coverage, and reiterate the time commitment involved. Orientation may also include a video presentation on board roles and responsibilities followed by discussion. It is helpful to go over committee job descriptions and goals and to orient new board members on how to be effective committee members. In addition to formal presentations, it's important to leave time for questions and the opportunity for board members to get to know each other.

Here are some board orientation ideas:

- Hold at least part of the orientation at the organization's main office, to get a feel for the working environment and to meet key staff.
- In addition to more formal presentations and discussions with the board, accommodate members' different learning styles by offering reading materials, CDs, or videos to be reviewed at their own pace.
- Pair a new board member with a more seasoned member as a mentor to make the new member feel welcome, address questions that crop up from

time to time, encourage active participation, and explain the background of current controversies or the history behind issues that the board needs to address.

- Schedule a follow-up session several months into the new board member's term to respond to questions and ask for feedback on the board's operation.

Table 6.2 reviews the information to be conveyed during orientation with suggestions of various ways in which the information may be communicated. Some issues may be presented in person and other items in writing only or via video or on the Web site. Much of the information can be included in the board manual, but it should also be discussed or at least referred to during orientation sessions.

TABLE 6.2. BOARD ORIENTATION INFORMATION

Program	Describe what the organization does, whom it serves, and what difference it makes. Tour the facilities, observe programs, or hear a presentation by a client, member, or program participant.
Finances	Explain where the money comes from, how it is spent, and the state of the organization's financial health, including their role in fundraising.
History	Provide sufficient knowledge about the past so that the present makes sense. Also, help new board members see their own participation as part of the organization's ongoing story.
Strategic direction	Present a framework for new members to participate effectively. Clarify the mission, vision, values, and goals that inform the organization's actions.
Organizational structure	Help new board members understand who does what and lines of accountability.
Board roles	Ensure that new members understand the roles of the board.
Board member responsibilities	Ensure that new board members understand their own responsibilities as board members.
Board operations	Help new board members understand how the board operates so that they may participate effectively.
The board as a team	Facilitate new board members' integration with the other members.
Skills	Instruct new members on how to read a financial statement.

Step 5: Support Continuous Board Involvement

Experience indicates that board members want and need to feel a personal connection to the organization and its services—and that it takes inspiration to keep them involved and engaged. Some of this inspiration comes from realizing that the board makes a difference in helping the organization serve the mission and that they each personally make a difference in the work of the board. Inspiration for active engagement also comes from connecting one's own hopes and aspirations with the board's activities.

Create Participation Opportunities

Board meetings should be structured in such a way that board members feel that their time is well spent and that by the time they leave, something has been accomplished—something that will make a difference for the organization. Keeping board members engaged also means making productive use of committees and task forces so that everyone's time, talent, and interests can be effectively used. Giving board members a specific job to do—whether on a standing committee that meets throughout the year or on a task force with a short-term project—can mean the difference between their feeling connected to a worthwhile endeavor and being a detached spectator. It is important to remember that when board members accept an assignment outside of their board work, they function as volunteers with no more power or authority than other volunteers and should not impose their authority or intervene in the directives set by the chief executive or other staff.

To learn more about committee roles and effective meetings, see Chapter Four, Governance Structure, and Chapter Fifteen, Board Meetings.

Make Information Easily Available

Effective use of technology can help keep the board informed about subjects it needs to address. To make sure that some board members are not placed at a disadvantage by their geographic distance or by the travel demands of their jobs, board and committee meetings may sometimes be conducted by teleconference or videoconference. E-mail keeps board members informed and involved between meetings, and the password-protected Web site mentioned earlier ensures easy access to information.

Develop the Board as an Inclusive Team

Building an effective board means building and developing a team composed of the diversity of perspectives, expertise, and other resources needed to accomplish the mission. However, it is not enough to *recruit* a diverse board. The board must become a cohesive unit that makes use of what every board member can offer. Such boards are well positioned to enable creative thinking, innovation, and problem solving and to provide leadership in meeting organizational challenges and identifying new opportunities. The more diverse the board, the more important it is to nurture understanding by creating opportunities for social and interpersonal interaction. There are two caveats to creating an inclusive board: avoid tokenism, and manage differences of opinion.

To avoid tokenism, involve new members right away and assign them tasks that are independent of their cultural or ethnic background. For example, refrain from turning to the sole Asian board member only when questions come up that relate directly to the Asian community. Ask the member to address general questions posed to the board as well as questions related to the member's special expertise—which may or may not have anything in particular to do with the Asian community.

A natural by-product of inclusiveness may be wider disagreement among members, which is not necessarily easy to deal with. With the board chair as moderator, the board needs to cultivate an atmosphere of acceptance by encouraging wide-ranging opinions and molding them into creative solutions. See Chapter Sixteen, Board Dynamics, especially the sections on developing a culture of inquiry and maintaining civility in the boardroom. By exploring a variety of perspectives and options, the board is more likely to make effective decisions.

Promote Informal Interaction

To support the development of the team, the board needs to create opportunities for members to interact more informally than is possible during regular board meetings. Members need time to get to know each other by sharing stories and comparing experiences. They need to discover the things they have in common and to explore some of the differences between them. Occasional retreats with all board members attending can serve as powerful team-building events (see Chapter Fifteen, Board Meetings). Whether the focus is on particular topics, such as strategic planning, leadership training, or board assessments, or on a more thorough exploration of important issues, these retreats give board members the chance to gain a better understanding of the board's work and of each other—in other words, to become a more effective team. Informal dinners together before board meetings, or icebreaker activities as meetings begin, are other ways to promote relationship building and build camaraderie and trust among board members. See Chapter Sixteen, Board Dynamics, for more strategies that help the board work together effectively.

Be Clear About Responsibilities

By getting to know each member of the board and establishing an open line of communication, the board chair fills an essential role in ensuring members' effective inclusion and engagement. Smart chairs will assign board members to committees according to interest, skill, and time available and will check in with new board members after a few months to find out whether they need additional information and invite their feedback on board operations.

The chief executive engages board members by providing necessary information as well as suggesting ways in which a member's expertise and interests might be of particular service to the organization. For example, the board chair of a youth service organization may ask a board member who lives in the neighborhood of its youth center to serve as the organization's eyes and ears and to keep the staff informed of issues that could lead to conflict. This type of involvement often leads to a board member's greater sense of contribution and commitment.

Particularly with larger boards, committees and small groups provide board members, both old and new, with opportunities to get to know each other and to be part of a team. However, no matter what the size of the board, all leaders share in the responsibility of actively involving and mobilizing their members in the work of the board.

Barriers to Board Member Involvement

New and current board members come to meetings eager to participate in meaningful discussions. Boards should make sure they've considered (and overcome, where possible) the following barriers to involvement so that they can have efficient and productive meetings:

- The board is too large. Some board members do not feel needed.
- The board is too small. Board members feel overwhelmed or suffer from insufficient stimulation or limited perspectives.
- The executive committee is too active. If it meets too often, the rest of the board may feel underutilized or disengaged.
- Members received insufficient or ineffective orientation. Agendas are weak. They lack substance, are too long or too routine. Board members fail to see the relevance of board meeting topics to organizational performance.
- Members do not feel well used or important. They will decide that they have better things to do.
- There is little or no opportunity for discussion. Board members feel bored or frustrated.

- A few board members are allowed to monopolize discussion, take up disproportional amounts of airtime, and carry disproportional weight in decisions. The board lacks social cohesiveness. Board members have little in common except board service and do not have opportunities to get to know each other. Status differences get in the way of team development
- Board members lack passion for the mission.
- Board participation has become routine after many years of service.

Step 6: Educate the Board

Continuous learning is a defining characteristic of boards that stand out from the crowd. Such boards understand the need for expanding and deepening their members' knowledge about factors that will affect their planning and decision-making capabilities and the organization's success in the long run. They build educational activities into board meetings, schedule retreats for exploration of complicated issues, and encourage their members to attend outside workshops and seminars. In such ways organizational leaders learn and grow, and in turn their organizations learn and grow.

Topics for board education might range from internal issues such as fundraising, strategic planning, liability issues, or how to read a financial statement to external issues such as demographic trends, mission-related challenges, and emerging competition. Instead of looking at financial statements only to discover whether income and expenses are in balance, learning-oriented boards look for information that gives clues about the organization's long-term financial health. Instead of looking at changes in the community's population from the perspective of determining who will need the organization's services, learning-oriented boards seek to understand how such changes will have an impact on economic and political structures as well as on the community's culture.

Field trips are an excellent learning opportunity. Having board members see programs and services in action, meet with individuals benefiting from these programs, or travel to the organization's different sites makes the issues and needs come alive. Participating as a group in one of the organization's programs will serve the same purpose.

No board can afford to believe that it has arrived at perfection, that it has no more to learn about being a great board. When a group feels that it has arrived and can begin to coast, circumstances can change and the sands can start to shift underneath the group.

Some topics can be scheduled for discussion as part of regular board agendas throughout the year; others may emerge suddenly because of decisions that need to be made. For example, if a board realizes that it needs to develop or revise its conflict-of-interest policy, a short educational piece on the board's legal duties might be very effective because of its immediate relevance.

Boards stay in a learning mode by encouraging members to suggest topics that would help them and the board do a better job. Some form of education should be on the agenda of nearly every board meeting, whether a presentation by an outside consultant or a briefing by a staff member on developments in the organization's mission area. A museum board might enjoy a presentation about the way another museum increased attendance. An education organization might invite an educational researcher to present new findings related to gender issues in elementary education. In another approach, board members might be assigned as individuals or as groups to explore certain subjects and then report their findings to the full board.

Board meetings should always include time for discussion. Rather than just asking for questions and comments after a presentation, it is usually more effective to ask the board to discuss the possible implications of the information presented, to consider how the topic relates to the strategic plan, or to brainstorm questions that need further exploration.

Tips for Promoting Board Learning

- Invite outside consultants or internal experts to discuss trends in the organization's mission area, the community, or the larger society.
- Conduct a periodic review of how the mission statement is related to the organization's programs and services.
- Present special board training workshops on topics such as fundraising, planning, and finances.
- Feature presentations and question-and-answer sessions with program staff throughout the board meeting calendar.
- Distribute articles, videos, CDs, and links to Web sites that individual board members may view at home.
- Plan a discussion on a facet of the board's operations, such as the committee structure, the content and conduct of board meetings, or how to increase board diversity.
- Promote team building by scheduling and carefully planning a board retreat that combines educational activities with work and social interactions. Attend governance workshops offered by management assistance providers or other experts.
- Create a well-crafted Web site with links to other sources of information related to the mission or guidance about governance policies and practices.

Step 7: Evaluate the Board

There is no such thing as a board that has "arrived"—that cannot or should not continue to grow. Wise boards take time for regular check-ups to discover ways to strengthen their performance. Using regular board meeting evaluations, formal self-assessments, and feedback from outside consultants, these boards keep discovering ways in which to increase their value to the organization and to their own members.

Board Meeting Evaluation

It takes just a few minutes at the end of the meeting to fill out feedback forms or for a quick round of member comments about whether the meeting dealt with issues of substance and strategic importance, whether it was run efficiently, and whether it used board members' time wisely. To make effective use of meeting evaluations, a board could start out by determining what would constitute a very good board meeting. A list of these characteristics can then easily be turned into a simple board meeting evaluation form. For more about evaluating board meetings, see Chapter Fifteen.

Board Assessment

Board assessments can measure the board's progress, identify areas that need improving, and establish goals for the future. They can also remind members of their responsibilities as board members and help reshape the board's operations. Discussion of the results can also help the board to build trust and facilitate communication among its members and the chief executive. Board assessments represent time and effort well spent and, in the long run, can save money by making better use of limited resources and helping to ensure the organization's health and viability in a changing world. To learn more about board self-assessment as part of an organization-wide culture of evaluation, see Chapter Thirteen, Evaluation.

Individual Board Member Assessment

Assessments of individual board member performance are particularly useful when a board member's term is about to end and he or she is being considered for reelection. As the governance committee prepares for an upcoming board election, it is wise to ask each incumbent who is eligible for another term to complete a self-evaluation. Some boards now engage in peer evaluations, particularly in connection with renomination of current members. Chapter Thirteen, Evaluation, also addresses individual board member evaluation.

Feedback from Consultants

Hiring consultants is of no value unless the board listens to their suggestions for improving performance and then implements those suggestions. It makes sense to gather the board in a retreat setting after it has carried out its self-assessment. In this neutral setting, a consultant can point out strengths and weaknesses in the board's processes and can suggest ways to change course, if it seems that is in the best interest of the board and organization.

Step 8: Rotate Board Members

In the early stages, board membership can be exhilarating and challenging. However, over time, if the board remains largely unchanged, it can grow stagnant. There are many ways to keep a board fresh and interesting. Some involve shifting board members' roles within the board, and others involve bringing in new members to introduce novel ideas and challenge old assumptions.

Keep the Board Engaged

Allowing ample opportunity for change will keep board members from burning out during their tenure. One source of variety is assigning board members to different committees over time and providing opportunities for leadership roles to help keep them interested. Giving board members the chance to chair committees or assume other leadership positions not only helps to hone their skills and keep them active, but also contributes to leadership development and facilitates succession planning. To add diversity to board tasks, board members can represent the organization on outside committees or advisory councils.

Make Room for New People

The regular infusion of new board members ensures fresh insights and ideas and prevents board members from going stale. Rotation can be a matter of board practice, board policy, or a bylaws requirement. Setting term limits offers the advantage of regular turnover. Term limits also provide a graceful exit point for board members who are often absent, ineffective, or simply overwhelmed by other responsibilities. The organizations that responded to BoardSource's *Nonprofit Governance Index 2007* survey report an average board term of 3.1 years, with board members eligible to serve an average of 2.3 consecutive terms. When adopted, term limits should stagger the terms of individual board members so that all current members will not retire from the board in any given year.

Step Down and Say Goodbye

Asking an ineffective or difficult board member to step down from the board is not an easy task. The board chair, not the chief executive, should deal with such board members. In some cases, a member of the governance committee may want to initiate the conversation. Sometimes board members are aware of their inadequate performance but don't quite know how to handle the idea of resigning. They may feel that resigning implies that they don't care, but they may actually feel relieved when the chair suggests that resigning would be the honorable and generous thing to do. At other times, a friendly conversation can clear up any misunderstandings or false assumptions that may have arisen.

Saying goodbye to the board does not have to mean saying goodbye to the organization, or for that matter even entirely to the board. As members leave the board, exit interviews may identify ways in which they could remain connected to the organization. Whether or not an organization imposes term limits, there are several ways to ease someone out of a spot on the board without forever losing their support and influence. They can be invited to join a committee, an ad hoc task force, or an advisory council, or they can be asked to raise money or volunteer in another capacity.

Removing a Difficult Board Member

Occasionally a board member needs to be removed because he or she is preventing the board from doing its work. In some cases, a conflict of interest or unethical behavior may be grounds to remove an individual from the board. In other cases, a board member's behavior may become so obstructive that the board is prevented from functioning effectively. More frequently, the behavior of a problem board member discourages others from participating, and the board may find that other members attend less frequently or find reasons to resign. Although board member removal is rare, organizations should provide for it in their bylaws. See Chapter Sixteen, Board Dynamics, for a discussion of dealing with troublesome board members.

Step 9: Appreciate Efforts and Celebrate Achievements

Although celebration is not actually a step in the board-building cycle, it certainly is part of the process. It may be better described as a way of infusing a certain spirit of affirmation and hope into the steps involved in building an effective board. It needs to be part of everything a board does throughout the cycle to strengthen its performance and to add meaning to the lives of its members. The trick is to recognize the things worth celebrating: when board members do a good job, when the organization completes a project, when an individual board member has good news to share, or when the board has reached a milestone.

The board chair and chief executive may pay tribute to an individual board member in a variety of ways for a job well done, ranging from an informal but public thank-you at a board meeting to a certificate or award at a special event or a special mention in the newsletter. However it is handled, the leadership should look for opportunities to recognize each member of the board for their unique contribution, even if they don't play particularly visible roles.

Boards can show appreciation with special board recognition events, from simple to elaborate. Tokens of appreciation—such as useful (not merely decorative) items imprinted with the organization's logo—can be handed out at a board retreat or at the annual meeting. Surprising the board with special refreshments at a board meeting can help celebrate particular achievements. A celebratory toast (alcoholic or nonalcoholic) shows appreciation for departing board members and welcomes new members.

Boards that make time for members to get to know one another, share stories, and compare experiences from their lives are more likely to work through their disagreements and find creative solutions. Boards that celebrate their potential for learning and growing and for making a difference in the world will attract the resources needed to carry out their mission. Celebration is not, therefore, the last step in the board-building cycle—it is a spirit that should be infused in every step of the cycle for a lasting and successful outcome.

Chapter Exercises

- How should a board react to an unsolicited request from an individual who wants to serve on the board?
- Is it a good idea for a board to use application forms as a recruitment method?
- Discuss how boards could best achieve diversity of thought. How does this relate to diversity of the composition of the board?

- Should family members serve on the same board?
- Give examples of how a board member can increase the organization's social, intellectual, and financial capacity.
- How do you convince a new member to go through orientation if he has already served on numerous boards and feels he understands what board service is all about?

CHAPTER SEVEN

LEGAL AND ETHICAL RESPONSIBILITIES

When joining the board of a nonprofit organization, a board member takes on a set of responsibilities and duties defined by law. Along with attention to programs, finances, and fundraising, nonprofit board members need to understand the regulatory environment in which their organizations operate, including the fundamental legal principles and complex tax laws that govern the work of boards and board members.

Nonprofit organizations and their boards do not function in a vacuum. They are important players in the country's societal, economic, and legal framework, and they must adapt to—and sometimes act as the impetus for—environmental change. At other times, they may fulfill obligations and expectations common in the for-profit and government sectors.

For example, the Sarbanes-Oxley Act of 2002, passed by the U.S. Congress in the aftermath of corporate and accounting firm scandals, raised the standards of scrutiny in the private sector for matters such as auditor independence, corporate responsibility, financial disclosure, and conflicts of interest. Aspects of this heightened concern for accountability and transparency have carried over into the nonprofit sector, more by practice than by legal requirements (although some states have passed similar laws related to nonprofits).

Thus the board of a nonprofit organization is challenged with two seemingly contradictory mandates: advancing the good work of the organization and deciding the extent of its accountability to the public. This tension makes board service both difficult and rewarding.

Fulfilling Fiduciary Responsibilities

Fundamental to the legal aspects of board membership is the concept of fiduciary responsibility. The control of a nonprofit organization is usually vested in its governing body, typically called the board of directors. The members of this board, charged with exercising responsibility over the organization and its resources, are considered fiduciaries. This concept of fiduciary responsibility extends to the accountability that board members have assumed both to advance their organization's mission and to oversee its assets.

Fiduciaries are held to a standard known as the test of reasonableness and prudence. This centuries-old test has its basis in English common law and the standards developed concerning governance of charitable trusts. In contemporary terms, this standard means that board members are expected to regard and treat the nonprofit organization's assets and other resources with the same care with which they would treat their own resources.

Most state laws, by statute or court opinion, impose the standards of fiduciary responsibility on directors of nonprofit organizations, whether or not the organizations are trusts (and often whether or not they are charitable). Thus personal liability can result when a board member, officer, or key employee of a nonprofit organization breaches the standards of fiduciary responsibility.

Because the board of directors is ultimately responsible for a nonprofit organization's activities, when problems arise it often becomes the prime target. The general argument often made against boards in these circumstances—and the one against which board members should defend themselves—is guilt by omission. This situation arises when board members have been passive or otherwise inactive in overseeing the activities of the nonprofit organization and consequently may have failed to adhere to the standards of fiduciary responsibility. To protect against these charges, board members must demonstrate that they appropriately discharged the requisite duties. Ignorance is not an acceptable excuse when a legal problem demands the board's attention.

A chief responsibility of board members is to maintain financial accountability and effective oversight of the organization they serve. As trustees of the organization's assets, board members must exercise due diligence to see that the organization is well managed and that its financial situation remains sound. Fiduciary duty requires board members to be objective, unselfish, responsible, honest, trustworthy, and efficient. Board members, as stewards of the organization's resources, should always act for the good of the organization, rather than for their personal benefit. They need to exercise reasonable care in all decision making, without subjecting the organization to unnecessary risk.

Collective and Shared Responsibilities

The distinction of legal liability between the board and an individual board member relates to the responsibility of *the board* for the organization and responsibility of *individual board members* for their actions. The board as a collective entity is responsible and liable for what happens in and to the organization. As the ultimate authority, it must ensure that the organization operates in compliance with the law and its own policies.

Boards make decisions in a legally structured meeting. One critical element of a legal meeting is the existence of a quorum—the minimum number of voting members who need to be present before the meeting can take place. The quorum is defined as the reasonable number of board members who can attend a meeting at any given time. If the quorum is defined with less demanding parameters, and a majority vote of those present is required, it is possible that a few board members will end up making major decisions for the organization. If legal action ensues, it can often be traced to an inattentive, passive, or captive board. For example, an attorney general may proceed against a public charity for payment of excessive compensation to an executive, even when the board was entirely unaware of the compensation arrangement. Or the organization may be involved in employment discrimination or the making of defamatory statements, with the board wholly in the dark as to these practices.

To avoid legal action, board members should attend meetings regularly; make independent and justified decisions, rather than simply voting with the majority; and, before approving any meeting minutes, review the document carefully to ensure it truly reflects what happened in the meeting. As government regulators grow more aggressive in demanding accountability, boards must become correspondingly more vigilant and active in establishing and implementing sound policies. In turn, the board's shared legal responsibilities depend on the actions of its individual members. All board members are liable for their own acts and deeds—particularly if those actions are alleged to be civil or even criminal offenses. In practice, this requires board members to hold each other accountable.

Board members do not, individually, have unilateral authority to make decisions about the organization's governance. Rather, the board has collective responsibilities, as the U.S. Congress emphasized in 2007 when it passed legislation that amended the congressional charter of the American Red Cross. Aimed at modernizing the organization's structure and strengthening its governance, the legislation called for the American Red Cross to substantially reduce the size of its board, delegate day-to-day operations to management, eliminate distinctions regarding the election of board members, and form an advisory council. Because the American Red Cross is a federally chartered organization, Congress was given the opportunity to enumerate the responsibilities listed as follows. These responsibilities as outlined by Congress are good reminders for nonprofit boards in general.

- Review and approve the organization's mission statement.
- Approve and oversee the organization's strategic plan and maintain strategic oversight of operational matters.
- Select, evaluate, and determine the level of compensation of the organization's chief executive officer.
- Evaluate the performance and establish the compensation of the senior leadership team and provide for management succession.
- Oversee the financial reporting and audit process, internal controls, and legal compliance.
- Ensure that the chapters of the organization (if any) are geographically and regionally diverse.
- Hold management accountable for performance.
- Provide oversight of the organization's financial stability.
- Ensure the inclusiveness and diversity of the organization.
- Provide oversight of the protection of the organization's brand (this is a responsibility rarely found in a list of this nature).
- Assist with fundraising on behalf of the organization.

As for determining compensation, board practices differ. Some boards are involved in setting the compensation only of the chief executive; others at least approve the compensation of the senior staff. At a minimum, however, boards should approve the items of compensation that appear on the organization's annual information return, Internal Revenue Service Form 990 (for more information about Form 990, see Chapter Eight, Financial Oversight).

Duties of Care, Loyalty, and Obedience

The duties of the board of directors of a nonprofit organization are described as the duty of care, duty of loyalty, and duty of obedience. Defined by case law, these are the legal standards against which all actions taken by directors are held.

These collective duties adhere to the entire board and require the active participation of all board members. Boards demonstrate accountability by showing they have effectively discharged these three duties.

Duty of Care

The duty of care requires that directors of a nonprofit organization be reasonably informed about the organization's activities, participate in decisions, and do so in good faith and with the care of an ordinarily prudent person in similar circumstances. The duty of care is carried out by

- Attending board meetings and meetings of appropriate committees
- Preparing in advance for board meetings, such as reviewing reports and the agenda before arriving at the meeting
- Obtaining information, before voting, to make sound decisions
- Exercising independent judgment
- Periodically examining the credentials and performance of those who serve the organization
- Frequently reviewing the organization's finances and financial policies
- Ensuring compliance with state and federal filing requirements, particularly annual information returns

Duty of Loyalty

The duty of loyalty requires board members to exercise their power in the interest of the organization and not in their own interest or the interest of another entity, particularly one with which they have a formal relationship. In practice, the duty of loyalty is carried out by

- Adhering to the organization's conflict-of-interest policy
- Disclosing any conflicts of interest
- Avoiding the use of corporate opportunities for personal gain or benefit
- Maintaining the confidentiality of information about the organization

Duty of Obedience

The duty of obedience requires that directors of a nonprofit organization comply with applicable federal, state, and local laws; adhere to the organization's bylaws; and remain the guardians of the mission. The duty of obedience is carried out by

- Ensuring compliance with all regulatory and reporting requirements, such as filing the annual information return (IRS Form 990) and paying employment taxes
- Examining all documents that govern the organization and its operation, such as the bylaws
- Making decisions that fall within the scope of the organization's mission and governing documents

Protecting the Board

Generally, directors who carry out their duties faithfully and in adherence to the three duties will not be found personally liable. Unfortunately, however, there are no guarantees. Individual responsibility and the responsibility of the board overlap. The demarcation can often be indistinct, and in legal action, under certain circumstances, an individual board member may end up paying the penalties or being hit with other sanctions.

If, for example, an organization fails to pay employment taxes (or taxes that should have been withheld), board members (or at least the officers responsible for employment and financial matters) are likely to be expected to personally make the appropriate payment to the IRS. As another example, board members who are directly involved in employment discrimination may be personally liable for damages.

Legal and Ethical Compliance

Nonprofit directors and executives know their organizations must meet federal and state laws and regulations governing their activities. Compliance as a function must be addressed regardless of an organization's size. Compliance with integrity requires more effort. Exceptional boards seek to meet this standard by addressing not only the details of what is legally required but also by going further to ensure that the organization's operations and undertakings are conducted in a truly ethical, open, and responsive manner. This is the foundation of strong organizations. A nonprofit should focus on six key areas as it lays that solid foundation: ethical values and standards, risk management, internal controls and audits, insurance and emergency plans, performance evaluation, and conflicts of interest.

Ethical Values and Standards

A statement of ethical values and standards adopted by the board is brought to life by the board's adherence to the principles and its actions to ensure that they are known and referenced regularly by staff. A statement and code guide board members and staff in compliance with legal and regulatory requirements by affirming the importance of meeting all such obligations (see the Appendix, Code of Ethics, for an example). But beyond that, they direct board members and staff to aspire to the highest ideals for openness, honesty, and integrity in all they do.

Risk Management

Awareness and management of risk is a serious board obligation. Boards can stay aware of current and foreseeable risks, in both program and operational activities, through regular reports from management. The process can be formalized: one organization established a task force for board review of certain activities that had come under criticism. This task force reviews activities that present reputational risk to the organization. Boards can also obtain information from whistle-blower hotlines, ensuring that reports of wrongdoing are promptly shared with the board. Less formally, board members can stay apprised of risk issues through visits to the organization's worksites and discussions with staff.

Internal Controls and Audits

Many boards designate an audit committee to pay specific attention to risk issues. In some organizations, the functions of the audit committee are interwoven with those of a finance or executive committee. But specifically designating a group of board members, particularly those with audit, accounting, or other relevant expertise, to address these issues elevates this function of the board both symbolically and in fact. Chapter Eight, Financial Oversight, reviews the role of the audit committee and the importance of an independent audit.

Insurance and Emergency Plans

Identified risks must be managed, including ensuring adequate insurance coverage. Board members should be covered by sound directors' and officers' (D&O) policies and should further ensure that the organization has the insurance it needs to cover employees, programmatic and operational activities, and property. This is not a static undertaking; insurance must be reviewed on a regular basis, and whenever an organization makes a change in activities or location.

Staff responsibility for this function should be clearly established. Organizations are encouraged to seek the help of professional advisers in reviewing and selecting various policies, as coverage issues can be exceedingly complex. If the organization has overseas offices or activities, the complexity deepens considerably.

In addition to adequate insurance, board members should query management to make sure there are emergency preparedness plans for natural or other disasters and that these plans are reviewed regularly, revised as needed, and known and understood by staff.

How Directors' and Officers' Insurance Works

Indemnification clauses in the bylaws and state and federal laws may provide some protection for some causes of action, but purchasing directors' and officers' (D&O) insurance is highly recommended, particularly if your nonprofit has employees.

Directors' and officers' insurance is a specific insurance policy to safeguard board members and the organization for causes of action not covered by a general liability policy. D&O insurance is a separate policy from the general liability policy. An important benefit of D&O insurance is broad coverage for employment-related claims.

Typically, a D&O policy will provide defense and indemnification for the individual directors and officers and for the organization. Because each insurance company offers a different policy form, with distinctions that could dramatically alter coverage, it is important to check the specific language in the policy.

Performance Evaluations

Boards need to give particular care to the selection and evaluation of the chief executive and senior executives, determination and review of compensation, and succession planning (see Chapter Twelve, Succession Planning and Chief Executive Transition, and Chapter Thirteen, Evaluation). Performance evaluations must be thorough, and compensation analyses should be made against relevant market standards that take into account the full measure of compensation, including additional insurance, pension contributions, and other benefits and perks not strictly limited to business use (for example, vehicles, cell phones, and home internet access). Boards ignore at their peril their obligations in this area: the highly publicized case in 2005 of the compensation of the president of American University (including his personal use of university resources) and the Senate Finance Committee's focus in 2002 on chief executive compensation in the American Red Cross underscore the importance of ensuring that compensation is not excessive.

Conflicts of Interest

A touchstone of compliance with the need for integrity is a strong conflict-of-interest policy for board and staff. Board members' duty of loyalty to their organization requires that they put the interests of the organization above any self-serving interests. Transactions with any director and/or the director's family members, or with any company with which a director has a direct or indirect interest, must be subject to the organization's conflict-of-interest policy. The policy should be reviewed and acknowledged in writing by board members when they first join an organization and annually thereafter. (A sample conflict-of-interest policy is included in the Appendix.) All potential conflicts must be disclosed and considered by the board or designated committee before any agreements are made or actions taken that might involve competing interests of the board member and the organization. Even if there is no actual conflict, board members should be mindful that even an appearance of conflict can erode the public confidence and trust on which every nonprofit ultimately depends. Here are some examples:

- *Financial conflict.* Some board members feel they are entitled to use their position to obtain a financial benefit from the organization—by, for example, entering into an advantageous transaction with the organization, individually or through a business owned by the board member, a close friend, or a family member.
- *Loyalty to multiple organizations.* Some individuals serve on two or more boards at the same time. If these nonprofits were to consider a major transaction—significant grant, joint venture, merger—with each other, it would be extremely difficult for a board member to serve both organizations with equal devotion.
- *Conflicting roles and relationships.* When a nonprofit board member plays more than one role with respect to the same organization, conflict may arise. Serving as a board member while providing professional services to the organization, even for a below-market fee, makes it difficult to give disinterested advice.

Tips for Avoiding Conflict of Interest

- Keep board composition diverse and board size adequate to encourage good discussion and to bring all points of view to the table. Don't allow a major conflict to dominate the board.
- Deal with the issue before it becomes an issue. Discuss potential conflicts and how the board should deal with them during the recruitment of new board members.
- For organizations with government or publicly mandated board positions, talk about conflict of interest with the authority responsible for choosing those board members.
- Familiarize board members with the duty of loyalty.
- Have a comprehensive conflict-of-interest policy in place and follow it.
- Require each board member to sign an annual disclosure form listing all financial, professional, and other relevant affiliations that might affect decision making during the coming year.

Getting Sound Advice

Charged with oversight, board members inevitably struggle with the limitations created by their part-time (at best) involvement and their volunteer status. No board member can know everything. Boards must rely, to various extents, on independent professionals that the organization may retain.

Acknowledging that sound legal advice requires legal counsel, most organizations consult attorneys. An organization may have an ongoing relationship with one or more attorneys, who may be in private practice or employed by the organization. The attorney may serve as a volunteer (perhaps as a board member) or be compensated (at full or reduced rates) for services rendered. In any case, board members should have access to the organization's counsel, within reason; legal fees can mount if access to the attorney is not monitored and limited.

The matter of attorneys on the board is tricky business. Like all of the other board members, they serve primarily as fiduciaries. Their role is not simply to provide free services for the board or the organization but to bring a new perspective and exercise vigilance. Although they will certainly speak up in the face of legal issues that come before the board, to the extent that those issues are within their range of expertise, board members with legal experience are not a substitute for the use of inside or outside legal counsel. Attorneys are sometimes asked to give opinions on the propriety of a board action, so having a lawyer on the board may put that person in the awkward position of passing judgment on his or her own actions.

Most attorneys specialize, so an attorney on the board is not necessarily competent to advise an organization on nonprofit law. Finally, having an attorney on the board—even one who specializes in nonprofit law—does not absolve the rest of the board members from being aware of their own responsibilities and duties under the law.

A Legal Liability Checklist

In the wake of the collapse of—and major damage to—large corporations and accounting firms in the early 2000s, regulators, legislators, watchdog groups, and the media heightened their focus on matters of corporate governance. Statutory law was enacted, followed by sweeping rules and regulations. Litigation on the subject is widespread. The IRS launched a concerted effort to promulgate and impose numerous governance standards on public charities.

As a result, every board must understand the framework within which its organization functions—which laws and regulations must be respected and how it can carry out its duties to meet all organizational, collective, and individual legal obligations. These responsibilities are grouped into three areas of vigilance for nonprofit boards and board members: mission, oversight, and personal action. By using this checklist, a nonprofit board can help protect the organization, the board, and its members from liability.

1. Be a Guardian of the Mission

Every organization needs to define its fundamental purpose, philosophy, and values, and find appropriate ways to tie them into meaningful activities. Without a purpose and mission, an organization has no mandate. The primary role of the board—and indeed, its most important duty—is to act as the guardian of that mission by fulfilling these requirements.

- *Fully understand and be able to articulate the organization's mission.* By drafting a clear and concise mission statement, the board has a tool for judging the success of the organization and its programs. This statement helps to verify whether the board is on the right track and making the correct decisions. It provides direction when the organization needs to adapt to new demands. Attention to mission helps the board adhere to its primary purpose and resolve conflicts during decision making.
- *Understand the overall operations of the organization.* Board members need to be familiar with the programs and services that carry out the organization's mandate. They also need to understand the various business activities the organization undertakes—such as fundraising, lobbying, and unrelated business—to ensure that the activities are appropriate and do not jeopardize the tax-exempt status.
- *Read and understand materials prepared and distributed by the organization.* Board members receive annual reports, promotional materials, publications, catalogs, newsletters, and fundraising materials. Keeping up to date helps the board ensure that the organization is represented accurately to the public and familiarizes board members with the organization's programs and services.

2. Ensure Compliance with Laws and Rules

Most nonprofit organizations function within the legal framework created by the federal government and the state in which they do business. An organization must also operate according to its own formal documents and the commitments it has made to various stakeholders. If the board is not familiar with and sensitive to the applicable laws, rules, and guidelines, it becomes vulnerable to liability and jeopardizes the organization's legal status.

- *Understand the organization's form   corporation, unincorporated association, or trust.* Board members should also know what is required to maintain that form and see to it that the necessary action is taken to respect that form (see Chapter One, Introduction to the Nonprofit World).
- *Feel comfortable about the IRS regulations affecting the tax-exempt status of the organization.* The IRS does not grant the status (Congress does that), but it recognizes it if appropriate forms are filed correctly and the organization continues to meet the appropriate legal requirements.
- *Periodically review the bylaws to ensure that the organization is in compliance with its governing documents.* These documents set the rules that help provide legal protection to the board members. Additional policies and resolutions provide even more specific guidelines for board and staff action. (See Chapter Fourteen, Bylaws and Policies.)
- *Know the jurisdictions in which the organization does business.* In addition to the state in which the main office is located, a nonprofit organization may also do business in other jurisdictions. If so, the board should know about those locations and ensure that appropriate registrations and reporting take place.
- *Understand the relationship between and among the organization's related entities and assess their purpose.* A membership association may have a related foundation, a political action committee, or a for-profit subsidiary. A charitable organization may have a separate organization that functions as a lobbying arm, or an advocacy organization may have a separate educational foundation. These organizations are likely to have different kinds of tax-exempt status.
- *Engage an auditor to attest to the reliability of the organization's financial condition.* Except in the case of federally funded programs, no federal law requires a nonprofit to have an annual independent audit. Only one state, California, has such a requirement (the California Nonprofit Integrity Act). Still, by commissioning an audit, the board provides an added incentive for proper resource management and helps produce a tool to encourage open communication with stakeholders. Small nonprofits with a simple and straightforward financial structure—and limited resources—can rely on reviews or even compilation of financial statements by a certified public accountant. (For more information on audits, see Chapter Eight, Financial Oversight.)
- *Safeguard the organization's tax-exempt status.* The board must ensure that the organization withholds employee income taxes, respects employment-related laws, and files IRS Form 990 and necessary state forms accurately and on time. If the board is not vigilant about these practices, the government may impose

serious financial penalties and excise taxes on individual board members and possibly revoke the organization's tax-exempt status. Also, the board must be aware of and follow all safe harbor measures when overseeing any financial contracts or compensation.

3. Promote Collective and Individual Vigilance

One approach a nonprofit board can take to guard against legal liability is to focus on actions individual board members can take. Some basic ideas and processes help board members stay organized, knowledgeable, and cautious about fulfilling their duties.

- *Have an up-to-date board handbook.* It need not be formal or fancy; a simple three-ring binder will suffice. The handbook should include, at a minimum, the following documents: a board roster and address (including e-mail) list, the organization's articles, bylaws, IRS determination letter, other documents with legal implications, recent board meeting minutes, a copy of the most recently filed Form 990, and the latest financial statements. In addition, a board handbook should include job descriptions for the board and a list of expectations for individual board members. (See Chapter Six, Building a Board, for sample board handbook contents.)
- *Keep up with issues that affect the functioning and future of the organization.* Periodic board retreats and educational seminars help place the nonprofit organization's activities in perspective and help board members understand more fully the board's structure, operations, and responsibilities. Continuous board education, starting with comprehensive orientation, is one of the most effective ways to give board members the incentive and the requisite tools to do their job conscientiously. Ninety-three percent of board members who responded to the BoardSource *Governance Index 2007* survey expressed interest in receiving additional governance training and information. (For more about board education, see Chapter Six, Building a Board.)
- *Regularly attend board meetings.* Obviously, schedule conflicts will arise at times; if the board member cannot attend a meeting, the minutes should reflect that fact and why. A board member cannot exercise the requisite degree of fiduciary responsibility without attending meetings and interacting with the other members. (See "Attendance" in Chapter Fifteen, Board Meetings.)
- *Actively participate in the decision-making process.* Silence is deemed to be concurrence. Board members who oppose an action to be undertaken by the organization at the behest of the board should speak up and be certain that the minutes note their dissent.

- *Ask questions.* Whether in the boardroom or outside of a meeting, failure to ask questions is one of the worst omissions of a board member. Board members who merely pretend to understand what is happening only fool themselves— and place themselves in a position to cause harm to the organization or personally. Questions may be asked of other board members, the organization's officers, staff, legal counsel, and other professionals. Questions may be posed during the course of a board meeting or on other occasions. (See "Culture of Inquiry" in Chapter Sixteen, Board Dynamics.)

- *Give careful consideration to board minutes.* There should be minutes of every board meeting, prepared with a heavy dose of common sense and perspective. Minutes are not verbatim transcripts of the proceedings but summaries of important actions taken during the meeting. A good test of the format is whether someone, years later, could grasp the essence of what took place at the meeting and the nature of the decisions made.

  When subject to legal action, organizations often must produce their minutes. Consequently, minutes should be written with an expectation that someday the document could serve as an exhibit in a court case. Board members should carefully read draft meeting minutes before approving them. (See "Board Minutes" in Chapter Fifteen, Board Meetings.)

- *Stay within bounds.* When acting in its volunteer capacity, the board should not exceed its proper authority. The members of the board serve as overseers, not day-to-day managers. Their role is to make extraordinary, not ordinary, strategic decisions. The board oversees the activities of the organization's staff, but it does not meddle in tasks that it has delegated to the chief executive.

How this works in practice will vary considerably. If the organization has a chief executive, that person will provide most of the information the board needs. (Still, questions should be asked.) Some boards prefer to meet only when the organization's chief executive is present. Others reserve time to meet in an executive session, without the chief executive or other staff present. The chief executive may be an ex officio but nonvoting member of the board or may be a voting member. In the latter case, the chief executive may recuse him- or herself to facilitate an executive session.

Being Accountable to the Public Trust

As a collective body, the board ensures that the organization functions within the framework of—and in advancement of—its mission, makes sure that the organization's resources are adequate and appropriately protected, and provides sufficient oversight. Whether or not accountable to another body, such as a membership or a parent organization, a board is *always* accountable to the public trust.

When a board neglects its legal and moral obligations, the entire sector suffers because the public trust in nonprofit organizations is weakened. On the other hand, board members who carry out the tasks assigned to them, come to meetings regularly and fully prepared, make independent and unbiased decisions, and disclose any conflicts of interest help advance the nonprofit sector as a whole and the organization they serve in particular. Board member service should be a richly rewarding experience—and it will be, for a board that diligently educates itself on its individual and collective legal duties and responsibilities.

Protecting the Board from Intermediate Sanctions

Traditionally, revocation of tax exemption was the IRS's only tool for punishing a nonprofit that had exploited its status in some way. The revocation of tax exemption not only disciplined the organization but also penalized its customers and clients by discontinuing the services. Also, this disciplinary action lacked any built-in warning mechanism or intermediate steps, which would allow the organization to correct its performance.

In 1996, the IRS installed *intermediate sanctions*, a system of excise taxes that are levied directly on the organization as well as on those making the inappropriate decisions. Since then the IRS has expanded its focus on misconduct to include any type of financial transaction that benefits those in positions of influence within the organization.

The IRS's intermediate sanctions rules provide a *safe harbor mechanism* for directors serving on nonprofit boards when they determine compensation for the chief executive or engage in other financial transactions with a "disqualified person." The safe harbor has three steps, all of which must be satisfied:

1. Reliance on appropriate, objective comparability data (for organizations with revenue under $1 million, the IRS recommends three data points; for organizations with revenue over $1 million, five data points). Comparability data may come from the nonprofit or for-profit sector, when appropriate. The board may also rely on advice from independent experts, such as attorneys, CPAs, compensation consultants, and valuation experts. There is no requirement that comparability data come only from the nonprofit sector; there may be many circumstances in which the appropriate data include for-profit comparisons.

2. Approval of the transaction by disinterested board members, with the interested person absent during debate and voting.
3. Adequate documentation by the board of the basis for its decision in its corporate records.

Should Nonprofits Have Business Relations with Board Members?

It is not uncommon for board members to recommend their own business services to the organization on whose board they serve. Although it is sometimes appropriate for a nonprofit organization to have business relationships with board members, it is extremely important to follow proper and ethical procedures before this kind of a relationship is established.

A conflict-of-interest policy with board members' annual disclosure of personal and professional affiliations ensures that no facts remain unchecked. The organization needs to openly seek bids to procure services, keeping in mind that what is best for the organization must be the determining factor. Sometimes a board member is willing to provide services at a discount. In any case, it is important to be able to document that the final decision was made in the best interests of the nonprofit and that the board was aware of the potential conflict.

Private Benefit and Private Inurement

The Internal Revenue Service defines private benefit and private inurement as unacceptable practices for nonprofit tax-exempt organizations. The IRS expects nonprofits to exist for the public good and not to be created or operated for the benefit, financial or otherwise, of a private individual. Violation of these doctrines can result in heavy taxation and/or loss of nonprofit status.

Private Benefit

Private benefit is a broad concept that applies whenever any individual, whether associated with the organization or not, reaps a benefit that is not within the parameters of the organization's exempt purpose. Private benefit does not have to be financial. The IRS does not see private benefit in absolute terms. It is allowable when it is insubstantial or incidental to the main service being provided. It is not acceptable when a service or a financial transaction is purposefully aimed to benefit an individual or a narrowly defined group rather than the public.

Here are some examples of unacceptable private benefit:

- Keep Our City Beautiful, a membership organization, plants a city alley with elaborate flowering bushes. The alley is not heavily traveled, but the decorations increase the attractiveness of a restaurant whose owner is a member of the organization.
- A nonprofit sets up a scholarship fund that supports only staff members' children.
- A hospital offers joint venture incentives to physicians to entice them to join the medical staff in order to bring more patients to the facility.

Private Inurement

Private inurement is an important part of private benefit; it happens when an insider—an individual who has significant influence over the organization—enters into an arrangement with the nonprofit and receives benefits greater than he or she provides in return. The most common example is excessive compensation, which the IRS condemns through intermediate sanctions (significant excise taxes). Other examples of private inurement:

- A nonprofit's chief executive is paid a reasonable and comparable salary with health benefits. In addition, the organization pays the chief executive a lavish living allowance that brings the total compensation to an amount not in line with comparable for-profit and nonprofit positions of the same nature.
- Five individuals, who are also board members, lease property to a school. The school funds or finances major improvements that greatly increase the property value beyond the life of the lease.
- A nonprofit art gallery exhibits paintings of members for a fee but grants board members the same service without cost.

Insiders—referred to in IRS parlance as "disqualified persons"—can be high-level managers, board members, founders, major donors, highest-paid employees, family members of any of these parties, or a business in which the listed persons own a more than 35-percent interest. If a nonprofit is organized to benefit an individual, even while fulfilling its tax-exempt purpose, it cannot be a tax-exempt organization. Under state law an organization may lose its nonprofit status.

Chapter Exercises

- Veering off the mission is one of the key challenges in the boardroom. Why is mission focus so essential to an organization?
- List specific examples of a board not meeting the duties of care, loyalty, and obedience.
- Corporate board members are compensated for their service. Why do nonprofits generally see board service as a volunteer commitment?
- Should every board have directors' and officers' insurance? Why or why not?
- Discuss differences between private inurement and private benefit. Why do nonprofit organizations need to differentiate between these two concepts?

CHAPTER EIGHT

FINANCIAL OVERSIGHT

Board members may think of their responsibilities in terms of how much money they should give to the nonprofit organization or what committees they will serve on. They may not realize that their responsibilities encompass far more. Ultimately, board members are responsible for the financial viability, the program success, and the very survival of the organization. Most important, they have a fiduciary responsibility.

As custodians of something of value to the community, the governing board has the ultimate responsibility for the organization's success, which includes every aspect of what happens with the organization—including the financial aspect. The board can delegate some details to a finance committee and some to an audit committee, but the full board always retains the final responsibility.

Dealing with financial matters requires board members (and staff, too) to communicate in another language. Accounting has its own vocabulary, grammar, and rules of construction—and nonprofit finances and fund accounting have a different dialect from those in the for-profit world. Unless board members have already been trained in it, this language takes some effort to learn to speak and understand well.

What Board Members Need to Know

Board members must understand the issues important to financial integrity and solvency, safeguards and procedures to protect the organization, and signs of financial trouble. They must know how to read and understand financial information—such as distinguishing the important numbers and relationships—and, most important, how to make decisions based on the information. Developing this knowledge enables board members to recognize impending problems and tell the difference between minor ripples and major crises.

Of course, board members inevitably have different levels of expertise. Training provided by an expert will give every member at least a basic understanding of nonprofit accounting and the organization's financial side. In addition, all board members need to feel comfortable asking questions when they don't understand something and be able to make sense of the answers (and realize when the answer doesn't make sense).

Financial information is, of course, not the only type of information used in decision making. But it plays an essential part in all important decisions—even those that may, at first glance, appear nonfinancial in nature (such as the example mentioned earlier involving keeping our clinic open an extra hour in the evening so people can get there after work). Armed with this knowledge, decision makers can better protect and enhance the nonprofit organization's capacity to serve the community.

Questions Board Members Should Ask

- Is the financial plan consistent with the strategic plan?
- Is the cash flow projected to be adequate?
- Does the organization have sufficient reserves?
- Are any specific expense areas rising faster than their sources of income?
- Is the organization regularly comparing its financial activity with what it has budgeted?
- Are the organization's expenses appropriate?
- Does the organization have the appropriate checks and balances in place to prevent errors, fraud, and abuse?
- Is the organization meeting guidelines and requirements set by its funders?

Financial Issues for Board Members

The entire board of a nonprofit is legally responsible for the organization's financial success. This responsibility calls for the board to focus on certain areas that involve the basic financial health and welfare of the organization: planning and budgeting, revenue and expenditures, and available cash and reserves.

Planning and Budgeting

Many nonprofits try to do too much with too few resources. As part of the planning process, the board should work with the staff to define the organization's mission, develop a strategic plan, and identify and implement programs. For every activity, including all programs, fundraising, and general management, the plan should address the financial implications. The planning process (see Chapter Ten) should include

- Evaluating existing and potential financial resources
- Examining internal and external environmental forces affecting the organization and its funding
- Reviewing the cost and effectiveness of existing programs
- Examining alternatives and their financial implications

The staff responsible for implementing the programs should develop the revenue and expense budgets needed to get the job done. Budgets should cover at least one year and preferably two years or more—although the budget for the second year need not have the high degree of detail required for the immediate year's budget.

During the budgeting process, staff should seriously consider clearly outlining for the board all major assumptions that underlie the numbers. It may take at least six months to plan and develop a sound budget, but the result is a better budget with more of the key issues worked out.

Unlike for-profit organizations, in which profit is the measure of success, nonprofit organizations measure their success by the good they do for the community as well as how well they manage to meet (or make) their budgets. Fulfilling the mission is the bottom line; balancing the budget makes it possible.

Some organizations help balance their budget through revenue-generating activities that do not directly relate to their mission: selling advertising in their publications, selling general merchandise in their gift shop or bookstore, or participating in a joint venture with a for-profit organization. The organization will have to pay taxes on the net income from such activities, often referred to as the unrelated business income tax (UBIT). Still, it is usually better to have the net income after tax, which can be used to further the mission, than to not have the income at all. Because of the various financial and legal implications, an organization should obtain professional advice before undertaking any unrelated business activities.

> ## Facts About UBIT
>
> A major benefit to being a nonprofit is the exemption from federal and state income taxes. However, certain activities, considered unrelated to the organization's core mission, *are* subject to taxes. This tax is called unrelated business income tax (UBIT). To be subject to UBIT, the profit-making activity must
>
> - Be conducted on a regular basis
> - Constitute a generally recognized trade or business
> - Not be an activity that is substantially related to the organization's tax-exempt status—meaning the activity does not further the mission of the organization
>
> Royalties usually are not taxed. Income from selling membership lists to a for-profit organization and from affinity programs is subject to UBIT. Even though unrelated, profit-making activities are permissible, they may not consume too much of the nonprofit's resources. In extreme cases, the IRS may determine that the organization has abandoned its tax-exempt purposes and may seek to revoke its exempt status.

Revenue and Expenditures

A variety of circumstances can lead to the organization's making either more or less than the amount budgeted. For example, if the organization makes more than was budgeted, perhaps it spent too little on programs or padded the budget with extra expenses just to be on the safe side. Of course, a surplus can also mean that the organization succeeded beyond expectations in enlisting grants or other revenue. Similarly, if the organization makes less than was budgeted, it might have taken on unanticipated tasks or allowed expenses to get out of line. Or revenue may have fallen short of expectations.

The board needs to review the budgeted income and expenses periodically and compare those figures to actual income and expenses, with staff providing explanations for significant differences. Only when it knows the full story can the board respond with appropriate action.

When the board's review indicates that the organization's expenses are rising or falling at the same pace as its revenue, the expenses are said to be "in line." Problems generally arise when expenses rise more quickly than revenue; if the organization is not already running at a deficit, then at some point it will be.

Similarly, certain items of expense directly relate to certain sources of income. For instance, it is important to ensure that publication expense is not running far ahead of publication revenue—unless the board has stated an intention to subsidize publications from other resources. There are two different and valuable perspectives to keep in mind.

The first is a *programmatic* perspective: Does this program's income exceed its expense? This analysis can be done at a broad level (for example, total meeting income versus total meeting expense) or at a more specific level (for example, annual meeting income versus annual meeting expense). To obtain this type of information, the organization must set up its accounting system to produce the necessary data. This calculation should include all relevant expenses, including noncash expenses such as depreciation and expenses covered by donations. Care should be taken to include all these expenses; otherwise, the organization may believe it is making a profit in areas where it actually is not.

Unlike for-profit businesses, nonprofits do not automatically change or discontinue an activity that loses money. As long as the activity is an important part of the organization's mission, and as long as the organization has adequate resources (such as contributions, endowment income, profits from other activities, or reserves) to draw on to cover the loss, the board may decide to stay the course and continue the activity. But this must be a conscious decision on the board's part, be revisited regularly, and not simply be an abdication of decision making. On the other hand, as part of its strategic planning, a board should not hesitate to pull the plug on an activity if it no longer represents a significant part of the mission or if adequate resources to cover a deficit are simply not available or in prospect.

The second perspective involves so-called *natural classifications of income and expense*. Examples include membership dues, interest income, and professional and maintenance expenses. These items are more difficult to compare because they relate not to a specific product or program but to the organization as a whole.

Nevertheless, monitoring the larger of these income and expense items in relation to each other will prove valuable. For instance, because salaries and other personnel costs (such as payroll taxes and fringe benefits) usually represent one of the largest expense areas for a nonprofit organization, the board should pay special attention to keeping them in line. To obtain a useful comparison, divide total personnel costs by total income for both current and historically comparable periods. This ratio should either improve (get lower) between periods or stay in a range appropriate to the organization. If it doesn't, the board should understand the variance.

Many different revenue and expense ratios can be computed, depending on what the organization determines is most important and meaningful. It is also possible to make comparisons with other organizations—if useful data can be obtained. This is not always easy in the nonprofit sector, although some nonprofit organizations (such as the American Society of Association Executives, the Council on Foundations, and the American Hospital Association) collect and compile these financial statistics.

Available Cash and Reserves

Although wide variations exist, many nonprofit organizations typically hold enough cash in a checking account to pay salaries and expenses for at least one month—or more, depending on circumstances, such as the likelihood of an unexpected sudden need for cash. Mitigating factors include the ability to quickly obtain cash through the prompt sale of assets and/or gifts from one or more dependable donors. If the organization doesn't have sufficient cash in the bank, it should have liquid investments that can readily be converted into cash. Organizations that have cyclical or irregular cash flow should maintain a line of credit or other borrowing ability to ensure they have enough cash available on a year-round basis.

If an organization is short of cash, it should project the amount of cash it should have on hand at the start of each future period, how much will be received or spent during that period, and what will remain at the end of the period. Cash-flow projections should be done on a monthly basis for the ensuing twelve months, then perhaps annually for the following two or three years (see the sidebar below). Some organizations will project weekly or even daily estimated cash on hand if they are truly cash poor. Cash-flow projections also enable the organization to plan for the purchase of new equipment, possible expansion of operations, increased staff compensation, and other essentials.

How to Compute Available Cash

Take the current cash balance, subtract all bills that must be paid in the near future, and divide the remainder by the annual budget. When the result is multiplied by twelve (number of months in a year), the answer will be the number of months that the organization could continue to operate at its currently projected level, assuming the worst case of a total cessation of income, before it would run out of cash.

Here is a hypothetical calculation:

Current cash balance	$400,000
Less bills due in near future	($100,000)
Available cash	$300,000
Annual budget	$1,200,000

Divide 300,000 by 1,200,000 = 1/4

Multiply 12 times 1/4 = 3 months before cash runs out

Financial reserves are a safeguard for rainy days and permit an organization to adjust to seasonal variances in expenses and income. Market forces, economic downshifts, natural disasters, or other unexpected expenses are not within the control of nonprofit managers, but these expenses can be managed. Reserves allow an organization to continue activity when income falls unexpectedly—for instance, when customers are unable to pay their bills on time or when major funding falls through. And financial reserves let an organization seize an unexpected opportunity—such as financing a new venture, making an advantageous capital purchase, or expanding a program at an opportune moment.

The optimal level of operating reserves is different for every organization. The following lists of pros and cons can guide decision making.

High Level of Reserves: Pros

- Makes capital available for program expansion or research development
- Permits the organization to be innovative and test new ideas with a reduced sense of financial risk
- Diminishes the urgency for fundraising

High Level of Reserves: Cons

- May result in an inefficient use of funds in meeting an organization's present needs
- Creates the potential for fundraising difficulties due to the public's perception of accrued wealth

Low Level or No Reserves: Pros

- Allocates funding toward fulfilling its mission and present needs immediately
- Obtains maximum benefit from public funds by using them for an expressed purpose

Low Level or No Reserves: Cons

- Puts the long-term sustainability of the organization at risk
- Makes the organization vulnerable to unforeseen circumstances
- Prevents the organization from capitalizing on great opportunities
- May cause stress and worry about the future

There are many accounting techniques to measure needed reserve levels. Some organizations calculate how many months they can operate without income (see sidebar on previous page). Others calculate various ratios. Some organizations rely on three months' worth of unrestricted net assets. Many experts recommend six months' worth.

Appropriate reserve levels may be very different for a museum, a homeless shelter, or a garden society. Consideration of generational equity—meeting today's needs at the expense of future ones—may affect the decision. Organizations at different phases in their life cycle have quite different needs. Stable income lowers an organization's vulnerability and thus the need for substantial reserves. Astute risk management acts as a defense mechanism. Reserves can also generate income through short-term investments to help cover operating costs. All these factors contribute to the need assessment.

Five Steps to Ensure Adequate Reserves

1. Determine the necessary level of cash reserves, and be prepared to defend the conclusion.
2. Create financial policies supporting the goal.
3. Monitor and adjust expenses regularly, allocate part of the assets to liquid or short-term funds, and have the board direct the expected surplus to a board-designated reserve fund.
4. Review the organization's risk management procedures and tools to diminish risk.
5. Activate the search for funds, and seek unrestricted income.

The Sarbanes-Oxley Act

In 2002, the U.S. Congress passed the Sarbanes-Oxley Act in response to several abuses in the for-profit business world. By its own terms, this federal law does not apply to organizations other than public companies, with the exception of two significant provisions: prohibition of retaliation against whistle-blowers and prohibition of the alteration or destruction of documents that are relevant to a lawsuit or regulatory proceeding. Organizations can facilitate compliance with these two provisions by having a whistle-blower policy and a document destruction and retention policy. Several states have passed similar laws that do apply to nonprofits. The California Nonprofit Integrity Act of 2004—which requires an audit committee in charities with budgets of more than $2 million—is one example.

The rest of the Sarbanes-Oxley Act sets forth a number of good practices for most organizations. These practices include

- Having an audit committee of the board, preferably separate from the finance committee
- Having at least one financial expert on the audit committee
- Making the audit committee completely responsible for the relationship with the outside auditor (if one is used)
- Having both the chief financial officer and the chief executive publicly attest to the adequacy and effectiveness of the organization's internal controls and the fairness of the presentation of its financial statements

Sarbanes-Oxley also has implications for the internal control systems (discussed later in this chapter) that nonprofit organizations establish and maintain in order to retain the trust of their constituents.

Major Financial Roles

Every nonprofit organization shares certain basic financial management functions:

- Protecting the assets of the organization
- Collecting income
- Paying debts that have been properly documented
- Recording receipts, disbursements, and necessary adjustments
- Providing accurate, timely reports (produced within ten days of the end of the month)

An organization must clarify how the board and the staff interact when handling the financial issues affecting it. Solid job descriptions, appropriate policies and procedures, and a system of checks and balances will ensure that the financial management and oversight are in good hands. The specific duties can vary greatly in individual organizations.

Board

The principal financial role of board members is to act as fiduciaries for the organization. This role entails securing organizational viability through planning and assessing the effectiveness of the plan. The board oversees the overall financial activity of the organization and ensures that appropriate internal controls are in place. The board approves the budget and must receive timely and accurate reports from staff to be able to survey the financial development and achievement of the fiscal goals. Setting financial indicators, asking pertinent questions, and staying vigilant about environmental factors that might affect the financial performance of the organization all allow the board to stay on top of its oversight responsibilities.

Treasurer

The treasurer's duties usually are spelled out in the bylaws. The treasurer is the gatekeeper of financial information for the board and in general ensures that board members are well versed in important financial issues. If the board has a finance committee, the treasurer may be its chair, but another board member may take this responsibility to distribute the duties more widely. The treasurer communicates directly with the staff chief financial officer and assists, when needed, with preparing the budget and introducing it to the board. He or she reviews the audit process and answers any questions board members might have about the audit report. A good treasurer is familiar with the activities in the organization, understands nonprofit accounting requirements, and is able to convey financial information to the rest of the board members in a clear and down-to-earth manner.

Financial Committees

Many boards benefit from having a standing committee that is permanently engaged in helping the board focus on its fiduciary duties. A finance committee may recommend financial policies, help review the budget, and take a first look at financial statements. If there is no separate audit committee or task force, the finance committee may take the role of overseeing the audit process, although it is usually wise to separate these two functions. If there is no separate investment committee, the finance committee could draft investment policies and hire and oversee the performance of an outside investment manager. See Chapter Four, Governance Structure, for sample committee descriptions.

Chief Financial Officer

In a small nonprofit the chief financial officer may be the chief executive; in a larger organization he or she may be another staff member whose main duty is to manage the financial aspect of the organizational affairs. The CFO is principally responsible for preparing the budget, ensuring that the organization has viable business plans, keeping abreast with new developments in the nonprofit accounting laws and principles, making sure that all staff members follow appropriate ethical standards when dealing with money issues, and serving as the designated contact person for the treasurer or the finance committee when the board needs additional financial data. As the need arises, the CFO hires additional staff to help with the details of financial management. These positions could include financial directors and managers, a controller, a bookkeeper, and other accounting assistants.

When There Is No Staff

Many start-up organizations have no staff but have a working board with multifaceted roles. The board must figure out how to implement and oversee at the same time. Board members handle daily tasks while serving as the governing entity. The greatest challenge in the area of finances usually is putting in place appropriate checks and balances. Even if fear of fraud is not the main motive for setting up an efficient financial monitoring system, internal controls (see the next section) help eliminate vulnerability to and opportunity for fraud while strongly increasing the organization's accountability. The key point is to share duties so that financial tasks are not concentrated under one person. As soon as the organization hires staff, it should check the bylaws and verify whether the roles of board members and officers need to be redefined. The treasurer's role, in particular, often needs readjustment.

Systems That Protect Nonprofit Organizations

The most difficult internal problems for an organization to recognize are those that result from gradual accumulation of bad habits rather than through gross mismanagement or malfeasance. For this reason, certain systems should be in place to help ensure safe and efficient operation.

Internal Controls

The board, with the help of staff, must insist on the creation of internal controls: those processes and procedures that protect the assets of an organization and promote its efficient operation. For example, a bill-paying process that is highly efficient, but occasionally pays invoices that should not be paid, sacrifices too much in protection of assets to justify an otherwise valuable efficiency.

Good controls both deter and detect improper behavior by staff and volunteers. They also protect the innocent from suspicion when something improper occurs. The key to good internal controls is segregation of duties—separating incompatible elements of certain transactions. The general rule is that no one person should be in a position to completely control all aspects of a transaction from its initiation through approval, handling of assets, and recording. For instance, whoever approves invoices to be paid should not prepare checks to pay the invoices, and vice versa. Separating these functions reduces the risk of paying an inappropriate invoice.

It becomes more difficult to achieve or maintain good internal controls in small organizations with fewer staff. Board members of these organizations must therefore work harder to gain as much asset protection as possible. Even when it is not feasible to have the strongest controls, it is usually possible to institute other procedures that mitigate a control weakness.

It is especially important to have strong controls, including adequate segregation of duties, in these areas:

- Receiving and processing incoming cash—including checks and electronic transfers (for a large volume, use of a banking service such as a lockbox or caging house is often an effective control)
- Processing and approving invoices to be paid and signing checks or approving outgoing electronic transfers
- Approving employee and volunteer expense reimbursement requests (no one should ever approve his or her own expense report)
- Having custody of petty cash and other cash funds, such as change funds, church collections, and other gifts
- Maintaining records of amounts owed to the organization (pledges and other receivables)
- Approving purchases, having custody, and maintaining records of inventories of supplies and property
- Having access to, and the authority to change, computer programs used to maintain accounting records
- Reconciling bank and investment accounts (this is one of the most important controls, especially in the absence of other desirable controls)
- Maintaining the basic accounting records (journals and ledgers)
- Analyzing the variance in budgets from one year to the next

Board members should ask whether the organization has an up-to-date accounting manual that details the correct procedures. If the board has any doubt about the adequacy of the internal controls, it should address questions to the external auditors. If the auditors are not reasonably satisfied with the state of the controls, the board should consider a special internal control study by the outside auditors.

Boards should not be lulled into believing that, just because the organization's controls are considered good, nothing bad can possibly happen. Unfortunately, some nonprofit organizations have experienced the ill effects of inadequate internal controls.

One large organization, for example, saw its chief executive go to jail for using organizational funds to pay for excessive and lavish personal travel and entertainment expenses. For several years afterward, as donors reacted to the negative publicity about the chief executive's behavior, the organization experienced a significant decline in contribution revenue—one greater in magnitude than the actual losses from the excessive expenses. Another organization had to refund millions of dollars of federal grants when it could not document the appropriate use of the money. Yet another found itself the victim of simple embezzlement: the chief financial officer wrote and signed large checks to herself, cashed them, and covered up the missing money by making fraudulent journal entries to fix the books—a clear case of inadequate segregation of duties and weak oversight by the chief executive.

Nonprofits work hard to develop whatever assets they have. Good internal controls will help to ensure that these hard-won assets are not lost or consumed inefficiently—and it is the board's responsibility to see that this happens.

Accounting Policies and Procedures

Every nonprofit should have written policies and procedures governing how it does business. Two documents are the most important.

An *accounting manual*, prepared by the accounting staff, contains guidelines for processing transactions and maintaining good internal controls. It analyzes each step in the fiscal process and describes the appropriate procedure for handling that step. The idea is that an accountant unfamiliar with the organization should be able to come in and, without access to any current personnel, fully understand what is happening and why. (This could be necessary in an emergency.) The manual should indicate which staff positions are responsible for which steps in the process and even who is to substitute in case of an absence. This manual, either prepared or reviewed by professionals, should be kept up to date.

Cash management procedures and *investment policies* help safeguard cash, ensure its liquidity, and employ it productively. A good investment policy will

- Delineate a specific philosophy of investment management and establish parameters for investment risk and return
- Assist and protect the designated investment manager by setting up practical guidelines and clear performance objectives

- Establish a process for regularly reviewing investment objectives and strategies and reviewing the manager's performance

The board is responsible for formulating an investment policy, ideally with outside professional advice if it does not have appropriate expertise among its members.

Some policies, especially those for organizations with smaller reserves, indicate which investments are allowed. For example, a rather conservative investment policy might allow only FDIC-insured bank accounts with balances under the $250,000 limit and short-term U.S. Treasury Bills. (Please note that the standard insurance amount of $250,000 per depositor is in effect through December 31, 2013. On January 1, 2014, the standard insurance amount will return to $100,000 per depositor for all account categories except IRAs and other certain retirement accounts, which will remain at $250,000 per depositor.) Policies for organizations with larger reserves might exclude certain high-risk investments or state what proportion of the reserves may be in stocks (equities) rather than in bonds (debt instruments). Organizations of all sizes often have a policy that requires outside advisers to select any investments that carry more risk than certificates of deposit or Treasury Bills.

External Audits

An audit is the process by which certified public accountants form an opinion as to whether the organization's financial statements fairly reflect its financial position, the changes in its net assets, and its cash flows. This lengthy and thorough study of financial records and procedures not only looks at the numbers but also determines whether appropriate accounting principles were used, and if so, whether they were applied consistently.

Although there is no law requiring nonprofits to conduct an external audit, having an audit gives the board the comfort of knowing that an outside professional has looked at the books and procedures. In particular, boards of larger or more complex organizations, or those that operate many different programs or facilities in geographically diverse areas, appreciate this added comfort factor.

An external audit may be required by

- Funders, such as United Way and the federal government (if $500,000 or more of federal awards are expended in a year).
- Individual states, if the organization solicits contributions from the public in the state. A few states require an audit of charitable organizations that solicit

contributions. Thresholds that must be reached before an audit is required vary from state to state, beginning at $150,000 and topping out in excess of $2 million.

- A parent organization (for example, if the nonprofit is a chapter or affiliate).
- A lender, if the organization has borrowed money.
- An organization's own bylaws.

Auditors must be absolutely independent of management. They must, by the rules of the profession, avoid financial inducements and resist pressure of any kind from management to alter their opinion. Note that an audit does not guarantee that the financial statements are perfectly accurate, because it is concerned only with material or significant amounts. Nor does it ensure the competence, wisdom, or honesty of management or the long-term financial health of the organization.

For organizations that cannot afford a full audit, a CPA can perform a review of the financial statements. A review takes less time—and costs less—but does not provide as high a level of assurance that things are in order. A review does ensure that the financial statements have been prepared on an acceptable basis of accounting and that this year's numbers make sense given the prior year's performance. However, the lack of substantial assurance makes a review less popular with nonprofit boards and funders.

An organization may ask financially astute volunteers to undertake a members' audit. Two or more knowledgeable individuals visit the organization and test some of its fiscal activities and records, such as cash disbursements and cash receipts, whether key assets actually exist, and whether the payroll records are in good order. As with an external audit, no area of activity can be sacrosanct for a members' audit. The volunteers undertaking this effort must feel free to look where they please and be creative in their investigations. Some organizations that use member audits have an external auditor accompany the volunteers to aid or guide their efforts.

Financial Statements and Reports

All board members—not just those who are CPAs or serve on the finance committee—must understand the financial condition of the organization in order to serve and protect it. Financial insight contributes to wise decision making on most board matters.

Even board members who are already skilled at reading financial statements may have difficulty understanding information from nonprofit organizations, because accounting practices differ somewhat from those of profit-making ventures. If board members aren't satisfied with their understanding of the financial statements and explanations provided, they should ask questions until they are comfortable.

Tips for Communicating Financial Information

- Communicate less (but more meaningful) information rather than providing detailed information with no explanation.
- Include a staff-written narrative describing the highlights of the reporting period to accompany the financial report.
- Use charts and graphs to point out the most important trends or relationships.
- Use dashboard reports for quick overviews of status and overall direction. Like an instrument panel on a car, dashboard reports provide critical measures of success, which vary from one organization to the next according to what each is trying to achieve.

Financial Documents for the Board

There is no single standard regarding which financial documents the board should receive. Here are the documents a board typically reviews:

- *Financial statements for internal use.* Larger nonprofit organizations should prepare internal financial reports each month. While certainly needed for management, this information may not require board review. In fact, many boards find it sufficient to review quarterly internal financial statements. In organizations with satisfactory reserves, the finance committee might analyze the monthly or quarterly reports, while the full board reviews only the annual internally prepared statement and the external audit. Boards with no finance committee should review the organization's financial statements at least quarterly.
- *Financial statements prepared for external distribution.* The board should always review year-end audited financial statements. If an audit has not been performed, the board reviews the unaudited statements. These year-end statements include

  - *Statement of financial position* (balance sheet). Shows assets and liabilities of the organization at a given point in time, in this case at year end. When possible, this statement should include comparative figures from the previous year.
  - *Statement of activities* (statement of revenue and expenses). Shows revenue and expenses for a specified period of time, usually one year, and whether

there was a net excess or deficit for the period. This statement should include comparative figures from the previous year.

- *Statement of changes in net assets* (statement of change in fund balance). Frequently combined with the statement of activities. It reflects the beginning net assets, plus the current period's excess or deficit, and may include other adjustments to reach the ending net assets.
- *Statement of cash flows.* Focuses on where cash came from and how it was used. It can be a good early warning sign of an impending cash crisis.

Every group of audited financial statements must be accompanied by footnotes that help the reader understand the organization's financial situation. The notes highlight significant accounting policies, major acquisitions or changes in operations, pension requirements, lawsuits, and details on other significant matters. Sometimes the board or management will want more detailed information—such as additional details of expenses or details by individual program or fund—than is required in the basic audited statements. In these situations, the auditors attach to the report a separate opinion, followed by additional statements or supplemental schedules. This opinion indicates the level of assurance the auditors are providing on this information, which may differ from the level of assurance provided for the basic audited statements.

Key Financial Statement Definitions

Assets: Things that the organization owns (cash, securities, accounts receivable, inventory, long-term fixed assets)

Liabilities: Things that the organization owes (accounts payable, mortgages, notes payable, bonds payable)

Net assets: The difference between assets and liabilities

Income: Revenues from operations or grants, gifts, and bequests

Expenses: Costs incurred in the operations of the organization

Financial results: The difference between income and expenses

---

Audit Opinions

Most organizations receive a clean (or unqualified) opinion following an audit, but some do not. Various types of opinions may result:

- *Unqualified (clean) opinion.* The highest level of assurance the auditor can provide, used when the auditor is satisfied with the financial statements.

- *Qualified opinion.* Provided when the auditor expresses reservations on a specific issue. Qualified opinions result when the organization is following accounting principles that are not generally accepted, according to the American Institute of Certified Public Accountants, or when the auditor was unable to complete all of the audit work deemed necessary to issue an unqualified opinion.
- *Adverse opinion.* A negative opinion, issued when the financial statements are misleading and management will not correct them. These are exceedingly rare and should alert the board to the need for strong corrective action.
- *Disclaimed opinion.* The auditor is unable to form an opinion, either because of a lack of independence or because the auditor has been unable to gather enough information. This type of opinion can also result when the organization's internal controls are unsatisfactory. When a board receives a disclaimed opinion, it should promptly investigate the cause.

In addition to providing an opinion on the financial statements, auditors generally provide a management letter, sometimes called an internal control letter. The board should always receive this document, which provides the auditor's observations on any control deficiencies, significant deficiencies, or material weaknesses in the internal control structure of the organization discovered during the audit. Significant deficiencies represent serious matters, and material weaknesses are very serious matters. Both require the board's immediate attention, followed promptly by corrective action.

IRS Form 990

In addition to the nonprofit organization's audited financial statements and the management letter, the federal and state governments, grantors, donors, or affiliated organizations may request to see the organization's Form 990, an annual report filed with the Internal Revenue Service. A revised and expanded Form 990—introduced for the 2008 tax year—has a summary page that gives a quick snapshot on the organization's mission, major programs, and key factors about board composition. Part VI (Governance, Management, and Disclosure) is of particular interest to board members because it poses questions to either encourage the adoption of good practices or reveal where these practices are missing.

Based on the details now required on Form 990, most organizations want to ensure they can answer the questions the way the IRS prefers. Board members should review the Form 990 before it is filed. The IRS also requires nonprofit organizations to make the Form 990 available for inspection or duplication to anyone requesting access to it. If the organization makes its Form 990 widely available—on its own Web site, for example, or on a public Web site such as GuideStar—then it may refer requesters to that posting. The organization, however, must still comply with any requests to inspect the form in person.

Other Financial Reports

The finance or audit committee should also review the reports from the OMB A-133 audit, which is required for organizations expending $500,000 in federal funds in a single fiscal year. In a series of up to five separate reports, the auditor must attest to the fact that there is "reasonable assurance that the organization or institution is managing federal awards in compliance with applicable laws and regulations." Whether or not board members review other required year-end reports is largely a matter of the report's significance to the organization. Whenever a report involves the potential of substantially increased or reduced funding, for example, board review is advisable. Reviewing insignificant reports, however, draws time and attention away from other matters. Board members should focus their attention where it will do the most good.

Signs of Financial Distress

Long before reaching the point that it has to close its doors, an organization gives off financial distress signals. Board members should be alert to the following signs of financial trouble:

- *Decline in critical income sources*, such as membership dues, publications, contributions, or grants. Although an organization may appear financially sound with a healthy surplus, its expendable resources may not be adequate to cover a significant decline in income.
- *Increase in certain expenditures.* Certain expenses require more scrutiny than others—especially salary and benefits, which represent a major portion of expenditures. If the miscellaneous expense account increases, the cause may be either hidden costs or less-than-adequate bookkeeping. A noticeable rise in consulting fees may reflect activity that could be better brought in-house. Or an increase in consulting or legal costs can signal an undisclosed major issue.
- *Private inurement.* When the IRS audits a nonprofit organization, it invariably attempts to ferret out incidents of private inurement, or private benefit (see Chapter Seven for a discussion of this concept). If it finds any appreciable amount, it can revoke the entity's tax-exempt status.

- *Unplanned auditor turnover.* An external auditor's resignation may indicate a substantial disagreement between management and the auditing firm, or it may point to financial problems within the organization, which the board must promptly identify and address. The board, either directly or through its finance or audit committee, should hold a private meeting with the auditors without management present. The board may find the problem is simply a matter of the organization's inability or unwillingness to pay a fee that the auditor finds satisfactory. Whatever the case, the board needs to understand the reasons behind the auditor's departure.
- *Board micromanagement.* When there is an appropriate level of staff, board members can focus on the big picture and minimize their involvement in operational management. A board that becomes involved in many small-dollar decisions creates enormous inefficiencies. Micromanagement generally arises when a board has traditionally received too much detailed financial information on an ongoing basis—in a real sense, it has been trained to micromanage. By concentrating on the details, the board loses its ability to focus on the risks facing the organization and to identify the strategies to survive in a rapidly changing world. The board must seek a broader overview, such as a dashboard, to tell it that all is well or to identify any problem areas. Weaning the board away from its accustomed level of detail and encouraging its members to adopt a strategic focus can be difficult but is essential (see Chapter Sixteen for more about board micromanagement).

The other leading cause of micromanagement is the discovery of embezzlement. Once the board becomes aware of this type of loss, no matter what the amount, it inevitably goes into micromanagement mode. After all, the loss occurred on the board's watch. Once the organization has taken corrective measures, however, board members must put the matter behind them and return to their strategic work. True leaders will encourage others to move on—the organization's staff has real work to do, and so does its board.

Finance and Investment Policies

Finance and investment policies serve as guidelines and protection for board and staff as they address both the complicated and the routine questions relating to financial management and oversight. These policies act as reference tools for appropriate action, ethical decision making, and dealing with potential or actual conflicts. Some of these policies can paraphrase a legal or accounting regulation, explain a procedure, clarify a principle, or express a desired goal. When properly used, they help diminish embarrassing or potentially harmful situations, improper behavior, and ineffective decision making.

The following are some typical policies:

- *Budgeting.* Budgeting policies vary from outlining respective responsibilities during the budgeting process to providing more detail to guide staff in fund allocation.
- *Capital expenditures.* The board should define the level of spending that constitutes a capital expenditure along with any approval processes. These policies should govern routine expenses, such as office equipment, computer upgrades, and building maintenance.
- *Financial controls.* If the organization does not have a single, all-encompassing financial policy, the board should ensure that some specific polices are instituted. Such policies include controls put on check-signing authority, transfer of funds, cash disbursement, and other financial transactions.
- *Investment.* Investment policies provide direction for how accumulated funds should be invested. Some organizations simply need a statement to clarify how any cash surplus is treated; others require a comprehensive policy defining the purpose and use of a substantial endowment. A basic investment policy identifies the assets available for investing, defines general investment objectives, sets asset allocation parameters (such as diversification), and clarifies the organization's tolerance for risk (by defining required ratings).
- *Reserves and endowment.* A reserves policy sets an appropriate level of reserve funds for the organization, given its mission. An endowment policy guides the board in making decisions about how the endowment should be invested and used.
- *Financial audits.* Policies requiring an annual financial audit range from a simple acknowledgment of the board's responsibility for the audit to more detailed requirements about the process.
- *IRS Form 990 and 990-PF.* Establishing a policy on public disclosure of Form 990 or 990-PF emphasizes the organization's commitment to public transparency and compliance with the law.
- *Risk management.* A comprehensive risk management policy identifies potential risks to the organization, evaluates their prevalence, and selects suitable techniques to deal with them. These techniques may include ways to avoid the risk (fix broken railing), modify its presence (install burglar alarm), accept the level of possibility for the risk to materialize (low probability for floods), or transfer the consequences to someone else (purchase insurance).

See Chapter Fourteen for more about board policies.

Financial Direction in Uncertain Times

Board members hold in trust the economic engine that is the nonprofit's ability to continue to serve the community. A well-functioning nonprofit organization provides services or products of such great importance that the community dedicates time and money to help it achieve its purpose. Board members are custodians not only of the organization's assets and liabilities but also of the accumulated efforts of those who preceded them in founding and expanding the entity they now serve. In any challenging economic climate, it is essential that board members focus on this aspect of their duties. No matter what the mission of the nonprofit, the organization will be successful only if financial underpinnings remain sound. If board members are to truly fulfill their fiduciary responsibility and pass on an even stronger organization to future boards, they must maintain a close eye on both the financial direction of the organization and its economic stability.

Chapter Exercises

- How do you define "fiduciary duty"?
- What level of financial acumen is adequate for a board member? Why?
- Discuss effective ways to increase the board's capacity to deal with complicated financial issues.
- What questions should the board ask when determining adequate operational reserves for the organization?
- When does it make sense for an organization to consider forming an endowment? How would an endowment influence the need for fundraising?
- Draft an internal controls flow chart for a humane society with four staff members and seven board members. Which aspects of handling of cash, accounting, budgeting, financial statements, and financial policies belong to the staff and which to the board?
- When should an organization consider conducting independent audits?

CHAPTER NINE

FUNDRAISING

Henry J. Rosso, a fundraising consultant and founder of the Fundraising School, referred to fundraising as "the gentle art of teaching the joy of giving." Fundraising is about much more than asking for money. It is about helping others to find ways to reach beyond themselves. When soliciting gifts, board members are a conduit that connects those who want to make a difference with a tangible way of doing so. Their enthusiasm for the organization's mission and commitment to supporting it equip them to promote, advocate for, and solicit on its behalf—that is, to teach the joy of giving through their own example.

Fundraising begins with the board, because board members hold the level of understanding and commitment necessary to fulfill the organization's mission. They are current donors who have made thoughtful commitments (or should be challenged to do so) to sustain the work of the organization. The board's oversight gives it the necessary knowledge, integrity, and credibility in making the case for support to peers, corporate and foundation leaders, and others who might care about the cause. As primary advocates and vested donors who are committed to the organization, board members are in the best position to ask others to make gifts and to secure volunteers to seek gifts from others. Their participation sends a clear signal of the organization's commitment to the fulfillment of the mission.

With the democratization of philanthropy—in which passion, networking, and advocacy cross economic, social, demographic, and other previously identified barriers—relationships with donors are changing. The old "checkbook philanthropy" is giving way to a twenty-first-century generation of donor-investors (or social investors) who want information, a relationship, and heightened accountability for program, financial, and board performance. (See sidebar below.)

Increasing Board Members' Fundraising Comfort Level

Today's donors have different expectations of the organizations in which they are investing: transparency, accountability, evidence of results or impact, a "return on investment" based on the values that inspired their giving, a focus on issues, and evidence of progress toward vision. As board members broker the relationships that lead to heightened investor participation, organizations can support their efforts in these ways:

- Engage them in tasks for which they feel comfortable and confident.
- Brush up the case for support to make sure that it is current, highlights the relevance and urgency of the need the organization is meeting, and focuses on effective solutions.
- Help them become better stewards to all donors, not just major donors (or rising major donors).
- Let them know about the trends in philanthropy and how the development program is responding to those trends in its planning.

Philanthropy in the twenty-first century presents a remarkable landscape. Though often difficult to navigate, it offers board members and donors a journey that is more satisfying than ever before. Fundraising today requires a high level of board involvement to reach its potential. Such involvement increases the breadth and depth of an organization's reach because each additional person who becomes involved contributes contacts, time, and ideas to the effort.

The board may have fundraising responsibilities in these three areas:

- *Strategy.* The board provides overall strategic guidance and direction to the entire organization through written statements of mission, vision, and values and a strategic plan. The specific goals and objectives in a strategic plan, with their costs and timetables, are the basis for a fundraising action plan— how the organization will seek the financial resources necessary to support its priorities.
- *Participation.* Board member participation is essential for identifying the resources to meet the organization's fiscal responsibilities.

- *Oversight.* In the fundraising area, board members have the responsibility for stewardship to oversee the faithful use of all funds received in accordance with donor restrictions, accounting standards, and legal and ethical requirements.

The First Step: A Commitment to Personal Giving

The board's responsibility for ensuring adequate financial resources begins with the individual board member. In *Managing the Nonprofit Organization: Principles and Practices*, Peter Drucker notes, "The board is the premier fundraising organ of a non-profit organization. If a board doesn't actively lead in fund development, it's very hard to get the funds the organization needs. Personally, I like a board that not only gets other people to give money but whose members put the organization first and foremost on their own list of donations."

Most organizations ask board members to place it as one of their top one or two charities during the period of their term of office. By establishing a policy of personal giving by board members, the organization's board sends a message that its members believe in the cause. (See Chapter Fourteen for guidelines for developing such a policy.)

This duty is not about the amount each board member can give; rather, it is about achieving full participation. For example, a constituent of the organization may make an excellent board member, lending perspective and valued opinions to the group, yet be unable to afford to donate a large sum of money. In some nonprofits, sizable gifts *are* expected and may even be required of board members. In those cases, prospective board members need to be informed of the specific giving expectations during the recruitment process.

Board members should be encouraged to make an annual stretch gift that is within their means. It is both their personal and their collective example that encourages others to make gifts. In particular, some grantmaking organizations, including foundations and corporations, require 100-percent board giving and 100-percent participation in fundraising as a prerequisite for receiving a grant. In a similar fashion, when board members are asking others for gifts, they must be prepared for the question, "Have you made your own gift?" If they cannot answer "Yes," there is little reason for another person to give to an organization its own board members do not support.

The job description provided to every potential board member should clearly state the board's personal giving policy, so everyone is clear about the expectations.

The board chair and development committee chair should take a lead position in soliciting personal gifts from board members after making their own personal gift decisions.

Alternatives to the Three Gs

Some boards live by the maxim of the Three Gs: give, get, or get off. They expect their members to bring in money by making a personal contribution or participating in fundraising or both. If a board member does none of these, he or she may be asked to leave. However, strict adherence to the Three Gs is not common on boards today—at least when it comes to "getting off" the board. Instead, boards are taking a more holistic approach—accepting instead the Three Ts (treasure, time, and talent) or the Three Ws (wealth, work, and wisdom). Besides participating in securing finances (treasure and wealth), board members are expected to participate in activities (time and work), and contribute their knowledge and expertise (talent and wisdom.) Boards that eliminate the third G sometimes ask board members to sign a give-and-get commitment form each year. This should include the following elements:

- A personal giving pledge/contribution—the amount of the board member's annual gift. Gifts of all sizes are considered valuable. Ask each board member to make a meaningful and significant gift according to his or her capacity.
- A personal getting goal—the minimum amount each board member commits to raising annually in addition to his or her own gift. Staff can help board members meet this goal by giving them opportunities to host prospective donors at special fundraising events.
- Participation in "non-ask" activities—assistance with prospect research, cultivation of prospects, introductions to business leaders or foundations, and expressions of appreciation for gifts.

Board-Staff Partnership

Fundraising is a partnership between an organization's board and its staff. Board members rely on the staff to educate and inform their thinking, coordinate planning, and ultimately support their ability to raise money. In exchange, the staff relies on board members to follow through on their commitments and to have confidence in the staff's management of support activities.

The role of staff is best characterized as *development*. Development is the provision of support for the fundraising effort, including prospect research, database management, gift recording and processing, accounting, special events planning and oversight, coordination of fundraising efforts across entities within larger nonprofits, and donor relations. The development staff instigates fundraising via the development plan, and they play a role in getting the board involved. The staff coordinates and manages the fundraising process, ensuring that fundraising goals and processes are aligned with the growth and strategic planning of the nonprofit as a whole and that the board is involved.

Fundraising focuses specifically on raising money to support the organization's achievement of its mission. The board defines the context for fundraising by clarifying the organization's mission, supporting its stability, identifying its leadership, approving its budget, and planning for its future. The board must also be comfortable with the overall fundraising plan drafted by the development staff. If no specific development staff exists, it makes sense for the board to form a development committee that works on this task and presents it to the full board for input and approval.

Development Committee

Many boards look at development as a process whose end result is successful fundraising. This concept allows the organization to take a totally new approach to development committees. Instead of forming a board fundraising committee, it might make sense to form an organizational committee that can be mostly composed of nonboard members and that works directly with and reports to development staff. Board members with special skills and contacts would also serve on this committee.

In addition, boards may want to form fundraising committees or task forces as the need arises. As every board is responsible for the overall policy formation, this task force can take the lead in drafting the necessary organizational fund development policies. If the board decides that each board member needs to be individually engaged in fundraising efforts, the task force can serve to motivate the board. For more about committees, see Chapter Four, Governance Structure.

The Case Statement

The foundation of successful fundraising is a well-articulated case for support of the organization. With a carefully crafted case statement, an organization outlines the need or problem that it is addressing and a proposed plan of action. A compelling case statement can turn a potential donor into a committed partner. The case statement may include information on the organization's values and mission and a statement of its value to the community. The case statement also describes the impact that a donor's gift will have on both the organization and the constituency it serves, in terms that appeal to donor interests and motivations.

A case statement is not an annual report, a grant proposal, a list of the organization's financial needs, or the history of the nonprofit. A case statement is a tool to educate, inform, and encourage a potential donor to partner with the organization. While answering the questions that a donor might pose, a case statement also raises interest in the case and persuades the potential donor to provide financial assistance by making it urgent, personal, and real. The case statement is a complete and independent document, making it a key tool for the development staff or committee. The nature of this document allows development staff to adapt it for grant proposals, major gift visits, and general solicitations. Internally, it can also be used to recruit volunteer leadership and seek contributions from board members.

Whether a case statement is an illustrated brochure or a simple document, it should address the target audience and be appealing, convincing, easy to read, and accurate. These tips help make a case statement effective:

- Use examples to show the organization's needs and intended results.
- Make the statement easily adaptable for targeted audiences.
- Limit the fundraising jargon and use common terms.
- Mention the dollar figures being sought, allowing potential donors to understand the amount of money needed and to think about what they need to contribute.
- Use language that gets the donor excited, inspired, and motivated.
- Clearly define how the donor will benefit from this gift.
- Convey a sense of urgency.

The Fundraising Process

Fundraising is a marathon, not a sprint. It is a process of cultivation, solicitation, and stewardship that takes place over time. By engaging actively in these three activities, the board establishes an environment in which relationships with donors are developed and maintained, resulting in meaningful contributions to the organization over time. A board that makes fundraising a priority and participates in the process can create a long-term culture that transforms a nonprofit.

Cultivation

Cultivation describes the way an organization builds relationships with individuals and foundations. It is often referred to as "friend raising" because the relationships that are developed lead to greater community visibility and more individual involvement with the organization, as well as greater success in solicitation.

Board members' involvement can include verifying the potential interest and ability of the prospect, identifying the best team to call on the prospect, arranging an appointment, and more. Board members also can assist development staff by supplying details to the prospect's profile record, such as known special areas of interest, prior gifts and service to other charities, family interests, occupational details, and leadership skills. These are all necessary first steps to take with each new prospect.

Current and past donors require this same level of respect and preparation before being asked for their next gift. All these details, when collected together, are quite sensitive. Therefore they must be treated in a confidential manner and used only as appropriate to benefit the organization. Because this information has been accumulated from public sources, neither the source nor the data require security. The overall collection of personal and professional details, however, requires sensitive treatment by all board members, volunteers, and staff. Those who will contact each prospect need only the details essential to their cultivation and solicitation efforts.

Solicitation

Soliciting contributions is a planned and strategic process that depends on collaboration, coordination, and communication among board and staff. As an organization's investors, donors deserve the same level of attention and service that any financial investor would receive from a for-profit corporation—if not more. Donors do not provide money to the organization solely because they were asked; they invest their money and trust in the organization's ability to deliver quality programs and beneficial services.

Given this mind-set, the best solicitation requests explain what donors' money can do and how those funds will benefit others. Donors are less interested in appeals that appear to help the organization serve itself. For example, appeals will fail to inspire serious gift decisions if they emphasize internal objectives without demonstrating how the funds would be used to benefit those whom the organization aims to serve through its mission.

The board duties of setting fundraising policy and procedure and approving solicitation activities are not as simple as they may seem. That's why orientation and training of board members must address these details—especially when new board members have limited experience with a nonprofit organization and its fundraising process.

Board members may participate in solicitation activities in a variety of ways. They may add personalized notes to direct mail letters; invite friends and colleagues to special events; or work with the organization's staff on proposals, tailoring the text based on their knowledge of the target foundation or corporation. In addition, of course, board members may solicit contributions directly themselves, either face-to-face or through a personal note or telephone call.

Stewardship

Stewardship is the notion that relationships with donors need to be maintained as well as cultivated. Stewardship begins at the board level. Any board members involved in the cultivation and solicitation steps leading to a gift should remain involved through continuing contact with these donors.

Board members help foster continued good relations with donors, beginning with their personal thank-you letter, telephone call, or e-mail along with occasional notes to keep them informed of the organization's progress and how the donor's funds have made a difference to the organization and to those it supports. While donors may appreciate recognition from the chief executive or a senior executive of the organization, receiving an additional, personal expression of appreciation from a board member can help cement their resolve to continue supporting the organization and perhaps to increase their generosity in the future.

Board members may participate in stewardship by sending personal thank-you notes, calling current donors to update them on the organization's activities, or meeting with them to request their ideas and input. However board members choose to express appreciation, they must be sincere and do more than simply follow a standard list of follow-up activities. When a donor wishes to remain anonymous, the organization must respect the donor's wishes regarding public notice. Still, board members and staff should continue to maintain personal contact, report on how their funds were used, issue invitations to public events, send copies of annual reports, and so on.

Types of Fundraising

There are four types of fundraising campaigns. The following sections describe them and offer guidance on how to implement them. The information will help boards and staff determine which types are appropriate for them and whether they have the level of support necessary to initiate them.

Not all methods of raising funds are appropriate for every organization. The development plan should clarify whether solicitation from individuals is an effective way to approach donors. Major gifts are most successful when there is a personal contact. Capital campaigns are lengthy and complicated ways to create or supplement funds for capital needs. Each fundraising type is most effective when it is directed to the appropriate kind of audience.

Annual Fund

The annual fund typically is used to support the annual operating expenses of an organization, including program-related expenses and overhead. Gifts to the annual fund are raised through an annual campaign that results in unrestricted revenue—that is, revenue that is not designated for a specific project or use.

An annual campaign involves soliciting gifts from individuals, foundations, and corporations. In planning the campaign, the organization identifies both potential donors and the solicitation strategies that will be used for each. These strategies are combined over a twelve-month period to ensure a continuous revenue stream:

- *Personal solicitation.* Board members and staff develop and maintain personal relationships with specific individuals (both current and potential donors) on the basis of mutual interest in the organization and the constituency it serves.
- *Special events.* Many organizations use special events to introduce people to the organization and its work, as well as to thank certain donors and to solicit contributions.
- *Direct mail, e-mail, and telephone appeals.* These appeals draw on the organization's database of current, former, and potential donors and may be structured in ways that encourage current donors to increase their giving or former donors to renew the relationship.
- *Internet marketing.* This method involves using the organization's Web site to attract donors and enable them to give online. It also involves registering the organization with online resources such as the Network for Good (www.helping.org) to take advantage of their outreach capability.
- *Proposals to foundations and corporations.* These requests target benefactors whose interests are aligned with the nonprofit's mission.

To implement an effective annual campaign, the board develops a plan that sets specific fundraising goals for the year and outlines steps for achieving them. The goals should be based on a careful assessment of how much can be raised from whom, based on both past experience and knowledge of future prospects.

Tailoring the Case for Support. The case for support for the annual campaign needs to appeal to a variety of donors, many of whom will make small or modest-sized gifts. It also needs to argue convincingly that the organization's operating costs, as well as its programs, are worthy of support. The case thus needs to articulate the connection between the funding of annual operating expenses and the organization's ability to provide programs, so that donors see that even small gifts can have an impact on those the organization serves.

Board and Staff Roles. Both board members and staff play vital roles in planning and executing an annual campaign. In the planning stage, board members help set fundraising goals and provide input for the case for support. They pinpoint individual donors who might be asked to increase their gifts, work with staff to identify effective strategies for reaching different types of donors, and develop untapped sources of donations. Staff members determine the fundraising plan. They provide information about past donors, outcomes of past fundraising activities, effectiveness of various solicitation strategies, and research on prospects, and take the lead in developing the master calendar. The chief executive and development staff identify appropriate opportunities for board member participation.

In the execution stage, board members solicit contributions in person, host guests at events, host small receptions or dinners in their homes, and thank donors by phone or mail. Staff members provide coordination and logistical support for all activities. They develop solicitation letters and grant proposals, design and produce direct mail materials, conduct telephone appeals, manage special events, track donations, maintain the donor database, and produce thank-you letters for tax purposes.

Together, board members and staff form a team with shared responsibilities and functions in the annual campaign. As paid workers, staff members carry out the detailed work that makes an annual campaign happen. As volunteers, board members connect with donors in ways that paid staff cannot. Each group thus is essential to the success of an annual campaign.

Major Gifts

A major gifts program is a natural extension of an annual campaign because it draws on the organization's current donor base. An organization may solicit major gifts as part of its annual campaign, to secure lead gifts. It may also conduct a major gifts campaign that is separate from the annual campaign, to raise funds for a special project or need.

The definition of a major gift depends on the nature of the other donations an organization receives, as well as the goal and budget for fundraising. A major gift to a small start-up organization may be $500, whereas a large university may consider $100,000 or more to be a major gift. Major gifts may be pledged or given outright, and may come in the form of cash or appreciated assets.

It is possible to receive a major gift as the result of first-time interaction with a donor, but usually major gift opportunities will develop over time as donors gain trust in the organization, are treated in ethical and appropriate ways, and are approached with their interests in mind. Such donor development requires long-term commitment on the part of both board members and staff. Most important, a successful major gift effort relies heavily on personal contact and solicitation of donors by board members.

Major gift fundraising develops in three stages:

1. *Formative:* Board members and staff develop donors' *interest* by making them aware of the organization's work and its contributions to the community.
2. *Normative:* Board members and staff invest significant time in ensuring that donors feel a sense of *involvement* with the organization. Such involvement can include making major gifts, either as lead gifts in the annual campaign or as designated gifts for specific purposes.
3. *Integrative:* Board members and staff seek to develop donor commitment to making an *investment* that will ensure the organization's ongoing health. At this point major gifts may segue into planned giving, as donors give or pledge assets rather than cash.

Tailoring the Case for Support. The building of a relationship that leads to major gift donations proceeds at a different pace with each individual donor. Board members and staff must therefore be willing to recognize each donor as an individual and take the time necessary to cultivate the relationship so that the donor feels connected to the organization's work and able to play a significant role in its success. With major gift donors, the case for support is a two-way street that articulates both what the donor can do for the organization and the impact the donor can have with this generosity.

Board and Staff Roles. An efficient staff that can effectively monitor donor relationships is essential to the success of a major gifts program. The staff is responsible for tracking donors, maintaining records, and identifying annual fund donors who might be approached for major gifts. However, the heart of a major gifts program is the commitment and contributions of board members who are both willing advocates for the organization and donors to it themselves. By investing time in building and maintaining donor relationships, and especially in determining how providing a major gift will reward the donor, board members ensure the continued success of the organization's major gifts program.

Capital Campaigns

A capital campaign is an effort over a multiyear period to raise a large amount of money for a new building, a new wing, or renovation of an existing structure. A capital campaign may raise money for equipment that will be used in the building, for the organization's operating expenses, or for an endowment to support the project long term. The project's dollar goals not only represent the specifics of the project, but can also represent a huge stretch for an organization compared to what it raises annually. In most cases, funds are sought from all available sources—individuals, corporations, national and community foundations, and governments. Usually some, if not all, of the money is raised in face-to-face solicitations. Other, typically smaller, gifts can come through direct mail, grant writing, or special events.

It is common for an organization to spend one to two years planning a five-year campaign. If the board is considering a capital campaign, this arduous and long-term project may require fundraising skills different from those that board members now possess. The board can work on developing members' proficiency and comfort levels with major campaigns, and it can also engage other resourceful and skillful individuals to help on committees.

The ultimate key to success is thorough planning. So much is at stake that without detailed preparation the organization risks losing more than just time and initial expenses. A plan for success includes the following:

- *Set the goal.* The campaign must be clear about its financial target.
- *Set start and end dates.* The feasibility study should help determine the right moment and the time needed to reach the financial goal in the most cost-effective manner.
- *Prepare support documents.* Capital campaigns usually need their own case statement, brochures, letters, and pledge cards that reflect the competent approach and the professional stature of the organization.
- *Plan the budget.* Include the cost of running the campaign and the cost of the feasibility study in the budget. Grants may be available to cover the costs of the feasibility study.
- *Calculate the hierarchy of gifts.* The study will help to determine how many lead gifts will be needed and in what denominations.
- *Divide the tasks.* Appoint a campaign chair and chairs for special activities. In addition, assign duties to staff, board members, and volunteers. Hiring an outside consultant may be advisable. Above all, hold people accountable.
- *Develop contingency plans.* Anticipate unplanned challenges, so an organization planning a capital campaign should make sure that its homework is done. Practice what-if scenarios and make sure that assignments are being accomplished.

Should We Launch a Capital Campaign?

It is the board's job to judge whether a capital campaign is worth the effort and whether the organization will be better off after finishing the project. Consider these questions:

- Will the project have a positive impact on the organization?
- Is the project necessary?
- Is the project urgent? Is it essential that the campaign be done now?
- Is the moment right to launch a capital campaign?
- Who will benefit from the project? How will it benefit the organization's constituency?
- Is the project consistent with the organization's mission and goals?
- Can the project be developed in a prudent manner, with careful planning and professional advice, if necessary?
- Will the campaign strike potential donors as exciting and vital? If donors don't approve or are not interested, the campaign could backfire.
- How will the campaign be funded? All campaigns—even those run entirely by volunteers—have expenses. How will the cost of the campaign be underwritten? Donors often want to know what percentage of the money raised will go toward the campaign.

Tailoring the Case for Support. Many donors are less interested in the actual brick-and-mortar facilities for which the capital fund is needed than in the impact those facilities will have on people. The case statement for a capital campaign needs to focus on people as much as or more than it focuses on bricks and mortar. It needs to convince donors that the project is solidly grounded in the values and objectives of the organization, and that its completion will increase the organization's ability to serve its constituents and contribute to the quality of life of the community. Instead of telling donors how the capital improvements will extend the life of a building, therefore, tell them how the work in the refurbished building will benefit people.

Board and Staff Roles. During a capital campaign, the active support and endorsement of the board is essential. In fact, if the board is in any way uncertain about the viability of the effort or its value to the organization, the campaign should not move forward. The organization's staff is instrumental in developing the project concept, obtaining architectural plans and cost estimates, and managing the logistics of the project and the capital campaign.

Board members must set a personal example by giving to the best of their ability before inviting others to make their best gifts. Further, successful capital campaign efforts require board members to assist staff with specific tasks such as the following:

- Endorsing, supporting, and participating in the preparation of the strategic plan
- Identifying specific fundraising objectives along with campaign policies and procedures
- Supporting marketplace research surveys, development program audits, and precampaign planning or feasibility studies that test the public's response to campaign objectives
- Selecting qualified campaign counsel and recruiting qualified and experienced fundraising staff
- Supporting funding requirements for campaign budget, staff, space, and systems
- Identifying, cultivating, and arranging opportunities to meet with major gift prospects
- Resolving the need for other, ongoing fundraising requirements for annual operating support during the campaign period

---

Reenergizing a Slow Campaign

If goals are not met as planned, the organization may need to reinvigorate the campaign and extend its deadlines. This might mean that donors are approached once again and asked for challenge gifts. It may be necessary to extend the pledge period and send out reminders for outstanding pledges. Increasing public relations activities can help to bring the campaign back to the front pages, but the leaders must also know when to cut their losses and stop short of the original goal.

Planned Giving

Planned or *deferred giving* is the current gift of future assets through vehicles such as bequests, charitable trusts, or annuities. Ninety percent of planned gifts are bequests. The difference between a present and a deferred gift is a matter not of when the gift is made, but when the organization can use it.

The practical reason nonprofit organizations solicit deferred gifts is that the variety of deferred giving options allows a much larger number of donors to contribute substantial amounts, especially donors who have assets but cannot afford present giving. The purpose of a planned giving program is not the immediate acquisition of funds, but the establishment of the organization's long-term financial security.

Funds generated by deferred giving programs are typically used to cover long-term expenses. Some organizations use the proceeds of deferred gifts to fund obligations that will generate income to cover long-term overhead and other types of expenses that are not usually covered by grants or other short-term sources of income. Funds obtained through planned giving may also be used to increase an organization's endowment or support special projects. The only legal restrictions on the use of the funds, once they are received, are those imposed by the donor that are contained in the trust or other legal document governing the gift.

There are a number of ways to structure a planned gift. Board members need not know the details—that function usually belongs to a staff member or a planned giving consultant—but they do need to know the general types of planned giving (see sidebar below), as well as information such as when the organization can expect the funds or what restrictions may be placed on a gift.

Planned Gifts: A Quick Reference

Current Planned Gifts. The decision and the gift are made today, with the funds invested and managed by the nonprofit for the donor's lifetime (or other term as described in the contract). The donor derives income by transferring a current financial asset, by contract, to a charity, with the residual principal delivered to the nonprofit organization following the donor's death. Types of current planned gifts include charitable remainder trusts, charitable lead trusts, and charitable gift annuities.

Future Estate Gifts. The decision is made today, but the organization does not receive the funds until after the death of the donor. For example, a donor may decide today to stipulate a specific gift for a favorite charity in a will or living trust. The gift may be in the form of a specified cash amount, specific asset, or percentage of the overall estate, all decided at the time the will or living trust is created—but not transferred to the organization until after the donor's death. Future estate gifts include bequests and gifts of retirement plan assets.

Tailoring the Case for Support. Planned gifts benefit both the organization and the donor, and the key to tailoring the case for support lies in being able to make this clear to potential donors. Donors benefit from deferred giving because they are able to make gifts without reducing their current income or undermining their financial security. Deferred gifts can augment, rather than reduce, a donor's current cash flow by reducing taxes or enabling the donor to diversify assets into those that produce income. The benefit to the organization has to do with its long-term stability. Deferred gifts provide a source of future support that a nonprofit knows it can rely on. By making deferred gifts, donors thus make a commitment to and an investment in the future of the organization. This means that both the effect of a donor's gift and the recognition of the donor's generosity will continue for some time, particularly if the gift is structured as a trust with the donor's name on it.

Board and Staff Roles. Typically, the board's development committee and the chief executive take the lead in creating the program. Board members take the lead in identifying prospective donors (who often are their peers), deciding who should contact them, and developing long-term relationships with them. The board's fiduciary duty includes managing the organization's planned gift contracts and endowment funds by faithfully observing donors' wishes and being vigilant about investing and managing donors' money. Board policies should define whether it will act as trustee for each contractual agreement and, if so, what professional investment policies and procedures will be in place to ensure the donor's interests are reserved for the life of the contract.

Board members should thoughtfully include making their own planned gift by writing the organization into their wills. They can have an even greater impact if they are also willing to publicize their gifts and set an example for others to leave such a legacy.

A planned giving program demands a fairly high level of staff management. Staff members prepare board members for visits with potential donors by conducting donor research and suggesting possible strategies, including what type(s) of planned gifts might appeal to the potential donor. Staff can also help board members by answering technical questions and helping to finalize the donation.

However, planned giving programs are complicated undertakings, requiring technical skills and specialized knowledge that are often beyond the expertise of both board members and staff. In certain key areas—such as the financial administration of gift vehicles, investment of the principal of the planned gifts, life income payments, and planned giving prospect management—the organization will need to rely on one or more outside consultants. The degree to which an organization needs external assistance will depend on the level of staff expertise available.

Developing Board Members' Fundraising Skills

Many nonprofit board members feel anxious or reluctant to move their fundraising activities from friend raising to direct solicitation. The fears that they cite—of potential rejection, making a negative impression, and having the potential donor expect a donation in return to his or her favorite charity—can be very powerful. Board members can begin to overcome these feelings by doing three things:

1. *Role-play.* Practice cultivation and solicitation scenarios with other board members—a sympathetic audience—until they have mastered the elevator speech (a brief summary of what the organization is about) and can respond to a variety of questions about the organization and its programs. Feedback from colleagues helps refine approaches and techniques. Role-playing is also an effective way to practice dealing with difficult situations, such as in bringing a conversation to a close after a potential donor says no.
2. *Observe.* Accompany a more experienced board member on solicitation visits. Start with a visit to a longtime supporter, where the positive outcome is certain and only the amount of the gift is in question. Such a positive experience will help board members overcome anxiety by proving that it is possible to have a pleasant, collegial conversation that includes a request for money. The less-experienced board member may want to prepare a shortened version of the elevator speech so that he or she can contribute a personal perspective on the value of the organization and why he or she supports it.
3. *Try a general request.* Try soliciting support from a current or potential donor without naming a specific dollar figure. For example, when hosting a potential donor at a special event, the board member might talk about the organization's plans for the coming year and then say, "I hope that you will consider supporting us next year. It would make a big difference. I will follow up with you then." In this way the board member can practice solicitation while preparing the donor for a more specific request at a later time.

To increase new board members' fundraising comfort level and skills, they can also be introduced to relatively risk-free fundraising cultivation and stewardship activities. Such introductory tasks include the following:

- Participating in group planning and building activities, such as drafting the case statement, deciding on fundraising budget allocations, or using board committee membership to strengthen understanding of fundraising needs
- Providing the names of donor prospects, researching addresses and phone numbers, and suggesting ways to approach donors the board member knows personally
- Brainstorming innovative donor recognition methods
- Assisting in fundraising special events

- Facilitating introductions to individuals or groups where the board member has credibility or influence—for example, a service club, church, or synagogue
- Asking staff to provide success stories about clients that illustrate the impact of gifts on the organization

Fundraising Policies

Boards need several basic policies that guide fundraising activities:

- A *board member fundraising policy* establishes expectations for board members to make a personal donation and to participate in solicitation efforts. The policy may list examples of how board members can or should be involved.
- A *donor relations policy* provides guidelines for recognizing donors for their gifts and defining the levels and methods of recognition. This policy should be clear about proper handling of the confidentiality and anonymity desired by some donors. Additional guidelines should state how to treat donor contact information and how the donor prefers to be listed or named in recognition vehicles.
- A *gift acceptance policy* defines the types of gifts an organization will accept. Such a policy helps the board decide whether to accept controversial gifts. Because nonprofits also receive noncash contributions, clear gift acceptance policies provide guidance as to whether the organization should accept gifts of real estate, stock, art, or automobiles, and how those gifts will be liquidated or maintained.
- A *sponsorship and endorsement policy* defines the relationship between the nonprofit organization and its corporate sponsors. It provides guidelines on the types of companies the organization will work with.

Evaluating Fundraising Performance

The board, working with the chief executive and senior fundraising staff, establishes quantifiable goals for fundraising in the form of performance objectives. The criteria may include timetables for completion; documentation of stewardship activities; results for each fundraising method and technique; and reasonable cost guidelines for effective and efficient use of budget, staff, and volunteers.

Complete data are often difficult to capture—especially fundraising cost allocations by specific method or solicitation technique—so typical statistical analysis may be ineffective. This reality often results in simplistic bottom-line analysis of total funds raised compared to total cost—an approach that reveals nothing about how each solicitation method actually performed.

Understanding effectiveness involves measuring how many people responded to each solicitation made. Understanding efficiency involves measuring actual expenses against funds raised. Only then can the board fully understand fundraising performance and know where to focus efforts to improve.

Each month or quarter, board members should receive three types of gift reports to monitor the performance of the organization's fundraising program: sources of gifts, purposes and uses of gifts received, and results of each solicitation program in use. With clear information about actual results, board members and staff can more easily see where improvements lie and what adjustments might be necessary to meet annual operating goals. The development committee, in its review of these regular reports, will have sufficient results to begin forecasting consistent and reliable future returns. These results also provide reliable data for future budget planning and verify the valuable efforts of board members, volunteers, and staff working together.

Beyond Fundraising: Earned Revenue

Because most nonprofit organizations have high aspirations and are "on a mission," boards should ensure that reliable and diverse revenue sources are developed—perhaps through programs and services that generate income, if such activity is compatible with the organization's mission. For example, revenue streams may include membership dues, publications income, client fees, conference registrations, tuition for educational seminars, and merchandise or product sales.

Relying on just one or two of these areas to generate the majority of the organization's income can be risky. What would happen, for instance, if the number of dues-paying members dropped precipitously? The board should be willing to advocate or approve creation of appropriate new products, services, or activities that not only have the potential for net income growth but also are consistent with the organization's purposes.

Such new initiatives may call for a more entrepreneurial approach to generating income—such as establishing a for-profit subsidiary, creating corporate sponsorship opportunities, forming a limited liability corporation (LLC), or licensing the organization's intellectual property. They may also lead to forming alliances or formal partnerships with corporations, government agencies, or even other nonprofit organizations and sharing the financial risks and rewards of the joint undertaking.

If an organization's budget depends heavily on a signature activity or one big event—which could easily be affected by weather, timing, or competing activities—or if the biggest percentage of revenues is tied to individual or corporate donations that vary from one year to the next, then diversifying income beyond direct fundraising can provide short-term economic stability as well as long-term viability. Nonprofits have a variety of options for generating revenue, including those described in the following section.

Corporate Sponsorships

Corporate sponsorships typically involve a specific product or signature event, although sometimes they apply to an organization's activities in general. They don't necessarily have to take the form of a cash donation. For example, an airline may wish to provide corporate sponsorship by providing several round-trip tickets each year, which the organization can use as prizes. Some organizations have formalized corporate sponsorship programs with specified levels of involvement. That is, as a company invests more with the organization, it moves up the sponsorship ladder and in return receives additional recognition and public acknowledgments.

The Internal Revenue Service keeps a close watch on sponsorships, which, unlike advertising, are not subject to unrelated business income tax. Therefore recognition of sponsorships is allowed, provided it does not constitute advertising by granting substantial benefits to the company in return.

Cause-Related Marketing

In this situation, a corporation makes a designated contribution to the nonprofit organization every time a customer makes a particular purchase. A restaurant, for example, might donate $1 for every steak dinner it sells—or donate 1 percent of its total sales on a particular evening. Typically, the nonprofit organization is mentioned in the company's advertising and promotional materials, which can boost visibility of its mission. The organization should exercise caution so that it does not link its name and reputation with a company that might undermine its mission. For instance, a health-related organization probably wouldn't want to partner with a company connected to the manufacturing or distribution of tobacco or alcohol products. The connections are not always obvious, especially with multinational corporations, so careful research is important before undertaking cause-related marketing.

Entrepreneurial Ventures

An organization may have the expertise to launch its own business or commercial enterprise that addresses unmet needs within the community or sector. Often, a nonprofit's venture into the business marketplace is a natural extension of something it was already doing—such as a homeless shelter opening an employment agency. In fact, the board should ensure that any commercial or business venture supports or advances the main reason the organization exists. Some organizations self-finance such a venture by drawing on their reserves or redirecting funds from another activity. Others take a pure business approach and obtain traditional bank financing, usually using reserves or building equity as collateral. Some tap into a venture philanthropy source—a funder that provides technical assistance or consulting, as well as dollars, to assist nonprofits with ventures that have a promise of sustainability for the long term. Such funding typically comes with specific conditions the nonprofit must meet.

The board should ask staff to undertake a feasibility study, which includes preparing a financial analysis with projected expenses, revenues, implications for unrelated business income tax, and a break-even point for the business venture. These projections, when considered as part of the organization's financial picture, and the nature of the venture itself (how closely related it is to the mission and purpose) will help determine whether setting up a for-profit subsidiary is the best route to take. The feasibility study can form the foundation for a detailed business plan to guide the new venture. Although the board must approve the policies governing the types of income-generating activities undertaken by the organization, it should hold the chief executive accountable for overseeing all those efforts. The chief executive's duties should include approving contracts, approving the promotional language and images used in marketing efforts, tracking royalty or sponsorship payments to the organization, and ensuring that corporate sponsors or supporters are properly acknowledged.

Membership Program

A membership program is a practical way to integrate supporters or subscribers into an organization. As long as the organization structures its recruitment process efficiently and calculates the expense/income ratio accurately, it should be able to enjoy additional revenue. To entice new members to join or to keep old ones coming back, the nonprofit must offer something of value to them while keeping the expenses under control. A successful membership program has a stable or growing member base and the fees largely cover costs.

Chapter Exercises

- Discuss the validity of the "give, get, or get off" statement.
- Few board members were born with natural fundraising skills. What are the most effective ways to involve every board member in fundraising?

- Discuss the potential fundraising effectiveness of a board with or without a development committee.
- Why do capital campaigns start with a lengthy silent period? What is the board's role in a successful capital campaign?
- Draft elevator speeches for Greenpeace, Planned Parenthood, March of Dimes, and the American Institute of Certified Public Accountants (AICPA).

CHAPTER TEN

STRATEGIC THINKING AND STRATEGIC PLANNING

An effective nonprofit board commits to mission-driven strategic planning as part of its ongoing work and engages in strategic thinking about ways to move closer to the vision. With a strategic plan in place and strategic thinking as a rewarding, productive way of doing the board's business, this organization has a head start on its future. Peter Drucker wisely observed, "The best way to predict the future is to create it." Having significant conversations about the future and producing and implementing a strategic plan are actions that yield a greater sense of collective energy and focus. The result is a proactive rather than reactive response to the constantly changing workplace and marketplace.

This chapter addresses two related concepts:

- *Strategic thinking*—The ingrained practice of asking far-ranging questions to help clarify thorny problems, offer breakthrough insights on pressing issues, present new ways of thinking about challenges and opportunities, look at the ramifications of board decisions, and actively generate important strategic ideas.
- *Strategic planning*—A process conducted in partnership with staff in which the board draws on an understanding of organizational strengths and weaknesses and environmental trends to articulate priorities and monitor progress against financial and programmatic goals.

As an integral part of the board process, strategic thinking ultimately provides rich, high-quality content for the strategic plan.

About Strategic Thinking

Imagine two nonprofit boards: Board A and Board B. Board A has it all figured out. Agendas are distributed well before meetings, and meetings are efficient and predictable. Financial oversight is handled carefully. Things run smoothly. Occasionally, though, a bad strategic surprise occurs. When it does, the board pulls together with good spirit and does what it can to recover.

Board B operates differently. Meetings are more contentious, a bit livelier. Although it occasionally delves into management issues (when they involve a major financial expense or a top personnel matter), the board members are mainly interested in big questions about performance, future funding, how the organization is perceived, how it can improve its service to the community—topics that rarely lead to immediate decisions but definitely establish a strategic agenda for ongoing attention.

Board B engages in strategic thinking most of the time; Board A does not. Board B's discussions go beyond the ordinary process questions to more "thoughtful" inquiries that drive deeper: into competitive conditions, constituencies' interests, and value-laden concerns. Board B devotes time to what matters most for the organization and its development. Board A may be "buttoned up" but is much more dependent on management for strategic early warnings and proposed actions to be taken.

Making strategic thinking a habit takes time, effort, and discipline, but it enables the board to be much more helpful to the organization. Strategic thinking, in a nutshell, is critical reasoning applied to matters that most influence the future performance and viability of the organization—reasoning at a level of quality and value far above a perfunctory discussion of current conditions. Strategic thinking focuses on what matters most.

Board members individually and collectively can do this if they are:

- *Intentional about improving strategies and performance.* Board members explicitly search for issues, topics, and opportunities that will improve and defend the organization strategically. They choose carefully what they spend time on.
- *Disciplined about what and how to be thinking.* They adopt more effective ways of examining complex and provocative issues. They look at subjects in new ways and from different angles—not just looking backward to see where the organization has come from, or forward when they engage in strategic planning, but

over, under, and around the issues. They ask why, what if, and what do others do? They react to and interpret information in ways that lead to clear choices, decisions, and actions.

All of this makes regular meetings feel much more like retreats, where members are encouraged to take the time to focus on the big issues. Thoughtful conversations—about the external environment, community needs and perceptions, peers, and competitors—will identify crucial issues and lead to more relevant, timely, and constructive decisions—all this while also getting their fundamental fiduciary work done.

Getting Started

Done well, strategic thinking makes the board a significantly richer strategic asset. Board work is far more productive and satisfying to board members. And the staff will find it has more time to deal with significant issues, no longer being drawn by the board into operational or inconsequential matters.

The board is uniquely positioned to bring such perspective because of its experience, diversity of background, sector-wide connections, loyalty to the organization and its mission, and detachment from day-to-day operations.

Making strategic thinking an integral part of board behavior takes attention and time. The following suggestions will help the board get started:

- Retool meeting agendas by allocating sufficient time for thinking. Strategic matters take time; rich debate won't flourish if the entire meeting is absorbed in discussing operational issues or those of little strategic consequence. Try using a consent agenda—which groups routine items, such as previous meeting minutes and committee reports, under one umbrella that the board can vote on without additional discussion—so there is time for discussions of important issues. Ask whether the right—that is, the most important—items are on the agenda.
- Pose catalytic questions or use some other meeting devices to stimulate thinking and promote lively, robust debates (see the following two sidebars).
- Challenge others' thoughts and behavior. A useful strategic thought must lead somewhere; it should consciously aim to improve strategic results. To prevent complacency in discussions, some boards rotate the responsibility for one member to play devil's advocate at each meeting, challenging assumptions and probing traditional thinking. With practice, this process will become more natural and ingrained as board members see the value that such thinking produces.

- Strengthen the board's composition. Does it include people who can look at things differently? If board members are mostly technical, consider recruiting an artist or writer to bring a fresh perspective. Board members who have become jaded or bored may find it difficult to be energetic and creative. Consider adding some new blood.

These suggestions may not magically transform the board into one that thinks strategically. But they can initiate the transition to a high-performing team of board members. Nourished and practiced over time, with the right leadership, they will encourage strategic thinking to naturally occur—almost without thinking.

Catalytic Questions

Richard P. Chait, William P. Ryan, and Barbara Taylor, in their book *Governance as Leadership,* suggest posing catalytic questions that invite creativity and exploration, and do not depend largely on data and logic to answer.

- What three adjectives or short phrases best characterize this organization?
- What will be most strikingly different about this organization in five years?
- What do you *hope* will be most strikingly different about this organization in five years?
- On what list, which you could create, would you like this organization to rank at the top?
- Five years from today, what will this organization's key constituents consider to be the most important legacy of the current board?
- In five years, what will be most different about the board or how we govern?
- How would we respond if a donor offered a $50-million endowment to the one organization in our field that had the best idea for becoming a more valuable public asset?
- How would we look as a take-over target to a potential or actual competitor?
- If we could successfully take over another organization, which one would we choose and why?
- What has a competitor done successfully that we would not choose to do as a matter of principle?
- What have we done that a competitor might not do as a matter of principle?
- What headline about this organization would we most like to see?
- What headline about this organization would we least like to see?
- What is the biggest gap between what the organization claims it is and what it actually is?

Robust Discussions

These techniques help stimulate board deliberations that are highly participative and relatively spontaneous.

- *Silent Starts.* Take two minutes at the beginning of the board meeting for members to write (anonymously) the most important questions the board and management should address. Read and tally to identify the most crucial issues.
- *One-Minute Memos.* At the conclusion of each discussion item, board members take a minute to write down what they would have said if there had been more time. Collect for review by the chair and chief executive so there's no doubt about what's on the board members' minds.
- *Future-Perfect History.* In breakout groups, develop a future-perfect narrative of how the organization can move from its present state to its envisioned state. Compare story lines and pathways and detours.
- *Counterpoints.* Randomly designate two board members to make the most powerful counterarguments to initial staff recommendations.
- *Role-Plays.* Ask subsets of the board to assume the perspective of different constituent groups likely to be affected by the issue at hand. How would they frame the issue and define a successful outcome? What would each group regard as a worst-case scenario?
- *Surveys.* Prior to discussing a major issue, board members take an anonymous survey that includes questions like these:
  - What should top our agenda next year?
  - What are we overlooking?
  - What is the most valuable step we could take to be a better board?
  - What are the most attractive aspects of the proposed strategic plan?
  - What are the least attractive and most worrisome aspects of the proposed strategic plan?

    An analysis of the responses (not the loudest voice) drives subsequent discussion.

About Strategic Planning

Strategic planning is the process used to seek the strategic fit between the mission of an organization and its internal strengths and external opportunities. Strategic planning develops a shared dream among stakeholders and produces a blueprint for how to achieve that dream.

The strategic planning process is the perfect time for board members to consider their dreams and visions for an organization and to articulate the essence of its values. It gives board members the time and the permission to visualize, ponder, and debate the future within the context of known realities and facts.

Strategic planning is an organizational, political, and rational process: it examines all aspects of an organization, involves key internal and external stakeholders, and requires a certain level of logic and discipline. Although strategic planning incorporates a rational approach and requires analysis and critical thinking from its participants, creativity is also important. Creativity not only keeps the process interesting but also helps an organization envision the possibilities for itself.

Yet like the progression of a dream or the creation of a work of art, strategic planning is not an end unto itself. Just completing a planning process does not make a plan. An organization must be vigilant about keeping intact the balance between process and product.

Strategic planning must fit into an organization's culture. What's important to the organization? What are its environment and atmosphere like? How often does the board usually meet? These are important elements to consider when developing the planning process and determining how to accomplish the work of planning.

Overcoming Resistance to Strategic Planning

Convincing the board to buy in to strategic planning is not always easy. Here are some reasons for their reluctance:

- *"We didn't have a good experience in the past."* For all those who have experienced the benefits of successful strategic planning, there are others who regarded the process as burdensome, particularly if the ultimate results prove negligible. When the process is clearly defined in advance, people tend to find it less confusing and threatening. And when the process also includes ongoing performance monitoring, it is more likely the ultimate plan will have a significant impact.
- *"We don't have time to do this right now."* Committing to conducting a strategic planning effort, even when everyone involved agrees on its importance, does not always seem sufficiently urgent to take priority over other demands. There is a certain irony in this, considering that the frequency of crises diminishes when there are effective strategies to follow.
- *"We don't understand how all the parts fit together."* Most nonprofit leaders are familiar with at least some of the steps involved in strategic planning. What is often

missing, however, is a sense of the order in which these steps should unfold and how they come together in an integrated big picture.

- *"Strategic planning is exhausting."* Comprehensive planning *is* time consuming, but it is important to note that those discussions that take place during the process are indeed the very conversations that an effective, well-managed organization needs to conduct on a regular basis.
- *"We will just have to do this all over again in a few years."* Sadly, many organizations complete the lengthy process of strategic planning only to watch the final plan disappear into the office archives. A few years down the road, with new board members and new staff members, someone challenges the organization to, once again, conduct the entire exercise. But if the strategic plan includes continuous monitoring and evaluation, its recommendations are not only implemented but also become integrated into the permanent organizational DNA.

Often, dissent or conflict will diminish if the board addresses the problems and agrees on resolutions. Sometimes it is helpful to generate question-and-answer periods during board and/or staff meetings. It is imperative to discuss expectations, come up with a realistic process, evaluate the level of investment of time and money that will be necessary, and keep the process on track so that it does not become all consuming.

Why Strategic Planning Is Important

Strategic planning requires a deep and strong commitment from the leadership of an organization. The board must give a clear mandate to embark on a planning process, including an understanding of why it is planning now and what it hopes to achieve. That mind-set must also be communicated widely, because successful strategic planning seeks ownership at every level of the organization.

With the board grounded in the rationale and choices underlying the organization's long-term strategy, it is better able to govern. The strategic plan will eventually guide the board in future decision making, facilitate and inspire fundraising efforts, and help the board better understand how the organization operates.

Because a board must be clear about its motivation for embarking on strategic planning, it is useful to look at some reasons why planning is important. Organizations conduct strategic planning to

- Clarify the mission to all stakeholders
- Assess, reassess, and adjust programs

- Reaffirm that an organization is headed where it wants to go or should be going
- Focus thinking outside the box
- Develop a framework within which to make difficult programmatic and financial decisions
- Address external uncertainties and change
- Garner financial support (particularly from funders who require a strategic plan)

Building Evaluation into the Strategic Plan

Strategic planning allows the board to measure whether (or the extent to which) the organization has been effective in accomplishing its mission. It offers a road map and benchmarks to measure organizational effectiveness, because the measurements identified through strategic planning are key indicators of performance.

Many organizations include performance measures or evaluative components in their strategic plans to enhance the ability to successfully implement the plan. Performance measures for each strategic goal and the associated objectives define what success would look like if these goals and objectives were achieved. (See Chapter Thirteen for more about evaluation.)

For example, if XYZ Organization has a strategic goal to increase its visibility and an objective to develop new partnerships with government, educational, and community groups, it should determine how many new partnerships it seeks to develop and what evidence or outcomes will indicate an impact on the organization's visibility. Some nonprofits make the development of an evaluation plan an objective in the strategic plan.

Approaches to Planning

The assumption underlying nonprofit strategic planning is that the organization will continually have to adjust to unexpected environmental changes. The essence of the plan, then, is not to lock a course of action in stone, but to establish organizational practices and approaches to decision making that will be responsive to change.

There are two basic approaches to planning: *staff-driven* and *participatory*. In staff-driven planning, key staff and board members develop a plan in a reasonably short amount of time without much external input or extensive research. Participatory planning entails a more extensive, time-consuming process in which considerable research into such areas as performance analysis, needs assessment, and market evaluation is conducted in advance. In participatory planning, key stakeholders come together to develop the plan, which includes mechanisms for ongoing performance evaluation as one of its components.

In today's fast-changing environment, it is impossible to predict the future—and therefore unreasonable to expect such predictions to be made. Because the planning horizon has consolidated, the five-year plan, which was often used in the past, is no longer a rational approach to the strategic planning process. Strategic plans are designed to address long-range objectives, but they are now typically intended to unfold over a three-year period. *Operational plans* (also known as *action plans* or *tactical plans*) incorporate the strategies of the long-term plan and translate them into tactical objectives, which are implemented and evaluated annually.

In terms of scope, *institutional plans* incorporate the entire organization, including administrative and program departments. *Departmental plans*, directed to specific administrative and service groups within the organization, are subcategories of the institutional plan. They require specific project plans to be determined within each department in order to create clarity in task roles and responsibilities.

Roles in Strategic Planning

In all types of planning there is someone who has the vision for the desired outcomes, someone who decides what needs to be done, and someone who implements the final plan. Planning the future of an organization, however, is a major endeavor and involves a great number of people. It cannot happen in a vacuum. The success of the final plan—and of the actual planning process—depends on the engagement of the right people at the appropriate phases of the process.

Group Effort

Planning requires thinkers and doers. A multitude of skill sets and expertise is needed during each stage. The strategic plan, as an end product, must meet the needs of a wide variety of stakeholders. If stakeholders are left out of the process, the final plan may serve the needs of only a few, who are unaware of the actual impact made by their decisions. It is unrealistic for the decision makers to serve up a strategic plan on a platter and expect to get the necessary buy-in and enthusiastic reception. When there is interaction between those responsible for the health of the organization, those responsible for doing the daily work, and those who depend on the products and services, the final plan is more readily accepted and owned by all participants.

The Board

Without the full board's blessing and participation, the success of the planning effort is compromised. Whether the board or the chief executive introduces the need for planning, the board must be fully behind the decision to move forward and ultimately must approve the final directives. The board's role is to set direction and, with the chief executive, determine and fine-tune the mission, vision, and the values of the organization. The board is liable for the organization, and strategic planning cannot happen without the board's input and ability to make strategic decisions for the organization.

The board works in close partnership with the chief executive, but it must own the final results of the strategic plan. It is unreasonable to expect individual board members to organize the details of the process, but each board member should contribute to the strategy development and understanding of the consequences of board decisions. Essential board decisions before the planning process include choosing the right approach to fit the organization's phase in life and determining the feasibility of the planning at that moment.

Periodic planning is only one way boards are involved in strategic planning and direction setting. Strategic thinking—a key attribute of an exceptional board—is required not just during the planning process. It must be present in every board meeting. Strategic thinking (discussed earlier in this chapter) keeps the board one step ahead in identifying priorities. The board needs to proactively reflect on potential business items, whether or not they require an immediate decision.

The Chief Executive

The chief executive should be in the driver's seat, taking charge and managing the strategic planning process. He or she is often the visionary, articulating the ideas for the future, then seeking the board's blessing. The chief executive usually instigates the idea of planning, then oversees it to ensure that the plan is executed in a concrete manner. In addition to coordinating the participation of needed collaborators, the chief executive may delegate some of the individual tasks to the board or staff while ensuring that planning proceeds as expected.

Staff

It would be impossible to carry out successful strategic planning without the input, perspective, and support of the staff. Staff provide relevant context to planning, as they are the ones closest to the everyday workings of the organization. They are often tasked with researching the organization's external and internal factors and organizing meetings and retreats to bring all the players together. After the overall plan is defined, the staff drafts the operational plans for implementation—the next step to the strategic plan. Ultimately, the staff translates the board-approved strategic plan into workable directives and timelines.

Consultants

A consultant or a professional facilitator can add objectivity and autonomy to the process while also alleviating the stress of the additional workload. Small-scale planning does not automatically necessitate the use of a consultant, but if the organization is going to use planning to execute a major shift, a facilitator can ensure that all the necessary steps receive proper attention. A consultant can be brought in to work as a facilitator who directs the process and runs the meetings but does not impose his or her opinions in any way. A consultant may also act as the professional guide, taking the responsibility of defining the key issues through interviews and other methods, then steering the board and staff in the right direction.

Constituents

The more participants there are in strategic planning, the easier it is to connect cause and consequence. Rich information leads to wiser decisions; however, to keep the process under control, it is useful to justify the involvement of stakeholders or be clear about the extent of their engagement. Surveys or focus groups can include stakeholders when external environmental scans are studied or when user feedback on the quality of services is needed. Because planning is an internal exercise and deserves confidentiality, it is not usually necessary to bring representatives to planning meetings.

The Planning Process

The development of a strategic plan unfolds in a series of discrete stages:

- Planning to plan
- Understanding context
- Setting purpose, direction, and guiding principles
- Expressing strategies, goals, objective, tactics, and actions

- Writing the plan
- Monitoring the plan

Each stage builds on the previous ones.

Planning to Plan

The first step is to assess readiness for planning, define the participants' roles, and decide how to manage the process. The following questions guide the determination of whether the timing is right:

- *What is the history of planning?*
     Have there been previous strategic plans? What were the outcomes? Can the positive results be replicated and the negative ones avoided?
- *Who will be included in the planning process?*
     Participants can include staff, board members, volunteers, clients, peers, and community partners. As the number of involved stakeholders increases, so does the richness of the input to the plan.
- *What kinds of resources are available for the planning process?*
     How much staff time can be devoted to planning? Is there budget for an outside consultant or to conduct research? Are there enough funds to survey the different stakeholders? Is there a venue for holding the meetings?
- *Who will facilitate the process?*
     Is there someone in the organization with well-developed facilitation skills? (There is a distinction between facilitation skills and content expertise.) Effective facilitation does not allow for involvement in the content of planning, but requires sole focus on the process. On the other hand, should an outside consultant be retained to facilitate the process?

Understanding Context

To place the organization in the right context and evaluate the forces that affect its present and future functioning, it's important to understand the organization's external and internal environments.

 Much of the data that drives strategic planning comes from scanning the *external environment*. The planning task force gathers extensive background information, about both the organization and its competition, ranging from original founding documents to fundraising requests, annual reports, and case studies. Important questions to ask include the following:

- What critical issues does the organization face?
- What do the external stakeholders need or expect from the organization?

- How well does the organization perform against those criteria, and why?
- How well does the organization perform relative to its competitors?

An effective way to organize this information into actionable principles is by devising action scenarios—descriptions of how the organization will respond to possible situations suggested by external trends. Scenarios are not predictions, but vehicles to help frame the context for decision making. They provide a common language for talking about possible future developments by asking "What if?" Many organizations use SWOT (strengths, weaknesses, opportunities, threats) analysis to carefully examine the organization's advantages and disadvantages. Other useful sources of information include client satisfaction surveys, individual client interviews, and client focus groups.

Historical data about the organization's past—from the beginning phases to the present status—provide valuable information on the internal forces that have shaped and continue to shape the future of the organization. An organizational chart explains the hierarchical structure of authority. It helps to understand the culture of the organization, how decisions are made, and how people relate to each other. Policies and processes can clarify the effectiveness and efficiency of internal decision making. Outlining possible strengths and weaknesses within the internal framework provides the base for future corrective action and productive change.

Setting Purpose, Direction, and Guiding Principles

Mission, vision, and values statements (also discussed in Chapter Two) summarize an organization's purpose, direction, and guiding principles. Although they may be brief, the information compressed in these statements is concentrated and crucial. These statements constitute the DNA of the organization—the master templates from which specific actions and programs evolve. All three statements are factual and inspirational, describing the needs the organization was created to fill and its ultimate dream for the future. The beginning of a strategic planning process is a good time for the board to review these crucial documents. (It is not necessary, however, to change these foundational statements each time planning takes place.)

Mission Statement. Board members whose experience is rooted in the corporate world will be more comfortable with mission statements that focus on the what: "The mission of XYZ organization is to provide programs and services for those who suffer from hunger." The more powerful kind of mission statement, however, focuses on the *why*.

In the nonprofit sector, *why* becomes the critical question because we are engaging people at the level of their deepest values and asking them to provide time and financial support for which the only return on investment is the knowledge of how they are making a difference. Coupling the why with a simple *what* statement usually satisfies the needs of those who want to see a more traditional corporate statement. As an example, an organization that works with people who have sustained injuries to their hands created a powerful example of a mission statement combining the why with the what:

> Next to the human face, hands are our most expressive feature. We talk with them. We work with them. We play with them. We comfort and love with them. An injury to the hand affects a person professionally and personally. At XYZ Organization, we give people back the use of their hands.

Although this mission statement can stand alone, it was also ably incorporated throughout the organization, with minor wording changes, using compelling design and graphics. It appeared on the cover of a brochure and in other materials, accompanied by program descriptions, successful treatment and therapy stories, goals of the organization, and other supporting information.

What Makes a Mission Statement Compelling

- It uses bold, clear, and memorable language.
- It conveys the organization's values both explicitly and implicitly.
- It has both an emotional and a rational impact.
- It combines a "why" statement with a "what" statement.
- It describes the need being met in positive, not negative, terms.
- It uses verbs that are active, not passive.
- It inspires people to act, give, join, serve, and learn more.
- It can be adapted for both marketing and development.
- It summarizes the mission succinctly.

Vision Statement. A vision statement is a written inspirational declaration of values, beliefs, and concepts that reflects how society will be changed in the future as a result of the organization's work. It defines the dream, the long-term goal, and the unconditional direction in which the organization is heading. It should inspire and challenge, and stretch the imagination of board, staff, clients, customers, and other stakeholders. The statement is not tied to future funding, obstacles of any kind, or the present availability of resources. Although it describes a desired state, it should not be totally unrealistic. With a reachable goal—however far the goal lies in the future—the vision statement should be motivational and hopeful. For instance, it's unrealistic—no matter how noble the vision—for one organization to expect to eradicate poverty in the world or to make crime disappear.

If the mission statement functions as a tool to help with everyday decisions, the vision statement guides the organization's overall long-term thinking. Two organizations may have different mission statements but share similar visions. For instance, the missions of a homeless shelter and a job-training center for the unemployed are quite different; however, both may envision elevating decency and respectability in the lives of all community dwellers.

Even organizations with strong missions have their limits if they don't have a strong, clearly written vision statement. An organization's vision keeps its mission on the right track. The vision is there to remind board and staff that even after they are gone, the long-term purpose of the organization will endure. The mere process of creating a vision statement helps to focus the board. Creating a vision statement is a group process, enabling board members to share their perspectives on what the organization is working toward.

Values Statement. Values are embedded in both mission and vision. Values are what click with people when they read an organization's materials. Vision statements also have implicit and expressed values. As the board works to gain a sense of mission and to create and reaffirm a mission statement, it is imperative to know and communicate values, usually through a written statement of core values or guiding principles.

One seasoned corporate executive, when asked to define what values meant to his involvement as chair of a nonprofit science center's board, said they were his deeply held beliefs that inspire and guide both his involvement and outreach. He listed these beliefs as discovery, fiscal responsibility, education, and accessibility. That mix illustrates the wide range of values that board members, other volunteers, and donors may express.

People are drawn to organizations whose values they share. They seldom work for, give to, ask for, join, or serve organizations whose values they do not share. An organization's ability to embed values in its mission is key to attracting board members, volunteers, staff, and donors who want to support organizations working on the issues that are most important to them. Expression of those values will attract people's interest in a way that the description of what the organization does cannot.

As important as a values statement can be to an organization's strategic direction, it does not take the place of a code of ethics—a document describing a code of conduct for board and staff. With its explicit guidance about actions, behaviors, and decision making, a code of ethics sends a message about the culture and work of the organization.

Mission, Vision, and Values Checkup

MISSION STATEMENT

- Does the statement clearly connect with the values of the organization?
- Is it broad enough to allow flexibility?
- Is it as succinct as possible and short enough for people to remember and repeat?
- Is it a unifying force providing direction and guidance?

VISION STATEMENT

- Does it challenge—make the organization reach—while also being realistic?
- Does it create passion? Is it inspirational?
- Does it give all constituencies a clear sense of where the organization is headed and what the organization hopes to accomplish?
- Does it communicate its essential message directly and succinctly?

VALUES STATEMENT

- Does it articulate the most closely held beliefs of the organization?
- Are the values defined clearly to eliminate ambiguity about their meaning in relation to the organization?
- Do they inspire pride of association?
- Do they capture the distinctive nature of the organization?

Mission, Vision, and Values: Four Examples

WTVP PUBLIC TELEVISION

www.wtvp.org

Mission

Intellectual, creative, and technological capacity is a requirement of an engaged democratic society. WTVP uses the power of public telecommunications to inspire, enhance, and inform our community.

Vision

Central Illinois is reinventing itself as a learning-based community. WTVP will use its technology, facilities, and creative talent to play a leading role in our region's educational, medical, economic, and cultural transformation.

Values (A Selection)

We believe in the strength and the future of our community.

We believe in independence from political pressure and undue and inappropriate outside influence.

We believe that the pursuit of knowledge and access to diverse points of view are fundamental to a dynamic and informed community.

We believe the human spirit is uplifted and inspired by the arts.

We believe that lifelong learning is essential to a balanced and fair society.

We believe that strength of mind requires not only serious discourse and consideration of great ideas but also enjoyment and excitement of great entertainment.

GOODWILL INDUSTRIES OF AMERICA

www.goodwill.org

Mission

Goodwill Industries International enhances the dignity and quality of life of individuals, families, and communities by eliminating barriers to opportunity and helping people in need reach their fullest potential through the power of work.

Vision

Every person has the opportunity to achieve his/her fullest potential and participate in and contribute to all aspects of life.

Values

- Respect—We treat all people with dignity and respect.
- Stewardship—We honor our heritage by being socially, financially, and environmentally responsible.
- Ethics—We strive to meet the highest ethical standards.
- Learning—We challenge each other to strive for excellence and to continually learn.
- Innovation—We embrace continuous improvement, bold creativity, and change.

AMERICAN ASSOCIATION OF CRITICAL CARE NURSES

www.aacn.org

Mission

Patients and their families rely on nurses at the most vulnerable times of their lives. Acute and critical care nurses rely on AACN for expert knowledge and

(Continued)

the influence to fulfill their promise to patients and their families. AACN drives excellence because nothing less is acceptable.

Vision

AACN is dedicated to creating a healthcare system driven by the needs of patients and families where acute and critical care nurses make their optimal contribution.

Values

As AACN works to promote its mission and vision, it is guided by values that are rooted in, and arise from, the Association's history, traditions, and culture. Therefore, AACN, its members, volunteers, and staff will:

- **Be accountable** to uphold and consistently act in concert with ethical values and principles.
- **Advocate** for organizational decisions that are driven by the needs of patients and families.
- **Act with integrity** by communicating openly and honestly, keeping promises, honoring commitments and promoting loyalty in all relationships.
- **Collaborate** with all essential stakeholders by creating synergistic relationships to promote common interest and shared values.
- **Provide leadership** to transform thinking, structures and processes to address opportunities and challenges.
- **Demonstrate stewardship** through fair and responsible management of resources.
- **Embrace life-long learning**, inquiry and critical thinking to enable each to make optimal contributions.
- **Commit to quality and excellence** at all levels of the organization, meeting and exceeding standards and expectations.
- **Promote innovation** through creativity and calculated risk taking.
- **Generate commitment and passion** to the organization's causes and work.

AN URBAN PRESCHOOL PROGRAM

Mission

Children need a strong start on life's learning journey. When they are guided and engaged, children eagerly embrace education. At [name of organization], we make sure that a child's first experience with learning is the successful beginning of a challenging and satisfying lifelong journey.

Vision

Our vision is that every child in the greater [city] area will be ready when it is time to start school.

Values

- Permission to learn and dream
- Education as the key to knowledge and self-confidence
- Inherent curiosity in all children
- Creation of an environment for discovery
- Guidance in a child's first steps toward school

Expressing Strategies, Goals, Objectives, Tactics, and Actions

Strategies, goals, objectives, tactics, and actions give concrete form to the abstractions of the mission and vision statements. Early in the process, the aim is to generate as many strategies and goals as possible to address the critical issues that have been identified.

- *Strategies* are high-level options for direction to help your organization meet its goals and fulfill its mission.
- *Goals* are the accomplishments that allow your organization to meet its mission-related prerequisites.
- *Objectives* are the purposes and rationale that help your organization further define and support your strategic goals. They are the more immediate aims that need to be realized en route to achieving longer-term goals—interim steps and accomplishments that provide a specific roadmap.
- *Tactics* are detailed action steps that support strategies.
- *Actions* are the tactical items in the day-to-day work of the organization that, if accomplished, will allow it to be successful in its plan. Detailed actions are defined in separate operational plans.

When identifying these key strategic issues, the participants in the process take a proactive approach to change. These issues or challenges may address conditions that either prevent the organization from functioning to its fullest potential (changes in the demographic composition of the constituents or serious staff retention problems) or prevent it from taking advantage of new opportunities (positive changes in the legislature or profitable, money-saving collaborations with other organizations). It is important to consider defensive goals as well as positive ones to prevent possible negative consequences that can occur if a particular course of action is not pursued.

After a list of goals has been culled, all items are prioritized. Objectives are then devised to accomplish these goals in the most effective way possible. More detailed tactics can be quite explicit and tightly defined. Because these goals logically are not expected to be achieved immediately or simultaneously, it is necessary to look at scheduling and appropriate timing for needed actions.

Writing the Plan

The format and contents of the written plan can be customized to the requirements of the particular nonprofit, but all share the same intent—to provide direction and operational guidance to members of the organization as they conduct their daily business.

It is helpful to provide portions of the plan to all key stakeholders inside and outside the organization; these may include board members, all staff, volunteers, funders, and members of the community. Versions of the compiled plan can vary, depending on who receives it. The staff and volunteers who are responsible for implementing the goals should receive the entire document. The board, funders, and community stakeholders may not need all the details of the goals and objectives, but they will find that having the shared mission and vision, guiding principles, and strategies is pertinent to their role.

The contents of a well-formulated strategic plan could look like this:

- A letter from the board and/or chief executive supporting and introducing the plan
- Historical synopsis of the organization
- Completed trend analyses of external environmental factors
- Customer feedback results
- Future potential scenarios for the organization, discussed and documented
- Mission statement
- Vision statement
- Agreed-upon guiding principles of the organization
- Key strategies for reaching the vision
- Goals that support the mission and vision
- A list of prioritized goals in temporal sequence
- Objectives that support the prioritized goals
- Formal adoption of the strategic plan
- Procedures and metrics that will be used to monitor the plan

Monitoring the Plan

The preparation of a written document does not mean the strategic plan is complete. On the contrary, ongoing monitoring and continuous revision is one of the most important aspects of effective strategic planning. This continuous process includes

- Incorporating the tenets of the strategic plan into annual operating plans and budgets
- Reviewing overall performance of the organization and its adherence to the plan on a periodic basis and making appropriate revisions
- Focusing reports around relationships to the strategic plan—for example, a chief executive's report that connects his or her accomplishments directly to the plan

A strategic plan exists as a guidance system to offer parameters to decision making and to align activities and programs. As such, the plan is not rendered permanently frozen on the day it is composed; rather, it is meant to be a functional tool capable of evolution with changing circumstances. To repeat the point for emphasis, the objective of the planning process is not only to produce the formal, written plan itself but, more important, to codify the collective intelligence of the organization in a way that directs actions and behavior.

To maximize effectiveness of operations in accomplishing strategic objectives, appropriate evaluative metrics are developed during the planning process and used to review performance on a regular basis. These performance measures should be included in the plan to provide evaluation metrics as well as procedures for review. The plan itself should be evaluated on a quarterly basis. Procedures for periodic review of the strategic plan allow for corrective action at regular junctures to maintain the momentum of the plan. Strategic planning is never over. It is a cyclical process by nature, whereby continuous evaluation demands reality checks and regular adjustment.

Ongoing performance evaluation should also occur in a less formal way at regular organizational events such as staff meetings, committee meetings, and individual performance reviews. The chief executive should encourage staff members to refer to the strategic plan, to ensure that all actions are still in line and no aspects of the plan have been neglected. The board naturally must do the same when reviewing staff reports.

Leading Toward the Future

In periods of significant social and economic change, when many of the past assumptions on which organizations have been built appear to be breaking down and resources are limited, it is even more important for nonprofit boards and chief executives to provide decisive leadership. It is indeed challenging to make strategic thinking a habit and develop a strategic plan when major uncontrolled forces hover on the horizon, affecting your future, but it is the presence of those forces that makes the need for strategic thinking as a mind-set and strategic planning as a regular process even more critical.

Putting an organization on a continuous cycle of strategic thinking, strategic planning, and evaluation ensures that it will stay focused on mission. A commitment to strategic thinking is vital because it contributes to the success of the organization. Quality content for a strategic plan comes not from the planning process itself but from the active brain power of board members and staff applied to pertinent subject matter and analyses. An investment in strategic planning serves to align the different parts of the organization by providing a common, unifying perspective. In times of tight budgets, staff will be concerned not just with saving money, but also with taking actions that maximize the impact of limited resources on strategic objectives. An organization with a guiding plan is likely to end up where it wants to go. One without a plan risks splintering into disparate pieces.

In the final analysis, the ultimate reason for engaging in strategic thinking and planning is that it gives the organization a real chance to shape the future— instead of being overwhelmed by it.

Chapter Exercises

- Why do most strategic planning processes start with examining the mission? How are the mission and vision linked to each other?
- Choose an organization you know well and list the issues to which you should pay attention as you analyze its external and internal contexts.
- What is the difference between a board that is a strategically thinking board and a board that diligently goes through strategic planning every three to five years? Or is there necessarily a difference?
- Can you think of other methods of planning besides the traditional method mainly described in this book? When would an organization choose a different approach?

CHAPTER ELEVEN

COMMUNICATIONS AND OUTREACH

Communications is the art of expressing ideas combined with the science of transmitting information. It is presenting a message to motivate target audiences to act in a desired manner. It integrates different parts of an organization—including public education, advocacy, service marketing, fundraising, and membership services—into a disciplined, potentially powerful engine. It helps shape a positive image of the organization, raises public awareness, maximizes scarce organizational resources, and strengthens community partnerships.

Most nonprofits are skilled at the front-end approach to communications: disseminating information and building public awareness through outreach activities. A strategic approach links all communications and outreach practices within a single framework. Strategic communications prepares the board and staff to deal with the increased scrutiny that all nonprofits face, builds trust and credibility, and can even prevent controversial situations from turning into crises.

For nonprofit boards, strategic communications involves big-picture thinking, a clear understanding of appropriate roles, and hands-on participation when appropriate. The board ensures that the organization does not lose sight of how it is perceived in the community. With their broad perspective on the external environment, board members can stimulate creative thinking. Public speaking, relationships that support coalition building, and personal connections are all valuable assets that committed board members share with the organization, leaving the day-to-day work for the staff to do.

A board's most important contribution is to encourage an organization-wide understanding of the connection between communications and mission. As nonprofits are challenged to demonstrate the impact of their work, old assumptions about the public's perceptions and expectations may no longer be appropriate. By maximizing resources; focusing on potentially supportive audiences; and conveying the value, services, and impact of the organization—by being strategic about communications—boards can help their nonprofits find their niche and make their value known.

Who Is Involved, and How

Strategic communications—like many nonprofit practices—is a collaborative effort that combines some roles for the board, some roles for the chief executive and staff, and a considerable amount of board-staff teamwork. And as in other arenas, those roles may shift depending on the nature of the task or the size and staff capacity of the organization.

The Board

Strategic communications is strongly correlated with the board's basic responsibilities: upholding mission and values, allocating adequate resources, ensuring effective planning, enhancing the organization's public standing, and monitoring program effectiveness. The board's role encompasses the following actions:

Providing the vision to support strategic communications. In collaboration with the chief executive, the board provides the vision—the aspirations for the organization's future—that guides communications strategy. Because the board's job is to articulate and translate mission and purpose, it must have a clear view of the organization's image, actual or desired. Board members know where the organization is headed, what its strengths and weaknesses are, and what areas of opportunity exist. The board's knowledge and guidance help shape strategic communications planning and practice. They have a sense of current and potential challenges, and if they take their role seriously they are prepared to deal with unexpected situations.

Engaging in regular strategic planning. Although the board usually does not have extensive hands-on involvement in developing a strategic communications plan, it does participate, of course, in the overall strategic planning that provides the framework for communications planning. The active listening that takes place during a planning process—as the organization pinpoints issues in the external environment and among stakeholders that will guide its focus and direction—can have a positive impact on the work of the board. Then the board ensures that a written communications plan exists; is linked to the organizational mission, vision, values, and goals; and is reviewed regularly. A board member may sit on a strategic communications planning task force, and in smaller organizations the board may be more involved in the actual planning process.

Dedicating resources to implementing the strategic communications plan. Strategic communications helps make efficient use of limited funds and lays the groundwork for generating increased support. Although smaller nonprofits may believe it is unwise to spend scarce resources on communications, effective strategic communications can ensure that even a small organization uses consistent messages to reach the audiences that are most essential to its work.

Monitoring the impact of strategic communications efforts. As part of its responsibility for monitoring the impact of the organization and its work, the board ensures that strategic communications objectives are being met. The board should also identify when existing approaches are no longer working and should challenge itself and the organization to be open to new ways of thinking.

Participating in repositioning the organization. When crises arise, new opportunities present themselves, or old methods no longer work well, the board supports the chief executive to reexamine the communications plan, safeguard the organization's integrity and reputation, listen to the needs and concerns of stakeholders, and take positive action. It provides leadership for repositioning the organization, branding, and refining communications strategies and messages.

The Board Chair

The chair's leadership of the board and partnership with the chief executive are pivotal influences in the arena of strategic communications.

Initiating communications planning. The chair and the chief executive determine whether (1) the communications strategies of the organization are effective and need routine monitoring, or (2) a comprehensive strategic communications planning process needs to be undertaken. The chair monitors the plan for policy issues that need to be brought to the full board.

Involving the board and inviting its guidance and feedback. In their regular conversations, the chair and chief executive should confer about how to achieve each communications goal and how to capitalize on board members' expertise to support the organization. The chair ensures that board members tap their networks, accept assignments for speaking and outreach, work with staff as necessary, and report back to the board at board meetings.

Ensuring ongoing board discussion of strategic communications issues. Featuring communications strategy in board orientations and as a regular discussion topic on the board agenda increases board members' awareness of how the organization does its work. The board chair also identifies potential funding sources for communications work and confers with the chief executive about the use of outside consultants.

With the governance committee, recruiting board members who can enhance communications efforts. Targeted recruitment will build the board's leadership and outreach capacity in the area of strategic communication. If the chair decides to set up task forces to work on communications planning, branding, framing, or other special projects, he or she identifies the appropriate task force chairs and ensures coordination with staff.

Individual Board Members

Board members have the skills, resources, and credibility that help an organization succeed, as well as unique viewpoints to gauge the organization's image and impact.

Contributing diverse perspectives that reflect audience needs and interests. Boards often recruit new members specifically because of their ties to the community, so it's important to draw routinely on this community-based network to support the organization and reach out to constituents.

Being knowledgeable about the organization's core values and messages. Board members need to be knowledgeable about the organization's core messages and comfortable with delivering those messages to constituents, stakeholders, and the public. This means being able to

- Describe the mission, vision, and goals
- Explain what the organization does and for whom
- Give a thumbnail sketch of the organizational structure and overall financial situation
- Provide information about basic programs and services
- Articulate their personal commitment to the organization and their reasons for joining the board

Speaking about the organization and sharing their enthusiasm for its work. Board members can act as ambassadors by speaking about the organization in formal settings and by sharing information about its successes and needs in their everyday business and personal lives. They should be encouraged to convey their enthusiasm for the organization, promote its achievements, support fundraising programs, and recruit new board members.

The Chief Executive

Day-to-day decisions about strategic communications are the responsibility of the chief executive, who oversees the staff's work and is the connection between board and staff.

Conceiving the overall approach to strategic communications and managing staff functions. The chief executive decides—often in collaboration with the board chair—whether the organization has effective communications strategies or needs to undertake a comprehensive strategic communications planning process. He or she then ensures that the staff develops a plan and implements its communications goals. The executive also serves as the primary spokesperson for the organization, regardless of size.

Keeping the board informed. The chief executive makes sure the board is up to date on communications activities, tools, and results so that an atmosphere of board-staff collaboration prevails and board members can be knowledgeable ambassadors for the organization.

Involving the board and inviting its guidance and feedback. The chief executive facilitates the board's role by seeking opportunities for board members to serve as ambassadors, promote the organization's achievements, support its fundraising programs, attract new leaders, and help the organization fulfill its community role. In smaller organizations, the chief executive's role may be more hands-on. He or she may manage the drafting and implementation of a strategic communications plan and ensure that the organization has effective communications tools and resources, from press kits to a Web site. Staff resources dedicated to communications depend on the size of an organization. Whether the communications staff consists of one person or several departments, it is important to keep a strategic focus on marshalling a range of activities—marketing, media relations, and so forth—in pursuit of communications goals.

Internal Communications

Successful strategic communications depends on strong and consistent internal communications. The key internal relationships are between the chief executive and board chair, between the board chair and the board, among board members, between the chief executive and staff, and among staff departments and individuals. Open communication helps generate a common understanding of mission, goals, issues, and programs so that board and staff work together, not at cross-purposes. Working together, the board, chief executive, and staff can identify common issues, avoid duplication of efforts, and collaborate in a way that taps the strengths and resources of individual board members.

It is critical for each board member to understand and observe the appropriate internal communication patterns. Board members should receive information primarily through the chief executive and the board chair. Routine communications mechanisms—monthly reports, updates at board meetings, and e-mail or other alerts for priority items—ensure that the board receives a balanced flow of information about key happenings. Board members should neither be overwhelmed with details nor constantly have to ask staff for more information. The board chair should be accessible to board members and ensure that they do not circumvent the communications structure by going directly to staff, except in extraordinary circumstances.

Every organization will create internal communications tools that suit its culture and needs. Electronic communication adds speed and spontaneity, but face-to-face conversations are critical. Some organizations have e-newsletters for board members, organize regular staff discussion groups on key issues, and hold staff briefings for the board. Periodic retreats give the board and staff the opportunity to think about the broader strategic challenges facing the organization. The challenge is to ensure that the material the board receives truly informs their understanding of the organization and its work.

Engaging Board Members in Communications and Outreach

Board members can and should be their organization's best advocates. Committed board members are familiar with the work of the organization and knowledgeable about the issues it addresses. They have a clear sense of the organization's impact, gained from participating in or observing programs and services. By interacting with constituents, listening to their concerns and interests, and explaining why they should be involved, each board member is a critical force in advancing the communications agenda. Board members engage in strategic communications and outreach by

- Serving as ambassadors for the organization as they move through their personal and professional lives
- Speaking on behalf of the organization in formal and informal settings and sharing feedback with staff to enhance the communications effort
- Facilitating coalitions with other organizations that advance strategic communications for the organization's mission, programs, and services

Well-Connected Board Members

Entrepreneurial boards pay close attention to recruiting members with diverse interests and strengths, giving the organization even greater reach and credibility in the community. Board members often have ties to key business, government, media, and other community leaders whom the organization would like to tap for support. For example, the board member who serves an organization for parents of special-needs children regarding their schooling can be a useful representative to civic leaders, educators, and parents. The attorney who specializes in consumer law can use her community connections and legal expertise to help craft a consumer action group's agenda.

Too many boards miss the opportunity to enlist board members as advocates because they take a narrow view of the board's role, limiting involvement to meetings, fundraising, and committee work. The board chair, chief executive, and senior staff should work together to capitalize on the board's potential for contributing to strategic communications. Meeting personally with each new board member, they can ask: Who do you know? How does their work overlap with the work of our organization? Would you be willing to serve as the link that gets them involved?

A board member may have a special relationship with a particular organization or group. Or the organization may need a credible representative to reach out to diverse communities, young people, elderly people, or specific demographic sectors. In outreach to these communities, board members, as peers, will enhance the organization's effectiveness and lend credibility to targeted communications efforts. At every board meeting, board members should be invited to share news of their efforts to support the organization within their circles of friends and colleagues.

A board matrix is an excellent tool for finding out how each board member fits into the communications effort. (See Chapter Six, Table 6.1 for a board matrix worksheet.) A simple questionnaire, completed by each board member at the beginning of each board year, helps match individuals with assignments that line up with their interests and capabilities, and tells the staff more about board members' community connections, including memberships, affiliations, and personal and professional contacts. Because the governance committee often recruits board members based on their specific community ties, the committee chair could be another good resource when making board assignments.

Using the board profile that emerges from the matrix, the chief executive and staff can develop an action plan for board participation. If a communications goal involves building compatible partnerships with educational institutions, for example, then certain board members could have key roles: the law partner of the school board president, the retired community college dean, or the newspaper colleague of the education columnist.

Some boards ask members to agree in writing to a list of tasks—communications-related and others—that they will accomplish over a year's time. The board chair and chief executive should routinely check with board members to encourage their participation—and always ask for feedback.

Acting as Ambassador

One of the simplest communications and outreach roles for board members may also be one of the most overlooked. Board members have many informal opportunities in their daily lives—at work, at social events, in their faith communities, among friends—to share their pride in the organization and spread the word about its accomplishments.

In their role as ambassadors, board members should think of themselves as the organization's advocates and representatives twenty-four hours a day, seven days a week. They should ask themselves how they can translate the commitment and enthusiasm that made them join the board into their own personal messages.

Some board members feel more comfortable with informal communications than with public speaking. They take on assignments such as attending meetings of other organizations, joining a board team to meet with an elected official, or simply talking with friends and colleagues about the organization's issues, services, and value to the community. At special events and conferences, the mere presence of board members adds credibility and sends the message that the board is supportive and engaged.

Personal advocacy involves listening and learning as well as actively communicating. Feedback from stakeholders, transmitted back to the organization through board members, helps shape board discussion about communications priorities. If every board member adopts this approach, opportunities for benefiting the organization will multiply.

As part of the strategic communications planning process, the chief executive and the board chair can help board members identify the contacts and skills they have to support the organization and its mission. Basic materials—including a one-page fact sheet, simple talking points, issue position papers, and brochures and flyers—will help board members prepare for informal outreach. Role-playing exercises can increase their comfort with talking about the organization and its programs and services.

Board members must be encouraged to stay on message in their informal interactions about the organization. And if they speak to issues outside of the mission, they should be clear about when they are presenting their personal opinions. Board members should be able to articulate the organization's official positions, but they should not take an official position if the organization has not issued one.

Public Speaking

Board members are positive representatives and advocates when invited to speak in formal settings. Public speaking is a proven mechanism for focusing attention on issues, educating the community about a specific concern, promoting programs and services, and building community support for and commitment to the organization's goals. It is also an excellent way to recruit volunteers, donors, and board members. If one goal of the strategic communications plan is to increase public and community awareness, for example, the board may want to consider creating a speakers' bureau for board members, providing opportunities for coaching and issuing reviews to help them address the range of issues important to the organization.

Board members should remember that every organization designates an official spokesperson—usually the chief executive—as its public voice. The media and the public should hear directly from the chief executive on all major issues, such as position statements or leadership changes. The communications director or another appropriate staff member is the lead contact person on day-to-day issues and can make statements and provide information in the spokesperson's name. Media interview requests always go to the spokesperson via the communications director.

When the organization receives a speaking invitation, the chief executive may decide to choose a board member who is a good match with the audience's interests and characteristics. The chief executive or a staff member briefs the board member about the audience and the goal for the event. In larger organizations, a staff member may prepare the speech, accompany the board member, handle press if they are present, circulate supporting materials, draft thank-you notes, and brief fellow staff members. In smaller organizations, the chief executive works with the speaker to develop talking points, provides materials to leave behind, and is responsible for follow-up. In every organization, the chief executive or staff members should be available to share success stories, prepare speakers with responses to frequently asked questions, and help board members practice their presentations.

A board member who makes a formal presentation should be

- A confident and enthusiastic public speaker
- Knowledgeable about the organization and able to represent its priorities

- Willing to work closely with staff to develop suitable strategies
- Able to work with the board chair or chief executive in unique or delicate situations to address issues requiring candid or off-the-record discussions

---

Speaking Tips for Board Members

Skilled public speakers keep two points in mind: What is the message I want to leave with the audience? What are two facts I want them to remember? The intent is to explain what the organization stands for, the people or cause that it serves, and the link between the organization and the audience. Are audience members unfamiliar with the organization, and do they need to be informed? Or are they already engaged on some level and need to be motivated to step up their involvement?

The following guidelines can help board members shape effective presentations:

- Understand the audience, the strategic goal for the speech, and the logistics for the event.
- Work with staff on the key talking points, and ensure that there is a specific "ask" or request for the audience to support the organization in some way.
- In the speech, describe why the organization is important to you, why you joined the board, and what personal commitment you have made to help the organization fulfill its mission.
- Always include time at the end of the presentation for questions and answers.
- Determine whether the press will be present at the event, and assume that the event is on the record.
- Leave behind brochures and other basic information that encourage the attendees to follow up with the organization. After the presentation, report to staff about the speech, the outcomes of the meeting, and any contacts that may require follow-up.

Facilitating Collaborations and Partnerships

Nonprofit organizations are increasingly reliant on coalitions to strengthen organizational capacity, provide services efficiently, and meet community outreach goals. As part of the communications strategy, partnerships and collaborations help organizations accomplish what they can't on their own. They can attract public attention or support beyond the organization's traditional sphere of influence. They can demonstrate the breadth and depth of this support to community leaders, policymakers, and other stakeholders. Coalitions are strategic when they are purposefully designed and implemented, and involve organizations with complementary missions and clientele. Many funding partners, policymakers, and community leaders look to nonprofits to work together in order to maximize the investment of resources and prevent duplication of effort.

The Board's Role

The board's experience and connections are vital to the creation of a successful partnership. As a group and as individuals, the board can broaden the range of collaboration possibilities by introducing the chief executive and other staff to prospective partners. The board must also continue to support the staff's efforts to build and sustain these coalitions and monitor the effectiveness of these relationships. In addition to identifying potential community partners and ensuring financial support for coalitions, the board's key responsibility is providing oversight. It should be prepared to ask probing questions about existing partnerships, including

- What does the organization gain by working with the partner(s)? What does the partner gain?
- Is the organization involved in the partnership for the right reasons?
- Does the partnership advance the organization's goals?
- Are the logistics of the partnership efficient?
- Do the rewards match the investment of time, energy, and money?

The board's perception strengthens the organization's oversight of its coalition work. Because the board is not absorbed in day-to-day work, it can see the organization from the perspective of its constituents and stakeholders. Coalitions need to change when they lose their effectiveness or when other groups emerge that may be more compatible. As part of the strategic planning process, the board may ask the staff to review existing relationships, decide whether some are no longer useful, and investigate potentially fruitful new alliances.

Individual Board Members

Board members bring a diverse mix of personal experience and connections to the table. Board contacts are a valuable coalition-building asset. When a board member is knowledgeable about another organization, he or she can advise the chief executive on the relative merits of a partnership. The board profile described earlier in this chapter yields useful information about board members' connections.

Board members contribute to coalition building as team players. Working closely with the chief executive—never independently without the chief executive's knowledge—board members can have conversations with board and staff in other organizations, discuss potential working relationships, and help negotiate partnership terms. The chief executive or a staff member can provide background materials and join the board member at meetings or in phone calls.

Positioning the Organization

As part of its responsibility, the board should pay consistent attention to image and identity. Board members should monitor how their issues and their organization are portrayed in the media, in the community, and by the organization. Staying abreast of current events and participating in community activities gives board members additional insight into the effectiveness of the organization's communications work.

Framing

From time to time, it is important for the board to sit back and look at how the community at large is discussing its issues. "How do people who are not connected with us look at our issues, the people we serve, the organizations we work with, and the policies we advance? Do they see our concerns the same way we do? Are they passionate about them for the same reasons? Or are their concerns different from ours? If so, how should we change our work to address their concerns and connect the community to our organization?" By asking these questions and understanding the community's values and concerns, board members can evaluate the frames that shape public perceptions of their issues and their organization.

Leadership at the board level provides the impetus for framing or reframing issues. The board can be involved in the following ways:

- Schedule board time to discuss how the media influence the organization's work. Explore new issues and current events that shape the community's values and perceptions of the organization. Framing analyses on particular issues can stimulate these discussions and may help identify new communications opportunities for the organization.
- Monitor how the media cover the issues of importance to the organization. Listen to outside perspectives, watch television, and listen to programs watched by the audiences the organization tries to reach.

- Encourage the board and staff to use the framing analysis model when presenting its communications recommendations to the full board. Test the hypotheses with the board members as representative of the communities that the organization serves.

Branding

In the nonprofit sector, branding involves developing a clear, consistent identity—a set of messages, images, and experiences—that stimulates positive feelings about an organization among its donors, members, constituents, and other stakeholders. A nonprofit needs a brand identity in order to translate those good feelings into trust, loyalty, and support.

The following scenarios may prompt a board (in partnership with the chief executive) to launch a branding initiative:

- The mission needs revision as part of strategic planning.
- Issues need reframing in response to changing public perceptions.
- The organization would like to reach new groups of donors.
- A new program or service is being introduced to a new client base.
- A communications audit shows that the current brand identity is not being consistently applied or is no longer effective.

Although the staff is involved in the day-to-day production and dissemination of educational and promotional materials for the organization, the board plays an essential role as follows:

- *Providing commitment, leadership, and oversight.* The board may determine that there is a problem with visual image. It endorses the need for a branding initiative, empowers the chief executive to conduct one, ensures that resources are available, contributes ideas and expertise, and reviews the results.
- *Establishing organizational identity.* The board clarifies organizational identity—the qualities that make it distinctive and worthwhile—through mission review and goal setting. Identity is often addressed in a positioning statement, which becomes the framework for developing a visual identity.
- *Supporting the brand identity in communications on behalf of the organization.* To be effective, brand identity must be supported and promoted from every corner of the organization, beginning with the board. An introduction to brand identity should be incorporated into all board orientation and training. The board also assumes oversight for ensuring that all new materials honor the integrity of the brand identity.

- *Building brand equity.* In their role as ambassadors for the organization, board members lead the effort to build the brand's impact and value, or brand equity.

Lobbying and Political Activity

Advocacy, lobbying, and political activity by nonprofits are frequently confused with each other. So far, this chapter has described advocacy: representing the organization in the community, articulating its mission, and supporting and defending its message.

Lobbying refers to particular activities that try to influence legislators to pass laws that are favorable to one's cause. There are two categories of lobbying. *Direct lobbying* occurs when an individual or organization has direct contact with legislators. *Grassroots lobbying* tries to influence legislation indirectly by attempting to mold the general public's opinion on an issue or prompt it to contact the legislative body. *Political activity* can be defined as involvement in a political campaign, whether it is in support of or against a political candidate. Nonpartisan voter education or get-out-the-vote drives are not considered partisan political activity.

The IRS allows 501(c)(3) groups to engage in lobbying so long as it is not a "substantial part" of their activities. As this definition is quite ambiguous, charities (except churches) have an option to elect an expenditure test under Section 501(h) of the Internal Revenue Code. Political activity is strictly prohibited for any 501(c)(3) group, and private foundations may not engage in any lobbying or political activity at all. Federal grant funds may not be spent on lobbying activities.

What Lobbying Is *Not*

Many activities resemble lobbying but are not, because they do not fulfill the right criteria. By carefully drafting the message, it is possible to communicate effectively with the constituents without its becoming lobbying. The following activities do not count as lobbying:

- Communicating with the judicial or executive branch or administrative agencies
- Discussing broad issues that do not refer to a specific piece of legislation
- Providing a strong opinion on a specific piece of legislation but omitting a call for action
- Naming legislators in favor of or against an action and omitting a request to contact them

- Preparing and distributing a nonpartisan analysis of a legislative proposal
- Testifying for or providing assistance to a legislative committee after a written request
- Self-defense lobbying when the organization's future is threatened
- Lobbying as private citizens and not as representatives of the organization

When choosing the 501(h) option, an engaged charity may find itself in a better position for surveying and controlling its lobbying activities. Under this election, lobbying expenses can account for up to 20 percent of its first $500,000 of exempt expenditures. The dollar limit on total lobbying expenditure is $1 million, but only 25 percent of the permitted amount can be devoted to grassroots lobbying. Under the "substantial part test," the organization must include volunteer participation as a percentage of activity; under the expenditure test, only actual money spent or staff time expended counts. The expenditure is calculated over a four-year period, not annually.

Social welfare, or 501(c)(4) organizations, and 501(c)(6) trade associations may engage in lobbying activities without limits; in fact, that can sometimes be one of their main functions. These organizations are allowed to participate in political campaigns but may not exclusively operate for the benefit of one political party or candidate.

A violation of the IRS regulations may result in the nonprofit losing its tax-exempt status and/or an obligation to pay excise taxes on the money improperly spent. Naturally, an individual, even when associated with a nonprofit, can participate in any legal activity as a private citizen.

Nonpartisan Voter Participation

Nonpartisan voter activity involves providing assistance in voter registration without screening voters and planning voter participation drives without trying to affect the outcome. Specifically, this means that the organization does *not*

- Name candidates when encouraging people to vote
- Use registration lists to identify unregistered voters to target Republicans or Democrats
- Select areas in which to work because a certain candidate is a favorite there
- Define subgroups by political or ideological criteria

The organization may focus on specific minority groups even if statistical data indicate a political preference, subgroups tied to discrimination (race, gender, language, poor, unemployed), or subgroups sharing common problems (farmers, businesspeople). The organization must be able to provide contemporaneous reasoning for its activities and not rely on after-the-fact rationales. If questions arise, it must be able to show what motivated it to make decisions before the event.

Voter Education

When planning educational programs, an organization should pay attention to the following guidelines:

- Don't introduce new issues close to an election.
- Don't coordinate activities with a candidate's schedule.
- Focus on broad issues and avoid high-profile issues that already divide candidates.
- When organizing candidate forums, the organization should
  - Show no bias when choosing the location, assembling the expert panel, and allowing the candidates to express their opinions
  - Address issues that have regularly been concerns of the organization
  - Invite all viable candidates to the forum, even if they ultimately are not able to attend
  - Avoid editorializing in informational reports

Crisis Communications

When there is a crisis in a nonprofit organization, the board may be called on to perform nontraditional and unexpected duties in the communications arena. In an extraordinary situation, the board should expect to step in (temporarily) to help manage a crisis if the staff's ability to manage it may be questioned. Additionally, in any crisis, board members should work to convey consistent messages to their network of contacts in the community, letting them know that the issue is being well managed, promising updates on the situation, and inviting feedback to convey to the chief executive and staff.

Nonprofits generally deal with two types of crises: emergencies and controversies. Emergencies are unpredictable events that can cause havoc for an organization or the people it serves and harm its ability to deliver on its mission. They tend to cluster in one of five key types of disruptions:

- Physical or psychological injury to people
- Inability to continue important organization operations

- Damage to or destruction of facilities
- Financial loss
- Spillover effects from something that has affected some other person or organization

The responsibility for handling emergencies rests primarily with the staff, guided by disaster and risk-management plans, with board members providing collateral support where appropriate.

Controversies are crises that threaten the organization's reputation. Since the passage of the Sarbanes-Oxley Act, many nonprofits have updated their policies to ensure effective management oversight. But controversies can still blindside even the most prudent organization. Fraud accusations, legal disputes, or leadership conflicts can be devastating to an organization's integrity and effectiveness.

Responding to a controversy usually requires board involvement. The best way to deal with a crisis is before it happens, by preparing for the unexpected. Understanding that a problem may arise even though checks and balances are in place, the board and chief executive should make crisis communications planning an integral part of strategic communications planning.

Crisis Communications Planning

A crisis communications plan addresses five essential questions:

1. Who is responsible for managing the crisis, and what are his or her duties?
2. Where should the command center be for responding to the crisis? What resources will it need?
3. Who should be part of the crisis control team, and what are their responsibilities?
4. What information is appropriate to give to the public?
5. Who will speak for the organization?

A spokesperson (usually the chief executive) is designated to issue public statements, but a crisis control team should be formed to lead the planning, monitor ongoing crisis mitigation, and manage a crisis if one occurs. The team can be board driven or staff driven; a collaborative approach to crisis planning and management will ensure that both perspectives are involved. Team members could include a human resources specialist, a financial officer, and a legal authority for the organization. Above all, the team should comprise trusted people who can remain focused under pressure.

A good starting point in crisis communications planning is a board discussion centered on the following questions:

- What are the emergencies and controversies that could affect our organization?
- Where is the greatest possibility for us to encounter a problem?
- What are the questions we would least like to answer in the press?
- What would we not want to react to in a public forum?

With this foundation, the board and chief executive can lead the board in strategic thinking when considering crisis prevention and response strategies. Consider each type of emergency and identify possible crises that could affect the organization, how to mitigate them, and how to respond. What is the worst-case scenario? What should be done if the unthinkable actually happens? Consider controversies that could affect the organization as a whole. When should the board be involved, and when can the chief executive initiate actions independently?

The written crisis communications plan should include two parallel action plans: one that is staff driven and one that is board driven. The plan should also include the information needed for dealing with a crisis:

- Contact information for crisis control team members
- Contact information for key stakeholders (donors, members, government, media, policymakers, coalition or partnering organizations, and so on), in priority order, with contact information for the board or staff member designated to speak with each one
- Media strategy, including a press kit with fact sheets
- Essential policy statements
- Talking points or responses to frequently asked questions
- Logistics for establishing a command center, including location and materials needed
- Logistics for convening an emergency board meeting
- A communications tree or circle of contacts that spells out whom the crisis control team contacts, who notifies the press, who notifies board members, and who contacts key stakeholders; the strategy should include timelines for single-event and continuing controversy scenarios

In crisis communications planning, clear roles are essential. The three basic rules are to prepare for the worst, have a plan of action, and remain calm and in control if a crisis does occur.

The Board's Role in a Crisis or Controversy

Crises and controversies are rarely one-day stories. Events happen, people ask questions, more information becomes available, differing perspectives begin to emerge, and subsequent events shape perceptions of the original triggering event. It happens all the time. It is impossible to know in advance exactly how things will go wrong, or what sequence of events will occur. Thus it's essential to have a plan that ensures that, whatever the critical circumstances the priority stakeholders are kept informed, that all factual information is stored in a central location, and that there is a single spokesperson.

The board's fundamental task in a controversy is to ensure that the organization operates legally and ethically. Oversight mechanisms and internal controls should be in place before a crisis occurs—in particular, an explicit set of ethical values and standards that has been candidly discussed, established, and clearly communicated to stakeholders of the organization. The board should ensure that legal counsel and the auditor understand that their primary obligation is to the board. Risk assessment and administrative oversight procedures should be routinely reviewed.

The board should also consider whether there are policy controversies or other issue-related controversies in the event of which the board could have the authority to overrule the decisions of the chief executive and the staff. These situations need to be clearly defined, and policies should be developed that inform staff and the board what circumstances would trigger such extraordinary board intervention.

Board members play an essential role in communicating to the public during controversial situations. Because of the high sensitivity of these situations, the board must strike a careful balance between being appropriately transparent and not over-communicating before action has actually been taken. The following guidelines will help members manage during these fragile times:

1. Identify a crisis communication team that will be in charge of notifications and scripts.
2. Keep an updated list of the organization's key stakeholders.
3. Identify a spokesperson and a backup spokesperson for your organization—is this the chief executive or the board chair? Both? Someone else? Under what circumstances?
4. Train the spokesperson to deal with interview questions, trick questions, and tough questions.
5. Gather, and keep updated, information about your nonprofit organization (annual reports, fact sheets, news releases, phone books, and the like).

The board chair or secretary can serve as the repository for critical backup information.

6. Develop key messages (scripts), tailored to each internal and external stakeholder group.
7. List several alternative message dissemination modes available to you and match them to each stakeholder group.
8. Drill and rehearse the crisis communications plan.

Although planning cannot be expected to prevent a crisis, it can minimize the impact and prevent the collateral damage that happens when people are caught in a tense or desperate situation.

Eight Steps to a Crisis Communications Plan

1. Refer all inquiries to the identified spokesperson for the organization.
2. Clearly define the controversy, its scope, how it came to light, and what has been done to contain the situation.
3. Accept responsibility for what happened. Do not appear to be covering up. Do not minimize the seriousness of the problem.
4. Provide a quick analysis of the situation and its impact.
5. Be straightforward and candid. Acknowledge the situation and show appropriate emotions.
6. Indicate what steps are being taken and will continue to be taken to rectify the situation.
7. If appropriate, involve the community in taking action.
8. Commit to change, and explain how the organization will prevent a recurrence of the problem.

Monitoring Effectiveness

The board and staff share responsibilities for monitoring the effectiveness of strategic communications in this way:

• The staff conducts systematic strategic communications assessments to evaluate communications practices, determine what works well, and recommend improvements.

- The board monitors communications effectiveness, using the results of the assessments to determine whether strategic communications goals are being met and how communications efforts have helped the organization have a greater impact on its targeted audiences.

It is much easier to measure communications activities than it is to measure the overall impact of communications efforts. Boards routinely receive quantitative reports on staff activities: the number of people who attended events, the number of articles that occurred around a particular press release, or the dollar amounts generated by a particular donor appeal. But an organization must be able to measure impact—how an audience responds to communications activities. The goal is to assess the change resulting from an activity, not simply the amount and type of activity.

To measure impact, the board and staff must ask different questions: Did the targeted audience take action based on our communications efforts? How many people who attended the event signed the petition? Did the press releases use the organization's messages? Did press coverage generate phone calls or an increase in contributions? How did the latest donor appeal compare to donations received in response to other messages and outreach?

Nonprofit organizations that embrace a strategic communications approach will find themselves rewarded for their efforts. The development of a thoughtful communications plan ensures that everyone, board and staff alike, is working toward common purposes with a clear understanding of roles and responsibilities. The challenge to board members is to know what it really means to be an ambassador for their organization; to understand when and where it is necessary to have a proactive attitude rather than "business as usual"; and to support and work in concert with the staff in integrating all aspects of the organization into a strategic communications approach.

Chapter Exercises

- When we say that board members should act as the organization's ambassadors, how do you think they could best fulfill this role?
- Do you think a board member is always a board member, whether in the boardroom or carrying on private activities? Why or why not?
- If the media contacts a board member in reference to the organization, what should her response be?

- Do you think that private foundations should encourage and be allowed to fund lobbying activities? Why or why not?
- List ways that a charity could cut costs when involved in lobbying.
- Public charities are strictly prohibited from engaging in political campaigns for or against a candidate. Why do you think this is the case?

CHAPTER TWELVE

SUCCESSION PLANNING AND CHIEF EXECUTIVE TRANSITION

The search for a new chief executive is an extraordinary opportunity for a board to have a lasting impact on the growth and success of the organization it governs. If the process is approached as a journey about possibilities, it can be satisfying and even enjoyable for the participants. Yet there's no denying that it also tends to be a labor-intensive, high-stakes, and stressful institutional passage.

In addition to attending to the mechanics of the search, a board can alleviate the uncertainty that surrounds its choice—and thus avoid costly hiring mistakes—by putting into place a well-conceived succession plan. "Succession planning" does *not* refer to the practice of grooming an individual to become the next chief executive. Rather, it is an ongoing, systematic process that boards, with the help of their chief executives, can use to create an environment for chief executives to succeed from the very beginning of their terms until the cycle is repeated with their successors.

Succession planning is a cyclical process that starts with the hiring of a new chief executive and the development of an evaluation process with that new leader. It is also a proactive process that keeps management constantly aligned with the organization's strategic framework. The board should discuss and revise the succession plan regularly. Only then is it possible to create a culture for positive succession that allows the board to react wisely and in a timely manner when it needs to support the present chief executive or to choose the next leader.

About Succession Planning

Succession planning helps ensure that the most qualified person is always running the organization. Its aim is not necessarily to groom a successor or to determine ahead of time who the next chief executive should be. A good plan proposes guidelines and options for action when that action is necessary. The steps of the plan are activated regardless of whether the present chief executive's departure is planned or unexpected.

To stay on top of things, the board should continually and faithfully evaluate its own performance, the performance of the present chief executive, and the success of the organization in fulfilling its mission (see Chapter Thirteen, Evaluation). The results of these three assessments are the underpinning of effective succession planning. They provide the reasoning and direction of the plan, and they help foster a healthy atmosphere in the organization and among board members.

A succession plan includes the following elements:

- An up-to-date job description for the chief executive
- Clear annual performance expectations for the chief executive
- Measurable indicators for the performance of the entire organization
- Determination, at regular intervals, whether the organization is going in the right direction and what the key qualities of the chief executive should be
- Assumption that the chief executive must be capable of taking the organization to its expected level of performance
- A process for hiring a new chief executive
- Options for managing the executive transition period
- Emergency measures for unexpected loss of the chief executive
- Safeguards for keeping the board undivided and focused on the future

Benefits of Succession Planning

Every chief executive leaves the organization sooner or later—because of retirement, health, death, or reassessment of personal priorities, or because the board decides that it is time for the chief executive to go. By having a process in place to guide its actions, the board can avoid knee-jerk solutions or quick-fix decisions. Being prepared allows the board to save time, because it can focus immediately on preevaluated options and eliminate unnecessary steps that do not fit the present situation. By maintaining succession planning as a part of its regular strategic approach, the board can reduce the human drama of a leadership transition.

Who Is Involved

The board is ultimately responsible for creating a succession plan, keeping the plan up to date, and executing the plan. Naturally, it never is wise to proceed in isolation. Feedback from those affected by the final decision (staff, donors, other constituents) helps the board to stay on track and choose the right options as the plan is implemented. An exit interview with the departing chief executive can provide invaluable information. When assessing organizational performance, an outside consultant can offer an unbiased view.

Obstacles to Succession Planning

Probably the main stumbling block for a workable plan is the tendency to misunderstand its scope. Succession planning is not limited to hiring a new chief executive or even planning for the executive transition. These important components of the plan must be addressed properly, but to focus on only one segment of the process would be to ignore the preparation that makes these steps successful.

Another obstacle is equating succession planning with internal grooming. In the for-profit sector it is common to train an insider for the leadership position. In the nonprofit world, where the bottom line is not the only criteria for success, it is impossible to determine the wanted qualities and characteristics of the next leader until a new person must be chosen. Limited resources, however, are not an excuse for failing to determine what skills the next chief executive should possess, how that leader will be found, and what kind of environment the board will create for the chief executive.

A Chief Executive Succession Planning Checklist

1. Is there a current and adequate written job description that clearly spells out the responsibilities of the chief executive?
2. Is there a climate of mutual trust and respect between the board and the chief executive?
3. Do board members understand their roles and responsibilities?
4. Is there agreement between the board and the chief executive on their respective roles and mutual expectations?
5. Does the board have a constructive process for reviewing the chief executive's performance, salary, and benefits on a regular basis?
6. Does the board have a regular and effective process for assessing its own performance?

(Continued)

7. Do board members support the current mission statement?

8. Do the board and the chief executive have a collective vision of how the organization should be evolving over the next three to five years?

9. Does the work of the board and staff reflect defined institutional directions and goals?

10. Does the board have a clear understanding of the financial condition of the organization?

11. Does the board have in place emergency transition management policies in the event that the chief executive is not able to serve or departs suddenly?

Developing a Compensation Policy

Before the executive search gets under way, the organization should have in place a well-thought-out compensation philosophy—expressed in a compensation policy (see Exhibit 12.1 for an example)—that provides ongoing guidance to the organization on staff compensation in general and supports the immediate goal of developing a chief executive compensation plan. For a discussion of compensation policies and guidance for developing one, see Chapter Fourteen, Bylaws and Policies.

Chief Executive Transition

Successful executive transitions require solid planning and good thinking about where the organization is, where it wants to go, and what kind of leadership it needs to get there. Here are some guidelines:

- *Don't rush the process.* If a board is concerned about a potential gap in executive leadership, it should consider hiring an interim executive. Rushing the process can lead to sloppy decision making and cause the board to settle for a lesser candidate.
- *Strive for a good ending; it leads to a good beginning.* Taking the high road with an executive who has behaved badly sets a positive, intentional tone for the future. If the departing executive is a beloved leader, the board needs to make sure that person is appropriately acknowledged; this allows people to come to closure.
- *Engage the staff and reap rewards.* Engaging staff in the transition helps ensure that the board's decisions reflect the organization's actual needs. It also helps

to reduce staff members' anxiety and to build their buy-in for the transition outcome. Consider including staff members on the transition committee.

EXHIBIT 12.1. SAMPLE COMPENSATION POLICY

- The compensation structure and systems of our organization will support our mission, strategy, and values.
- We will pay for performance, skills and competencies, development and growth, and effective visible commitment to the organization.
- The compensation system will encourage recruitment, retention, and motivation of outstanding employees so that the organization can achieve its mission and objectives.
- The compensation system will reward truly outstanding performers and provide appropriate feedback to staff members who need improvement.
- Our compensation structure will be a mixture of base salary, performance-based "at risk" pay appropriate to the nonprofit marketplace, retirement and other benefits, and special recognition awards as merited by performance.
- A portion of each employee's pay will be tied to the achievement of organizational and individual objectives. Unusual individual achievement may also merit special financial awards.
- Our compensation system will include annual adjustments to pay ranges based on changes in the marketplace (subject to financial constraints). Adjustments to individual base pay will be based on job performance and growth in mastering job competencies. All adjustments to pay will be consistent with practice in the nonprofit marketplace.
- The compensation system will have a coherent structure based on pay practices consistent with our not-for-profit mission and status, but will recognize that parts of our organization are in different markets and that the compensation for each position must be based on the appropriate marketplace for that professional area.
- We will pay as close as possible to the median (midpoint) of the appropriate external marketplace, while recognizing that internal equity and financial constraints can justify some deviation from the market.
- The marketplace adequacy of the structure will be judged in terms of total compensation, including benefits; the total package will be competitive with the marketplace.
- The compensation structure will be linked to an effective performance management system with individual growth and development as well as professional achievement goals. The goals will be accompanied by effective benchmarks for measuring success.
- Executives and staff will receive regular and comprehensive training in the compensation system.

- *Begin with the end in mind.* The transition process is an opportunity to put the organization on a stronger footing. Boards should enter the process with the following goals:
  - Finding and hiring an executive who fits the organization's current and future leadership needs
  - Addressing organizational issues that surface during the transition and working to resolve them
  - Securing the board's and staff's commitment to work effectively with the new executive
  - Achieving agreement between the board and the new executive about priorities, roles, expectations, and performance measures

- *Come to terms with history.* While honoring what's been accomplished and applying lessons from the past, the board should close the books on the departing executive's tenure and give the new executive a fresh set of pages to work with. The board risks a failed transition if it isn't attentive to the environment that the new leader is stepping into. The organization may need to come to grips with persistent issues or past behaviors that could inhibit the effectiveness of the new executive.
- *Step up and support the new executive.* The first few months are the most critical of the new executive's tenure. The board and executive should clarify goals, roles, expectations, and performance measures. The board also should provide the executive with any needed support, such as professional development to round out skill sets and/or coaching or mentoring to address specific challenges.

Steps in the Transition

Although each transition occurs under somewhat different circumstances, boards can prepare to take certain steps to manage the transition in the most seamless way possible. The board that has thought through the entire process, from the first inkling of change to the last, will be far better prepared for that change than the board that leaves the process to chance.

Managing the Departure

Every transition begins with a departure. It could be a planned departure, for which the executive has given ample notice. On the other hand, it could be an abrupt departure, with the executive leaving quickly to pursue a new opportunity.

Or the departure may involve challenging circumstances such as the firing of the executive because of poor performance, improprieties, or perhaps even a scandal. In some extremely unfortunate circumstances, the transition may have been precipitated by the death or serious illness of the executive. The advice of an attorney or a human resources professional can help clarify state and federal laws governing such issues as dismissal and confidentiality.

Managing an Executive Transition: The First Five Days

The first five days after an executive's departure becomes official are a crucial time. Regardless of the circumstances, the departure management process is the same: organize, stabilize, understand, plan, and execute. However, these steps will necessarily differ depending on whether the departure is abrupt or planned.

The Planned Departure. When the executive is giving several months' notice, the board has more time to launch and execute its transition plan. But the initial planning and assessment process is just as urgent.

Organize

- Appoint a transition committee.
- Hold organizing meeting(s) to address the steps that follow.
- Define the departing executive's role during the transition.

Stabilize

- Attend to the staff.
- Consider having the board chair and/or other board leaders meet with the staff along with the departing chief executive, if necessary.
- Review plans for addressing any current staff vacancies.

Understand

- Assess the organization—its finances, systems, staffing, governance, and current strategic direction.
- Unpack the current chief executive's job and encourage delegation of extraneous duties.
- Ask the departing executive to develop a handoff report that outlines key contacts, grants and contracts, major deadlines, internal and external liabilities and obligations, and the executive's sense of the organization's current situation and future direction.

Plan

- Develop an initial timeline covering at least the first phase of the transition, including assignments for board and staff. (This can be a living document that the board updates as the situation becomes clearer and uncertainties have been addressed.)
- Prepare a public statement and talking points about the departure to ensure that all board members are on the same page in their communications.
- Identify a spokesperson, typically the departing executive and/or board chair, to respond to media inquiries, if necessary (see the Execute elements for more on communications).

Execute

- Work the plan.
- Communicate with the staff and key stakeholders.
- Provide assurance that the board is working diligently to plan a successful transition.
- Work with the departing executive to inform any funders with whom the organization has grants or contracts.

The Abrupt Departure. If an executive has left or is leaving abruptly, the first step for the board should always be to pull out its emergency succession or backup plan for the executive role, if one exists, and begin to follow it. If a plan does not exist, this is the time for the board to carefully—but swiftly—determine who will be in charge of the daily affairs until a more comprehensive approach has been defined.

The key to success in these challenging circumstances is for the board to strive for a good ending so there can be a good beginning. This means trying for the best possible ending with the departing executive so there is a sense of completion, with no unfinished business. Key elements of each of the five process steps are as follows:

Organize

- Appoint a transition committee (traditionally known as the search committee).
- Hold organizing meeting(s) to address the steps that follow.
- Resolve any key problems with the exiting leader before transition planning can begin in earnest.
- Address the need for interim leadership by hiring an interim chief executive or appointing an acting chief executive.

Stabilize

- Address any financial crises facing the organization.
- Attend to the staff by arranging a meeting in which the board chair and/or other board leaders can hear the staff's story and concerns, provide appropriate assurance, and inform staff of initial plans for the transition.
- Meet with or contact key funders to make sure they are informed and aware that the board is taking decisive action.

Understand

- Make sure the board understands the organization's financial situation, its contracts, and other external obligations.
- Review personnel policies to ensure that the board understands the organization's obligations to the departing executive for unpaid leave, insurance, and so on.
- If possible, conduct an exit interview with the departing executive to acquire critical information, such as the status of contracts.
- If the board is discharging the executive, secure legal advice to discuss the terms of separation and to review related documents.
- Inform the auditor of the situation and determine whether a special audit may be needed.

Plan

- Develop an initial timeline covering at least the first phase of the transition, including assignments for board and staff. (This can be a living document that the board updates as the situation becomes clearer and uncertainties have been addressed.)
- Prepare a public statement and talking points about the departure, to ensure that all board members are on the same page in their communications.
- Identify a spokesperson to respond to media inquiries, if necessary (see the Execute elements for more on communications).

Execute

- Work the plan.
- Communicate with the staff and key stakeholders.
- Provide assurance that the board is working diligently to make sure the organization will come out of this situation in good shape—and even stronger.
- Update any funders with whom the organization has grants or contracts.

- Secure keys and computer passwords from the departing executive, as well as any organizational property, such as credit cards, laptop, and cell phone.
- Change the signatories on all financial accounts.

Announcing the Departure

An organization's key stakeholders—including major donors, key institutional funders, and any collaboration partners—will want to hear about the transition early and from the board directly. Allowing these stakeholders to find out about the departure through the grapevine might have a serious negative effect on the organization's important relationships.

The goal is to communicate with clarity and in a way that inspires confidence among stakeholders. The board does not need a detailed transition plan at this point, just a list of top-level actions that will help stakeholders see how the organization plans to handle the transition, along with a rough timetable. If appropriate, the board also can inform stakeholders about how they can be helpful to the organization during the transition.

Except in cases of involuntary separation, the executive is usually the one who drives the departure communications. The executive and the board chair should work together on a rough outline or understanding about how the departure communications will be handled.

In challenging circumstances involving the involuntary departure of an executive or a scandal or organizational crisis, communications with staff, key funders, and others takes on heightened importance. It's a natural tendency for the board to want to deal with the messy ending first and get things settled, *then* communicate. But a better approach is to communicate appropriately while the board is dealing with the circumstances. Priority should be given to providing key constituencies with what they're looking for: assurance that the board is on top of the situation and engaged in thoughtful planning.

Communicating with staff. Of any group, the staff probably has the most at stake in the transition—professionally and personally—and probably feels the most vulnerable. The board will want to ensure stability and calm among the staff members. It is important to have a board member, ideally the board chair, on hand to announce the departure to the staff and answer questions. The announcement also could be made by the departing chief executive (if that person is leaving on good terms). The board chair would then speak to the organization's plans for the transition, the role that staff might play during the transition process, and other issues.

If the departure involves some controversy, or if the chief executive has been terminated, several board members might be involved in the departure announcement and then have follow-up, one-on-one meetings with management team members and other key staff. Abrupt departures are unsettling and potentially destabilizing to the staff. It typically takes more than one session with the staff to help settle things down.

Clarifying Roles in the Transition

Executive transitions call on the board to step up to a higher level of engagement and to lead the organization through a crucial period that will determine its future course. Although much of the board's work will be carried out through the work of the transition committee, the larger board still has an important role. At the same time, there is also an important role in the transition for the departing chief executive—again, assuming that person is leaving the organization on friendly terms.

The Board. The board's role is to set out the expectations that define success for the transition and to ensure that the process addresses any legacy issues facing the organization. The board ensures that

- Transition planning considers where the organization stands and where it is headed so that the job of the incoming executive is calibrated to address the future
- Diversity and cultural competency considerations are factored into planning
- The organization is stable during the transition (especially in situations of an abrupt transition or a messy departure)

At the same time that the board is stepping into its leadership role in the transition, it also must engage in a thorough assessment of its own practices and the extent to which it is prepared to work with a new executive. What is the board's strategic contribution toward the vision of the organization? How should the board govern in light of that vision and the type of executive it is trying to recruit? The answers to these questions will go a long way toward shaping constructive preparation work and providing the energy and enthusiasm the board needs to push forward with any changes in its structure, practices, or approach.

The Transition Committee. This is an ad hoc committee whose purpose is to plan and oversee the entire executive transition process. Typically, the duration of the committee's appointment is from the beginning of the transition through the successful completion of the installation of the new executive.

Ideally, the transition committee is a small team of five to seven people. It should include past, current, and prospective future board leaders. Many organizations include a senior member of the staff on the committee, but this person should not be a prospective candidate for the chief executive position. In these instances, the staff member usually is not involved in interviews—especially the final interview—nor in selection deliberations when the board needs to speak very frankly about the finalists' merits. In most cases, the board chair or another officer chairs the committee.

The transition committee has five key responsibilities:

- Planning and overseeing communications with internal and external stakeholders
- Ensuring healthy closure with the departing executive and clarifying that person's role in the transition process
- Planning the hiring and transition activities
- Managing the hiring and transition process
- Providing a healthy start for the new executive

The Departing Chief Executive. The departing chief executive should focus on leading and managing the organization, not leading the transition. Typically, the departing executive supports the transition process through a range of activities and responsibilities, such as these:

- *Preparing the platform for the successor.* This may include strengthening the organization's financial position, staff, and systems, and helping to strengthen the board.
- *Acting as a key information resource during the planning and execution of the search and selection.* This may include taking part in the planning work leading up to the search, meeting with the finalists to answer questions, and providing information that will help them and the board make a better choice. However, the departing executive should not sit in on interviews.
- *Ensuring a successful handoff to the incoming executive.* This may include working with the transition committee to plan the orientation process for the new executive; consulting with the new executive on the handoff; and proactively handing off key relationships, particularly those with donors.

Organizations often find it valuable to have an ongoing relationship with the departing executive—for example, by signing a consulting contract that makes the departing executive available as a resource to the new executive for a short time. However, the succeeding executive must be in charge of the relationship. It is not advisable to have the departing executive move into a board role or assume a fundraising or programmatic leadership role.

Working with Consultants

Sometimes the board lacks members with prior experience in hiring executives or in human resources. In such cases, organizations sometimes retain one of three types of consulting assistance to bring expertise, time, and ready contacts to help the board meet the transition challenge:

- Specialty consultants with subject-matter expertise and skills in strategic planning, board development, human resources, and other areas identified as priorities for the organization during the transition
- Executive transition consultants, who marry expertise in transition management and planning with the capacity to conduct an executive search
- Executive search consultants, who focus exclusively on helping organizations find a new chief executive

The decision about which type of consulting help it needs—and whether it needs outside help at all—will depend on an honest assessment of the situation by the transition committee and the larger board.

Acting and Interim Chief Executives

Every nonprofit organization going through a transition needs to clarify who's in charge. Appointing an interim or acting chief executive can give the board the breathing space it needs to make a good choice about the permanent executive and ensure that the organization is prepared to work more effectively with that new staff leader. Not every organization in transition will need an interim executive, but a good interim executive can be a powerful partner with the board to build the capacity of the organization during the transition period. Both research and practice demonstrate that groups that employ a skilled interim executive emerge from the transition as stronger organizations.

Organizations generally turn to one of the following approaches for ensuring temporary coverage of the chief executive's role:

- *Acting chief executive.* A senior manager or other insider who is appointed to provide bridge management during the interim period, with a temporary salary adjustment. He or she then returns to the previous role on the staff. In some cases, the acting executive is a candidate for the permanent position.

• *Interim chief executive.* Typically a seasoned executive from outside the organization who, like the acting chief executive, provides bridge leadership during the interim period. An important responsibility of the interim executive is to help prepare the organization to work more effectively with the incoming permanent executive. A good interim executive deals with the day-to-day affairs of the organization, while at the same time building the platform for the permanent successor. As a rule, the interim executive should not be a candidate for the permanent position.

• *Transition chief executive.* An executive from inside or outside the organization who is appointed for an extended period, often twelve to twenty-four months or more. The transition chief executive's job is to turn around an organization experiencing serious problems or to realign an underperforming organization.

Other options for ensuring bridge leadership for the organization include (1) making no change, based on the assumption that the staff can continue without a chief executive for a limited period; (2) temporary leadership by a board member; or (3) leadership by a management team of senior staff.

Boards should consider the following key points when hiring or appointing a temporary chief executive:

• *Look for management experience, not just familiarity with the organization's programs.* The interim chief executive's role is not a job-training opportunity. Typically, the most successful interim executives are mid- to late-career professionals. Management experience is paramount; experience in the organization's particular program area is probably less essential.

• *Don't look through the same lens the board will use for the permanent executive's position.* Look for a match between experience and transition priorities. If, for example, the organization is laboring under an inadequate financial information system, the board may want to look for a temporary executive who has particular strength in that area as well as the capacity to bridge the leadership/management role.

• *Consider cultural competency.* Boards should consider hiring an interim executive whose background and demographic profile reflect the community served by the organization. Such an individual can bring cultural competency and important insights to the organization that can help ensure the success of the transition.

• *Look for a leadership style that matches the dynamics of the transition.* Successful interim executives tend to be action-oriented but collaborative in their approach, with well-honed listening skills. They help the organization pursue its change agenda, but always in close collaboration with the board and in consultation with the staff. The interim period typically is not a time to take on bold new initiatives, nor is it a time for the interim executive to pursue that person's solo agenda or vision for the organization.

- *Look for flexibility.* Executive searches often take longer than anticipated. Boards should ensure that the interim chief executive is available beyond what may be an optimistic timeline.
- *Think twice before appointing a board member as the acting or interim executive.* Sometimes a board member will throw a hat into the ring, or the board will actively seek the candidacy of a board member believed to have the time and interest to lead the organization on a temporary basis. But as the board considers what it needs in a temporary executive, familiarity with the organization should not supersede the executive skills needed to manage and lead during a time of transition.

Conducting the Search

All of the organization's planning, as well as all of its hard thinking about the future and the kind of leadership it needs, will now come to a head as the board sets out to find the best candidate for the chief executive job. A successful search requires the board to always refer back to the goals and vision laid out earlier in the transition process. An organization may never find the "perfect candidate" for the job, but the board should not compromise as it looks for someone with the fundamental skills and qualifications that are required to stabilize the organization and create a successful future.

Pre-Search Assessment

If the board has been engaged recently (and deeply) in strategic or long-range planning, then transition planning might start with revisiting key elements of the strategic plan and moving directly into a discussion about what skills and characteristics the organization needs in a chief executive in order to accomplish its goals. If a strategic plan is nonexistent or out of date, the transition planning work will have to begin at a more fundamental level.

Board and staff leaders can clarify current and future leadership needs by focusing on the following three sets of strategic questions in a series of meetings or a mini-retreat:

1. *Where do we stand as an organization?* What's our mission? Who are our customers? What are our successes? What are our core competencies? What are our strengths and weaknesses?

2. *Where are we headed?* What's our long-term strategic direction? What is our vision for the next three to five years? What challenges are we facing on the immediate horizon? What opportunities can be captured? What does future success look like?

3. *What kind of leadership do we need?* If there is a gap between our present and our desired future, what kind of leadership will it take to close the gap? What does our assessment of where we stand and where we are headed tell us about any pivots or changes the board may need to make? What does it tell us about the priorities for the first year of the new executive's tenure?

Listing the Desired Characteristics

At a minimum, the board should sign off on a description of the desired competencies, character, personality, and experience that a new chief executive should have. Even better, a number of people—including staff members, board members, major donors, and leaders in your sector—can list what characteristics a new chief executive should have for the current stage in the organization's life cycle (see the following sidebar for some suggestions).

It's important to define what the organization needs *before* focusing on particular candidates and their personalities. If the organization has been on a growth trajectory, for example, it may want to look for a chief executive who has experience leading a larger group. Or perhaps, given the board's recent approval of a capital campaign case statement, someone with a fundraising background would be a good fit.

Characteristics of a Chief Executive

VISION BEARER

The chief executive must be skilled at articulating and promoting the vision and mission that guide the organization. People follow men and women who know where they are going. In startup organizations, the chief executive is often the founder and keeper of the vision that attracts board members, volunteers, and donors. The vision creates excitement. Sustaining that initial excitement depends heavily on the chief executive. In a mature organization—one that has had, say, five or more chief executives—the chief executive must sometimes move slowly in changing the vision because so many are now aware of it and believe in it. But he or she must embrace the vision and find new ways for people to relate to it.

Persuasive or Motivational

A chief executive, by definition, must motivate other people to accomplish activities in support of the vision or mission. A board needs a chief executive who can explain, persuade, and empower others to do their best. Paid and volunteer staff members need to know why they do what they do. Donors must understand the purpose and the opportunity to help financially.

Many different styles seem to work for chief executives in meeting this test. Some quietly model what they want others to see and follow. Many are particularly gifted at oral persuasion or at wielding a creative pen. A few can persuade by the sheer strength of their domineering personalities, although depending on guilt, intimidation, or obligation is typically a short-term leadership style. Motivation comes after the first wave of enthusiasm. Being a good persuader and being a motivator go hand in hand.

Ethical

The best chief executives don't stop at what they perceive to be expected ethical behavior. They go the extra mile, challenging board members, staff, and donors to be above reproach in all areas.

Many ethical traps lurk for participants in a nonprofit organization. Sometimes a law is misunderstood; sometimes a donor tempts one to compromise in return for a gift. Friends may ask for favors they shouldn't be given. But people see the successful chief executive as committed to what is good and honest. When mistakes are uncovered, this type of chief executive is willing to face the music and correct what is wrong.

Focused on Strengths

Top chief executives do not try to do all things or be all things to all people. They focus on their strengths to achieve the productivity they enjoy, and they manage their weaknesses—often through delegation.

Decisive

After gathering information and involving other key people, the chief executive must be able to make decisions in a timely fashion. Whether it is a quiet, personal decision following private reflection or a group decision facilitated by the chief executive, the fundamental role of good leaders is to make the call.

Startup organizations are often managed by visionaries, who reach their goals by being flexible. As their organizations grow, however, a decision made late—or never made at all—has a negative effect. One way to compensate is to appoint a chief operating officer who makes decisions easily and put him or her in charge of daily operations. Then the strategic decisions are left to the chief executive, but routine decisions are someone else's responsibility.

(Continued)

Organized or Disciplined

Discipline in personal life carries over to discipline in organizational life. Well-organized chief executives know how to manage their schedules to keep family, friends, leisure, and work in balance. They manage their finances well enough to keep themselves and their organizations free from constant money crises. They track their work so they know when goals are reached. They delegate tasks that others can do as well or better.

A chief executive who is not well organized needs a solid staff structure as a support and to get the day-to-day tasks accomplished.

Strategic

In the corporate world, buying, selling, merging, joint venturing, subcontracting, and outsourcing are common practices because they increase profits. Nonprofits, too, can improve their bottom line by reaching out to other groups in the independent sector, to businesses, to media corporations, and to government agencies. They need a chief executive with the strategic vision, inventiveness, and diplomatic skills to bring together very different organizations to accomplish a shared goal.

Energetic

Chief executives always have new people to meet, literature to read, travel to schedule, and meetings to attend. If a chief executive is not naturally endowed with high energy, he or she must learn how to generate energy through proper exercise, diet, and rest and how to conserve energy through good planning, wise decision making, and a readiness to delegate.

Writing the Position Description

Any chief executive is asked to achieve the intended results within the policy parameters set by the board. But candidates will want to see what the board expects the chief executive to accomplish, how the position relates to the board, and what the specific duties are. Each search should begin with a new description that reflects the organization's current and evolving needs.

The description of the board's style in governing the organization should be clear, as should the duties of the job itself. A prospective chief executive must understand and agree with the board's expectations for how their roles work together to accomplish the organization's mission. If that doesn't happen, another executive search will be on the horizon.

Identifying Candidates and Narrowing the Field

Contacting a broad group of people who know good prospects is the primary way to build a list of potential candidates. An e-mail or letter inviting nominations, sent to several hundred key constituents and leaders in the field by the board chair or the transition committee chair, is well worth the effort. Often, top candidates are satisfied with their current jobs and are contacted because someone nominated them without their knowledge.

Well-placed ads and announcements in print publications and online non-profit employment sites can also help get the word out. As applicants and nominees become known, the transition committee should send information on the organization's mission and goals and the desired qualifications of a new chief executive. Include a request for a letter of interest, a resume, and the names of references.

The candidates for the chief executive's position may include a senior staff member or two. But even if the transition committee suspects that an internal candidate might be the best choice for chief executive, it should complete all the steps in the search process; an even better candidate might surface along the way. Board members should fully expect the departure of any staff member who applies for the chief executive position but isn't selected.

When the announced deadline has passed, the transition committee narrows the field to a short list of three to seven candidates who appear to meet the criteria set early in the process. The transition committee chair or committee members should call these individuals to ask whether they wish to be considered active candidates. Some of them may be happily situated in their current positions and need more information about what the organization has to offer. It's desirable to have candidates who are drawn to the mission. And the board should expect a challenge in winning the interest of some good nominees.

Depending on time, distance, and funding, candidates on the short list typically are screened at length by phone after a few reference checks. Questions should be thoughtfully selected in advance and given to the transition committee members who make the phone calls.

The committee will arrive at the final two or three candidates after conducting a personal interview, several phone interviews, six to eight reference checks, and perhaps a credit check. They'll need to keep the process moving, but still be thorough.

Negotiating with the Final Candidate

The full board votes on the final selection, as recommended by the transition committee. On behalf of the full board, the transition committee should present a written offer. Give the candidate a few days to review the draft appointment document, which will be signed by both parties, and to suggest changes. When the board and the new chief executive make verbal agreements, too many assumptions result, and uncomfortable situations can arise later.

Launching the New Chief Executive

The board and organization have made a significant investment in finding a new executive. The post-hire process is about making the most of that investment. It is the board's responsibility to help the new executive start off on the right foot, to structure the board-executive relationship in a positive way, and to make sure it achieves the priorities identified in the planning stage of the transition.

Announcing the Appointment

The new executive's appointment will be of interest to a range of stakeholders in the organization's work, from clients and community members to major donors and the press. Planning the announcement involves targeting the organization's audiences, identifying the vehicles to reach those audiences, and developing messages and materials for the announcement. At a minimum, the announcement materials might include a press release, a biography and photo of the new executive, and a letter to stakeholders.

The announcement of a new chief executive is an opportunity to do more than simply tout the incoming leader's credentials. It is also a chance for the board to signal a new direction or vision for the organization, particularly for those organizations that are making a significant pivot or change with this transition. Similarly, the announcement can be an opportunity to create further alignment and buy-in among key stakeholders in the organization's success.

Providing Support and Beginning to Build the Relationship

Early investment in developing the board-executive relationship is important. This takes attention and work from both the board and the executive, but the payoff can be enormous in terms of increasing the mission impact of the organization, not to mention the clarity and resulting job satisfaction for board members and the new executive alike.

In addition to facilitating the new executive's adjustment to the job, the board should continue the conversations about expectations for the chief executive's performance. This feedback is essential for the chief executive's success in his or her leadership role. For a discussion of evaluating performance, see Chapter Thirteen.

The following key steps ensure that the board is providing necessary support:

- A thorough orientation for the new executive
- Carefully assembled essential information and materials about the organization's finances, policies, and more

- Introductions at community forums, executive sessions with other nonprofit leaders, and other events
- Joint visits by board members and the new executive to key donors and organizational partners
- Training, coaching, or other professional development opportunities for the new executive, as needed
- A ninety-day entry plan for the new executive, identifying key short-term challenges and opportunities, along with orientation and learning priorities
- A collaborative leadership agenda for the organization identifying short-term strategic priorities
- A plan for monitoring the new executive's performance

Chapter Exercises

- What differences distinguish succession planning, chief executive transition, and emergency planning?
- How should the leaving chief executive be involved in the succession planning and transition process?
- Discuss the benefits of hiring an outside interim chief executive. What are the pros and cons of a board member acting as the interim chief executive?
- Think of good questions to ask the finalists for the chief executive position.

CHAPTER THIRTEEN

EVALUATION

Evaluating mission achievement ranks high in importance among a board's responsibilities. As mission stewards, board members do more than monitor financial performance and receive programmatic updates. Results-oriented boards take on the more difficult task of measuring overall efficiency, effectiveness, and impact. Taking care to collaborate with staff without micromanaging, they focus on outcomes, not inputs. And they think purposefully about indicators of excellence and the infrastructure that excellence requires.

Evaluation, at a basic level, is figuring out something's value or worth by looking at it carefully. The term suggests a subjective process. But evaluation that is implemented systematically by a results-oriented board helps an organization move beyond subjectivity and introduces a level of objectivity to important management decisions.

Meaningful evaluation is a form of internal learning. When organizations conduct evaluation only to prove that they've done what they said they would do, they miss a significant opportunity for mission achievement. It's up to the board to promote a culture of continuous evaluation, beginning with assessing their own effectiveness and including evaluating the performance of the organization and its major programs and services.

The board's responsibility for evaluation focuses on measurement of organizational effectiveness; self-assessment for the full board; self-assessment for individual board members; and performance evaluation for the chief executive. The staff is responsible for evaluating an organization's core programs, as well as areas such as fundraising, finance, marketing, and human resources. The board ensures that these assessments take place regularly, while respecting the clear boundaries between board and staff roles. For both board and staff, evaluation results provide a learning tool to gain a comprehensive view of whether the organization is effective at achieving its mission.

Ten Ways Boards Can Use Evaluation Findings

1. *Assessing the chief executive:* Use program evaluation findings to hold the chief executive accountable for decreases or increases in client outcomes and program quality.

2. *Fundraising:* Use findings to inspire potential donors by telling and showing the mission story with facts and figures.

3. *Recruiting board members:* Share the organization's successes and challenges from a mission perspective, motivating individuals to bring their experience to bear in a way that is mission-focused.

4. *Strategic planning:* Use evaluation findings to assess the strengths and weaknesses of the organization's programs, identify opportunities and threats to the programs, and make resource acquisition and allocation decisions for mission success three to five years down the road.

5. *Managing finances:* Use findings about nonmonetary but essential resources (such as time, experience, expertise, facilities, and equipment) to ensure that money is allocated for them.

6. *Assessing the organization:* Use findings about program success as a yardstick for assessing how well key organizational functions (such as knowledge management, program staff assessment and development, volunteer management, and joint programming efforts with other nonprofits) support program delivery.

7. *Celebrating success:* Use findings to provide praise and recognition to staff.

8. *Business planning:* Use findings to develop replicable programs and services that could generate a fee-for-service revenue stream.

9. *Managing human resources:* Use program quality findings as a tool for providing more directed professional development and for conducting annual performance reviews.

10. *Deciding to engage in a strategic alliance with other nonprofits:* Use findings to identify resource needs for improving service delivery that could be addressed by collaborating or partnering with other nonprofit organizations.

Evaluating Organizational Effectiveness

Nonprofit organizational effectiveness describes the capacity to sustain the staff, infrastructure, resources, strategies, and other elements that support achievement of mission. Corporate boards always keep an eye on the bottom line to maximize return on investment for shareholders. Now nonprofit organizations are increasingly being asked to document and assess results or bottom-line indicators so that funders and the public can determine whether an organization is achieving the kind of results its clients and constituents demand—and doing so efficiently and effectively.

Many nonprofit boards are used to monitoring financial performance and program progress, but fewer boards pay attention to the broader and more complex task of measuring impact. Evaluating organizational effectiveness is directly linked to expressing and monitoring mission. In fact, it seems clear that a board can't know whether the organization is fulfilling its mission without an intentional commitment to assessing impact. Board and staff work together to decide on critical indicators based on mission, vision, and strategic priorities, as well as a consideration of community needs, comparable organizations, and the operating environment.

A Basic Formula

This simple formula illustrates the components of an organizational evaluation:

Internal effectiveness + external results = orgnizational effectiveness

Organizational effectiveness takes into account performance in a variety of organizational areas, including

- Program impact and outcomes
- Service coordination (including systems such as management information)
- Financial stability
- Staff qualifications, tenure, and turnover
- Visibility (including the ability to get the word out and attract clients or audiences)

The SWOT analysis or the analysis of the organization's external and internal contexts, conducted during strategic planning (see Chapter Ten), are evaluation tools that can also contribute useful information (especially qualitative data) to an analysis of organizational effectiveness. Sometimes, in preparing for an analysis, an organization surveys its internal and external stakeholders for their perceptions of its strengths and weaknesses. The information external stakeholders provide can be more a matter of perception, but the information internal stakeholders provide highlights what is and is not working in an organization. Two other types of evaluation—discussed later in this chapter—are linked to organizational success: assessing the chief executive's performance and assessing the board's performance.

The Organizational Evaluation Process

Five questions guide development of an organizational evaluation process:

1. *What do you currently measure?* There's no need to reinvent the wheel. Many organizations collect data from their Web sites, customer or constituent surveys, and other sources that can form the basis of ongoing measurement.
2. *What or who is driving the need for measurement?* Whether it's a new funder, the board chair, or the chief executive who's asking, being clear and honest about why the organization needs information is the first step toward a positive, effective review.
3. *Are you measuring "process" or "outcomes"?* Process focuses on what the organization does and how well; outcomes identify the difference it makes. This distinction is an important step toward confirming the vision of success and developing key indicators that reflect progress toward that vision.
4. *Is the information you collect mission-critical?* Some information is easy to quantify but ultimately says little about what the organization really accomplishes. The process should narrow your scope to what's truly important—and relatively easy to obtain.
5. *Can you attribute your outcomes to your work?* The mission is likely aimed at a long-term objective, such as improving the lives of people in the community. But what are the short-term goals? For example, think about how the organization increases awareness through education, promotion, or advocacy.

Ultimately, organizations have to decide what success looks like for them. What goals have they established during their planning cycle that outlines that success? What evidence and results will indicate that they have been effective? Organizational effectiveness is the extent to which an organization has met its stated goals and objectives—the key link in strategic planning—and how well it performed in the process. Quantitative measurements don't always tell the whole story of success. Sometimes progress toward mission goals is best revealed in the compelling stories about the difference an organization is making in its community.

One organization whose mission involves empowering women to reenter the workforce invited ten of its clients to speak at an annual fundraising event. They told inspiring stories about how the organization had given them confidence and helped them on the road to self-sufficiency. Words speak more eloquently than numbers about progress toward mission fulfillment.

The information a board obtains from an organizational assessment becomes part of the evaluative data that guide the next strategic planning process, seamlessly supporting a continuous cycle of planning and evaluation. An organization may consider examining its overall effectiveness every three to five years, thus corresponding with its strategic planning cycle. In doing so, the board has established a natural plan to assess progress on the journey to its envisioned future.

Dashboard Reporting

One of the most helpful tools for monitoring and evaluating an organization's advancement in fulfilling its mission and meeting its goals is a *dashboard report.* Usually this report, attached to a board meeting agenda, is a one- to two-page document with graphs, charts, tables, or columns—and limited text. The document presents visual information consistent with and compared to previous data so the board can easily spot changes or trends in performance. All the necessary information is in one place, not scattered in separate documents. The charts can be color-coded with dots or arrows to allow the board to immediately see when the results are on target, exceed expectations, or lag behind.

There is no single set of right things to measure for every organization; each board must choose what's best in regard to its current circumstances. After evaluating the overall performance and life cycle of the organization, it is easier to determine which specific undertakings need the board's attention and what criteria—benchmarking, growth, risk management, achieving strategic goals—the board should use in determining its approach. The board naturally needs to monitor the finances of the organization, but plenty of other issues may prove just as important. Specific indicators that the board may want to monitor include the following:

- *Finances:* revenue and expenses, cash flow, budget projections, contributions
- *Programs:* client and customer participation, satisfaction levels, client flow from program to program, graduation/program completion rates
- *Quality control:* number of mistakes, accidents, complaints
- *Human resources:* turnover rate, growth of staff, compensation comparisons

Benefits of dashboards include

- *Supporting planning.* Performance indicators allow the board to see seasonal variations and patterns in activities, detect trends, and become sensitive to demographic changes.

- *Identifying performance drivers.* Carefully chosen data manages to link efforts to results (inputs to outputs) and align activities with each other (funding, sales, marketing) to better reach common goals.
- *Prioritizing information.* When the staff guides the board's focus to a few key strategic areas at a time, it avoids diffusing board members' attention, delivering too much information, and sharing unnecessary or inappropriate information.
- *Identifying problems early.* By following the evolution of activities in a graph format and comparing it to previous data, it is easier for board members to detect shifts or see a sudden change in the results.
- *Increasing efficiency.* Because the staff has already created a process for capturing data and presenting it in a standard, consistent format, there is no reinventing the wheel when a board meeting approaches.

Dashboards cannot replace traditional communication and information sharing with the board. Other documents present the background support for the numbers and figures and cover issues that are not addressed in the dashboard report. A board member must always understand the context within which data are shared. Numbers and charts are not meant to convey all types of information. A chart cannot explain the reason behind high staff turnover or what actually motivates people to renew their subscriptions. Qualitative data do not translate well into graphics, and the appropriate stories need to be told along with and in addition to the data.

From time to time it is necessary to determine whether the right indicators are capturing the board's attention. Over time, the reports may need to change focus or the board may want to experiment with different levels of detail, identify alternative indicators, or discover new approaches to digesting the data. Exhibit 13.1 shows a sample summary-style dashboard report that reviews forty key performance indicators on a single page. It works well in printed form and online. By scanning the icons in the third column, the user can quickly spot where the organization is performing positively in relation to the goal (arrow pointing up), where it is performing not so well (arrow pointing down), or where there is some indication of negative performance (diamond).

Program Evaluation Strategies

Boards often view their role as setting direction and ensuring progress at the organizational level, focusing on the financial and operational leadership and management of the nonprofit. As a result, boards leave program decisions to staff

EXHIBIT 13.1. SAMPLE DASHBOARD REPORT

Sample Medical Center
Board of Trustees Quarterly Dashboard
Year to Date / Second Quarter 20XX

Indicator			Actual	Goal or Target	Variance: ( ) = Unfavorable	Comparison
Finance						
1	Adjusted Discharges	◆	5,184	5,236	(52)	Budget
2	Controllable Cost Per Adj. Discharge (CMA)*	▲	$3,824	$3,905	$81	Budget
3	Net Patient Revenue Per Adj. Discharge	▲	$6,451	$6,124	$327	Budget
4	Net Income	▲	$3,315,979	$2,381,115	$934,864	Budget
5	Core Earnings	▼	$1,080,177	$1,280,667	($200,490)	Budget
6	Days in Accounts Receivable	▲	63.30	58.02	(5.28)	Budget
7	Days Cash on Hand	▲	384.65	225.39	159.26	Budget
8	Supply Expense Per Adj. Discharge (CMA)*	▲	$918	$927	$9	Budget
Volumes						
9	Inpatient Acute Admissions	◆	3,378	3,447	(69)	Budget
10	TCU Admissions	▼	113	120	(7)	Budget
11	Outpatient Visits (Includes OB)	▲	12,920	12,307	613	Budget
12	Emergency Room Visits	▲	8,922	8,100	822	Budget
13	Inpatient Surgery	▲	1,083	1,055	28	Budget
14	Outpatient Surgery	▲	1,423	1,234	189	Budget
15	Home Health Visits	▲	13,864	11,400	2,464	Budget

(Continued)

EXHIBIT 13.1. (Continued)

Sample Medical Center
Board of Trustees Quarterly Dashboard
Year to Date / Second Quarter 20XX

Indicator		Actual	Goal or Target	Variance: ( ) = Unfavorable	Comparison
Customer Satisfaction					
16	Willing to Return ◆	93.0%	95.1%	-2.1%	Prior Year
17	Willing to Recommend ◆	91.9%	94.1%	-2.2%	Prior Year
18	Quality Index Score ◆	4.25	4.28	(0.03)	Prior Year
19	Waiting Time Registration ▲	80.3%	80.0%	0.3%	Less Than 10 Min.
20	Empl. More Concerned with Patient Than Selves ◆	4.23	4.29	(0.06)	Prior Year
Clinical Outcome					
21	C-Section Rate ▲	20.1	22.7	2.6	State Dep. Health
22	Nosocomial Infection Rate ▲	3.05	3.15	0.10	Prior Year
23	Number of Deaths / 1,000 Discharges ▼	35	32	(3)	Prior Year
24	Fall Rate / 1,000 Patient Days ▼	4.03	3.23	(0.80)	Prior Year
25	Medication Errors / 1,000 Patient Days ▲	2.01	2.76	0.75	Prior Year
Utilization					
26	Acute LOS (All Payors) ▲	5.14	5.19	0.05	Budget
27	Acute LOS (Medicare) ◆	6.62	6.59	(0.03)	Budget
28	TCU LOS (All Payors) ▲	12.98	20.00	7.02	Budget
29	Drg 106 LOS (All Payors) ▼	11.92	10.16	(1.76)	Target
30	Drg 107 LOS (All Payors) ▲	6.54	6.87	0.33	Target

Safety/Risk Management

31	Patient Occurrence Reports	▼	239	143	(96)	Prior Year
32	Visitor Occurrence Reports	▼	7	2	(5)	Prior Year
33	Employee Injuries	▲	59	145	86	Prior Year
34	Days Lost	▲	9	148	139	Prior Year
35	Workers Comp. Claims	▲	9	26	17	Prior Year
Managed Care						
36	Covered Lives	▼	3,987	5,339	(1,352)	Budget
37	PHO Net Income (Loss)	▼	($395,104)	$0	($395,104)	Budget
Human Resources						
38	Employee Turnover Rate	▲	4.0%	4.9%	0.9%	Healthcare Advisory
Ethics						
39	Number of Ethics Education Programs	▲	1	1	–	ASI Standard
40	Number of Ethics Committee Meetings	▲	5	3	2	ASI Standard

▲ On or Ahead of Target   ◆1–5% Below Target   ▼ >5% Below Target
* CMA = Case Mix Adjusted

Source: The Nonprofit Dashboard: A Tool for Tracking Progress, BoardSource, 2007.

leaders, who will set program direction and ensure that programs achieve desired outcomes for people they serve.

Although the board should not get involved in day-to-day program decision making, it should understand whether programs are successful and, if so, the reasons for their success. After all, the financial and operational functions of any nonprofit organization should be in service to the mission. Sustaining and strengthening the organization is not the end but rather the means to the end: mission success. The only way to determine mission success is through program evaluation.

Program evaluation is a practical tool that an organization uses to track and assess what it does. It is essential to improving programs and services for constituents. Although program evaluation designs may resemble some research designs, evaluation need not be considered theory-based academic research. Program evaluation is simply a learning tool for the board and management to use to help them make decisions about the future. Program evaluation also provides concrete evidence to support advocacy and fundraising efforts.

Nonprofits sometimes conduct program evaluation because a funder has made it a requirement of program funding. When the funding ends, so does the evaluation. Using program evaluation as an accountability tool for funders is less likely to help nonprofits learn about what works, but rather helps the funder know whether its investment was worth it.

Systematic program evaluation that includes outcomes measurement takes the subjectivity out of justifying an organization's existence and introduces objectivity by enabling an organization to report valid results. Ultimately, program evaluation helps an organization and its board ensure the integrity of programming in pursuit of mission. Evaluation also helps staff and the board determine which programs remain valid because they are closely tied to fulfilling the mission and which programs exist simply because they have always been there.

Responsibility for program evaluation belongs to the organization's program staff, with oversight from the chief executive or executive management. But the board, as the organizational leader, should insist on evaluation and require staff leaders to identify and set aside resources for conducting evaluation on an ongoing basis. It is the board's role to agree on expectations, allocate funds in the budget, and get and review information so that it can see how the organization is doing.

Comprehensive program evaluation has two components. *Outcomes measurement* determines how a program is working by demonstrating actual results. *Performance measurement* measures program inputs and outputs to determine the quality and effectiveness of program implementation. By measuring outcomes and implementation, an organization will get a better idea of total program performance. Because the board is not involved in the detailed analysis of program outcomes, it needs to make sure it gets adequate information on the success of the overall program.

The board should expect program evaluation to be based on qualitative and quantitative data gathered through a variety of methods, including surveys, interviews, focus groups, pre- and post-tests, observations, and assessments of products developed from program participation. Many nonprofit organizations use a logic model as a framework for both planning their programs and evaluating the extent to which those programs are (or aren't) working to achieve the desired outcomes. Because of its visual component, a logic model helps staff envision all the various components of a program and how they interrelate. Then it becomes easier for staff to draw logical conclusions or connections between the resources the organization needs to deploy and the activities it must engage in to eventually arrive at its intended results.

Board Self-Assessment

Self-assessment gives the board an opportunity to step back from its everyday business and address larger, more fundamental issues. In addition to allowing boards to reflect on how well they are meeting their responsibilities, a self-assessment helps them focus on integral aspects of their work—from strategic direction setting and oversight to fundraising and community outreach. Self-assessment can have the following benefits:

- Diverting boards from micromanaging the organization's work and redirecting their focus to governance issues
- Leading to a more engaged and higher-performing board
- Developing the board's team-building skills and providing a better problem-solving structure
- Signaling to funders and constituents that board members take their responsibilities seriously

Self-assessments are designed to be constructive sessions from which board members emerge with a better understanding of their own and other board members' roles and a clear set of board action plans. Despite the evident benefits, however, only about half of all boards—52 percent of respondents to the 2007 BoardSource Governance Index survey—formally assess their own performance.

When to Conduct a Self-Assessment

Self-assessment can be particularly useful if the board is exploring its roles and responsibilities and identifying gaps in its performance. The self-assessment can be a forum for discovering problems and developing plans for the future.

Board assessments can be especially critical at these times:

- In the early stages of the organization's life, especially when the organization has hired staff after having been largely volunteer-run
- When there is some confusion about which responsibilities belong to the board and which to the staff
- During changes in leadership (either on the board or in the chief executive position)
- In connection with strategic planning

Assessments are too comprehensive for most boards to perform every year. More likely, a stable board might assess itself every two or three years. It is best to schedule the evaluation for a retreat or a special board meeting, rather than undertake it when the organization is in crisis or experiencing personnel issues within the board.

The Self-Assessment Process

Boards use a variety of informal and formal tools and processes for assessments. Informal evaluations help the board stay focused on self-improvement, using one or more of the following techniques:

- *Regular board discussions.* Add to each board meeting agenda a ten- to fifteen-minute item called "Ideas for Improving the Board." The board chair should be a champion of board improvement. The morale and loyalty of board members are stronger when the board is given the freedom to make suggestions. However, frank discussion also raises expectations that things will change. When a consensus is evident, the chair must be prepared to take action or refer ideas to a committee or task force for further consideration.
- *Board training.* Training sessions can provide the stimulus for taking an in-depth look at board members' roles, individually or collectively. A session or two of board training—using a book, an outline, a veteran board member, or a consultant—can help set standards against which the board can measure its own performance.
- *Mini-assessments.* Easy-to-complete surveys distributed at a board meeting are a way of getting board members to think about their perceptions of the board's performance (see Table 13.1).

The board should spend most of its time discussing issues and formulating new, better ways of self-governance, rather than simply focusing on collecting information and compiling the results.

Board members should review the list of basic board responsibilities in Table 13.1 and indicate whether they think the board currently does a good job in an area or whether the board needs to improve its performance. (*Note:* This survey is abbreviated, and most boards will want to conduct complete self-assessments, available from BoardSource and other organizations.)

When conducting a formal self-assessment, the board decides what kind of instrument to use for gathering feedback from its members and identifies who will be responsible for collecting and compiling responses. All board members are asked to complete the assessment survey in a candid, thorough manner. To encourage candid responses, most boards prefer to keep responses anonymous.

TABLE 13.1. MINI BOARD SELF-ASSESSMENT SURVEY

	Does well	Needs work	Not sure
Organization's Mission Do we use it as a guide for decisions? Does it need to be revised?			
Program Evaluation Do we have criteria for determining program effectiveness?			

Financial Resources
Do we understand the organization's income
    strategy?
Do all board members participate actively in
    fundraising efforts?			

Fiscal Oversight and Risk Management Does the budget reflect our strategic priorities? Do we have a firm understanding of the organization's financial health?			

Relationship with the Chief Executive
Is there a climate of mutual trust and respect
    between the board and the chief executive?
Does the executive receive a fair and
    comprehensive annual performance review?			

Board-Staff Relationship
Do all board members refrain from attempting
    to direct members of the staff?
Do board and staff treat each other with
    respect?			

Public Relations and Advocacy
Are all board members actively promoting the
    organization in the community?
Do we understand the organization's public
    relations strategy?			

Board Selection and Orientation
Does the board have the necessary diversity of
    perspectives and other resources needed?
Do new board members get an effective
    orientation?			

Board Organization
Do board meetings make effective use of the
    time and talents of board members?
Do our committees contribute to the effective
    functioning of the board?			

Board members' responses are then compiled in a report that should give a fairly accurate impression of how the board views its own performance. For instance, the findings may point to board members' desire to make better use of their time, focus more on meaningful issues rather than administrative tasks, interact more with one another, or simply enjoy their positions more. The report will indicate areas of consensus and areas where board members differ about how well the board is doing in exercising its responsibilities. The assessment should culminate in an extended board session or a retreat where the board has time to discuss and identify steps toward increased effectiveness.

External Governance Audits

A board can facilitate a more thorough evaluation of its governance practices by engaging an expert on governance. Typically, an external governance audit includes reviewing the articles of incorporation and bylaws; observing board and committee meetings; and interviewing officers, other board members, former board members, and the chief executive. The consultant may also create and administer a premeeting or in-meeting survey and then facilitate a board discussion about key issues that emerged from the survey.

By contracting with an expert who knows how other boards function, a board improves its chances of focusing on positive changes and increases its own level of interest and participation. A consultant is more objective than a member of the board and can offer alternatives for addressing problems. In addition, employing an external consultant is usually perceived as less threatening than having your own leaders conduct a peer evaluation.

Using Self-Assessment Findings

A successful self-assessment can energize board members and make them eager to return to their leadership roles—and lower-performing board members may realize that it may be time to move on. It can improve board and staff relations by clarifying division of labor within the organization. And it can identify board structures that need to be improved. But none of these results will happen without effective follow-up.

The board as a whole should discuss the findings of an evaluation and what can be done to improve its effectiveness or productivity. For instance, the results of a self-evaluation may prompt the board to consider making some governance changes, such as reducing the number of standing committees, or to modify its communication practices with board members. The assessment meeting should lead to an action plan that answers such questions as, What will be done, by what time, and by whom? Likewise, board leadership must ensure that it follows through on the action plan.

Five Strategies for Overcoming Board Resistance to Self-Assessment

Commitment. Get the full board's buy-in. Ensure confidentiality to encourage honest responses. Understand that a self-assessment is designed to improve, not punish.

Process. Determine together which tool is appropriate. Fine-tune the tool to address issues and questions that are important to the board. Determine how to include individual evaluation for the purpose of self-reflection. Address general resistance to change.

Planning. Devote adequate time to planning. Schedule a special retreat to discuss results.

Competency. If this is the board's first self-assessment effort, form a task force to explore how others have done it. Learn how to give feedback constructively. If possible, bring in an outside facilitator.

Follow-up. Make sure the final recommendations will be implemented. Give board members opportunities for self-improvement. Clarify expectations and overall duties of board service. Commit to repeating the process.

Individual Board Member Self-Assessment

In addition to evaluating the performance of the board as a whole, there is also the question of individual board member performance. Individual assessments are particularly useful when a board member's term is about to end and he or she is being considered for reelection. As the governance committee prepares for an upcoming board election, it is wise to ask each incumbent who is eligible for another term to complete a self-evaluation.

This self-evaluation may be based on the board member letter of agreement (if any) that members signed at the beginning of their term, the board member job description, or the individual board member section of the board self-assessment instrument. The self-evaluation and a subsequent conversation with the board chair serve several purposes: to assist incumbents in considering whether they ought to stand for reelection, to remind them of their responsibilities if they were to be elected for an additional term, and to help the governance committee determine whether to nominate a member for an additional term.

See the questions in Table 13.2 for a sample of an individual board member evaluation. Board members answering yes to these questions are likely to be fulfilling their responsibilities as board members. (*Note:* This survey is abbreviated, and most boards will want to conduct complete self-assessments, available from BoardSource and other organizations.)

Peer Evaluation

Because of the current emphasis on accountability and the increased awareness of boards operating as teams, some boards now engage in peer evaluations,

TABLE 13.2. INDIVIDUAL BOARD MEMBER SELF-EVALUATION

	Yes	No	Not sure
1. Do I understand and support the mission of the organization?			
2. Am I sufficiently knowledgeable about the organization's programs and services?			
3. Do I follow trends and important developments related to this organization?			
4. Do I assist with fundraising and/or give a significant annual gift to the organization?			
5. Do I stay informed about the organization's financial health?			
6. Do I have a good working relationship with the chief executive?			
7. Do I recommend individuals for service to this board?			
8. Do I prepare for and participate in board meetings and committee meetings?			
9. Do I act as a goodwill ambassador for the organization?			
10. Do I find serving on the board to be a satisfying and rewarding experience?			
11. Do I attend at least 75 percent of board meetings during the year?			

12. Write short answers to these questions:
    a. What could the organization do to make my board service more productive and satisfying?
    b. What could I do to make my board service more productive and satisfying?

particularly in connection with renomination of current members. Peer evaluation forms are usually brief and commonly ask about attendance, preparation, follow-through on assignments, and quality of participation in board discussions and interaction with other board members and staff. Most commonly collected and summarized by the chair, the results are shared with each individual evaluated and also with the governance committee in preparation for possible renomination.

Individuals who are evaluated by their peers gain valuable insights into how they are perceived by others, and they have the option of modifying their behavior accordingly. However, because board members serve on a voluntary basis, many may feel uncomfortable or resentful of being held up for judgment by their peers. For this reason, the practice of peer evaluation is still fairly uncommon.

Board Chair Evaluation

Boards need to be accountable in all areas, including the board chair position. The board chair should receive feedback on how to modify his or her performance to best achieve a high-functioning board. Although this is a challenge when dealing with a volunteer lay leader, a board chair evaluation framed as being in the best interests of the organization can be useful.

Like any evaluation, the process gives the chair a clearer view of this leadership position and specific requirements related to the position.

Evaluation clarifies what works and where improvement is desired. It can focus on the chair's facilitation skills, relationships and interactions with board members, use of board work structures, and governance practices. It allows the chair to see how his or her peers perceive his or her approach to chairing meetings, communication style, and serving as an example. A board chair evaluation can also help a board avoid informal mumblings or private discussions that blur the line between truth and fiction and negatively affect the work of the board.

The chair evaluation is to be handled by fellow board members. It is never the responsibility of the chief executive. It is rarely an easy task for peers to evaluate each other's performance; therefore, special tact is necessary. Often the task is delegated to the executive committee (or, if there is none, to the governance committee). The committee may or may not seek comments from others on the board. Keeping the process anonymous allows everyone to provide feedback as honestly and straightforwardly as possible.

The overall comments are communicated directly to the chair in a private discussion. This discussion can also help the chair redirect a course of action if it is necessary.

Evaluating the Chief Executive's Performance

Chief executive performance evaluation can benefit the chief executive, the board, and the entire organization. The chief executive benefits by getting constructive feedback on his or her performance. The board benefits by showing support for the chief executive—one of the board's main duties. The evaluation process helps to enhance the communication between the board and the chief executive and facilitates the board's oversight function. The entire organization benefits because evaluation ensures that the right hands are guiding the organization in the right direction. It is important that there be a perfect fit between the organization's goals and a chief executive who is able to achieve them.

The Foundation for Evaluation

Three elements ensure that the performance evaluation is well structured: job description, expectations, and process. Like any evaluation, the practice is cyclical. Outcomes must be incorporated into the next evaluation cycle to feed into future improvement efforts.

- *Job description.* The chief executive needs a clear and unambiguous job description in order to clarify the primary duties and responsibilities of the position. The skills needed to carry out the duties of the job define the competency of the person being hired for the position.
- *Expectations.* Establishing annual expectations helps to identify the priorities and specific projected accomplishments for the coming year. The chief executive and the board must mutually agree on these expectations, as they serve as the final device for assessing achievements or shortcomings.
- *Process.* Implementation of a performance evaluation starts with the decision to do it. The evaluation process needs to fit the organizational culture and enhance the working relationship between the board and the chief executive. The board and chief executive together should determine who should be involved, what evaluation tools to use, and how the results will be communicated, to make them useful as building blocks for the future.
- *Participants.* The full board must be familiar with the evaluation results and feel comfortable with them; however, a committee, a task force, the chair, or an outside facilitator may handle the actual process. The chief executive's self-evaluation is an integral part of the process. If the board wants to use a 360-degree approach, other feedback may come from senior staff, key clients, funders, or other stakeholders.

When and What to Evaluate

The evaluation may be conducted at the end of the fiscal year, or there may be intermittent discussions throughout the year, or both approaches may be used—as long as it is understood that constructive criticism is part of positive feedback and the evaluation is based on previously set goals. Documentation of the discussions and agreements protects both the board and the chief executive if disagreements or misinterpretations occur.

A comprehensive assessment looks at qualitative and quantitative factors that shape individual performance and measurable indicators that link goals to results. A chief executive's intangible qualities should also be calculated into the assessment, as they may have a critical impact on the success of the organization. Some of the areas to evaluate include

- The chief executive's success in meeting the overall goals
- The strategic alignment with the board's directives and accomplishment of management objectives
- Programmatic and fundraising achievements
- Fiscal management
- The chief executive's relationship with the board, staff, and the community

The Evaluation Process

The process can be informal or structured. A self-evaluation prompts the chief executive to reconcile his or her own strengths and weaknesses and then to discover ways to improve them or to build on them. This opportunity for reflection can also help the executive to clarify expectations and outline priorities for the coming year. Board members may complete a questionnaire, relying on the predetermined performance objectives when forming their opinions of the executive's accomplishments. Usually board members' comments are compiled, tabulated, and shared with the chief executive. These comments, along with those of the self-assessment, are the basis for a discussion. If the board seeks opinions from outsiders, their comments should be integrated into the feedback. The board chair should prepare a written document summarizing the evaluation results, which is given to the chief executive and placed in his or her personnel file. The document should include a performance improvement plan detailing expectations for measurable results, accompanied by a timeline and a commitment to provide adequate resources for improvement.

Boards that may want to be less structured about the process should still ensure that continuous or intermittent feedback reaches the chief executive.

Communication may take place via scheduled phone conversations or e-mails. Note taking is still wise, as records help refresh the memory about the discussion and provide documentation for human resources or for legal purposes.

To prevent the process from becoming too cumbersome, each board and chief executive should determine the most productive and comfortable approach that allows open communication to make the evaluation a tool for enhancing performance and recognizing accomplishments. The ultimate intention of the evaluation is to strengthen the organization by improving its management.

Chapter Exercises

- Why is it difficult for many nonprofits to measure and evaluate their impact? Can you think of any nontraditional ways of assessing the effectiveness of an organization?
- List some qualities of a productive board meeting.
- How often do you think boards should evaluate their own performance? Why?
- Peer evaluations are a controversial and sensitive issue on many boards. What is your opinion about them and why?
- Discuss the pros and cons of a 360-degree evaluation of the chief executive's performance.
- What would you include in a dashboard report for a university, a museum? For a land trust? For a professional association?

CHAPTER FOURTEEN

BYLAWS AND POLICIES

An effective nonprofit organization depends on policy development and oversight tied not only to its mission and operations but also to its governance. Bylaws and policies that reflect the culture and expectations of the organization and are carefully considered and implemented can be a powerful tool in this effort. These valuable resources are capable of promoting sound decisions under the range of circumstances that a board may encounter. In addition, they are the operating rules, and they streamline governance by codifying existing agreements that affect decision making. And as one part of a coordinated strategy—including a strategic plan, oversight of operations, continuous assessment of opportunities and challenges, and the range of talents of board members—bylaws and policies contribute to the long-term institutional strength of the nonprofit.

Bylaws are significant written rules by which an organization is governed. With minor exceptions, they are largely similar in structure for all organizations, as the mission of the organization does not ordinarily affect the structure of the governance document. The content does vary—sometimes significantly—depending on the organization. Bylaws define the duties, authority limits, and principal operating procedures for the board and board members. The highest-level board policies—such as those concerning conflict of interest—can be embedded in the bylaws. Revising bylaws requires following a specific process (explained in the bylaws document) and approval by the full board and probably by members in a membership organization. Thus they should not contain overly detailed procedures or restrictions.

Policies serve as operating principles at various levels. Some set out organizational guidelines for board and staff behavior, such as whistle-blower and gift acceptance policies. Others supplement the bylaws and guide board practices and oversight procedures, such as investment, internal controls, and executive compensation policies. Still others direct staff operations, such as personnel and communications policies. Many policies not only apply to the work of the staff but also have implications for the board.

Although bylaws are the foundation for the organization's structure, policies add greater detail to cover the many situations that are not addressed in the bylaws. Many organizations intentionally make bylaws hard to amend so that fundamental structures cannot be overturned by majority rule. Policies, however, are more flexible, so that decision makers can respond to immediate needs and the majority of the board can establish and change policies.

This chapter explains the context for bylaws and policies and provides an overview of the issues and areas they should address. Although the recommendations and examples included in this chapter can serve as a starting point, bylaws and policies should be tailored to each organization's circumstances.

The Context for Bylaws and Policies

Bylaws and policies are part of the core organizational documents that reflect how a nonprofit fulfills its mission and carries out its business in an orderly, legal manner. They fall into a hierarchy of rules that flow from government regulation and other compliance requirements. The following structure is one way of understanding how policies relate to an organization's other operating guidelines:

- *State corporate law.* Most nonprofit organizations are legally organized as corporations. The highest authority governing their organizational documents is the state corporation act. If there is a contradiction between the bylaws and these other regulations, that part of the bylaws is considered invalid. For example, if state corporate law provides that the maximum single term of office for any officer is three years, a provision in the bylaws allowing for four-year terms of office is illegal and can be challenged.
- *Articles of incorporation.* This legal document outlines the general purpose and structure of the organization and its intent to operate exclusively with a nonprofit purpose. The articles are filed with the state government if and when the nonprofit is incorporated. They usually follow a standard form and contain

a minimum of detail because they are cumbersome to change. (See Chapter One for more about articles of incorporation.)

- *Bylaws*. Bylaws are always subordinate to the articles of incorporation. If there is a conflict, the articles always prevail.
- *Policies*. Common policy areas are programs, financial management, fundraising, personnel management, public relations, and board operations.
- *Resolutions*. A resolution is a specific board decision that describes an action to be taken or a principle to be adopted. Resolutions are specific to a particular board for a given situation. They range from broad statements about organizational values (such as protecting the environment) to elevated recognition of significant contributions (of exemplary board members or retiring staff, for example).
- *Recommendations and guidelines*. These documents, often nonbinding, suggest actions or behavior. Coming from the board, the language is more suggestive than directive, as it would be for a policy in which the statement is clear and resembles an order. For example, after a lengthy discussion, the board might establish criteria to guide the staff in launching a new program; these criteria may not warrant a formal policy or procedure, but will be taken into consideration.
- *Procedures*. Procedures define a process for implementing a general policy. There is often a blurry line between policies and procedures because it can be difficult to separate *what* gets done from *how* it gets done. In practice, policies set the broadest parameters, and procedures are used at the staff implementation level. But because the process sometimes matters as much as the results—to ensure transparency, participation, and accountability—some procedures are treated more like policies.

Creating and Amending Bylaws

The board creates bylaws at the time the organization is established. It is not wise to operate without them. Each state has different statutes that apply to a nonprofit's bylaws; some dictate specific provisions, whereas others give more general guidelines.

Bylaws are not static, and the board should review them regularly and amend them so that they accurately reflect how the organization works. Keeping bylaws simple in language and content can help ease this process. Some organizations periodically appoint a task force to review the bylaws and make suggestions for revision by the whole board. If the board votes to amend the bylaws, the revisions are marked on the bylaws, and the date they were amended is recorded. The revised document is attached to the next IRS Form 990 filed by the organization, and any major changes are explained in the form.

During governing controversies that focus on the organization's mission, bylaws take on particular importance. These disputes can take many forms: a board member who is voted out of office seeks reinstatement, a dissident group within the organization attempts to gain control of the board, or a faction mounts a legal challenge to a board decision. In these difficult situations, carefully crafted bylaws and adherence to them can help ensure the fairness of board decisions and provide protection against legal challenges.

What Bylaws Include

Bylaws are individual to an organization, but should cover certain issues:

General
Official name of the organization
Location of principal office
Statement of purposes
Limitations required for tax exemption, such as prohibitions against political campaign participation and inurement or private foundation provisions for 501(c)(3) organizations
Procedure for amending the bylaws
Procedure for dissolving the organization
Disposition of assets upon dissolution

Members (If the Organization Is a Formal Member Organization)
Qualifications for membership
Admission procedures
Dues obligations
Classes of membership and their rights and privileges
Notice required for membership meetings
Quorum requirements
Frequency of meetings and meeting procedures
Circumstances under which members may be expelled
Voting procedures

Board of Directors
Size of the board
Qualifications for membership
Terms of office and term limits

Selection process

Process for filling vacancies

Frequency of meetings

Quorum and voting requirements

Meeting procedures

Powers of the executive committee—if one exists

Other standing committees or a statement that allows the board to form them

Compensation of board members

Circumstances under which board members may be removed

Conflict-of-interest procedures

Officers

Qualifications for holding office

Duties of officers

Process for selecting or appointing officers

Terms and term limits

Provision for a chief executive on the board

Circumstances under which officers may be removed

Fiscal Matters

Audit committee and audits

Fiscal year of the corporation

Indemnification and insurance for officers and directors

About Policies

Policies are written rules, statements, principles, or directives for making decisions and taking action. Their purpose is to serve as a guide as the board carries out its governance duties and as staff conducts the organization's daily operations. Policies also establish a standard and recommended way of acting in challenging situations. They function as a protective mechanism for the organization and for individuals when a decision is questioned; those responsible can explain how they reached their conclusion by pointing to an approved policy that was followed.

Policy statements on issues related to an organization's mission are not the same as the organizational policies described here; rather, they are action-oriented advocacy messages that communicate the organization's official position or recommendations on a matter of public interest or concern. The board approves them in the context of an overall communications plan.

For nonprofit organizations, policies are tools for setting priorities, making decisions, and defining and delegating responsibilities. Too often, policies are reactive—created to make sure a bad decision made during a crisis is never repeated. But policymaking is far more effective when done proactively. It often begins with the need to address situations that are common to all organizations, such as conflict-of-interest policies. It is also done preemptively to handle situations that are anticipated as part of a significant organizational change (such as starting an endowment) or opportunities that emerge over time (such as sponsorship). Boards that practice proactive policymaking can save themselves a great deal of anguish in a crisis situation that demands instant response.

The primary policies for an organization are most likely found in its bylaws. These policies define the role of board members, how they are elected, how they function during board meetings, and how their work is structured. However, bylaws usually only create the very basic structure for the board's operative functioning and should not be cluttered by every conceivable rule and recommendation.

Organizational size, complexity, and maturity inevitably shape policies. A smaller, relatively young organization with few staff may operate with simpler policies than those of a more established organization with a large staff and considerable financial resources. Policies should be selected based on what is appropriate for the organization at that particular time in its life. As an organization evolves, the board and staff should review its policies for relevance and update them as necessary.

Policies are also influenced by mission-based practices and community expectations. Museums need to manage their collections, social service agencies need to protect their clients, foundations need to oversee their investment portfolios, and associations need to address industry standards. Although the nonprofit sector shares a set of generally accepted policies, each organization also operates within its own realm of practice. Again, the board and staff should ensure that policies are in keeping with the organization's particular circumstances.

Last and most important, policies may also depend on government regulations, which vary from location to location. Policies are not one-size-fits-all documents. Professional advisers—lawyers, accountants, investment managers, and consultants—can be helpful in developing appropriate policies.

Types of Policies

An organization needs to identify the policies necessary to direct its activities and decision making. Here is a list of policies (grouped in categories), by no means exhaustive, that can prepare the organization to function in a more effective and accountable manner.

Ethics and Accountability

- Mission
- Vision
- Values
- Code of Ethics
- Conflict of Interest
- Diversity/Inclusiveness
- Confidentiality
- Whistle-Blower Protection
- Record Retention and Document Destruction

Role of the Board

- Role of the Board
- Board Member Agreements
- Board Chair Job Descriptions
- Other Board Officer Job Descriptions
- Compensation of Board Members
- Board Member Expense Reimbursement
- Board Self-Assessment

Chief Executive

- Chief Executive Job Description
- Chief Executive Performance Evaluation
- Executive Compensation
- Executive Transition
- Emergency Succession

Finance and Investments

- Budgeting
- Capital Expenditures
- Financial Controls
- Investments
- Reserves and Endowments
- Financial Audits
- IRS Form 990 and 990-PF
- Risk Management

Fundraising

- Board Member Fundraising
- Donor Relations

Gift Acceptance
Sponsorships and Endorsements

Personnel
Responsibility for Human Resources
Equal Employment Opportunity
Nepotism
Sexual Harassment
Workplace Environment
Substance Abuse
Solicitation
Electronic Communication
Complaints
Performance Review

Communications
Media Relations
Crisis Communications
Electronic Media
Lobbying and Political Activity

Committee Responsibilities
Governance Committee
Financial Committees (Finance, Audit, and Investment)
Development Committee
Executive Committee
Other Common Committees
Advisory Councils
Committee Chair Job Descriptions

Policymaking Participants

It is an oversimplification to say that boards make policy and staff implements it. Depending on the nature of the policy, the chief executive or even other staff may develop and implement policy without consulting or notifying the board. Policies established by the staff must support—and not conflict with—organization-wide policies established by the board. However, this does not excuse the board from its responsibility to stay apprised of the organization's policies.

Usually boards are involved in setting the major policies and then delegate the standard operating procedures to staff, except in the area of board-specific policies. In staffed organizations, too much board involvement in establishing standard operating procedures for the staff risks board micromanagement. In all-volunteer organizations, however, the board is likely to be directly involved in defining and implementing all operating policies and procedures for the organization.

The chief executive and board are responsible for establishing policies concerning their governance roles and responsibilities. The macro issues of how the board operates—board size, officer positions, and committee structure—are usually set forth in the bylaws. But many micro areas are not covered in the bylaws and should not be—areas such as board member fundraising requirements and executive compensation. Boards need policies in these and other areas to clarify expectations and establish guidelines for handling the multitude of complicated situations that arise.

Policymaking Approach

A few organizations document their policies diligently, and the board periodically reviews and updates them as necessary. Many, however, have accumulated policies haphazardly and maintain them in various places. When dealing with a difficult issue, some suffer from the absence of policies and create them retroactively. Whatever the situation, the following key elements are part of a thoughtful, comprehensive approach to developing and maintaining organizational policies:

1. Start with the End—an Up-to-Date, Comprehensive Policy Manual—in Mind. A manual puts all policy documents in one place, in writing. These policies should be shared with new board members during orientation, and board members should be encouraged to reference them appropriately throughout their tenure. For example, the board should establish policies on executive compensation and review them when it comes time to conduct the chief executive's performance review. Likewise, all board members should sign their conflict-of-interest disclosure statement annually.

2. Take Inventory and Identify Policies. Look first for policies in the organization's bylaws. Among the policies that you may find are mission statements, board officer duties, and committee charters. Extract clauses that are, themselves, policy statements or that relate to policy issues. Then search board meeting minutes from recent years for explicit policy decisions and examples of decisions that implicitly suggest policy.

3. Develop an Outline of Core Policies. Identify the main policy areas. The section headings in this book serve as a good starting point. In the end, the policies will cover a core set of issues common to all types of organizations, such as codes of ethics, and some that apply only to certain kinds of nonprofits, such as membership voting for associations and spending policies for foundations.

4. Draft and Discuss Policy Recommendations. Someone has to take the first steps: collect and draft policies, identify the discussion issues for each policy, and compile the actual policy manual. This responsibility is often delegated to the governance committee or an ad hoc task force. Inevitably, it will require support from staff and professional advisers (such as lawyers, investment managers, accountants). No commitment to developing policy is real without a deadline for review and consideration. The board should allot time at board meetings to discuss and approve one or more policies.

The board should adopt each policy only after appropriate adaptation and thorough discussion, answering these questions: Does this proposed policy reflect the organization's values, mission, and goals? How often should it be monitored? Board members should define the policy in its own context, explore situations where the proposed policy will be used, consider what problems it will head off and what problems it might create, and discuss any concerns.

5. Finalize and Formalize Policies. Approaches to policy document formats vary, and a number of formats are incorporated in this sampler. Common components of a policy document might include:

- Organization name
- Policy number or policy area within hierarchy
- Policy name
- Introduction or statement of purpose
- Policy statement
- Definitions
- Examples
- Assignment of responsibility
- Monitoring and review schedule
- Date approved
- Date last modified

6. Use the Policies. Harder than crafting policies is bringing them to life. They should guide decisions and actions; that is, they should not gather dust on a bookshelf but should be part of the organization's routine operations. They need to be accessible to staff for reference, at committee meetings for direction, and during key board deliberations for guidance.

7. Review and Update Policies. Policies may change over time. In fact, if they don't, the board is probably neglecting them. Some changes are minor—fixing a typo or revising a date. Others are major—adopting a new audit policy. Policy review is more than just comparing the words of a document against basic regulatory requirements. More important, it ensures that the policy is being followed. Did the board review the chief executive's performance in a timely, thoughtful manner? Did the organization observe the gift acceptance policy with the new donor? To manage the daunting task of regularly reviewing policies, it may help to delegate the actual policy review to an appropriate committee or a special task force and to stagger the review cycles for different policies.

Unfortunately, nonprofit boards sometimes spend precious time handling avoidable crises, micromanaging competent staff, or remaking decisions. In the end, time invested in making policy now frees up future time for the board to engage in work more productively and directly related to the mission. The purpose of policies is to help nonprofits improve their governance and thus increase their ability to achieve their mission—to make a difference.

Creating a Policy Manual

A simple method for keeping track of policies is a manual containing all the ongoing policies that the board has adopted, organized for easy accessibility. The policy manual should be a fixture at every board meeting, providing the most up-to-date versions of board policies and decisions. A searchable electronic version—housed in a password-protected section of the organization's Web site—is a convenient reference. The manual should contain all standing policies of the organization as they have been added to or modified over time, as well as an ongoing record of when policies were revised.

Policy Guidance

Some policies common to nonprofit organizations are described in detail in the following sections. Each section explains the key elements of the policy and includes a list of practical tips that boards should keep in mind when creating and implementing policies.

Conflict of Interest

A conflict of interest exists when a board member or employee has a personal interest that may influence him or her when making a decision for the organization (see Chapter Seven, Legal and Ethical Responsibilities, for more about conflict of interest). Although the law focuses primarily on financial interests and provides some guidelines, nonprofit organizations contend with a variety of potential and perceived conflicts of interest, only some of which may be detrimental to the organization. The key for nonprofit boards is not to try to avoid all possible conflict-of-interest situations, which would be impossible; rather, boards need to identify and follow a process for handling them effectively.

Both board members and employees must abide by conflict-of-interest policies. Generally, conflict-of-interest policies should clarify what a conflict of interest is, what board members and employees must do to disclose possible conflicts of interest, and what board members and employees should do to avoid acting inappropriately if and when such a conflict does arise. How an organization ensures open and honest deliberation affects all aspects of its operations and is critical to making good decisions, avoiding legal problems and public scandals, and remaining focused on the organization's mission.

For a sample policy, see the Appendix.

Every organization needs a conflict-of-interest policy. Remember, conflicts of interest are not uncommon and not inherently illegal; rather, they create situations that call for careful attention—and a process for handling them appropriately.

Key Elements

- Conflicts are not only financial in nature. Issue conflicts (for example, if a board member takes a position or supports another organization that is counter to the organization's mission and principles) may have to be addressed as well.
- Conflict-of-interest policies should be applicable to the board and key staff, at a minimum; they may also include other employees and key constituents with influence over the organization (such as major donors).
- A conflict-of-interest policy should clearly define a consistent process for dealing with conflicts. This process should include, at a minimum, disclosure and recusal. It also often includes the expectation for the board member in question to leave the room for the discussion and voting and, in extreme situations, to resign.
- Ultimately, the policy should clarify the consequences for violating the policy, which may include dismissal.
- Some organizations, instead of using the term *conflict of interest*, use the term *duality of interest*. A duality of interest recognizes that, under certain circumstances, even if a board member has multiple interests, those interests do not necessarily create a conflicting situation.

Practical Tips

- Conflicts of interest are sometimes quite obvious and other times more obscure. To provide better guidance, consider including examples of what constitutes a conflict of interest for the organization. These examples may be lengthy, organization-specific, and/or distinguish among real, perceived, or potential conflicts.
- On the administrative side, determine who will maintain proper documentation of signed conflict-of-interest disclosure statements, as well as who has responsibility for determining whether or not an actual conflict of interest exists. Often these responsibilities are shared between the chief executive and a board committee.
- Board members, being busy and engaged people, are involved in various activities in the community, and these affiliations are likely to collide at times. At least annually, consider requiring board and staff members to disclose—in writing—any relationships that might constitute a conflict of interest. By openly and preemptively disclosing these potentially conflicting connections, the organization is better able to carry out proper due diligence.

Role of the Board

A nonprofit board is well served to establish policies to guide it. Policies relating to the overall role of the board remind board members that they are part of a group with authority over, and liability for, the organization. These policies often involve duties of the board as a whole or of individual board members. Although these documents take many forms—from general lists, to job descriptions, to letters of understanding—they serve a common function: to clearly communicate the board's responsibilities as a governing body.

Defining accountability for the organization is one of several key elements in defining the board's role.

Key Elements

- Although there are many ways to describe the role of the board, its fundamental responsibilities derive from three duties—care, loyalty, and obedience. These duties mean that board members must make prudent, educated, and independent decisions; place the organization above their personal preferences; and remain faithful to the mission of the organization.
- The policy should speak to the board as a group with collective duties. Board responsibilities fall into three broad areas: setting direction, overseeing the affairs of the organization, and ensuring adequate resources.

Practical Tips

- Draft these policies to include legal requirements, but frame and style them according to your own board culture.
- Realize that policies evolve as the organization and the board evolve. Start with the basics, but ensure that these documents are constantly reviewed and amended and that new policies are added as they become relevant.

Executive Compensation

The chief executive's compensation package is an important component of a board's responsibility for managing the executive, and putting together a compensation package is a complex activity. It is tied to who the chief executive is expected to be as a professional and to what the chief executive is expected to do for the organization. Although very personal for those involved, it is also very public; if over $100,000, the total amount of compensation must be disclosed on the IRS Form 990, and it must comply with stringent legal requirements.

For a sample policy, see the Appendix.

Key Elements

- Compensation includes salary and benefits. When developing a compensation policy, the board should list all components of the package. Often, the original employment contract (if any) establishes the chief executive's base compensation, and the board determines annual raises and bonuses each year. All compensation and benefits should be shown in the employment contract; there should be no unlisted, "off-agreement" benefits.
- Compensation is linked to experience, performance, and industry. A compensation policy may list those factors that the board feels are most important, such as prior experience and education level. It should also establish performance goals and compensation adjustments based on accomplishments. Last, it should take into account the complexity of the organization, requirements of the job, and market rates.
- A compensation policy should also address the process for determining the chief executive's compensation, such as who communicates with the chief executive, how adjustments will be determined (for example, cost of living, merit increases, bonus rewards), research into compensation in comparable organizations, and use of external consultants.
- Fair and reasonable compensation is one of the key elements to attract and retain the most qualified chief executive for the organization. Although the full board is responsible for determining appropriate compensation, it may

delegate certain tasks—such as negotiating with the chief executive (during the hiring process) and reviewing comparable salaries—to a committee or an independent consultant. The full board or a committee of the board must approve the final compensation package.

- The policy should be developed to satisfy the IRS Intermediate Sanctions safe harbor requirements of independent decision making, reliance on comparables, and documentation. (See Internal Revenue Code section 4958 and the regulations thereunder.) The Intermediate Sanctions safe harbor requirements provide that there is a rebuttable presumption of reasonableness that applies to a financial arrangement with any person with substantial influence over an organization, if the financial arrangement was approved by an independent board (or an independent committee comprised of board members) that:

  - Was composed entirely of individuals unrelated to and not subject to the control of the disqualified person(s) involved in the arrangement.

  - Obtained and relied upon "appropriate data" as to comparability. For compensation, data might include compensation levels paid by similarly situated organizations (both tax-exempt and taxable) for functionally comparable positions; the location of the organization, including the availability of similar specialties in the geographic area; current compensation surveys compiled by independent firms; or actual written offers from similar organizations competing for the services of the disqualified person. For property transactions, relevant information includes current independent appraisals and offers received as part of an open and competitive bidding process.

  - Adequately documented the basis for its decision when the actual decision was made. For example, the board minutes should include the terms of the transaction and date of approval, the members present and voting, the comparability data relied on and how it was obtained, and any actions taken regarding consideration of the matter by anyone on the board or committee who had a conflict of interest.

Practical Tips

- In addition to paying close attention to the legal requirements for setting appropriate compensation, be sensitive to the public's perception of what is acceptable or reasonable.
- Do your homework: there are numerous national and local nonprofit compensation surveys available.
- For smaller nonprofits that can't afford consultants or published national surveys, do local research and investigate compensation packages in similar organizations. Contact the organizations directly, or rely on GuideStar for

posted Form 990s. Other information sources include professional associations, management support centers, and nonprofit resource centers.

- Equally, when financial benefits must be limited, there are many other ways the board can compensate and support the chief executive. Consider a more flexible working environment, opportunities for professional development, and sabbaticals.
- Many of these suggested guidelines should be considered when reviewing compensation of other executive staff, particularly the president, chief operating officer, chief financial officer, and anyone else with substantial influence over the organization or a major section of the organization.

Financial Controls

As part of its financial oversight of the organization, the board is responsible for ensuring that appropriate internal controls are in place—and adhered to—to protect the organization. (For further discussion of financial controls, see Chapter Eight.) These internal controls ensure that the organization is using generally accepted accounting principals, complying with applicable laws and regulations, providing reliable financial information, and operating efficiently. More specifically, financial controls are designed to segregate financial duties, protect against asset loss, protect cash receipts, keep track of inventory, ensure an efficient bidding process, produce timely reports, and maintain accurate recordkeeping.

For a sample policy, see the Appendix.

Key Elements

- Good financial practice requires boards to have policies for the handling of money by staff and board alike. Such policies include controls put on check-signing authority, transfer of funds, cash disbursement, contracts, and other financial transactions.
- Financial controls provide broad guidelines for significant financial transactions, but the board should not get involved in determining (or monitoring) how the staff handles daily transactions.
- An area of financial concern is the approval of capital expenditures, such as for equipment and other tangible assets, made by the staff. Nonprofit organizations often have financial limits beyond which a chief executive cannot go without board approval.

Practical Tips

- Depending on the scope of the organization's other financial policies, consider ensuring that certain internal management controls are established and requiring that they be reviewed annually.

- In managing funds, the board generally delegates day-to-day control to staff; however, the board should keep control of borrowing money. Excessive borrowing is not in the interest of the organization and may signal a lack of sufficient financial controls on the part of staff and board.
- Review the organization's financial policies and procedures regularly. This task can be delegated to the audit or finance committee.
- If the board approves the establishment of credit card accounts for the organization, the chief executive must establish clear processes to ensure proper use of the cards for business purposes only.

Board Member Fundraising

Board members have a crucial role to play in raising funds for the organization they serve (see Chapter Nine). They are volunteers dedicated to the mission of the organization and the people served by the organization. And they have contacts in the community. The expectation of board member involvement in fundraising continues to rise, yet many boards have not created a policy that specifies what that involvement should entail. A board fundraising policy can take the form of a narrative or a specialized agreement or contract in which board members indicate the amount they expect to contribute to the organization in the coming year and how they will participate in the fundraising efforts of the organization.

For a sample policy, see the Appendix.

Key Elements

- Personal giving policies state whether a board member is expected to give a certain amount or to give according to his or her means. Funders often ask whether 100 percent of board members give and 100 percent participate in fundraising.
- Fundraising policies establish expectations for board members to make a personal donation and to participate in solicitation efforts. The policy may list examples of how board members can or should be involved, such as providing names of potential donors, writing or signing fundraising letters, thanking donors personally, accompanying the chief executive on donor and foundation visits, or making the ask themselves.
- Some organizations use a special pledge form that guides board members in thinking about the array of fundraising activities taking place throughout the year and asks them to make an annual fundraising commitment.
- Some nonprofits incorporate board member fundraising expectations into more general job descriptions.

- If the organization has a separate fundraising body (maybe a supporting organization), it is still important to outline the role for board members and how they relate to this body—and vice versa.

Practical Tips

- To become a committed fundraiser, a board member must first make a contribution. This requirement is the cornerstone of individual fundraising because it allows a board member to use himself or herself as an example of someone who supports the organization.
- Not every board member will be able to give the same size gift. Some organizations stipulate a minimum gift amount; most do not. The policy should encourage each board member to make the organization a priority in his or her personal giving plan or to make what is, for that person, a substantial financial contribution. The policy should not, however, eliminate capable and valuable individuals from joining the board and contributing other skills and expertise.
- Board members possess different skill levels and aptitudes for solicitation. To help each board member gradually assume more responsibility, members should be given training in fundraising and practical tools like checklists, sample elevator speeches, and steps for approaching a potential donor. Providing mentors and coupling inexperienced board members with staff or more seasoned board members is another way to increase everybody's comfort with personal solicitations.
- Some individuals, because of their profession or position (for example, journalists and judges), may be prohibited from certain kinds of fundraising solicitations (such as workplace campaigns). The board should seek other activities for these board members to pursue so they can still support the organization in a meaningful way.

Human Resources

The board is ultimately responsible for the personnel policies of the organization. In practice, this means that the board should periodically review the personnel policies to ensure that they are appropriate and up-to-date. The board may also consider overarching employment policies that reflect the organization's values and desired interactions with its stakeholders—clients, volunteers, staff, and/or the public. That said, except for its supervision of the chief executive, the board does not usually get involved with human resource management. In practice, this means that the board delegates general responsibility to the chief executive for the nonprofit's employment practices.

Personnel policies cover such things as hours of work, paid holidays, paid leave for illness and personal reasons, and employment status. They also cover issues that may lead to litigation, such as employee complaints, discrimination, and sexual harassment. It is especially important for the board to provide guidance on these areas. So, in delegating responsibility to the chief executive, the board should be sure to articulate core elements related to human resource issues and the workplace environment.

For a sample policy, see the Appendix.

Key Elements

- A simple policy helps to delegate responsibility for the organization's employment practices and procedures to the chief executive. The chief executive may in turn carry out that responsibility himself or herself or by assigning it to another employee (such as a human resource manager).
- Nonprofit organizations often borrow personnel policies—from more established organizations and/or those with similar programs—to serve as guidelines, but the personnel policies of each organization should reflect the values of that particular organization. The board should ensure that any borrowed policies meet the requirements of the state laws that are applicable to them.
- In young nonprofit organizations, with their first paid staff, the board may be reluctant to create personnel policies out of fear that the policies imply a lack of trust. Although board members may want to maintain the collegial work environment, they should not underestimate the value of clear guidelines in helping the organization function better and avoiding potential problems in the future.

Practical Tips

- Make certain that the dissemination of policies to employees does not constitute a contract between management and employees that could result in legal liability under state laws if the policies are not followed. In states where policy manuals may be deemed to constitute contracts, employers can protect themselves by adding a waiver in prominent language, preferably at the beginning of the manual, which states that the manual and/or the policies stated in it do not constitute a contract. Often, this waiver clarifies that employment with the organization is at will, meaning that employees can be terminated for any reason that does not violate federal or state law.
- Adapting personnel policies from a comparable organization is an efficient strategy. It's important to have specialists in human resource management and employment law review all personnel policies to make sure they are fair

and equitable and that they include all legally required elements. Sometimes a board member with special expertise may serve as a resource for reviewing and updating the policies.

Chapter Exercises

- List specific bylaws clauses that are bound to change as the organization evolves. How might these issues be handled in a start-up board and then in a more mature board?
- How do you draw the line between what is too detailed for the bylaws and what processes should be explained in that document? Why is this an issue?
- If the bylaws give the members specific rights to influence how the board functions, why should a bylaws clause also give the members the right to approve amendments to the document?
- What types of financial policies should the board regulate and what types belong to the staff?

CHAPTER FIFTEEN

BOARD MEETINGS

A board cannot perform without meetings. Regular meetings are the place for a board to make decisions, a place where individual board members "fuse" into the group that is responsible and liable for the organization. Meetings are where the board carries out its role as policy maker, sets direction for the organization, defines and follows its own ethical guidelines, oversees operations, and takes care of its own well-being. Together, individuals act as the board.

Meeting attendance is not optional. Preparing for and participating in board meetings is a duty that comes with board service. Generally, all of the board's activities cannot be accomplished in a meeting that lasts only a few hours, so individuals, task forces, and committees carry out decisions made in the boardroom or prepare work for the full board to act on at the next meeting. All this action culminates in a masterfully conducted board meeting in which every minute is spent on issues that advance the mission of the organization. This may sound idealistic, but with a solid objective as a guide, any board can improve its performance, and members can leave the meeting with a sense of real accomplishment and personal satisfaction.

The faster pace of society and the presence of younger and more assertive board members have pushed boards to streamline their structures and operations, including meetings. Busy executives and energetic young professionals want to get in, get the job done, and move on. But each board needs to strike an appropriate balance that will ensure fast-paced, efficient meetings while maintaining the spirit of teamwork and collegiality among board members. The collegial spirit can disappear when meetings become too structured, but valuable board members may leave if they feel their time is not used productively.

Achieving the all-important balance requires careful organization and preparation for board meetings. The most effective boards plan their meetings to focus on the important matters of governance while preserving the sense of community and mission that brings the organization together. Operating efficiently should allow more time, not less, for personal interaction among board members to build mutual understanding and respect. Dealing with issues that allow board members to use their skills and expertise makes board meetings more informative and interesting, thus providing a greater incentive for members to attend and participate in them.

Sunshine Laws

Nonprofits that receive government funding or government contracts are usually affected by sunshine laws, or open-meeting laws: state laws intended to bring transparency to nonprofit processes and show the public how they carry out their business. Board meetings are covered by these regulations.

Sunshine laws vary in their specificity. Some serve as general guides; others address every conceivable detail of your meeting arrangement. For example:

- In California, meetings must be held within the boundaries of the jurisdiction of the organization.
- In Oregon, an executive session may constitute the entire meeting.
- In Wisconsin, a meeting notice must be announced at least two hours before the meeting starts.
- In Utah, names and content of those commenting during the meeting must be included in the minutes.
- Virginia lists more than twenty different situations in which closed meetings may be held.
- In Colorado, if e-mail is used to discuss public business, it counts as a meeting and is therefore public information.

The Reporters Committee for Freedom of the Press (www.rcfp.org/tapping/index.cgi) provides state-by-state guidelines on sunshine laws. It is important to know your state laws and set them as the minimum requirement for your board.

> ## What Should the Bylaws Say About Board Meetings?
>
> An organization's bylaws provide the framework for board meetings by providing clear guidance for how a board goes about making decisions—for example, explaining that the board uses the consensus-building method to reach agreements. The bylaws should not, however, get into the nitty-gritty aspect of process and procedure, such as where and when the meetings should take place, who drafts the agenda, or what goes into a consent agenda. Those issues should be discussed separately and clarified in guidelines, policies, and resolutions, when appropriate, and these should be shared with new board members in a separate policy manual or the board handbook.

Planning the Meeting

Successful board meetings begin long before the board chair calls the meeting to order. The chief architects of the meetings, the board chair and the chief executive, should shape each meeting around the answers to two questions:

- What is the purpose of this meeting?
- How can we organize the meeting to fulfill that purpose?

Preparation includes establishing the time and place of the meeting, confirming it with board members, determining the issues to be covered, preparing and providing background information, and preparing and circulating draft proposals for action so board members have time to gather the information they need to determine their initial positions.

Most effective board meetings happen after successfully coordinated efforts of board and staff. There must be someone authorized or expected to call the meeting, compile materials, set the agenda, and handle all the logistics. And participants must do their share and do their homework. Orchestration of a board meeting requires time, resources, and selfless effort.

An organization's bylaws provide the framework for board meetings by providing clear guidance for how a board goes about making decisions.

Setting an Annual Schedule

Successful board meetings begin with an annual schedule so that all members know in advance when and where meetings will take place and what they will cover. Some organizations set their meetings as much as three years in advance, to give busy board members plenty of time to keep those dates clear and avoid scheduling conflicts.

Setting up a yearly meeting calendar should include taking time to determine if a meeting requires the full board's presence or if other groups (task forces, committees) can handle the business. Some procedures and issues must be covered at specific times, and scheduling them on an annual calendar of meetings enables the board and staff to plan accordingly.

Determining Meeting Frequency

There is no definitive number of meetings that can be recommended as applicable to every board. State laws, in many cases, require that a nonprofit board hold at least one meeting annually, but the boards of most organizations meet more frequently because one meeting per year hardly allows the board to pay proper attention to its fiduciary duties. The frequency of board meetings (monthly, bimonthly, quarterly) can depend on several factors, from geography and function to the board's life cycle and capacity to whether the organization is local, national, or international in scope. Some boards, for example, need enough time between their meetings to engage in committee or task force work and to review relevant reports related to upcoming board action items.

The amount of work to be accomplished in alignment with the organization's strategic plan will influence the frequency of meetings. When the organization has a very small staff and a "working board," or when the organization faces a crisis situation, meetings may need to take place monthly or on an as-needed basis. On the other hand, some boards may meet monthly even when such frequency is not necessary, either because committees and task forces do not function as they should or because the board has simply gotten in the habit of meeting every four weeks. These boards should have a serious discussion on the purpose of their meetings.

Take these steps to determine how frequently the board needs to meet:

- Develop an annual plan that assigns board tasks and functions to the time of the budget before the organization's fiscal year begins and review the audit results several months after the fiscal year ends. This scheduling enables all board members to see what contributions they will need to make and when.
- Assign routine functions that are not time sensitive—such as review of bylaws and policies or review of liability exposure and insurance coverage—to specific meetings as well, so that they are not all left until the last meeting of the year. Through this process, the board chair and chief executive may determine that committees and task forces can handle some tasks between meetings, reducing the need for the full board to meet.

- Consider policies regarding the frequency with which board members can participate by conference call. Too often they are simply disembodied voices to the rest of the board.

An organization might, for example, devote one meeting per year to basic board operating functions, including election of new members and board officers and the review of program evaluations and financial reports from the previous year. This meeting might also include a review of and adjustments to committee and task force memberships, as well as a presentation by a motivational speaker or governance consultant.

Meetings Without a Boardroom

If state law allows it, meeting by videoconference or teleconference can be an option when every board member is not able to sit around the same table. Electronic meetings should not replace face-to-face meetings, but they can bring the board together quickly in an emergency, save costs by cutting down long-distance travel and staff involvement, or keep committees and task forces in touch in between regular meetings. However, note that teleconferencing should not be used for major planning meetings or for sorting out a conflict, and videoconferencing should not be used by large boards (in general, more than fifteen members). The facilitator's role in this type of meeting is more complicated, but as long as all members understand the guidelines, this format can be a convenient way to encourage participation.

For a smooth teleconference:

- Be mindful of different time zones. Choose a convenient hour for everyone to be a part of the meeting.
- Start with a roll call to establish a quorum.
- Ask every speaker to identify himself or herself before making a comment.
- Pay special attention to how to involve all board members.
- Don't allow people to speak at the same time.
- Ask members to call from a quiet location and to speak clearly.
- Follow up with minutes if decisions were made.

For a well-organized videoconference:

- Have a contingency plan in case contact is lost or interrupted.
- Practice and test the system and tech sites ahead of time.
- Try to find convenient contact sites for members, or organize regional contact points.
- Include expenses for this method in the budget.

Meeting Communication and Documentation

Communication with board members happens on a continuum, and information exchange is a constant activity during and between meetings. Communication can be facilitated by accurate and comprehensive documents as well as a clear understanding of the boundaries between official and private communication dealing with board and organizational matters. Board documents provide a permanent record of the board's activities, discussions, and decisions and, if properly kept, can provide the board with some legal protection.

Agendas and Consent Agendas

In most organizations the chair and the chief executive draft the agenda. The chair ensures that topics included are appropriate for the board and that all relevant issues are incorporated. The chief executive adds topics that the board would not otherwise know of, such as the organization's operational challenges and successes since the last meeting, and possible future issues the board should be prepared to tackle. Together the two leaders can prioritize the issues while ensuring that the agenda is not too staff-driven or operational but still includes the chief executive's internal perspective. It also is helpful to highlight the items in the agenda requiring board voting—even provide a list of main discussion points.

The topics on the agenda should reflect the organization's strategic plan or framework to stimulate strategic thinking, inquiry, and analysis on core issues (see Chapter Ten for more about the value of strategic thinking). A future-focused agenda gives attention to the board's oversight responsibilities while dedicating a major part of the meeting to timely issue discussions geared toward the organization's next stage.

To increase efficiency and ensure that the board addresses important issues, many organizations have adopted a format that opens with a consent agenda, followed by substantive matters in order of importance. A consent agenda groups together uncontested items that require board action but not discussion or debate—such as approval of meeting minutes, acceptance of reports from committees and the chief executive, and final approval of other items on which the board has previously deliberated. Using a consent agenda reduces the amount of time a board must dedicate to handling routine matters, allowing it to discuss initiatives that will shape organizational strategy and actions.

Materials for the consent agenda should be included in the board book so that board members review the items and are prepared to approve them as a group, without discussion. Some boards use a password-protected online discussion group for board discussion of issues on the consent agenda prior to the meeting.

The consent agenda is the first item voted on during the meeting. The chair asks whether any items in the package require discussion; if so, the chair withdraws those items from the consent agenda for later discussion.

With all controversial items shifted out of the consent agenda, the board can approve the package and then move on to the rest of the meeting agenda, which should contain two types of items:

- Discussion items that share information or pose big-picture, what-if questions and ask for board members' input.
- Action items that convey information, knowledge, or data and require a board decision or vote. Examples include voting on the annual budget and setting strategic planning goals. Any printed material related to action items must be sent ahead to all board members so they can prepare accordingly.

Ideally, items should appear on the agenda in order of importance, not history, with top-priority items coming first. Most meetings have one or two items that require special attention, yet all too often these appear late on the agenda, when board members have started closing their notebooks to leave. (See Exhibit 15.1.)

EXHIBIT 15.1. MEETING AGENDAS

Sample Agenda One

[Name of organization]
Board of Directors Meeting
Monday, September 15, 20XX 8:30 a.m. – 4:30 p.m.
2000 Main Street, Suite 200
Our Town, VA 22222

A. Welcome and Chair's Remarks
B. Consent Agenda

- Approval of minutes of June 15, 20XX
- Approval of agenda
- Chief Executive's Report
- Treasurer's Report
- Committee Reports

C. Collaboration Proposal
D. Introduction to New Membership Program
E. Upcoming Planning Process
F. Adjournment

(Continued)

Sample Agenda Two

[Name of organization]
Board of Directors Meeting
Date: Monday, March 15, 20XX
Time: 6:00 p.m.
Location: 100 Main Street, Our Town, ME 01234

Agenda Items	Accountable	Purpose	Time
Welcome	Chair		5 min.
Introduction of new members	Chair	Information	5 min.
Consent agenda Previous minutes President's report Committee reports Leasing contract	Chair	Decision	1 min.
City contract proposal	John Murphy	Decision	15 min.
Summer program	Dianne Letts	Decision	15 min.
Relocation proposal	Cary Mann	Discussion	30 min.
Term limits	Becky Lowes	Discussion	20 min.
Adjournment	Chair		1 min.

The estimated amount of time allotted for each item can also help guide the meeting's pace. Some organizations list the phone number of the board member responsible for an agenda item, so any member who needs more information after reading the meeting materials can call. This practice eliminates redundant questions during the meeting itself, enabling the board chair to keep everyone focused on the most important or complex issues.

It is the job of the meeting facilitator to stay on time and on topic. If discussion lags with no sign of resolution, it makes sense to send the matter to a committee, along with a charge to bring a recommendation to the next board meeting.

Mission Moments

Without a connection to the fundamental reasons why the organization exists, board members can leave meetings knowing only about financial windfalls or shortfalls, personnel changes, capital needs, fundraising plans, and committee reports. By scheduling a regular "mission moment" (or two) that demonstrates the organization's relationship with stakeholders, the board can ensure that members don't lose sight of the organization's mission.

Schedule a mission moment during the middle of each board meeting. Invite someone whose life has been touched by what you do to give a short, personal testimonial: a client or client family, a grateful patient, a satisfied symphony patron, or kids who love camping. Here are some examples of effective mission moments:

- For the board of a learning disability center for children, a teacher from the school district came to tell the board what a difference she saw in learning skills development among children who had been in its programs.
- For a medical center board, members of a patient's family came to thank the board for creating the hospice program that had provided comfort and support for their grandmother and the entire family.
- For a baroque orchestra board, musicians from the orchestra came to each board meeting over a year's time to explain more about their rare and unusual instruments and to give a short concert.
- For a nurses' association board, a nurse discussed how the changes in accreditation requirements have improved the quality of care in her hospital.

Reports

All reports, including those submitted by committees, should be written and included in the board book (see sidebar below), ideally as part of the consent agenda if they are not separate discussion points during the meeting. This practice gives board members time to review the reports and formulate their questions and comments for the deliberation. It does not give them an excuse to ignore the information or provide the means for a small group to slip something past the full board.

What a "Board Book" Should Include

The board book is the main tool used to prepare members of the board for fruitful discussion. In addition to the agenda (with the consent agenda clearly noted), it should contain all of the necessary materials and documents that address issues listed in the agenda:

- Financial reports
- Committee reports
- Chief executive's report
- Minutes from the previous meeting
- Any relevant background information for discussion items
- Update on the issues to be voted on

(Continued)

- Related newspaper articles
- Update on relevant legal issues affecting the organization
- Organization's newsletter

Sharing board books electronically makes sense. Posting the materials on a member-secured intranet or web page also makes them accessible after the meeting. Board members are still likely to print materials, however, and may even need to have them available at the meeting. Projecting the documents on a screen during the meeting may gradually help board members wean themselves from this habit.

The purpose of a committee report is to keep the board informed on the evolution of a project, communicate the results of a specific task that the committee undertook, engage the board in discussion of an issue, or present recommendations for board action. If nothing has happened since the last meeting, no report should be necessary. The report is not the same as committee meeting minutes. The board does not need to know those details, but requires a consolidated message that the group wants to convey to the rest of the board. It makes sense to develop a format for all committee reports or at least set clear guidelines on what is relevant and essential.

Only reports that directly influence decisions on the agenda need to be presented orally at the meeting itself. Some reports might be updates—if, for example, the organization has a fundraising campaign underway or is engaged in negotiations to purchase or sell a property—while other reports would be included in the consent agenda and require no discussion. Only the action items call for oral transmission and deliberation.

Policy Compendiums

Board members and staff rarely know the policy history of the organization, and sometimes they initiate new proposals that contradict or duplicate existing policies. To avoid this trap, the organization could create a compendium of all policies ever adopted by the board. The compendium should include an index to facilitate location of existing policies on any subject.

A task force, a volunteer, or an intern can undertake this process, ideally producing an electronic product that is searchable and easily updated. Once the compendium is complete, board members can research the history and current policies on any subject before presenting new policy proposals.

Dashboards

Just as an automobile dashboard offers the driver a status report on key functions at a glance, a nonprofit dashboard provides a synopsis of the organization's "vital signs." In a graphic format, dashboards—described in more detail in Chapter Thirteen—show nonprofit boards where the organization is thriving and where it is struggling at a given point in time.

A single page included in the board book distributed before each meeting helps board members arrive with an indication of areas that may require special attention. Indicators might include historic comparisons and relationships with budgets and plans. Financial indicators might show year-to-date donations compared with budget projections and receipts at the same time a year ago. Similarly, rates of participation or attendance for programs or services can be presented in an easily understood graphic format.

Minutes

Minutes are the permanent record of a board meeting. They provide information about when the meeting occurred and the actions taken. Historically, the secretary writes the minutes, but today it is more common for a staff member to have that role. Some organizations follow strict rules regarding the format; others may be more informal. Minutes are a necessary legal document, but they are also a practical means of conveying information about what action was taken at a meeting. Some common uses of minutes are as reference material, as board history, as a legal review of the proceedings, and as a board orientation tool.

While content can vary, the basic elements of good minutes include

- Organization name
- Meeting date and starting time
- Board members in attendance and absent
- Existence of a quorum
- Motions made and by whom
- Voting results
- Names of abstainers and dissenters
- Reports and documents introduced
- Future action steps
- Time the meeting ends

The minutes are not a transcript, nor should they try to be a verbatim account of the meeting. They are simply a record of the decisions made and the action taken. When a debate or discussion is recorded, only the major points for and against the issue at hand are included. It is important for members to be able to have meaningful discussions without being concerned about individual liability; therefore, names or direct quotations should not be recorded in relation to the debate.

Minutes need to include enough information to be a useful resource. Someone looking at the minutes should be able to understand what decisions were made and the reasons why. Skeletal minutes that include only the motions and whether they passed do not provide an adequate record.

Taping the Meeting. Making an audiotape of the meeting can be a useful tool for the person writing the minutes, for long or involved meetings, but it should not replace the written minutes. If the person uses tapes—with the full board's consent—the board needs a written policy for how to deal with them after the minutes are written in order to protect board members from legal liability. If tapes are destroyed, a policy should state so.

Legal Considerations. Minutes are a legal record of a meeting. They can be used in court if questions of legal liability concerning a program or policy arise; therefore they should be an accurate reflection of what occurred at a meeting. If minutes provide the right information, they can be helpful to the organization during a legal review. Any actions or questions around a specific legal issue should be included, with appropriate detail provided. Issues such as a conflict of interest should be noted along with the action that board member took. Individual board members who disagree with a board decision and are concerned about personal liability should have their dissent noted in the minutes.

After the Meeting. The completed minutes are circulated to the board prior to the next board meeting so that members can review them for mistakes or missing information. If minor corrections can be made before the next meeting, then approval of the minutes can be part of the consent agenda. Otherwise, corrections should be addressed at the next meeting, and any changes voted on. The minutes are then approved, signed by the secretary and the chair, and archived. The archives of minutes should be organized and easy to locate.

Meaningful Minutes

Are your board meeting minutes detailing every second of your hours-long meetings? If so, it is time to take a hard look at the document and turn it into a useful and informative record that can be defended if ever put to a test by a board member or even the courts. Ask the following questions:

Do our minutes meet the legal test?

To serve as a legal document, your minutes should be accurate, state that your quorum requirements were met (as well as any other condition potentially demanded by your state laws), and address every action item during your meeting.

Do our minutes meet the practical test?

To make sense and prove useful, your minutes should be written concisely and in clear English. They should follow the sequence of events but not be a transcript of everything that was said or done during the meeting.

Is every board member willing to approve the document?

Each board member should consider the minutes a sound description of the meeting. Some board members may have disagreed with decisions made during the meeting, but they should feel comfortable that the decision is accurately recorded and, when applicable, their absence, disagreement, or active participation is correctly noted.

Would the document stand the test of time?

To confirm the outcome of a previous debate, see who was present or serving on the board years ago, or verify whether a policy actually was approved during a particular board meeting, you need to be able to find the information. Consider the minutes as part of your board and organization's history.

Communication Between Meetings

For most boards, communication continues between meetings as information and documents are shared. Minutes are circulated before the next session. Meeting planners need feedback on logistical issues. The chief executive carries on continuous conversation with the chair and the rest of the board. The chair follows up on board assignments. Some matters need not enter the boardroom and should be handled only outside of official sessions. Electronic communication is the most efficient mechanism.

Boards use a variety of options for facilitating communication between the senior staff and board and board members among themselves:

- E-mail for transmitting documents, suggesting future agenda options, and sharing personal news with board colleagues
- A special section on the organization's Web site, accessible only to board members, for archiving documents and providing a permanent contact place
- An online discussion group or a chat room for board members
- A blog written by the chief executive to communicate how the organization is connected and involved in the community
- Webinars conducted by staff on specific topics for board education

- LinkedIn networking under the organization's name as a tool for sharing information that is not confidential
- Twitter for quick project updates (not to be used for internal board matters)

Meeting Structure, Decision Making, and Voting

A board has total freedom to choose its method for conducting its meetings, as long as all legal requirements and genuine ethical expectations are met. No state law or federal law wants to regulate the very detailed processes—or lack thereof—in a private business meeting. Fortunately, the choice to follow a strict parliamentary procedure or take a more relaxed approach is an internal decision. Some structure and order are necessary to keep proceedings from getting out of hand and to help guide the decision-making process.

Chairing the Meeting

The role of facilitating the board meeting usually falls to the chair (or vice-chair, when necessary). The chair makes sure that the agenda fits the meeting and that the board members fulfill their roles and responsibilities to achieve the objectives set out on the agenda. The chair also sets the tone, the pace, and the process for board meetings. The goal is to ensure that members feel welcome, participate, and spend their time together productively by focusing on action and decision making.

To enable the board to make knowledgeable decisions, the board chair and chief executive can use provocative questions to prompt thoughtful discussion. They don't rush deliberation. They also incorporate executive sessions with and without the presence of the chief executive—not to escape difficult dialogue but to encourage frank discussion of confidential issues.

Qualities of a Good Meeting Facilitator

The board chair can rely on these tested principles to facilitate a productive meeting:

- Know board members thoroughly—what personal attributes they can contribute and who is in need of special attention.
- Own the agenda. The chair should be familiar with the items and seek a wide range of opinions.
- Explain any personal philosophies of running meetings to members, to create a mutual understanding of what is acceptable and where the limits lie.

- Engage every board member during the meeting. Don't let the timid escape or the tired sleep.
- Control the domineering characters. Do not let the verbose members dominate the floor. Try to bring out the best in even the difficult colleagues.
- Remain objective and fair. Let controversial issues and opinions come out. Don't let personal opinions influence facilitation.
- Be familiar with basic meeting procedures. Know the conventional process and when to safely break from the conventional.
- Earn the respect of peers. Even if the chair is part of the group, in the facilitator capacity the chair must function as a neutral leader.
- Use humor in the boardroom. If it does not come naturally, study ways to relax the atmosphere. There is no law dictating that board meetings should be stiff and boring.

The bylaws of most organizations indicate that meetings should follow *Robert's Rules of Order*. Few board members, however, have ever read these rules—and if they had, they probably would not have thought them appropriate for their boards. In fact, *Robert's Rules* were developed for a large parliamentary setting in which representatives look out for the constituents who elected them and do whatever is necessary to gain acceptance of their opinions. In such a setting, careful attention to process is necessary to guard against tyranny of the loudest and endless arguments over procedure.

Every nonprofit board meeting needs a framework, defined processes, and order, and the use of basic parliamentary procedure can keep things moving forward. But a nonprofit board meeting should focus on discussion and deliberation rather than structuring every expression into a specific order. In other words, each board should adopt a system of rules that still allows for flexibility. The rules should free the board chair to guide deliberation in a manner that invites open discussion and creative solutions. The board chair determines when all opinions have been heard and the group is ready to vote, puts the motion back on the table, and records the results.

Unless its bylaws stipulate the use of *Robert's Rules of Order*, a board should determine what rules and procedures it intends to follow for meeting management. At a minimum, rules should include

- Determining whether a quorum is present
- Declaring when the meeting starts and adjourns
- Making and seconding motions
- Allowing the chair to facilitate discussion and make judgment
- Handling dissension

- Tabling an agenda item
- Making calls when order is lost or unruly members dominate the floor
- Reaching a general understanding of procedure when an impasse occurs

---

Electing a Devil's Advocate and Devil's Inquisitor

To push a board into thinking more creatively or to unblock tendencies of stagnation, the board may want to create an official position of a "devil's advocate." By choosing a single member, or rotating the job among board members, the devil's advocate has the role of purposefully contradicting presented arguments. As long as it is understood that this is the intended role of the board member during the meeting, the board can turn the idea into a productive game. The devil's advocate does not need to feel left outside of the actual debate if that person simply makes sure his or her point of view comes up during the discussion or as one of the counterpoints or questions.

You may also encourage board members to serve as "devil's inquisitors." The role of these individuals is not to purposefully contradict a statement or position but to always ask the questions that nobody else wants to ask—those difficult questions that most of us normally find embarrassing or "dumb." The purpose of these questions is to clarify and simplify the issue under discussion and to ensure that everyone ultimately is on the same page and has at least a basic understanding of the details. These questions could come in handy particularly when the board is looking at the financial statements and not every member is a financial wizard.

Attendance

Board members must take meeting attendance seriously and make it a priority. They must attend board meetings to fulfill their duty of care—a legal obligation that defines the attention, thought, and consideration they must exercise in their role as guardians of the organization.

In addition, board members who miss meetings can affect the board's ability to have a quorum. State law often defines a quorum as a majority of voting members; an organization's bylaws may set a higher standard. Without a quorum, the meeting is not official and the decisions made cannot be regarded as binding on the organization.

Although this legal consideration is significant, many board members do not find it particularly compelling. Ultimately, board members convene because they have developed positive working relationships with one another and believe their participation is essential to maximizing the board's assets. Board members attend because the meetings matter to them and they feel their participation matters to the meetings.

In addition to board members, the chief executive naturally attends the entire meeting. The chief executive provides the insider perspective and information on the organization's activities and their outcomes, ongoing needs, and opportunities for growth or further outreach. The chief executive's participation enhances the board's ability to deliberate and make informed decisions.

Other staff members usually don't attend the entire meeting, but only those portions that relate to their areas of expertise or require the sharing of information relevant to specific agenda items. Although it can make chief executives and boards nervous, structured staff participation in board meetings enhances staff morale and helps build strong board-staff relationships. Having staff present also makes it possible to quickly answer board questions or verify details about finances, programs, and other issues for which the senior staff is responsible.

Decision Making

Board meeting decisions in no way differ from other decisions individuals make in their own lives. Without an open and careful study of the details that make up a case, one can end up relying on wishful thinking rather than on facts and experience. A diversified board that can bring a variety of opinions and expertise into the discussion has a better chance of guiding the organization in the right direction—a responsibility that weighs heavily on every board member's shoulders.

Deliberation drives good decisions; it is the meat and bones of a meeting. During deliberation, members of the board discuss all sides of an issue. Without a thorough airing of all aspects relating to the issue under discussion, it is difficult to end up with a conclusion that is sound, well founded, and fair.

Reaching consensus is another approach for making decisions. Building consensus—a general agreement to a proposed idea—is not always well understood because it is a complicated process. It demands a skillful facilitator and requires that the board fully understand the consensus-building process. Consensus building may be the most democratic way of coming to a final accord, although it may not be an easy or quick way to run a board meeting.

The principle of consensus building assumes that all points of view are valid, and minority views are incorporated into the discussion. The goal is to find a solution that everyone can accept and is willing to implement. Consensus eliminates the win-or-lose approach of a majority vote because it does not count votes. It takes a more qualitative approach, not forcing a compromise but seeking to eliminate objections. It also encourages alternative thinking and fosters innovative solutions.

During the process, the facilitator presents a proposal and invites all participants to express their concerns or reservations. This input may result in a modification of the proposal, gradually allowing it to become more and more specific. Modification moves from major points to fine-tuning the final agreement. Prioritizing points is a useful way of eliminating unacceptable solutions. Synthesizing opinions brings clarification to concepts. When the facilitator feels that a mutual agreement has been reached, this is articulated and the chair asks whether participants agree that the articulated statement accurately reflects the consensus. If there is no objection, it is recorded as the group's decision.

Voting

Most state laws require that a majority of the board members present (after a quorum is determined) must agree before a vote is carried. A majority means 51 percent—or, if there are ten voting members present, six will carry the vote. A board could also agree ahead of time on what kinds of decisions demand deliberation, when a simple majority is enough, or when the board must rely on a higher level of agreement, or when the board does not even need to address the issue. Here are some examples of the range of situations:

- A conceptual amendment to a bylaws clause must be discussed and a super-majority must pass it.
- Firing a chief executive should be deliberated by the full board, with a high degree of consent needed.
- Deciding to use an executive search firm can be determined by a majority during a normal course of the meeting.
- Determining the keynote speaker at the next conference does not need to reach the boardroom. The chief executive can approve the choice and the good news will be shared with the board.
- The full board approves—and ideally reaches unanimity on—the chief executive's compensation package.
- The bylaws may give the chair the right to decide on who chairs each committee.

State law often defines whether a nonprofit board may use proxy votes. A proxy generally refers to either the person with a power of attorney or the piece of paper that conveys this power to vote or make decisions on behalf of a board member in his or her absence. For-profit corporations and nonprofit membership organizations commonly use this practice during membership meetings. However, for nonprofit boards, proxy voting is generally not a good practice, as it conflicts with the practice of listening together and discussing issues before voting.

Executive Sessions

When the board needs to discuss confidential or sensitive issues, the board chair should call for an executive session. In addition, the board chair should clarify whether other board members can request an executive session—and how to do so. (See sidebar, When Is an Executive Session Necessary?)

The issue being discussed will determine who participates in an executive session. Normally, all board members are present. The chief executive is present only if the issue does not relate to the chief executive; others who have relevant information to contribute may participate at the invitation of the chair. Only board members would participate in an executive session devoted to discussing the chief executive's performance review and compensation. Similarly, an executive session with the auditor does not include any staff.

Some boards occasionally have an executive session without the chief executive, to establish the habit and procedure. Establishing this pattern can help avoid a crisis of trust if a problem does arise—so no one feels uncomfortable, startled, or surprised by the board meeting in an executive session. In addition, these sessions give board members uninterrupted time to talk solely with one another.

Another type of executive session focuses on what Keeps the President AWake at Night (KPAWN). It devotes perhaps fifteen minutes to the issues of greatest concern to the chief executive. This not only enables the chief executive to vent without judgment but also gives the board a better understanding of and appreciation for the chief executive's responsibilities.

Usually, in an executive session, the conversation remains confidential and is not recorded in the minutes. The purpose of the session must be established ahead of time; the minutes of the board meeting should indicate the time when the board met in executive session, the purpose of the session, who was present, and a list of any actions taken or decisions made.

Because nonvoting participants in a board meeting will be asked to leave when an executive session begins, it is best to schedule the executive session just before a break or at the end of a board meeting. An organization's bylaws or board policies should spell out the procedures, which also warrant review during board member orientation.

When Is an Executive Session Necessary?

The following circumstances may demand confidentiality, a candid exchange of opinions, or the protection of individual rights:

- Investigation of alleged improper conduct by a board member
- Discussion of financial issues with an auditor
- Preparation for a case with a lawyer
- Exploration of planning for major endeavors, such as mergers or real estate deals
- Discussion of the board's approach to a scandal or negative publicity
- Handling of personnel issues, such as chief executive compensation, performance evaluation, or disciplinary issues
- Handling of any other matters where confidentiality has been requested or is otherwise prudent
- Peer-to-peer discussions about board operations

Evaluating the Meeting

To be productive, board meetings need to matter. As the agent for board effectiveness, the governance committee assumes responsibility for evaluating meetings and, in discussion with the board chair, recommending improvements. Investing a few minutes at the end of each meeting to ask board members what went well—and what didn't—can reap a substantial return.

The evaluations need not be personal or critical. They can gather valuable feedback for the next meeting by asking questions such as these:

- Did this meeting deal with substantive issues of strategic import to our board?
- Did the advance materials and reports provide the information you needed to make informed decisions?
- Did the chair keep the meeting on time and focused on the written agenda?
- Was ample time allowed for discussion and deliberation of each agenda item?
- Did this meeting use your time and talents wisely?

Board Retreats

Retreats involve the board as a group. They are often used for purposes of education, training, reflection, planning, or socializing. A retreat brings board members (and frequently senior staff) together to provide an environment in which free communication and brainstorming is possible. Often an outside facilitator is brought in to lead the proceedings and give every board member the opportunity to participate fully. Retreats can last from several hours to several days, often taking place over a weekend. In addition to handling business, socializing usually plays an important role during retreats. They are an excellent opportunity to mix work and recreation so that board members can get to know one another more intimately in a setting different from the more formal boardroom.

A retreat can be organized around a board orientation, a strategic planning session, a fundraising workshop, a board self-assessment, or a discussion of major internal or external strategic issues that are important to the nonprofit. If possible, the retreat should not take place in an office setting. A different environment helps send the message that new ideas and innovation are in order and creativity is desirable. There are a variety of special retreat accommodations to choose from, and the board can be creative in selecting the location. A good mixture of programmatic brainstorming activities and entertainment can help board members leave the retreat with a personal and professional sense of satisfaction and accomplishment.

Toward Better Board Meetings

When it comes to meetings, the board itself determines what works best. A board must work collectively—members must learn from each other and teach each other—no matter how different the players are. Each board must figure out what processes bring about the desired outcomes and then be bold enough to follow through, even if the means do not correspond to the traditional norms. Each board member must keep an open mind while adapting to team culture. Individuality is an asset in a board member, but it's the collective body that determines the course of action.

If board meetings do not focus on real, important, and relevant issues, they can be a waste of time. No matter how impeccable and considerate the processes are, if the board is working on the wrong issues, it is only perfecting the outer framework. The purpose of the board meeting is to bring board members together to steer the organization to its next level of potential. If the meeting time is spent on trivial issues, members will lose interest and feel unappreciated. By being strategic in planning the meetings' focus, the board can stay one step ahead, be proactive, and productively advance the mission of the organization.

What are the signs of a successful board meeting? When the meeting is over, board members walk out, chatting with each other—even smiling—because they feel they added value, their decisions will push the organization forward, and ultimately there will be concrete results among those served by the organization. A good meeting is a meeting of minds that are able to rely on collective wisdom (see Exhibit 15.2).

EXHIBIT 15.2. FROM A BOARD CHAIR: SIGNS OF A SUCCESSFUL MEETING

I know we've had a successful board meeting when

- We engage in a healthy discussion of issues and recommendations developed by staff. For example, when we consider human resource policies, we need to recognize that staff recommendations may focus on employee needs, such as a grievance policy that allows for numerous appeals, but the board needs to discuss whether our policies meet legal requirements and offer adequate protection for everyone involved.
- We have a lively discussion focused on strategic questions, such as "What will our organization look like in five years?" and "Will our mission have changed in significant ways?" When we recently posed these questions, our answers were not only informative and fun but also resulted in our thinking about innovative ways to broaden our reach and create a stronger volunteer and donor network.
- Board action clearly relates to our overall purpose. For example, we recently reviewed our priority projects and discussed how they would help us achieve our goals. I believe that any board that facilitates an open discussion, while keeping strategy at the forefront, will make sound decisions that benefit the organization.

Chapter Exercises

- Discuss how a board's meeting frequency might change during the organization's life cycle.
- Study various states' sunshine laws and explain why specific clauses are included.
- List strategic issues and specific tasks a board should remember to include in its annual meeting calendar.
- Why should the chair and chief executive draft the meeting agenda together?
- Why should every board member make it a priority to attend every board meeting? Discuss the consequences of lax quorum requirements.
- Should boards ever vote by secret ballot?

CHAPTER SIXTEEN

BOARD DYNAMICS

Exceptional boards, energized by a deep commitment to the work of their organizations, constantly search for solutions and seek to add value, according to BoardSource. They focus on purposefully developing the critical elements of board leadership, composition, structure, and practices. They also pay attention to the development of individual board members and the board as a whole. They continually strive to promote a working environment that encourages collaboration, partnership, engagement, trust, respect, flexibility, and interaction.

The board chair and the chief executive take the lead, but every board member also contributes to the overall group dynamic. Only by attending as purposefully to the development of the dynamics of the group as to the work of the group—governing—can a board hope to realize the promise of each individual member, gather individuals into a harmonious group, and harness the group's potential.

This chapter focuses on five key issues that affect the dynamics of a board's work, along with solutions to help boards develop and sustain productive environments for governing:

- Building trust to support collaborative governance
- Developing a culture of inquiry
- Ensuring independent-mindedness
- Recognizing and avoiding micromanagement
- Dealing with the problem of troublesome board members

Building Trust

Any collaborative effort relies on trust among team members, and building this trust is critical to the team's ultimate success. Board members must be able to rely on each other—as team members—openly and without reservation. The chair, individual board members, and the board as a body must develop a trusting relationship with each other and with the chief executive to consolidate mutual efforts and objectives. In short, when trust is present, everyone is driven by a common goal and shares information openly, accepting positive interdependence.

Honesty, respect, caring, integrity, and accountability: these are all elements closely tied to trust. In a group setting, members depend on each other; their individual and collective performance is based on reliability. Each member is committed to contributing to the common goal and entitled to expect the same from others. Trust is a two-way street—give and take must be on equal footing.

Building Trust in the Boardroom

A board is not a static entity, because members come and go. Term limits continually test group dynamics. Under these circumstances, a board has a challenge to create a culture of trust and loyalty that survives the flux of membership. New members need to be incorporated in the team from the first meeting on. This may mean their taking an active approach to board participation in order to become fully integrated. By accepting assignments and following through, each new member builds a reputation as a trustworthy peer.

This culture of trust is present when board members feel free to debate, question, openly examine, and even argue with each other's points of view without turning the discussion into—or perceiving it as—a personal attack. Differing opinions should be a welcomed tool to get to the heart of the matter under consideration. Respect for each other's contributions is the true foundation for professional reliance and interdependence.

Trust in the boardroom also assumes that appropriate confidential issues remain classified. Without that basic principle, the reputation of the organization may be endangered, openness of deliberation may be compromised, and individual board members may worry about what they must not say instead of participating in a free exchange of ideas.

The Board and the Chief Executive

The board and the chief executive are connected by the need to support each other in their respective roles. Board decisions are deficient without the inside professional perspective that the staff leader provides. The board must be able to trust that the information it receives is timely, accurate, and unfiltered and includes all the elements that allow the board to make educated and wise decisions. The board has the fiduciary duty to oversee the activities in the organization. In that capacity, it needs a healthy dose of constructive skepticism that is reasonably balanced with trust in the integrity and competence of the chief executive to avoid intrusiveness and micromanagement.

The chief executive needs to feel empowered and trusted as he or she engages in accomplishing the mutually accepted goals without the board needing to second-guess management actions. Equally, the chief executive must be able to count on the board's support with confidence. He or she must be able to go to the board for guidance, direction, or protection if a situation so demands without losing face. Unhindered communication builds trust between the board and the chief executive, and that trust must be earned.

Trust in the Organization

Every tax-exempt organization must earn the trust of its constituents. The board has the responsibility to ensure that the donors, customers and clients, staff, and any other stakeholders—including the general public—can feel confident that the organization is focused on its mission, efficient in allocating its funds, and able to show that it makes a difference for the public good. The board must ensure that reporting is guided by appropriate transparency and that all the necessary processes and procedures are employed to achieve this: making the Form 990 easily available, sharing financial statements, presenting the organization truthfully in its materials and brochures, and so forth.

Mechanisms for Building Trust

As the board incorporates trust in its role as the organization's representative, in its own methods of operating and in its relationship with the chief executive, it should keep the following in mind:

- Disclosing and providing easy access to organizational documents that describe financial and programmatic achievements is essential to gaining the public's trust.
- Transparency of the processes for making appointments to board positions and hiring the chief executive eliminates concerns about unfair treatment or discrimination.

- Incorporating a culture of positive dissent in the boardroom encourages board members to share opinions and accept counter-comments without turning issues into personal conflicts.
- Regularly occurring executive sessions remove secrecy from these meetings, which allow board members to openly and in confidence discuss internal issues without staff present.
- Regular KPAWN (what Keeps the President AWake at Night) meetings provide a safe, trusting environment for the chief executive to share personal and position-related challenges with the board.
- Annual chief executive performance evaluations allow for honest feedback and assessment of achievements under fair conditions if they are based on mutually agreed-upon goals.
- Board self-assessment, as a collective effort to judge how the team is working together, builds trust and confidence among board members.

Developing a Culture of Inquiry

When there's trust, board members are comfortable sharing different points of view and feel respected by other board members who are listening and considering their comments. Boards that foster a culture of inquiry are not afraid to question complex, controversial, or ambiguous matters or look at issues from all sides. Inviting smart people to do this not only can make a difference to the quality of the outcome but also can make board service more interesting and gratifying. These boards make better decisions because members are better informed as a result of robust discussions in which multiple ideas are vetted. There is less rubber-stamping on such boards. Board members take full ownership of decisions—because everyone's engaged, there's less need to revisit previous decisions, and meetings become more productive.

Any board can develop a culture of inquiry, although members should not expect it to happen overnight. But the costs of *not* developing such a culture can be high. Boards that cannot engage in candid discussions of complex issues unwittingly encourage their members to suppress or channel dissent in destructive ways. Conversely, board members as well as chief executives who understand that dissent does not equal disloyalty and that consensus does not equal unanimity have a greater appetite for these kinds of conversations.

It is almost impossible to maintain a culture of inquiry if the chief executive and the board chair do not embrace it. When they serve as advocates and role models, they often invest time in building trust, followed closely by three other practices and behaviors: information sharing, generative thinking, and well-attended, well-run meetings.

Information Sharing

Chief executives who regularly distribute relevant and timely articles to their board members keep them informed about what's happening in their sector. Some also invite guest speakers to meetings to provide continuing education about topics related to the organization's mission, programs, and community.

Besides external sources of information, board members have rich experiences that deserve to be mined. They may have been withholding precious social, political, and intellectual capital because the culture didn't prompt them to share it.

Access to useful information is necessary so members can be informed and then engage in lively and challenging discussions. There's nothing like having to defend your point of view to make you consider all sides of it. Such discussions help everyone improve the quality of thinking and the ultimate decisions.

Generative Thinking

In their book *Governance as Leadership*, Richard P. Chait, William P. Ryan, and Barbara E. Taylor highlight the value of generative thinking as a means of producing solutions based on deliberation and analysis—not on gut feelings or personal preferences. Of course, it is not realistic or productive to enlist this practice at every board meeting; rather, this approach is especially suited to embryonic, high-stakes issues that have not yet been clearly framed. While generative thinking is an enabler for a culture of inquiry, it can be noisy, scary, and fast. People talk. They challenge. They build on the ideas of others. They frame and reframe situations to think about them in new ways. But it's not just about the solution; it's about making sure they've identified the right problem—possibly something quite different from what they first thought it was.

To stimulate the sharing of different points of view, it's best to start slowly, perhaps by designating someone to play the role of devil's advocate. This useful tool pushes people to examine traditional thinking and question assumptions. The devil's advocate role should alternate among different board members (as explained in Chapter Fifteen), which is why it's important to recruit members who bring candor and reflection to their board roles.

Another trick to stimulate generative thinking, suggested by Chait and his colleagues, is to begin meetings by asking open-ended questions such as these: What's the biggest gap between what the organization claims it is and what it actually is?

What three short phrases best characterize this organization? What do you hope will be most strikingly different about this organization in five years? The discussions that result will help everyone begin to frame issues in new ways.

Well-Attended, Well-Run Meetings

The time the board spends together should be spent productively. Because the tone at the top will influence whether a culture of inquiry will flourish, the chief executive's and chair's roles are critical variables. Ideally, the chief executive is secure in inviting a range of views, and the chair possesses the skills to manage group dynamics, facilitate discussions, and encourage those not participating to join in and share their perspectives. Together, the chief executive and chair can carry out their roles as the "chief board development officers" by monitoring as well as supporting the culture. Is everyone's voice being heard? Are people listening? Is the atmosphere one in which people feel safe and comfortable sharing unpopular ideas and questions? Is there an agenda, and does it provide time to focus on what's important?

As the chair's ability to facilitate group interaction will influence the success of the board, it is important to look for this skill set in officer succession planning. When these qualities are not present in the chair (and when a board agenda item cries out for generative thinking), another, more skilled board member or an outside facilitator might facilitate the board discussion.

Independent-Mindedness

Independent-mindedness is fundamentally about making decisions free of undue influence. In the boardroom, it requires a measure of detachment that seems to contradict the energetic embracing of mission at the heart of board service and a periodic distancing from the executive and other influential players that can easily feel ungrateful or untrusting. An independent-minded attitude must come across as helpful rather than merely irritable and be exerted steadily rather than in fits and starts. Independent-mindedness is a board quality that depends heavily on the ability of individual board members to appreciate its value and find constructive ways to exercise it.

The greatest challenge in building an independent board is getting all the elements of good governance to come together: a sturdy framework of policy and practice; a smart, secure executive; enough collective time together to build experience and a decent culture; and finally, a strong majority of individual board members who have overcome their hodgepodge of experience, style, and attention spans to work together as a unit. Easier said than done.

Policy and Practice

Good governance is not achieved through mind reading. Nuance may be useful, but, generally speaking, subtlety is not. The natural turnover that is part and parcel of board life requires that an organization take the time to articulate its values and be frank about what constitutes acceptable performance. Why leave these matters to the imagination or rely solely on goodwill or good sense to maintain the effectiveness of the board and its capacity to be independent-minded? A clear conflict-of-interest policy with sensible mechanisms for complying with it (see Chapters Seven and Fourteen) does not imply a lack of faith in board members' ability to detect and avoid these situations on their own. Rather, it expresses a common understanding of what will put a board member in conflict with the interests of the organization, and it allows board members, the board, and the organization to deal with these moments consistently and in a straightforward, open, and unembarrassed way.

The same could be said of values statements and the agreements board members reach about their own behavior. One association board, whose members could be characterized more for their clout than for their deference, compiled a list of boardroom values that went beyond important but expected concepts, such as mutual respect and integrity, to include less expected—but probably more necessary—behaviors for the group, such as listening and the pledge to keep issues in the room and on the table. How much easier it is to agree as a board to park bad habits, personal interests, and hobby horses at the door than it is to correct misguided enthusiasm or blind spots, instance by painful instance.

Similarly, what makes more sense for the organization and the board: to look at the executive's performance in a thoughtful and consistent way each year or to put a process in place only when the relationship is under stress? Someday, the annual evaluation of the chief executive will be seen as the best way to strengthen everyone's performance rather than as a judgment (and possibly a punishment).

A Culture of Independent-Mindedness

Independent-mindedness is like regular exercise: the temptation to avoid it should be gently resisted. It is a challenge to chair a board or committee and make it your job to insist on preparation and invite healthy debate. It's tough to look at a budget and express doubt that, given past performance, the projected income is realistic, or to look at the cost of a project and wonder if the money is well spent. Even constructive criticism may initially be interpreted as implying that someone's favorite child is homely.

It is easier to go with the flow, particularly when the flow is swift and positive and deliberation might slow it down. In one organization, an energetic and charismatic executive produced outstanding results year after year. But a moment came when the executive found this pattern impossible to maintain, and it was even more difficult to admit this to his board. The board, not wanting to appear to doubt the executive's abilities, ignored the warning signs, and the result was the undoing of the organization.

Nothing kills independent-mindedness more quickly than prizing comfort over stewardship or mistaking timidity for politeness. This is not a culture in which good governance can thrive. Board chairs and executives recognize such behavior and discourage it. Instead, they invite good questions, play devil's advocate, and have the stamina to withstand a few knocks along the way. The chair in particular should know the difference and strike a balance between acceptance that masks passivity and healthy disagreement that risks becoming a free-for-all.

Independent-mindedness also requires critical mass. If only one or two members of the board have it in them to bring this quality to the boardroom, it is much harder for the board as a whole to enjoy it. All board members have an obligation to be attentive and engaged rather than diffident and disconnected.

Seeing the Relationship Clearly

Perhaps the toughest aspect of being independent-minded is separating the emotional content of the board's relationship to the chief executive and other players in the organization—whether a founder, influential board members, long-tenured program staff, or volunteers—from the work itself. It is the board's role to step back periodically and provide a deliberately neutral perspective.

Many mechanisms can support the positive neutrality that ensures that missions are met and people are served. Boards need not sacrifice powerful emotions; goals that board and staff believe in; evaluations of results that are genuinely thoughtful and rigorous; an evaluation process for the executive that is respectful but thorough; regular board self-assessment; and the habit of holding individual members accountable, not just for showing up but also for the quality of their participation. This last element is particularly challenging but essential to include as part of a culture of independent-mindedness. A board is too easily captive to its least-effective members and must demonstrate the courage of its convictions in asking that all members do their part.

Boards That Micromanage

It is not always easy for a board to see the line between management and governance, between implementation and oversight. Monitoring of activities in the organization can be facilitated by clear reporting guidelines and deliberate clarification of the role of the board and the staff. But when boards overstep the line between governance and management, they can easily become micromanagers.

A micromanaging board steps out of its governance role and gets caught up in the actual operations of the organization. It forgets that the chief executive is responsible for daily management according to the guidelines set by the board. Boards that micromanage want to both set strategic direction *and* actively oversee the implementation of the details.

Why Some Boards Micromanage

Board members, especially those who deal with management issues in their daily jobs, may overstep the boundaries between governance and management because that is what they know best. In some cases, the board may be missing the necessary strong leadership that would help it focus on strategic issues.

Governing does not usually create immediate rewards; this can be difficult for some boards to live with. Strategic developments take time to show results; operational tasks can often produce faster tangible outcomes and personal satisfaction. Particularly in organizations with small staffs, board members can easily get drawn into daily operations.

In some instances, the chief executive may steer the board astray by bringing management issues to the board for approval. The executive may not be providing the board with adequate information, thus forcing the board to ask for additional detailed reports. Micromanagement can also happen when the board loses confidence in the chief executive's ability to manage the organization.

What Micromanagement Looks Like

A board is too meddlesome in management issues when it wants to:

- Approve the choice of vendors, office equipment, software, or office furniture
- Participate in staff hiring and defining job descriptions (besides the chief executive's)
- Approve individual staff salaries

- Verify receipts and invoices
- Contact staff members directly for information, unless explicitly invited to do so by the chief executive
- Have a key to the office to be able to come and go at will
- Create committees that duplicate staff work
- Send a board representative to staff meetings
- Publicly second-guess the chief executive's decisions

Micromanagement Solutions

When the board oversteps its boundaries, the chief executive needs to discuss the issue with the chair and work out a solution. The chair should remind other board members of their roles and how to communicate with staff. If the chair is micromanaging, the chief executive still needs to address the problem directly and remind the chair of their different responsibilities. The chief executive can prevent the most flagrant board interventions by being proactive, by not bringing detailed administrative issues to the board's attention, and by ensuring that the board receives regular and concise information.

All-Volunteer Organizations

When there is no staff, the board has to divide its time between governance issues and carrying out programmatic and administrative duties. This works out best when there is a clear distinction between the functions of the full board and the individual board members. The full board acts as the strategist. The board delegates specific tasks to individual board members, who follow the guidelines set by the board.

Micromanagement can be avoided when each board member is aware of which hat he or she is wearing at each moment. A board member must be able to differentiate; for example, taking part in drafting guidelines as part of the group, then allowing a colleague to finish a task independently as assigned by the group.

The Perfect Partnership

When a board hires a competent chief executive, it already has adopted the basics of role differentiation between board and staff. Delegating management duties to the chief executive also assumes that the board clarifies job duties. Like any supervisor, the board is there to support the manager, set performance expectations, and challenge him or her to propel the organization forward. How the staff gets its work done is the responsibility of the chief executive; how the board manages its own tasks is the responsibility of the chair. In a productive partnership, the chief executive uses the board as a sounding board. The two end up formulating strategic decisions together while leaving the details of implementation to appropriate individuals.

Keeping Civility in the Boardroom

Acceptable boardroom ethics and codes of behavior are not tied to any parliamentary order. They are generally valued, often-unwritten rules that allow board meetings to proceed with civility and good humor. Here are some tips:

- Arrive on time; stay until the end.
- Come to the meeting already prepared, having read the materials ahead of time.
- Don't make judgmental statements.
- Talk about issues, not people.
- Don't speak over others.
- Don't criticize those who are absent.
- Don't monopolize conversation.
- Ask questions when you do not understand; there are no stupid questions.
- Keep confidential information confidential.
- Talk about board issues in the boardroom, not in the parking lot afterward.
- Recognize when you have a conflict of interest and disclose it to the group.

Disruptive Board Members

When people join a board, they often have aspirations of helping the organization, making a difference, giving back to the community, getting involved in interesting activities and ideas, and working with similarly spirited and highly motivated people. Fortunately, most of the time this is what board service turns out to be. Unfortunately, sometimes troublesome behavior by a board member tests their tolerance and forces them to fulfill one unpleasant responsibility of board service.

Troublesome board members present a chronic problem, meeting after meeting, interfering with normal board (and staff) work and relationships. They are unresponsive to the standard tools of negotiation or conflict resolution.

Generally, troublesome board behavior falls into one of three categories. *Poor board member behavior* consists of role confusion, lackadaisical meeting attendance, micromanagement, failing to honor commitments, or ignoring conflicts of interest. These types of troublesome behaviors can be avoided or corrected through recruitment practices, board training, and ongoing discussion of expectations.

Troublesome behaviors based on *poor people skills* often interfere with team cohesiveness. People with controlling personalities tend to impose their own ideas on others, disrupt meeting procedures, or form cliques that divide the group. Bad manners—intentional or, more often, not—offend and discourage others. Team-building activities can emphasize the value of tolerance, consideration, and mutual goals in spite of individual differences.

Additional *delicate and troublesome circumstances* relate to behaviors that are illegal or unethical, to personal challenges or circumstances—say, in a board member's family or work environment—or to troubling situations caused by the board's leaders, who should be acting as peer models but who are putting the organization at risk by their behavior. These cases need individual solutions and delicate handling.

Most of the time, boards function as teams—attending to their serious legal obligations and liabilities. A team that produces results is able to do that, in part, because it is clear about the expectations for each member. Some expectations are clear-cut rules that state what to do; some deal with behaviors that allow the group to remain a congenial and interactive body, thriving on individual differences and dissimilarities. But if these individual differences become troublesome behaviors that interfere with the board's getting its work done, board members must take action to remedy the situation, even if it means asking a member to resign so that the board can refocus its attention on its duties and responsibilities. Exhibit 16.1 presents a sample document that one board used to establish standards for board member conduct.

EXHIBIT 16.1. ONE BOARD'S RULES OF ENGAGEMENT

Discussions

- Feel free to raise an issue or concern, and expect a considerate reply.
- Respect and learn from differences of opinion.
- Build on each other's ideas.
- Value the contributions of all members.
- Ensure that every person has expressed his or her views.
- Don't pontificate.

Decisions

- There are no reprisals for speaking your mind.
- It's okay to agree to disagree.

- Challenge groupthink.
- Check assumptions before running with or arguing against someone else's idea.
- Commit to board decisions.
- Disagree, then commit.
- Seek and respect the opinion or recommendation of staff management.

Interaction with Members

- It's okay to solicit ideas from the membership. Doing so does not violate board integrity.
- Individual members should not make commitments for the board.
- In the board meeting location, board members may participate in an event that has strategic advantage.

Interaction with Fellow Board Members

- Hold each other accountable (the executive director is not the board police).
- Provide feedback. If the feedback is specific, it should be given one-on-one.
- Speak in the first person only, not second-hand.

Before Meetings

- Attend all agreed-upon meetings and come prepared.
- Read documentation prior to meetings.
- Identify the outcome for proposed agenda items.

During Meetings

- Develop shared meaning on old and new ideas.
- Check to see that we're on the same page.
- Seek additional information or data before stating opinion as fact.
- Clarify content, implications, fit to strategic plan, and consequences.
- Test agreements frequently.
- Take time to look at the long-range view.
- Ensure that board committees and work groups are given proper authority and resources for completion of assignments.
- Maintain a strategic focus and establish supporting policy.
- Keep discussions inside the boardroom confidential.

After Meetings

- Minutes will capture agreements, actions/timing, and responsibilities.
- Follow up with stakeholders.

Source: International Society for Performance Improvement.

Chapter Exercises

- Group dynamics affect the culture of the board. What do you think are the key elements to take into account when a new member arrives?
- How would lack of trust between the board and the chief executive manifest itself? What would be the consequences for the organization?
- What does it look like when a board engages in groupthink? What are the pitfalls of such behavior? What are some techniques for overcoming groupthink?
- Discuss the impact of a charismatic founder on the board culture and processes.

SAMPLE POLICIES FOR NONPROFIT BOARDS

The sample policies in this Appendix are selected and reprinted from *The Nonprofit Policy Sampler*, Second Edition (BoardSource, 2006). They represent just a few of the policies most commonly found in the nonprofit sector. Each sample has been edited to eliminate any reference to the organization responsible for its submission. Although the original publication was vetted by a team of professional advisers and nonprofit practitioners, it is incumbent upon each organization to tailor policies to its own situation and have them reviewed by professional counsel.

Board Member Fundraising

Sample One

This general policy outlines expectations for board member participation that is beyond simply "giving and getting."

Board members are expected to give an annual monetary gift to XYZ and are asked to make XYZ a priority in their personal giving. Board members are expected to be involved in fundraising by using their personal and business connections when appropriate, by soliciting funds when appropriate, by serving on fundraising committees, and by attending fundraising events.

Sample Two

This brief statement not only establishes a minimum amount for personal contributions, but also separates fundraising obligations from personal giving.

Each board member is expected to

- Support XYZ by making a meaningful financial gift of at least $ each calendar year.
- Solicit the financial, in-kind, and political support of others and obtain at least $ in contributions made to XYZ each fiscal year in addition to his or her personal contribution.
- Attend as many XYZ program and fundraising events as possible.

Human Resources

Sample One: Philosophy for Staff Employment

This brief, affirmative statement sets the framework for the organization's employee philosophy and assigns responsibility for personnel policies to the chief executive.

With respect to the treatment of paid or volunteer staff, the chief executive is responsible for ensuring that working conditions meet all local, state, and federal legal requirements [and] are humane and safe, and that employees are treated in an equitable, professional manner. The chief executive should

- Ensure that employment decisions are based on the individual's qualifications and ability to perform the job.
- Hire quality people with known maturity.
- Pay compensation reasonably required to attract and retain employees with the skills and experience necessary to accomplish the organization's mission.
- Develop and maintain appropriate personnel policies in a handbook reviewed by legal counsel and available to all staff (and kept in the [Board Reference Book]).

Sample Two

This policy defines the management boundaries within which the chief executive must operate vis-à-vis employees and personnel policies.

In relating to staff, the chief executive shall not fail to

- Establish human resource policies and to acquaint staff with the organization's personnel procedures. In developing these policies, the chief executive shall not fail to consult with legal counsel.
- Seek gender, ethnic, and age diversity in the composition of staff consistent with the organization's staffing requirements.
- Ensure that the rights of the employees to equitable and humane treatment are not impaired, and establish procedures through which employee complaints will be resolved.
- Develop a plan for periodic and systematic review of employee performance and of compensation and benefits package for XYZ employees.
- Establish management policies and procedures that protect the rights of the employees and of the organization.

- Initiate appropriate intervention or advocacy on behalf of any employee or agent of XYZ who in the course of duty is unlawfully detained, subjected to physical harm, or otherwise placed in jeopardy.

In addition, the chief executive shall not

- Conduct the decision-making process of XYZ's administration in a secretive manner except as required for personal privacy and confidentiality of personnel records.
- Subject staff to unsafe or unhealthy conditions.
- Discriminate or retaliate *against* any staff member for expressing an ethical dissent, or discriminate *among* employees on other than job-related individual performance or qualifications.
- Allow any position descriptions to be vague, or to inaccurately reflect the responsibility and tasks given to the position.
- Hinder an employee from expressing a complaint to the board in cases where internal complaint mechanisms have been exhausted, and where the employee contends that
  - Board or administrative procedures have been erroneously or capriciously applied to his or her detriment; or
  - Board policies or administrative procedures are inhumane, unfair, or constitute a violation of the employee's legal rights.

Code of Ethics

Sample One: Policy for the Promotion of Ethical Conduct

This policy is a formal statement about ethical conduct.

As a nonprofit organization at the forefront of [purpose of organization], [Name]'s policy is to uphold the highest legal, ethical, and moral standards. Our donors and volunteers support [Name] because they trust us to be good stewards of their resources, and to uphold rigorous standards of conduct. Our reputation for integrity and excellence requires the careful observance of all applicable laws and regulations, as well as a scrupulous regard for the highest standards of conduct and personal integrity.

[Name] will comply with all applicable laws and regulations and expects its directors, officers, and employees to conduct business in accordance with the letter and spirit of all relevant laws, to refrain from any illegal, dishonest or unethical conduct, to act in a professional, businesslike manner, and to treat others with respect. Directors and officers should not use their positions to obtain unreasonable or excessive services or expertise from [Name]'s staff.

In general, the use of good judgment based on high ethical principles will guide you with respect to lines of acceptable conduct. However, if a situation arises where it is difficult to determine the proper course of conduct, or where you have questions concerning the propriety of certain conduct by you or others, the matter should be brought to the attention of [Name]. If you are an employee, you should contact your immediate supervisor and, if necessary, the Director of Human Resources. Board members should raise any such concerns with the Chair or the Treasurer of [Name]'s Board.

In all questions involving ethics and conduct, the Board of Directors will make relevant determinations, except that any individual whose conduct is at issue will not participate in such decisions.

Sample Two: Code of Ethics

This policy sets an affirmative tone with the introductory phrase, "We will do the following."

We, as XYZ professionals (staff and board members), dedicate ourselves to carrying out the mission of this organization. We will do the following:

1. Recognize that the chief function of XYZ at all times is to serve the best interests of our constituency.

2. Accept as a personal duty the responsibility to keep up-to-date on emerging issues and to conduct ourselves with professional competence, fairness, impartiality, efficiency, and effectiveness.

3. Respect the structure and responsibilities of the board, provide them with facts and advice as a basis for their making policy decisions, and uphold and implement policies adopted by the board.

4. Keep the community informed about issues affecting it.

5. Conduct our organizational and operational duties with positive leadership exemplified by open communication, creativity, dedication, and compassion.

6. Exercise whatever discretionary authority we have under the law to carry out the mission of the organization.

7. Serve with respect, concern, courtesy, and responsiveness in carrying out the organization's mission.

8. Demonstrate the highest standards of personal integrity, truthfulness, honesty, and fortitude in all our activities in order to inspire confidence and trust in our activities.

9. Avoid any interest or activity that is in conflict with the conduct of our official duties.

10. Respect and protect privileged information to which we have access in the course of our official duties.

11. Strive for personal and professional excellence and encourage the professional developments of others.

Conflict of Interest

Sample One

This brief policy provides general guidelines and definitions related to conflicts of interest.

Employees and board members have an obligation to conduct business within guidelines that prohibit actual or potential conflicts of interest. This policy establishes only the framework within which XYZ wishes its business to operate. The purpose of these guidelines is to provide general direction so that board members and employees can seek further clarification on issues related to the subject of acceptable standards of operation.

An actual or potential conflict of interest occurs when a board member or an employee is in a position to influence a decision that may result in personal gain or gain for a relative as a result of XYZ's business dealings. For the purpose of this policy, a relative is any person who is related by blood or marriage, or whose relationship with the board member or employee is similar to that of persons who are related by blood or marriage.

No presumption of a conflict is created by the mere existence of a relationship with outside firms. However, if a board member or an employee has any influence on any material business transactions, it is imperative that he or she discloses to an officer of the organization as soon as possible the existence of any actual or potential conflict of interest so that safeguards can be established to protect all parties.

Personal gain may result not only in cases where a board member, an employee, or a relative has a significant ownership in a firm with which XYZ does business, but also when a board member, an employee, or a relative receives any kickback, bribe, substantial gift, or special consideration as a result of any transaction or business dealings involving XYZ.

Sample Two

This example begins by explaining why a conflict-of-interest policy is important and then defines key components of the policy and the process for handling conflicts.

Reason for Statement

XYZ, as a nonprofit, tax-exempt organization, depends on charitable contributions from the public. Maintenance of its tax-exempt status is important both for its continued financial stability and for the receipt of contributions and public support. Therefore, the operations of XYZ first must fulfill all legal requirements. They also depend on the public trust and thus are subject to scrutiny by and accountability to both governmental authorities and members of the public.

Consequently, there exists between XYZ and its board, officers, and management employees a fiduciary duty that carries with it a broad and unbending duty of loyalty and fidelity. The board, officers, and management employees have the responsibility of administering the affairs of XYZ honestly and prudently, and of exercising their best care, skill, and judgment for the sole benefit of XYZ. Those persons shall exercise the utmost good faith in all transactions involved in their duties, and they shall not use their positions with XYZ or knowledge gained therefrom for their personal benefit. The interests of the organization must have the first priority in all decisions and actions.

Persons Concerned

This statement is directed not only to board members and officers, but to all employees who can influence the actions of XYZ. For example, this includes all who make purchasing decisions, all other persons who might be described as "management personnel," and all who have proprietary information concerning XYZ.

Key Areas in Which Conflict May Arise

Conflicts of interest may arise in the relations of directors, officers, and management employees with any of the following third parties:

- Persons and firms supplying goods and services to XYZ
- Persons and firms from whom XYZ leases property and equipment
- Persons and firms with whom XYZ is dealing or planning to deal in connection with the gift, purchase or sale of real estate, securities, or other property
- Competing or affinity organizations
- Donors and others supporting XYZ
- Recipients of grants from XYZ
- Agencies, organizations, and associations that affect the operations of XYZ
- Family members, friends, and other employees

Nature of Conflicting Interest

A material conflicting interest may be defined as an interest, direct or indirect, with any persons and firms mentioned in Section [ABC]. Such an interest might arise, for example, through

1. Owning stock or holding debt or other proprietary interests in any third party dealing with XYZ.
2. Holding office, serving on the board, participating in management, or being otherwise employed (or formerly employed) by any third party dealing with XYZ.
3. Receiving remuneration for services with respect to individual transactions involving XYZ.
4. Using XYZ's time, personnel, equipment, supplies, or goodwill other than for approved XYZ activities, programs, and purposes.
5. Receiving personal gifts or loans from third parties dealing with XYZ. Receipt of any gift is disapproved except gifts of nominal value that could not be refused without discourtesy. No personal gift of money should ever be accepted.

Interpretation of This Statement of Policy

The areas of conflicting interest listed in Section [ABC], and the relations in those areas that may give rise to conflict, as listed in Section [DEF], are not exhaustive. Conceivably, conflicts might arise in other areas or through other relations. It is assumed that the trustees, officers, and management employees will recognize such areas and relation by analogy.

The fact that one of the interests described in Section [DEF] exists does not necessarily mean that (1) a conflict exists, or (2) the conflict, if it exists, is material enough to be of practical importance, or (3) if it is determined to be material, upon full disclosure of all relevant facts and circumstances, it is necessarily adverse to the interests of XYZ.

However, it is the policy of the board that the existence of any of the interests described in Section [DEF] shall be disclosed on a timely basis and always before any transaction is consummated. It shall be the continuing responsibility of board, officers, and management employees to scrutinize their transactions and outside business interests and relationships for potential conflicts and to immediately make such disclosures.

Disclosure Policy and Procedure

Disclosure should be made according to XYZ standards. Transactions with related parties may be undertaken only if all of the following are observed:

1. A material transaction is fully disclosed in the audited financial statements of the organization;
2. The related party is excluded from the discussion and approval of such transaction;

3. A competitive bid or comparable valuation exists; and
4. The organization's board has acted upon and demonstrated that the transaction is in the best interest of the organization.

Staff disclosures should be made to the chief executive (or if he or she is the one with the conflict, then to the designated committee), who shall determine whether a conflict exists and is material and, if the matters are material, bring them to the attention of the designated committee.

Disclosure involving directors should be made to the designated committee.

The board shall determine whether a conflict exists and is material, and, in the presence of an existing material conflict, whether the contemplated transaction may be authorized as just, fair, and reasonable to XYZ. The decision of the board on these matters will rest in their sole discretion, and their concern must be the welfare of XYZ and the advancement of its purpose.

Confidentiality

Sample

This general policy provides board and staff members with broad guidelines for handling confidential information.

It is the policy of XYZ that board members and employees of XYZ may not disclose, divulge, or make accessible confidential information belonging to, or obtained through their affiliation with XYZ to any person, including relatives, friends, and business and professional associates, other than to persons who have a legitimate need for such information and to whom XYZ has authorized disclosure. Board members and employees shall use confidential information solely for the purpose of performing services as a board member or employee for XYZ. This policy is not intended to prevent disclosure where disclosure is required by law.

Board members and employees must exercise good judgment and care at all times to avoid unauthorized or improper disclosures of confidential information. Conversations in public places, such as restaurants, elevators, and airplanes, should be limited to matters that do not pertain to information of a sensitive or confidential nature. In addition, board members and employees should be sensitive to the risk of inadvertent disclosure and should, for example, refrain from leaving confidential information on desks or otherwise in plain view and refrain from the use of speakerphones to discuss confidential information if the conversation could be heard by unauthorized persons.

At the end of a board member's term in office or upon the termination of an employee's employment, he or she shall return, at the request of XYZ, all documents, papers, and other materials, regardless of medium, that may contain or be derived from confidential information in his or her possession.

Whistle-Blower Protection

Sample

This policy is written in simple language and focuses on the intent behind whistle-blower protection.

XYZ Code of Ethics and Conduct ("Code") requires directors, officers, and employees to observe high standards of business and personal ethics in the conduct of their duties and responsibilities. As employees and representatives of the organization, we must practice honesty and integrity in fulfilling our responsibilities and comply with all applicable laws and regulations.

Reporting Responsibility

It is the responsibility of all directors, officers, and employees to comply with the Code and to report violations or suspected violations in accordance with this Whistle-Blower Policy.

No Retaliation

No director, officer, or employee who in good faith reports a violation of the Code shall suffer harassment, retaliation, or adverse employment consequence. An employee who retaliates against someone whoM has reported a violation in good faith is subject to discipline up to and including termination of employment. This Whistle-Blower Policy is intended to encourage and enable employees and others to raise serious concerns within the organization prior to seeking resolution outside the organization.

Reporting Violations

The Code addresses the organization's open-door policy and suggests that employees share their questions, concerns, suggestions, or complaints with some-one who can address them properly. In most cases, an employee's supervisor is in the best position to address an area of concern. However, if you are not comfortable speaking with your supervisor or you are not satisfied with your supervisor's response, you are encouraged to speak with someone in the human resources department or anyone in management whom you are comfortable approaching. Supervisors and managers are required to report suspected violations of the Code of Conduct to the organization's compliance officer, who has specific and exclusive responsibility to investigate all reported violations. For suspected fraud, or when you are not satisfied or uncomfortable with following the organization's open-door policy, individuals should contact the organization's compliance officer directly.

Compliance Officer

The organization's compliance officer is responsible for investigating and resolving all reported complaints and allegations concerning violations of the Code and, at his or her discretion, shall advise the chief executive and/or the audit committee. The compliance officer has direct access to the audit committee of the board and is required to report to the audit committee at least annually on compliance activity. The organization's compliance officer is the chair of the audit committee.

Accounting and Auditing Matters

The audit committee of the board shall address all reported concerns or complaints regarding corporate accounting practices, internal controls, or auditing. The compliance officer shall immediately notify the audit committee of any such complaint and work with the committee until the matter is resolved.

Acting in Good Faith

Anyone filing a complaint concerning a violation or suspected violation of the Code must be acting in good faith and have reasonable grounds for believing the information disclosed indicates a violation of the Code. Any allegations that prove not to be substantiated and which prove to have been made maliciously or knowingly to be false will be viewed as a serious disciplinary offense.

Confidentiality

Violations or suspected violations may be submitted on a confidential basis by the complainant or may be submitted anonymously. Reports of violations or suspected violations will be kept confidential to the extent possible, consistent with the need to conduct an adequate investigation.

Handling of Reported Violations

The compliance officer will notify the sender and acknowledge receipt of the reported violation or suspected violation within ___ business days. All reports will be promptly investigated and appropriate corrective action will be taken if warranted by the investigation.

Record Retention and Document Destruction

Sample

This brief policy is framed as part of compliance with the Sarbanes-Oxley Act of 2002. It includes a list of documents and time periods.

XYZ takes seriously its obligations to preserve information relating to litigation, audits, and investigations. The Sarbanes-Oxley Act makes it a crime to alter, cover up, falsify, or destroy any document to prevent its use in an official proceeding. Failure on the part of employees to follow this policy can result in possible civil and criminal sanctions against XYZ and its employees and possible disciplinary action against responsible individuals (up to and including termination of employment). Each employee has an obligation to contact the chief executive or chief financial officer of a potential or actual litigation, external audit, investigation, or similar proceeding involving XYZ. The information listed in the retention schedule [see chart] is intended as a guideline and may not contain all the records XYZ may be required to keep in the future. Questions regarding the retention of documents not listed in this chart should be directed to the chief executive.

From time to time, the chief executive may issue a notice, known as a "legal hold," suspending the destruction of records due to pending, threatened, or otherwise reasonably foreseeable litigation, audits, government investigations, or similar proceedings. No records specified in any legal hold may be destroyed, even if the scheduled destruction date has passed, until the legal hold is withdrawn in writing by the chief executive.

SAMPLE RETENTION SCHEDULE

File Category	Item	Retention Period
Corporate Records	Bylaws and Articles of Incorporation	Permanent
	Corporate resolutions	Permanent
	Board and committee meeting agendas and minutes	Permanent
	Conflict-of-interest disclosure forms	4 years
Finance and Administration	Financial statements (audited)	Permanent
	Auditor management letters	Permanent
	Payroll records	Permanent
	Journal entries	Permanent
	Check register and checks	[7 years/Permanent]

File Category	Item	Retention Period
	Bank deposits and statements	7 years
	Charitable organizations registration statements (filed with [State] Attorney General)	7 years
	Chart of accounts	7 years
	Expense reports	7 years
	General ledgers and journals (includes bank reconciliations, fund accounting by month, payouts allocation, securities lending, single fund allocation, trust statements)	7 years
	Accounts payable ledger	7 years
	Investment performance reports	7 years
	Investment consultant reports	7 years
	Investment manager correspondence	7 years
	Equipment files and maintenance records	7 years after disposition
	Contracts and agreements	7 years after all obligations end
	Investment manager contracts	7 years after all obligations end
	Correspondence—general	3 years
Insurance Records	Policies—occurrence type	Permanent
	Policies —claims-made type	Permanent
	Accident reports	7 years
	Fire inspection reports	7 years
	Safety (OSHA) reports	7 years
	Claims (after settlement)	7 years
	Group disability records	7 years after end of benefits
Real Estate	Deeds	Permanent
	Leases (expired)	7 years after all obligations end
	Mortgages, security agreements	7 years after all obligations end
	Purchase agreements	7 years after disposition requirement
Tax	IRS exemption determination and related correspondence	Permanent

(Continued)

File Category	Item	Retention Period
	IRS Form 990s	Permanent
	Withholding tax statements	7 years
	Correspondence with legal counsel or accountants, not otherwise listed	7 years after return is filed
	Timecards	3 years
Communications	One set of all communication documents kept on-site and one set kept off-site:	
	Press releases	Permanent
	Annual reports	Permanent (5 copies)
	Other publications	7 years
	Photos	7 years
	Press clippings	7 years
Donor Services	Fund agreements (paper and digital copies)	Permanent
	Correspondence — acknowledgment of gifts and grant requests	Permanent
	Donor fund statements	Permanent
Community Philanthropy	Records from advisory committee or family fund meetings, including minutes, if any, and lists of grants recommended for approval	7 years
	Scholarship grant records, including applications if foundation staff participates in selection decisions	7 years
	Approved grants—all documentation supporting grant payment, including application/recommendation, due diligence, grant agreement letters, grant transmittal letters, and post–grant reporting information, if any	7 years after completion of funded program, or date of grant if general operating support
	Foundation funding requests, correspondence, and reports (funding received)	7 years after completion of program
	Declined/withdrawn grant applications	3 years
	Foundation funding requests (denied)	3 years
Consulting Services	Consulting contracts/filed	7 years after all obligations end

File Category	Item	Retention Period
Human Resources	Employee personnel files	Permanent
	Retirement plan benefits (plan descriptions, plan documents)	Permanent
	Employee medical records	Permanent
	Employee handbooks	Permanent
	Workers comp claims (after settlement)	7 years
	Employee orientation and training materials	7 years after use ends
	Employment offer letter	7 years after all obligations end
	Employment applications	3 years
	IRS Form I-9 (store separate from personnel file)	Greater of 1 year after end of service, or 3 years
	Résumés	1 year
Technology	Software licenses and support agreements	7 years after all obligations end
Library	Other foundations' annual reports	2 years
	Directories and periodicals	2 years
General Administration	Correspondence—chief executive and general	7 years
	Appointment calendars—chief executive	7 years

Executive Compensation

Sample

This sample outlines the organization's compensation philosophy and acceptable sources for comparable pay.

Program Philosophy and Objectives

XYZ's primary objective is to provide a reasonable and competitive executive total compensation opportunity consistent with market-based compensation practices for individuals possessing the experience and skills needed to improve the overall performance of the organization.

The organization's executive compensation program is designed to

- Encourage the attraction and retention of high-caliber executives.
- Provide a competitive total compensation package, including benefits.
- Strongly support and further transition to a "pay for performance" culture through the use of incentives for key employees.
- Reinforce the goals of the organization by supporting teamwork and collaboration.
- Ensure that pay is perceived to be fair and equitable.
- Be flexible to reward individual accomplishments as well as organizational success.
- Ensure that the program is easy to explain, understand, and administer.
- Balance the need to be competitive with the limits of available financial resources.
- Ensure that the program complies with state and federal legislation.

Program Market Position

While XYZ focuses on comparable nonprofit organizations in our area to benchmark pay, we also understand that the market for executive talent may be broader than this group. Market information from two additional market segments, private foundations, and published not-for-profit compensation surveys may be used as a supplement.

In addition, XYZ may also collect other published survey data, when appropriate, for for-profit organizations for specific functional competencies such as finance and human resources.

Together with data from the comparable local organizations, data from these market segments are used to form a "market composite" to assess the competitiveness of compensation.

In general, XYZ positions total compensation, including benefits, at the median of the market. Programs are designed to be flexible so that compensation can be above or below the median based on experience, performance, and business need to attract and retain specific talent.

Governance and Procedures

XYZ's executive compensation program is administered by the compensation committee of the board. The compensation committee is responsible for establishing and maintaining a competitive compensation program for the key executives of the organization. The committee meets as needed to review the compensation program and make recommendations for any changes to the board, as appropriate.

The compensation committee commissions an annual review by an independent consulting firm to evaluate the organization's executive compensation program against the competitive market. The evaluation is reviewed in the spring of each year and is intended to ensure that the compensation program falls within a reasonable range of competitive practices for comparable positions among similarly situated organizations.

Following this review, the committee reviews and approves, for selected key executives, base salaries and annual incentive opportunity adjustments, and objectives and goals for the upcoming year's annual incentive plan. The committee reviews and recommends to the board salary approval and incentive awards for the chief executive.

Investments

Sample

This basic set of investment policies establishes an investment committee, authorizes the retention of an investment consultant to guide and assist the committee in its work, and addresses standard investment policy issues. Reprinted from Robert P. Fry Jr., Who's Minding the Money? An Investment Guide for Nonprofit Board Members, *second edition (BoardSource, 2009).*

Preamble

It is the policy of the Board of Directors (Board) to treat all assets of the Nonprofit Organization (NPO), including Funds that are legally unrestricted, as if held by NPO in a fiduciary capacity for the sake of accomplishing its mission and purposes. The following investment objectives and directions are to be judged and understood in light of that overall sense of stewardship. In that regard, the basic investment standards shall be those of a prudent investor as articulated in applicable state laws.

Investment Assets

For purposes of these policies, investment assets are those assets of NPO that are available for investment in the public securities markets as stocks, bonds, cash, or cash equivalents, either directly or through intermediate structures. Illiquid assets are described in NPO's Gift Acceptance Policies, and are governed by those rules and not by these investment policies.

Supervision and Delegation

The Board of Directors of NPO has adopted these policies and has formed an Investment Committee, described below, to whom it has delegated authority to supervise NPO investments. The Board reserves to itself the exclusive right to amend or revise these policies.

Investment Committee

The Investment Committee ("Committee") consists of the chief financial officer, _____, Board members, and _____ non-board member(s), who serve at the pleasure of the Board. It shall be the responsibility of the Committee to:

Supervise the overall implementation of NPO's investment policies by NPO's executive staff and outside advisors

Monitor and evaluate the investment performance of NPO's Funds

Report regularly on NPO investment matters to the Board of Directors

Grant exceptions as permitted in these policies and recommend changes in approved policy, guidelines, and objectives as needed

Execute such other duties as may be delegated by the Board of Directors

Whenever these policies assign specific tasks to the Committee, the policies assume that the actual work will (or may) be performed by NPO's chief financial officer or other designated staff members, subject only to the Committee's overall supervision.

Investment Consultant, Advisors, and Agents

The Committee is specifically authorized to retain one or more investment advisors (Advisors) as well as any administrators, custodians, or other investment service providers required for the proper management of NPO's Funds. The Committee may utilize an Advisor as an investment consultant (the "Consultant") to advise and assist the Committee in the discharge of its duties and responsibilities. In that regard, a Consultant may help the Committee to:

- Develop and maintain investment policy, asset allocation strategies, risk-based fund objectives, and appropriate investment management structures
- Select, monitor, and evaluate Investment Advisors and/or investment entities
- Provide and/or review quarterly performance measurement reports and assist the Committee in interpreting the results
- Review portfolios and recommend actions, as needed, to maintain proper asset allocations and investment strategies for the objectives of each fund
- Execute such other duties as may be mutually agreed

In discharging this authority, the Committee can act in the place and stead of the Board and may receive reports from, pay compensation to, enter into agreements with, and delegate discretionary investment authority to such Advisors. When delegating discretionary investment authority to one or more Advisors, the Committee will establish and follow appropriate procedures for selecting such Advisors and for conveying to each the scope of their authority, the organization's expectations, and the requirement of full compliance with these Policies.

Objectives

NPO's primary investment objective is to preserve and protect its assets, by earning a total return for each category of assets (a "Fund"), which is appropriate for each Fund's time horizon, distribution requirements, and risk tolerance. NPO currently maintains [list Funds here; for example, Operating Reserves, Endowments, Charitable Trust Funds, Annuity Reserves] and may add other Funds in the future. These policies apply to all NPO Funds, although the specific objectives, risk parameters, and asset allocation will vary, as appropriate, from Fund to Fund.

Asset Allocations

Actual asset allocations for each Fund will be established and maintained by NPO on the advice of its Consultant and/or Advisors, within the ranges provided in the following table:

	Cash	Fixed Income	Equities	Alternative Investments
Operating Reserves	0–100%	0–50%	n/a	n/a
Retirement Funds	0–25%	0–25%	25–50%	n/a
Endowments	0–10%	0–20%	25–75%	Up to 25% if approved by committee

When appropriate, specific objectives for each Fund, including specific asset allocation parameters and performance standards, may be reflected in an appendix attached to these policies. Such specific objectives shall nonetheless be within the foregoing ranges, which can only be modified by the Committee with the approval of the Board.

Rebalancing Procedures

The Committee will monitor the asset allocation of each Fund based on reports provided by NPO's Consultant and/or Investment Advisors. The Committee may establish any reasonable rebalancing procedure based on either periodic reviews or departures from a range and may use its discretion to determine the timing of rebalancing actions. To achieve rebalancing, NPO may either move money from one asset class to another or may direct future contributions to and expenditures from particular classes as is most convenient.

Investment Guidelines

To accomplish its investment objectives, NPO is authorized to utilize any legal investment structure that holds publicly traded securities including separately managed portfolios, mutual funds, exchange traded funds, limited partnerships, and other commingled investment entities. This authority is subject to the requirements and restrictions contained in these policies.

When utilizing mutual funds or other commingled entities, the Committee shall see that NPO's staff, Consultant, and/or Investment Advisors have selected the investment entity appropriately based on the strategies and provisions contained in the entity's prospectus. In that event, the terms and conditions of the prospectus are deemed to control the entity's internal asset allocation, asset quality, diversification, and other requirements.

For purposes of these investment policies, all private (non–publicly traded) investments and all investments prohibited under the Risk-Based Restrictions, below, will be considered Alternative Investments. Alternative Investments may only be used with the approval of the Investment Committee granted in accordance with the exception processes described below.

Investment Restrictions

NPO's investment assets are to be managed with regard to the following restrictions for either tax, risk, or mission purposes:

Tax-Based Restrictions NPO is a charitable organization under § 501(c)(3) of the Internal Revenue Code. Consequently, its income is generally exempt from federal and state income tax with the exception of income that constitutes Unrelated Business Taxable Income (UBTI). Since UBTI can be generated by leveraged investments (resulting in "debt-financed income"), NPO will not utilize margin, short selling, or other leveraged investment strategies unless the Investment Committee grants a specific exception as described below.

Risk-Based Restrictions NPO will not engage in commodities transactions or option strategies (puts, calls, straddles) nor will it invest in any non–publicly traded securities including but not limited to managed futures funds, hedge funds, private equity funds, or other alternative investments unless approved by the Committee as provided below.

Mission-Based Investment Criteria

NPO desires to invest in companies whose business conduct is consistent with NPO's goals and beliefs. Therefore, NPO's Consultant and/or Investment

Advisors will use their best efforts to avoid holding securities of any company known to participate in businesses the Board deems to be socially or morally inconsistent with NPO objectives. The Committee will provide Advisors with a statement of NPO's mission guidelines and restrictions.

Exceptions to the Investment Restrictions

The Board recognizes the evolving nature of the investment world and that, under some circumstances, NPO may wish to utilize newer or more complex investment strategies. Therefore, the Investment Committee is authorized to grant exceptions to the foregoing restrictions. For tax-based restrictions, the Committee is to determine if a particular strategy or investment will generate UBTI, for which it may rely on advice of counsel.

When granting exceptions to the Risk-Based restrictions or otherwise approving Alternative Investments, the Committee must determine that the potential rewards outweigh the incremental risks and the Committee, or the Committee's retained investment consultant, must complete the additional Alternative Investment Due Diligence described in the exhibit to these policies. All such exceptions shall be made in writing and shall be communicated to the Board as part of the next regular Investment Committee report.

Proxy Voting

Subject to any specific instructions received from NPO or contained in NPO's mission guidelines (see Mission-Based Investment Criteria, above), each Advisor shall vote proxies according to their firm's established procedures and shall provide a copy of such procedures to the Committee upon request.

Custody and Securities Brokerage

The Committee will establish such custodial and brokerage relationships as are necessary for the efficient management of NPO's Funds. Whenever the Committee has not designated a brokerage relationship, then NPO Investment Advisors may execute transactions wherever they can obtain best price and execution.

Cash Flow Requirements

NPO will be responsible for advising the Consultant and each Advisor in a timely manner of NPO's cash distribution requirements from any managed portfolio or Fund. Each Advisor is responsible for providing adequate liquidity to meet such distribution requirements.

Reporting Requirements

Monthly—The Committee will obtain written monthly custodial statements. Such statements should contain all pertinent transaction details for each account that holds all or a portion of any NPO investment Funds. Each monthly statement should include:

- the name and quantity of each security purchased or sold, with the price and transaction date
- a description of each security holding as of month-end, including its percentage of the total portfolio, purchase date, quantity, average cost basis, current market value, unrealized gain or loss, and indicated annual income (yield) at market

In addition, if not included in the custodial reports, the Consultant and/or the Investment Advisor(s) should provide a report for each Fund or portfolio showing the month-end allocation of assets between equities, fixed-income securities, and cash. The monthly review of custodial statements may be delegated to NPO accounting staff.

Quarterly—The Committee should obtain from its Investment Consultant and/or Investment Advisors, a detailed review of NPO's investment performance for the preceding quarter and for longer trailing periods as appropriate. Such reports should be provided as to each Fund and as to NPO investment assets in the aggregate. As to each Fund, the Committee should establish with its Investment Consultant and/or Investment Advisors the specific criteria for monitoring each Fund's performance including the index or blend of indices that are appropriate for the objectives of each Fund and for the investment style or asset class of each portfolio within a Fund. The Committee shall meet with the Consultant to conduct such reviews to the extent it deems necessary.

Periodically—The Committee should meet with its Investment Consultant at least annually to review all aspects of NPO's investment assets. Such a review should include (1) strategic asset allocation, (2) manager and investment entity performance, (3) anticipated additions to or withdrawals from Funds, (4) future investment strategies, and (5) any other matters of interest to the Committee.

Financial Audits

Sample

This sample policy delegates certain responsibilities to the audit committee and requires periodic rotation of the auditors.

The financial records of XYZ shall be audited annually by an independent CPA firm that has a significant group of nonprofit clients. The finance committee shall be responsible for selecting the audit firm to conduct the annual audit. If the same audit firm conducts the audit for more than five consecutive years, the finance committee shall review the firm's services and decide if the firm or the audit partner needs to rotate.

The audit firm will not be hired to perform non-auditing services, except for tax preparation and Form 990 preparation and shall not perform substantial services for any officer or director personally. The audit firm shall be engaged to present annual audit findings to the chief executive and the finance committee, and if needed, the board. The finance committee shall review the audit and make its recommendation to the board.

Risk Management

Sample

This statement identifies general areas of risk that the chief executive is responsible for managing and provides some guidance on the level of protection.

The chief executive shall adequately protect and maintain from unnecessary risk XYZ assets. Accordingly, the chief executive shall

- Insure against theft and casualty losses of tangible personal property to at least 80 percent replacement value and against liability losses to board members, staff, or the organization itself at no less than minimally acceptable prudent levels
- Have sufficient employee dishonesty insurance and directors' and officers' liability insurance for personnel with access to material amounts of funds
- Ensure office and equipment is not subjected to improper wear and tear or insufficient maintenance
- Protect the organization, its board, and staff from exposure leading to claims of liability
- Protect intellectual property, information, and files from loss or significant damage
- Seek bids or demonstrate other prudent methods for any purchases over $ and protect against conflicts of interest
- Receive, process, or disburse funds under financial controls that meet the board-appointed auditor's (or other grant) standards
- Invest or hold operating capital in secure instruments, such as insured checking accounts and bonds of greater than __ rating, interest-bearing accounts (except when necessary to facilitate ease in operational transactions or where restricted by the funder)
- Acquire, encumber, or dispose of real property only with board approval, with the price set on any property to be disposed of following either a formal market appraisal or analysis of comparable properties by at least two reputable Realtors in that market
- Not endanger the organization's public image or credibility, particularly in ways that would hinder its accomplishment of mission, except when necessary to accomplish its mission

Media Relations

Sample One

This short policy is for a small organization that is concerned about consistency of the message.

To ensure the quality and consistency of information disseminated to media sources, the following policy shall be enforced:

- All media inquiries are to be handled by the chief executive or his or her designee, regardless of who the media representative is, whom he or she represents, or how innocuous the request.
- All press releases or other promotional materials are to be approved by the chief executive or his or her designee prior to dissemination.

Failure to comply with the XYZ's media policy shall be grounds for disciplinary action.

Sample Two

This brief policy provides additional guidelines, such as including the board president as an authorized spokesperson and requiring advance approval from the chief executive.

Only the chief executive, board president, board chair, or other individual(s) designated by the board are authorized to speak with the media. The chief executive and the board designate shall collaborate on message development and coordinate who will handle which press inquiries.

Employees, board members (other than the chair), and members acting in a capacity within a committee or a caucus shall not make statements, provide information for distribution, or provide background information unless specifically directed to do so by the chief executive and/or the board.

Provided that they have prior permission to do so from the chief executive or the board, employees, board members, and members acting in a capacity with a committee or a caucus shall speak publicly on behalf of XYZ only in accordance with established public-speaking procedures.

GLOSSARY

501(c)(3): IRS tax-exempt status defining public charities and private foundations.

501(c)(4): IRS tax-exempt status defining social welfare organizations.

501(c)(6): IRS tax-exempt status defining mainly trade and professional associations.

501(h) election: IRS option for public charities (except churches) to measure their permissible lobbying activity using an expenditure test.

527: IRS tax-exempt status defining political organizations, including political action committees (PACs).

accountability: A board's sense of responsibility, building of trust, and credibility with the public and constituents.

action organization: An organization whose primary objective may be obtained through lobbying and influencing legislation.

ad hoc committee: *See* task force.

advisory council: A group that advises or supports a nonprofit and its board and usually focuses on a specific issue; also called advisory group, advisory committee, and advisory board.

advocacy: Supporting and defending an organization's message and/or its specific policy issues.

affiliate: A local chapter, an auxiliary group, or a branch of a (usually) national parent organization.

agenda: A list of issues to be discussed in a meeting, including order of business; *see also* consent agenda.

annual campaign: A fundraising drive to support the annual operating expenses of an organization, including program-related expenses and overhead.

articles of incorporation: A document filed with a state agency to establish a corporation.

articles of organization: A charter for an unincorporated organization.

assets: All money and property owned by an organization.

association: In the nonprofit sector, usually a membership organization that may be incorporated or unincorporated.

attorney general: A senior state attorney; state government position to which nonprofits are accountable.

audit: An independent review of financial and/or legal transactions and activities of an organization.

AVO (all-volunteer organization): A nonprofit whose full board functions as the overseer while individual board members carry out the organizational activities.

board development: A process of building effective boards and educating board members about their governance role.

board handbook: A compilation of policies, procedures, and informational materials that board members use as a reference.

board matrix: A tool that helps identify desired characteristics and gaps on a board.

board member: A person sharing responsibility and liability for the organization with the rest of the members of the governing body.

board member agreement: A written commitment outlining board member expectations.

board of directors: The governing body of a nonprofit or for-profit corporation, which has specific legal and ethical responsibilities to the organization.

branding: A set of messages, images, and experiences that stimulates positive feelings about an organization among its donors, members, constituents, and other stakeholders.

bylaws: A legal document outlining the guidelines for governing a nonprofit organization.

capital campaign: A multiyear effort to raise funds for an endowment or capital projects; for example, a new building, a new wing, or renovation of an existing structure, including equipment purchase or operating expenses for the project.

case statement: A document used in fundraising to help articulate the purpose and goals of a specific campaign.

chair: The board officer who is the leader of the board.

chapter: A member or affiliated organization of a federated organization.

charitable contribution: A monetary or in-kind gift to a tax-exempt organization that can accept tax-deductible contributions.

charitable gift annuity: An annuity contract in which the purchaser receives an income stream for life, with the charity retaining the balance of the funds after the income stream ends.

charity: A tax-exempt nonprofit organization providing a public service as defined by the Internal Revenue Code, section 501(c)(3); see also 501(c)(3).

charter: The legal organizational document for a nonprofit; also known as the articles of incorporation or articles of organization.

chief executive: The top staff position of a nonprofit organization; common titles include CEO and executive director.

code of conduct: Ethical standards expected of every board member.

committee: A work group of a board organized to help manage the board's work; *see also* standing committee, task force.

community foundation: A foundation whose mission is to support a specific community.

confidentiality clause: A board policy defining unauthorized and improper disclosures of confidential information by board members.

conflict of interest: A situation in which the personal or professional concerns of a board member or a staff member affect his or her ability to put the welfare of the organization before personal benefit.

conflict-of-interest policy: A policy intended to protect an organization's interests when it is contemplating entering into a contract, transaction, or arrangement that might benefit the private interests of a board member, officer, or any other individual with substantial influence over the organization.

consensus: An agreement that all participants can accept by eliminating objections.

consent agenda: A portion of a meeting agenda that lists routine items for a single vote without further discussion; *see also* agenda.

consultant: An expert providing professional advice or services.

corporate foundation: A foundation whose funds are provided by a specific corporation; representatives of the corporation supervise disbursement of funds.

corporate sponsorship: A relationship between a nonprofit organization and a company in which the nonprofit receives monetary support, goods, or services in exchange for public recognition of the company.

corporation: A legal entity that exists in perpetuity or until it is dissolved; a "fictitious person," separate from its managers or governors, usually given the same rights and obligations as natural persons.

D&O (directors' and officers') insurance: Insurance that protects board members and top staff personnel from liability created by board decisions or actions.

dashboard report: A document presenting comparative data in graphs, charts, tables, or columns, used for monitoring and evaluating an organization's advancement in fulfilling its mission and meeting.

determination letter: An official notification by the IRS stating that a nonprofit is recognized as a tax-exempt organization.

development: All methods of obtaining funding or support for an organization.

disclosure requirement: Regulations requiring nonprofits to share financial or other information with the public, defining IRS Form 990 as a public document.

disclosure statement: A statement in which each individual covered by an organization's conflict-of-interest policy acknowledges his or her familiarity with the organization's conflict-of-interest policy and discloses in writing any existing financial or other material interests or co-investment interests.

dissolution: The formal procedure by which a nonprofit ceases to operate or exist; it involves filing with the state and distribution of assets.

diversity: Inclusivity; equal opportunity; collective mixture of participants.

domestic corporation: A corporation is considered domestic in the state where it has filed its articles of incorporation; it is considered foreign in any other state.

due diligence: The expectation that a board member will exercise reasonable care and follow the business judgment rule when making decisions.

duty of care: The expectation that a board member will perform his or her duties in good faith and with the care that an ordinary prudent person in a like position would use under similar circumstances.

duty of loyalty: The expectation that a board member will act in a manner he or she believes to be in the best interest of the organization.

duty of obedience: The expectation that a board member will keep the organization faithful to its mission.

emeritus status: An honorific title usually given to a former board member who is invited to stay on the board as a nonvoting member in an advisory capacity.

endowment: A fund or collection of assets whose investment earnings support an organization or a specific project.

ex officio: "By virtue of office"; a board position held by an individual because of his or her position in that or another organization.

executive committee: A committee that has specific powers, outlined in the bylaws, that allow it to act on the board's behalf when a full board meeting is not possible or necessary.

executive session: A meeting of a board to handle confidential issues; often no staff are present.

federated organization: An organizational structure composed of a national umbrella organization and smaller local chapters.

fiduciary: A person responsible for the oversight, administration, investment, or distribution of assets belonging to another person or to an organization. The duties of the fiduciary are termed fiduciary responsibility.

Financial Accounting Standards Board (FASB): The body that develops the recognized, authoritative concepts and standards for financial accounting and reporting for organizations and businesses.

Form 990: The annual information return that most tax-exempt organizations file with the IRS.

Form 990-PF: The annual information return that private foundations must file with the IRS.

Form 990-T: The annual tax return for tax-exempt nonprofits that generate unrelated business income.

foundation: A tax-exempt nonprofit organization that normally distributes funds rather than running its own programs.

fund accounting: A nonprofit accounting method that separates various restricted assets into different fund categories.

fund balance: An organization's claim to its assets; the net worth of the organization.

governance: The legal authority of a board to establish policies that will affect the life and work of the organization while holding the board accountable for the outcome of such decisions.

governance committee: A committee responsible for recruiting, orienting, and training of board members.

grassroots lobbying: The act of influencing legislation indirectly by attempting to mold the general public's opinion on an issue.

incorporation: A legal process in which a group is created and recognized by the state as an entity separate from the individuals who manage or govern it.

incorporator: A person or group who signs and delivers the articles of incorporation to the appropriate state agency.

independent contractor: An individual contracted to perform a specific project or service for a specified amount.

in-kind donation: A donation of products or services instead of money to a nonprofit by a company or individual.

insider: A board, staff, or family member of a board or staff member who has influence on the decisions made by the organization.

intermediate sanctions: IRS regulations creating penalties for nonprofit board members and staff who receive or authorize an excessive benefit transaction for an insider.

joint venture: A specific project or event conducted by two or more nonprofits or a nonprofit and a for-profit corporation.

liability: Any legal responsibility, duty, or obligation.

lobbying: Attempting to influence legislation through direct contact with lawmakers or with constituents.

management letter: From the independent auditor, an assessment of and potential guidelines for improving internal practices provided in addition to the audit report.

membership organization: A nonprofit that grants its members specific rights to participate in its internal affairs.

minutes: A legal written record of actions during a meeting.

mission: An organization's fundamental purpose and reason to exist, expressed in a mission statement.

motion: A formal proposal for action during a meeting.

mutual benefit organization: A nonprofit providing services to its members rather than to the general public.

nonprofit organization: An organization defined by state law as established for activities other than profit making; also called a nongovernmental (NGO) or not-for-profit organization.

officer: A board leadership position; usually the chair, vice chair, secretary, or treasurer.

open meeting laws: State laws that require government agencies and some nonprofit organizations receiving public funding to open at least some of their board meetings to the public.

operating foundation: A foundation that actively runs programs rather than just distributing grants.

operating reserves: A reasonable buffer against unforeseen, seasonal, irregular, or exceptional cash shortages.

planned giving: The current gift of future assets through vehicles such as bequests, charitable trusts, or annuities.

policy: A written plan used to determine decisions or actions about a specific issue.

political action committee (PAC): A separate organization or a segregated fund whose function is to influence federal, state, or local public office elections.

political organization: A party, committee, association, or fund organized and operated for the purpose of influencing federal, state, or local public office elections.

private benefit doctrine: Doctrine based on the rule that tax-exempt organizations may not benefit private persons, even though they are not "insiders," except to an insubstantial extent; *see also* private inurement doctrine.

private foundation: A tax-exempt 501(c)(3) organization, other than a public charity, with funds usually from a single source and established to maintain or aid charitable activities serving the common good, primarily through grantmaking.

private inurement doctrine: Doctrine based on the rule that tax-exempt organizations may not enter into arrangements with insiders, or individuals who have sizable influence over the organization, when the arrangement provides benefits greater than the individual provides in return; *see also* private benefit doctrine.

public charity: A section 501(c)(3) organization for the public good that receives support from a wide range of sources or meets other specific requirements, such as a church, school, or hospital.

public support test: An IRS regulation used to determine whether a nonprofit organization is a private foundation or public charity; it involves determining the source of the majority of funding for the organization.

publicly supported organization: A nonprofit organization that is exempt from federal income tax under section 501(c)(3) and that has passed one of the public support tests contained in section 509(a).

resolution: A formal, longer, or more complicated meeting motion presented in a written format for board action; a resolution is "resolved" rather than "moved."

retreat: A brainstorming or action-oriented meeting.

rules of order: Written parliamentary rules that guide meeting process; *Robert's Rules of Order* is the leading manual of parliamentary order.

Sarbanes-Oxley Act of 2002: Federal corporate reform law designed to protect the interests of shareholders and the public by preventing fraudulent practices and accounting inconsistencies. It focuses on the integrity of financial information, the adequacy of internal financial controls, and the independence of auditors. Provisions on whistle-blowing and record retention apply to nonprofit organizations.

secretary: An officer position that involves taking minutes and keeping records and archives of the board.

self-perpetuating board: Governing board whose members elect subsequent members.

social welfare organization: Tax-exempt organization that engages in social welfare activities and is organized under section 501(c)(4).

standing committees: Board committees that deal with ongoing issues, such as financial oversight or investments. Members rotate on and off, but the committees exist indefinitely.

strategic thinking: Board behavior that enables board members to explore the frameworks within which the organization operates and ask far-ranging questions that drive deeper decisions.

succession planning: An ongoing, systematic process that creates an environment for chief executives to succeed and prepares a foundation for their successors.

sunshine laws: *See* open meeting laws.

SWOT analysis: A planning and evaluation tool that focuses on strengths, weaknesses, opportunities, and threats.

task force: Board work group established to accomplish a specific objective and then disband; sometimes called an ad hoc committee.

tax-deductible contribution: A donation that a donor can deduct from his or her taxable income; *see also* charitable contribution.

tax-exempt organization: An organization that is exempt from one or more federal, state, or local taxes, most commonly income tax.

term limits: A restriction on the number of consecutive terms that a person can serve as a board member.

trade association: Individuals and companies in a specific business or industry organized to promote common interests.

transparency: A continuous flow of information from an organization to the public about the organization's mission, financial situation, and governance practices.

treasurer: A board officer position that is responsible for coordinating and ensuring financial oversight of the organization.

unrelated business income: Income from business activities that are not substantially mission related.

unrelated business income tax (UBIT): Tax obligation for income over $1,000 raised from unrelated business activities.

values: The beliefs, principles, and ethical guidelines that direct a nonprofit's planning and operations; they are expressed in a values statement.

vice-chair: A board officer whose main duty is to replace the chair when the chair is not able to carry out his or her duties.

vision: An organization's picture of its desired objective; expressed in a vision statement of the organization.

zero-based committee structure: A board structure that starts annually or biannually with no committees and establishes committees and task forces based on its current needs. These work groups disband once their objectives are met or when the board decides they should disband.

RESOURCES

Chapter One

Ansberger, Paul, et al. "The History of the Nonprofit Sector: An SOI Perspective." Internal Revenue Service. http://www.irs.gov/pub/irs-soi/tehistory.pdf.

Cheng, Willie. *Doing Good Well: What Does (and Does Not) Make Sense in the Nonprofit World*. San Francisco: Jossey-Bass, 2008.

Hall, Peter Dobkin. *A History of Nonprofit Boards in the United States*. BoardSource e-book. http://www.boardsource.org/dl.asp?document_id=11.

Internal Revenue Service. *Frequently Asked Questions About Tax-Exempt Organizations*. http://www.irs.gov/charities/content/0,,id=96986,00.html.

Internal Revenue Service. *Life Cycle of an Exempt Organization*. http://www.irs.gov/charities/article/0,,id=169727,00.html.

Powell, Walter W., and Richard Steinberg. *The Nonprofit Sector: A Research Handbook*. New Haven, CT: Yale University Press, 2006.

Renz, David O. "The U.S. Nonprofit Infrastructure Mapped." *Nonprofit Quarterly*, Winter 2008.

Starting a Nonprofit Organization. BoardSource e-book. http://www.boardsource.org/dl.asp?document_id=17.

Chapter Two

Barr, Kate. "Improving Nonprofit Decision Making Amid Economic Crisis." *Nonprofit Quarterly*, Spring 2009.

Chait, Richard P. "The Gremlins of Governance." *Trusteeship*, July/August 2009.

Chait, Richard P., William P. Ryan, and Barbara E. Taylor. *Governance as Leadership: Reframing the Work of Nonprofit Boards*. Washington, DC: BoardSource, 2005.

Connolly, Paul M. *Navigating the Organizational Lifecycle*. Washington, DC: BoardSource, 2006.

Lakey, Berit M. *Nonprofit Governance: Steering Your Organization with Authority and Accountability*. Washington, DC: BoardSource, 2000.

Renz, David O. "R-E-F-R-A-M-I-N-G Governance." *Nonprofit Quarterly*, Winter 2006.

"Shifting Tides of Nonprofit Governance: An Interview with Paul Light." *Nonprofit Quarterly*, Summer 2008.

The Source: Twelve Principles of Governance That Power Exceptional Boards. Washington, DC: BoardSource, 2005.

Chapter Three

Bradham, June. *The Truth About What Nonprofit Boards Want: The Nine Little Things That Matter Most*. Hoboken, NJ: Wiley, 2009.

Chait, Richard P. *How to Help Your Board to Govern More and Manage Less*. Washington, DC: BoardSource, 2003.

Charan, Ram. "When Directors Sweat the Small Stuff." *Conference Board Review*, Summer 2009.

Harrison, Yvonne, and Vic Murray. "The Best and Worst of Board Chairs." *Nonprofit Quarterly*, Summer 2007.

Ingram, Richard T. *Ten Basic Responsibilities of Nonprofit Boards*. Washington, DC: BoardSource, 2009.

Moyers, Richard L. *The Nonprofit Chief Executive's Ten Basic Responsibilities*. Washington, DC: BoardSource, 2006.

Orlikoff, James E., and Mary K. Totten. "Microgovernance: The Changing Roles of the Board and Management." *Trustee*, July/August 2008.

Tessier, Oliver, and Ruth McCambridge. "The Nonprofit ED's First 100 Days." *Nonprofit Quarterly*, Spring 2008.

Wertheimer, Mindy R. *The Board Chair Handbook*. 2nd ed. Washington, DC: BoardSource, 2007.

Chapter Four

Fernandez, Kim. "Pulling Together or Pulling Apart." *Associations Now*, October 2008.

Internal Revenue Service. "Section 509(a)(3) Supporting Organizations." http://www.irs.gov/charities/article/0,,id=137609,00.html.

Larson, Laurie. "The Power of Committees." *Trustee*, February 2009.

The Nonprofit Board Answer Book: A Practical Guide for Board Members and Chief Executives. 2nd ed. Washington, DC: BoardSource, 2007.

Various authors. *Committee Series*. Washington, DC: BoardSource, 2006.

Widmer, Candace, and Susan K. Houchin. *Governance of National Federated Organizations*. BoardSource e-book.

Chapter Five

Chait, Richard P. *How to Help Your Board to Govern More and Manage Less*. Washington, DC: BoardSource, 2003.

Cockerell, Lee. "Creating Leadership Magic." *Leader to Leader*, Summer 2009.

Howe, Fisher. *The Nonprofit Leadership Team: Building the Board–Executive Director Partnership*. San Francisco: Jossey-Bass, 2003.

The Source: Twelve Principles of Governance That Power Exceptional Boards. Washington, DC: BoardSource, 2005.

Williams, Sherrill K., and Kathleen A. McGinnis. *Getting the Best from Your Board: An Executive's Guide to a Successful Partnership*. Washington, DC: BoardSource, 2007.

Chapter Six

Brinckerhoff, Peter. *Generations: The Challenge of a Lifetime for Your Nonprofit*. Fieldstone Alliance, 2007.

Gazley, Beth, and Monica Dignam. "Are You In or Out?" *Associations Now*, August 2008.

Henry, Kristine. "A Place at the Table." *Chronicle of Philanthropy*, September 18, 2008.

Hrywna, Mark. "Youth Movement Critical for Boards." *Nonprofit Times*, June 1, 2009.

Lakey, Berit M. *The Board Building Cycle: Nine Steps to Finding, Recruiting, and Engaging Nonprofit Board Members*. 2nd ed. Washington, DC: BoardSource, 2007.

Lakey, Berit M., et al. *Governance Committee*. Washington, DC: BoardSource, 2004.

Marabella, Santo D. "Reaping the Benefits of Improved Orientation." *Board Member*, January/February 2006.

Chapter Seven

Bruder, Lee. "Nonprofit Dissolution: What to Do When Closing the Doors." *Nonprofit Quarterly*, Spring 2009.

Greene, Jan. "Directors and Officers Insurance." *Trustee*, June 2009.

Herman, Melanie. *Financial Risk Management: A Guide for Nonprofit Executives*. Nonprofit Risk Management Center, 2008. www.nonprofitrisk.org.

Hopkins, Bruce R., and David O. Middlebrook. *Nonprofit Law for Religious Organizations: Essential Questions & Answers*. Hoboken, NJ: Wiley, 2008.

Kurtz, Daniel L., and Sarah E. Paul. *Managing Conflicts of Interest: A Primer for Nonprofit Boards*. 2nd ed. Washington, DC: BoardSource, 2006.

Nonprofit Risk Management Center. www.nonprofitrisk.org.

Ober | Kaler. *The Nonprofit Legal Landscape*. Washington, DC: BoardSource, 2005.

"The Sarbanes-Oxley Act and Implications for Nonprofit Organizations." Revised ed. BoardSource and Independent Sector, 2006. http://www.boardsource.org/dl.asp?document_id=558.

Tesdahl, D. Benson. *The Nonprofit Board's Guide to Bylaws: Creating a Framework for Effective Governance*. Washington, DC: BoardSource, 2003.

Chapter Eight

Batarla, Rob. "How to Turn a Financially Clueless Board Member Into a Financial Whiz." *Associations Now*, March 2009.

Berger, Steven. *Understanding Nonprofit Financial Statements*. 3rd ed. Washington, DC: BoardSource, 2008.

Blazek, Jody. *Nonprofit Financial Planning Made Easy*. Hoboken, NJ: Wiley, 2008.

Common Fund. *Uniform Prudent Management Act Proposes Major Changes in Standards for Nonprofits.*
http://www.commonfund.org/Commonfund/Archive/CIO+Commentary/UPMIFA_
commentary.htm.

Greenlee, Janet, et al. "How to Steal from a Nonprofit: Who Does It and How to Prevent It."
Nonprofit Quarterly, Winter 2007.

Lang, Andrew. *Financial Responsibilities of Nonprofit Boards.* 2nd ed. Washington, DC:
BoardSource, 2009.

Ostrower, Francie. "Financial Transactions with Your Board: Who Is Looking?" *Nonprofit
Quarterly*, Summer 2008.

Panepento, Peter, and Grant Williams. "A Question of Calculation." *Chronicle of Philanthropy*,
February 7, 2008.

Chapter Nine

Association of Fundraising Professionals. *Donor Bill of Rights.* www.afpnet.org/ka/ka-3.cfm?
content_item_id=9988&folder_id=898.

Daubert, Erik J. *The Annual Campaign.* Hoboken, NJ: Wiley, 2009.

Drucker, Peter. *Managing the Nonprofit Organization: Principles and Practices.* Oxford: Butterworth-
Heinemann, 1990.

Foster, William L., Peter Kim, and Barbara Christiansen. "The Nonprofit Funding Models."
Stanford Social Innovation Review, Spring 2009.

Greenfield, James M. *Fundraising Responsibilities of Nonprofit Boards.* Washington, DC:
BoardSource, 2009.

Hall, Holly. "Raising Money in Hard Times." *Chronicle of Philanthropy*, February 26, 2009.

Hopkins, Bruce R. *The Tax Law of Charitable Giving.* 3rd ed. Hoboken, NJ: Wiley, 2005.

Speaking of Money: A Guide to Fundraising for Nonprofit Board Members. Video, hosted by Hugh
Downs. Washington, DC: BoardSource, 1996.

Sternberg, Dave. *Fearless Fundraising for Nonprofit Boards.* 2nd ed. Washington, DC:
BoardSource, 2008.

Warwick, Mal. *Fundraising When Money Is Tight.* San Francisco: Jossey-Bass, 2009.

Chapter Ten

Chait, Richard P., William P. Ryan, and Barbara Taylor. *Governance as Leadership.* Hoboken,
NJ: Wiley, 2005.

Collins, Jim. *Good to Great and the Social Sectors.* New York: HarperCollins, 2005.

Fishman, Raymond, Rakesh Khurana, and Edward Martenson. "Mission-Driven
Governance." *Stanford Social Innovation Review*, Summer 2009.

Grace, Kay Sprinkel, et al. *The Nonprofit Board's Role in Mission, Planning, and Evaluation.* 2nd ed.
Washington, DC: BoardSource, 2009.

Gross, Susan. *Seven Turning Points: Leading through Pivotal Transitions in Organizational Life.*
Fieldstone Alliance, 2009.

LaPiana, David. *Nonprofit Strategy Revolution: Real-Time Strategic Planning in a Rapid-Response
World.* Fieldstone Alliance, 2008.

Perrone, Michela, and Janis Johnston. *Presenting: Strategic Planning-Choosing the Right Method for
Your Organization.* Washington, DC: BoardSource, 2005.

Schmidt, Arthur "Buzz." "Escaping the Perpetuity Mindset Trap." *Nonprofit Quarterly*, Spring 2009.

Vergara-Lobo, Alfredo, et al. "The M Word: A Board Member's Guide to Mergers." CompassPoint Nonprofit Services, 2005. http://www.blueavocado.org/sites/default/files/The%20M%20Word%20A%20Board%20Members%20Guide%20to%20Mergers%20from%20CompassPoint.pdf.

Waechter, Susan A. *Driving Strategic Planning: A Nonprofit Executive's Guide.* 2nd ed. Washington, DC: BoardSource, 2010.

Chapter Eleven

"Advocacy: Oh Yes, You Can…And Should." *Nonprofit Quarterly*, Fall 2000.

Avner, Marcia. *The Nonprofit Board Member's Guide to Advocacy and Lobbying.* Fieldstone Alliance, 2004.

Independent Sector. "Nonprofit Advocacy and Lobbying." http://www.independentsector.org/programs/gr/advocacy_lobbying.htm.

Patterson, Sally. *Generating Buzz: Strategic Communications for Nonprofit Boards.* Washington, DC: BoardSource, 2006.

Chapter Twelve

Andringa, Robert C. *Presidential Transitions in Private Colleges: Six Integrated Phases Essential for Success.* Council of Independent Colleges, 2005.

Axelrod, Nancy R. *Chief Executive Succession Planning: Essential Guidance for Boards and CEOs.* 2nd ed. Washington, DC: BoardSource, 2010.

Corvington, Patrick, and Frances Kunreuther. "Next Shift: Beyond the Nonprofit Leadership Crisis." Annie E. Casey Foundation, 2008. http://www.aecf.org/KnowledgeCenter/Publications.aspx?pubguid=%7b5A026EAE-421A-4CC2-8BEE-046FFD275B9E%7d.

"Ready to Lead? Next Generation Leaders Speak Out." CompassPoint Nonprofit Services, Annie E. Casey Foundation, Meyer Foundation, and http://www.compasspoint.org/assets/521_readytolead2008.pdf.

Tebbe, Don. *Chief Executive Transitions: How to Hire and Support a Nonprofit CEO.* Washington, DC: BoardSource, 2009.

Tierney, Thomas J. "The Nonprofit Sector's Leadership Deficit." *Bridgespan*, 2006.

Vogel, Brian H., and Charles W. Quatt. *Nonprofit Executive Compensation: Planning, Performance, and Pay.* Washington, DC: BoardSource. 2010.

Wolfred, Tim. *Managing Executive Transitions: A Guide for Nonprofits.* Fieldstone Alliance, 2009.

Chapter Thirteen

ASAE and Center for Association Leadership. *Seven Measures of Success: What Remarkable Associations Do That Others Don't.* ASAE and Center for Association Leadership, 2006.

Bradach, Jeffrey L., Nan Stone, and Thomas J. Tierney. "Four Questions to Answer as They Seek to Thrive in Hard Times." *Chronicle of Philanthropy*, January 29, 2009.

Butler, Lawrence. *The Nonprofit Dashboard: A Tool for Tracking Progress.* Washington, DC: BoardSource, 2007.

Crutchfield, Leslie, and Heather McLeod Grant. *Forces for Good: The Six Practices of High-Impact Nonprofits*. San Francisco: Jossey-Bass, 2008.

Grace, Kay Sprinkel, et al. *The Nonprofit Board's Role in Mission, Planning, and Evaluation.* 2nd ed. Washington, DC: BoardSource, 2009.

Herman, Robert D., and David O. Renz. "Advancing Nonprofit Organizational Effectiveness Research and Theory: Nine Theses." *Nonprofit Management and Leadership,* Summer 2008.

Orlikoff, James E., and Mary K. Totten. "Using Competencies to Improve Trustee and Board Performance." *Trustee,* April 2009.

Saul, Jason. *Benchmarking for Nonprofits: How to Measure, Manage, and Improve Performance.* Fieldstone Alliance, 2004.

Chapter Fourteen

Bowen, William G. "The Machinery That Makes Good Boards Tick." *Corporate Board Member,* May/June 2008.

Crutchfield, Leslie R., and Heather McLeod Grant. *Forces for Good: The Six Practices of High-Impact Nonprofits*. San Francisco: Jossey-Bass, 2008.

Foundation Center. *Frequently Asked Questions: Where Can I Find Samples of Nonprofit Bylaws?* http://www.foundationcenter.org/getstarted/faqs/html/samplebylaws.html.

Lawrence, Barbara, and Outi Flynn. *The Nonprofit Policy Sampler.* 2nd ed. Washington, DC: BoardSource, 2006.

Tesdahl, D. Benson. *The Nonprofit Board's Guide to Bylaws: Creating a Framework for Effective Governance.* Washington, DC: BoardSource, 2003.

Chapter Fifteen

Cochran, Alice C. *Roberta's Rules of Order: Sail Through Meetings for Stellar Results Without a Gavel.* San Francisco: Jossey-Bass, 2004.

"Consent Agenda: A Tool for Improving Governance." Topic Paper. Washington, DC: BoardSource, 2005. http://www.boardsource.org/dl.asp?document_id=484.

"Executive Sessions: How to Use Them Regularly and Wisely." Topic Paper. Washington, DC: BoardSource, 2006. http://www.boardsource.org/dl.asp?document_id=555.

Flynn, Outi. *Meeting, and Exceeding Expectations: A Guide to Successful Nonprofit Board Meetings.* 2nd ed. Washington, DC: BoardSource, 2009.

Junker, Lisa. "Call to Order." *Associations Now,* December 2008.

Kaner, Sam. *Facilitator's Guide to Participatory Decision-Making.* Gabriola Island, Canada: New Society Publishers, 2005.

Robert, Henry M., et al. *Robert's Rules of Order.* Newly revised, 10th ed. Cambridge, MA: Da Capo Press, 2000.

Wertheimer, Mindy R. *The Board Chair Handbook.* 2nd ed. Washington, DC: BoardSource, 2007.

Chapter Sixteen

Axelrod, Nancy R. *Culture of Inquiry: Healthy Debate in the Boardroom.* Washington, DC: BoardSource, 2007.

Chait, Richard P., William P. Ryan, and Barbara E. Taylor. *Governance as Leadership: Reframing the Work of Nonprofit Boards.* Washington, DC: BoardSource, 2005.

Firstenberg, Paul B. *Transforming the Dynamics of Nonprofit Boards: From Passive to Active Agencies.* Baruch College, 2008.

Hewlett, Sylvia Ann, Laura Sherbin, and Karen Sumberg. "How Gen Y & Boomers Will Reshape Your Agenda." *Harvard Business Review,* July-August 2009.

Kennedy, Debbe. "How to Put Our Differences to Work." *Leader to Leader,* Spring 2009.

Macey, Jonathan R., and Steven A. Seiden. "Endnote: Advice and Consent." *Directors & Boards,* Annual Report, 2009.

Prybil, Lawrence. "What's Your Board's Culture?" *Trustee,* June 2008.

The Source: Twelve Principles of Governance That Power Exceptional Boards. Washington, DC: BoardSource, 2005.

INDEX

Note: Page numbers for glossary definitions are printed in boldface.

A

Accountability: board oversight for, 39, 42, 43–45; defined, **359**; increased demands for, 42, 44, 127, 136; policies for, 281, 287; to public trust, 140–141; shared board and chief executive, 84, 91. *See also* Ethics; Fiduciary responsibilities; Financial oversight; Legal responsibilities

Accounting. *See* Financial accounting; Financial oversight

Accreditation committee, 73

Action organization, **359**

Action plans: for board improvement, 268–269; in strategic planning, 197

Action scenarios, 201

Actions, in strategic plan, 207

Ad hoc committee. *See* Task forces

Adolescent stage, of nonprofit development, 26–27

Adverse audit opinion, 162

Advisory councils: characteristics of successful, 74–75; composition and structure of, 75; definition and scope of, 73, 106, **359**; former board members on, 52, 53, 123; functions and examples of, 74; staff involvement in, 75; wrong reasons for, 76

Advocacy: defined, **359**; engaging in, 224–226

Advocacy organizations, IRS classification of, 6. *See also* Social welfare organizations

Advocates, organizational: board members as, 38–39, 216–220; former board members as, 52

Affiliate, **359**. *See also* Chapters

Agendas: action items in, 301; consent, 300–302, 303; defined, **360**; discussion time in, 301; educational items in, 119–120; elements of, 300–303; sample, 301–302; strategic-thinking time in, 33, 191. *See also* Meetings

All-volunteer organization (AVO): board roles in, 18, 326; board-member professional services in, 109; defined, **360**; start-ups as, 26. *See also* Start-up organizations

Ambassadors: activities of, 218–219, 224; advisory councils as, 73; board members as, 38–39, 47, 214, 216–220; former board members as, 52. *See also* Outreach

American Association of Critical-Care Nurses, 205–206

American Express Foundation, 6

American Hospital Association, 150

description for, 248–250, 272; launching a new, 252–253; as official spokesperson, 219; policies on, 281; policymaking responsibilities of, 282, 283; responsibilities of, 50–51, 85–87; strategic planning responsibilities of, 198; transition, 246; voting rights of, 69, 93–95, 140. *See also* Board–chief executive relationship

Chief executive compensation: benefits in, 288; board responsibility for, 40, 130, 289–290; chief executive role in review of, 92; ethical and legal compliance in, 134, 143; IRS regulations and, 143, 288, 289; policy and guidelines for, 236, 237, 283, 288–290, 348–349; private inurement and, 143; researching, 289–290; sample policies of, 237, 348–349; transparency about, 44

Chief executive departure: abrupt, 238, 240–243; announcement of, 242–243; controversial or involuntary, 239, 242–243; management of, 238–243; planned, 238, 239–240

Chief executive evaluation, 272–274; board responsibility for, 40–41; chief executive role in, 92; as compliance measure, 134; contents of, 273; foundations for, 272; participants in, 272; process of, 273–274; self-assessment in, 272, 274; trust building with, 320; uses of, 256

Chief executive search and selection: advertising in, 250–251; board responsibilities for, 36–37, 247–251; candidate identification for, 250–251; conducting, 247–251; consultants for, 245; executive committee involvement in, 70; final negotiation in, 251; for integrity, 44, 134; internal candidates for, 233, 235, 251; job description for, 248–250; overview of, 36–37; pre-search assessment for, 247–248; for start-up organizations, 18; transparency in, 319. *See also* Chief executive transition; Succession planning

Chief executive transition, 233–253; board role in, 37, 243; consultants for, 245; departing executive's role in, 244–245; departure management in, 238–243; first five days of, 239–242; goals for, 238; guidelines for, 236–238; interim period in, 245–247; post-hire process in, 252–253; roles in, 243–245; search and selection steps in, 247–251; steps in, 238–245; transition committee for, 239, 240, 243–244, 251. *See also* Chief executive

departure; Chief executive search; Succession planning

Chief financial officer (CFO), 15, 66, 153, 154–155

Civility, in boardroom, 327

Cleveland Foundation, 6

Client fee income, 185, 256

Coalition building, 216, 220–222

Code of conduct, 328–329, **361**. *See also* Ethics

Collaborations, 220–222

Collegial spirit, 296

Colorado, meeting laws of, 296

Commercial ventures, 186–187

Committees: benefits of, 57–58; board chair's responsibilities with, 49, 86; chairs of, 61; chief executive involvement in, 86; composition of, 61–62; creating new, 59–61; defined, **361**; examples of, 60–61; former board members on, 52, 53, 123; involvement in, 62, 116, 118; meetings of, 61; non-board members on, 61–62; organizational *versus* board, 58–59, 62, 72; policies on, 282; reports of, 303–304; rotation on, 122; size of, 62; special, 71–73; staff involvement in, 57, 62; standing, 58, 59, 63–70, **365**; structures of, 57–58, 59, 60–61; term limits for, 62; zero-based structure, 58, **366**. *See also specific committee* headings

Common law, 12, 128

Communication(s): about chief executive appointment, 252, 319; about chief executive departure, 242–243; with advisory councils, 75; within board, 116, 300, 307–308; between board chair and chief executive, 84, 87–88; board members' responsibilities for, 214, 216–220; board size and, 56; board's role in, 212–213, 223–224, 231; chair's role in, 213; for chief executive search, 250–251; chief executive's responsibilities for, 215; crisis, 226–230; exercises on, 231–232; financial, 160; with former board members, 53, 123; front-end approach to, 211; impact assessment of, 230–231; internal, 215–216; knowledge required for, 214; linked with mission, 212; monitoring the effectiveness of, 213, 230–231; organizational positioning and, 213, 222–224; overview of, 211–212; planning, 39, 213,